W9-AHQ-010

AMERICA AND THE MONROE YEARS

AMERICA AND THE MONROE YEARS

EUGENE M. WAIT

Kroshka Books
Huntington, New York

Editorial Production: Susan Boriotti
Office Manager: Annette Hellinger
Graphics: Frank Grucci
Information Editor: Tatiana Shohov
Book Production: Donna Dennis, Patrick Davin, Cathy DeGregory and Lynette Van Helden
Circulation: Latoya Clay and Anna Cruz

Library of Congress Cataloging-in-Publication Data

Wait, Eugene M.
         America and the Monroe years / Eugene M. Wait
                  p.   cm.
         Includes bibliographical references and index.
         ISBN 1-56072-759-4
         1. United States--Politics and government--1817-1825. I. Title.
E371.W15   1999   CIP
973.5'4--dc21   99-054095

Copyright 2000 by Eugene M. Wait
         Kroshka Books, a division of
         Nova Science Publishers, Inc.
         227 Main Street, Suite 100
         Huntington, New York 11743
         Tele. 631-424-6682Fax 631-424-4666
         e-mail: Novascience@earthlink.net
         e-mail: Novascil@aol.com
         Web Site: http://www.nexusworld.com/nova

Printed in the United States of America

DEDICATED TO

EUGENE WAIT 1903-1987
VIRGINIA RICE WAIT 1908-1990

CONTENTS

ACKNOWLEDGMENTS

This book is the second in a long series on the age and life of Abraham Lincoln, with emphasis on the times. This series covers from 1809 to 1865; 13 volumes are finished extending to the fall of 1862 at the time this is written. They are meant to stand alone, each volume by itself.

My sincere thanks go to Marie Wait Featherston and her husband Harry Featherston , as well as my brother, H. Joe Wait, for their invaluable support of my efforts.

In addition I wish especially to thank Willeen Gray who works in inter-library loan at the Butt-Holdsworth Memorial Library in Kerrville, Texas. She encouraged me and obtained the necessary research books for me through the library. Mary Myers is her able supervisor, who has also put forth great effort to secure materials for my work.

The chief librarians there were Evelyn Jaeglli, then Victoria Mosty Wilson, and now Antonio Martinez. Also due appreciation is to Herb Peterson, James Rowe, Ann Eickenroht, Mildred M. Daniel, Fran Menzel, and Jon Patton. The important poetess Sarah Patton, sister-in-law to Jon, was encouraging. Winnie Whitaker and Clara Watkins loaned me books as did Jon. I extend my thanks and gratitude to the authors who have gone before me and whose books and articles used in research and writing.

Most of all I thank my deceased parents, Eugene Wait and Virginia Rice Wait, to whom this book is dedicated and to whom all of my works are dedicated. Their unstinting support made everything possible.

Finally a note on the author. Eugene Meredith Wait was born on July 13, 1936, in Longview Texas. He has lived most of his life in Kerrville. He got his AA at Schreiner College and his BA at the University of Texas at Austin. After serving his patriotic duty in the army, he returned to graduate school in Texas where he studied under Thomas F. McGann and the famous librarian and historian Nettie Lee Benson. She befriended him and he worked for her for two and a half years, having gotten his MA in Latin American History. He completed his doctorate thesis, lacking only oral examinations to receive his Ph.D., when illness struck in 1965. Since then, he has written 39 books.

Eugene M. Wait
Kerrville, Texas
May 15, 2000

Chapter I

MONROE

James Monroe took his oath of presidential office on March 4, 1817, after an overwhelming election of 183 electoral votes compared to the 34 of his Federalist opponent. This gave him a clear mandate and a chance to be president of the nation in a way which had not been done since Washington. He declared at the outset that the American people were one great family, having common interests. Although his course was not to be totally smooth and not the era of good feeling so lauded to the skies, there was an increased harmony and lack of major discord.

It was eleven-thirty in the morning of that day, when James Monroe and his vice-president D.D. Tompkins left the home of the former. They had had waiting for them a crowd, which followed them from there. The large cavalcade of people on horseback rode along the muddy and uneven streets towards the Capitol. Special deputies escorted the parade. Reporters estimated the crowd to be between five and eight thousand people. This was a larger crowd than any Washington DC had seen before this date. Monroe got off at the Capitol and made his way to the platform. The ceremonies were engaged and he gave his inaugural address. The numbers were indicative of the good will he was to receive from the multitude, although there were to be divisions among his cabinet of outstanding men.

The man of a widely spread party, Monroe could stand aside party feeling and stand for all of the people, that later presidents could envy if that was in their natures. Indeed, he condemned party spirit and became a man above party. He hoped that Americans would reach the highest degree of perfection without a divisive party system. This was the old idea of Washington and his associates before parties became important as a lever in the machinery of government and the nation. He believed that parties were not necessary for free government. But Monroe was bred by party spirit and won public office as a Republican. His broad based support in the nation enabled him to rise above party.

In the coming summer, Monroe made a show of a tour from Washington to Baltimore, Philadelphia, New York, and New England. Thousands cheered him on this journey and leaders of both old parties greeted him fondly. At Boston, some 40,000 people lined his route and John Adams and Timothy Pickering, old Federalists of importance, greeted him without any concern of ill-feeling or party spirit. He was after all a popular man of the people and a long time official. Behind this display was the undercutting of the Federalist party which was to end in his reelection by and all but unanimous vote. Also he did not accept every Federalist into this party and there was still some bad feeling and discord below the surface. This was soon to surface. Monroe was to have opposition within his broad based party. [1]

James Monroe took the eighteenth century republican view that political parties were symptomatic of defects in republics. George Washington also believed that parties were bad and the other founding fathers had not made any constitutional provisions for these associations in the Constitution. Doubtless, they were well aware that French philosopher Jean Jacques Rousseau, one of the leading proponents of the Enlightenment, believed that associations should not be allow to exist. Special groups, if formed, would lend to a single agreement. The vital general will, which was made up of a variety of opinions, would then be lost.

Because of the growing dissolution of the Federalist party and the weakening of Republican ideology. Monroe thought he would be the one to bring in a non-party state. For while, it seemed that the Republican party would dissolve into a partyless election of officials based upon the idea of election of the best man for the job than voting the party line. Instead the Republican party was to break into factions and later into a two-party system that was to affect the growing Abraham Lincoln, whose father was a Jeffersonian Republican and who followed Thomas Jefferson until he was influenced by Henry Clay and became a Whig. [2]

The new president was a practical politician, more so than his four successors. Washington, Adams, Jefferson, and Madison had all discovered that leadership required political action. However, Monroe was the first president to be a professional politician and official. The four were ruled by ideas, while Monroe had more flexible policies. Before coming to a conclusion, he sought support and made compromises. Because his party was so dominant, the members differed with each other rather than the crumpling opposition. Monroe had to take that into account, which made the process more difficult. John Adams lost the election of 1800 in part due to a party split. Monroe had to consult with more people because Republicans were splintered. Further, he tried to gain the support of Federalists for a consensus presidency. Recently, the Federalists had been labeled disloyal. Now they sought to be considered loyal and were soon to support Monroe, to Monroe's advantage.

Among the most common political concepts discussed in 1816-1817, reconciliation between Republicans and Federalists, was accepted by Monroe. It was observed that the Republicans had already adopted as their own such Federalist ideas as a nation-wide bank and the protective tariff. Harrison Gray Otis of Massachusetts believed that there was no reason for an opposition in the governmental process. This was true momentarily. Basic differences already existed and were to reach the spotlight of national affairs during Monroe's presidency. However, at the time Otis saw that the Republicans had taken over the Federalist programs. The Federalists still left would support their own ideas by voting for the Republicans. Madison was satisfied that the shift to Federalist principles was good. Peace was acceptable. Nicholas Biddle believed that voters were tired of endless party disagreements.

Advisers suggested Monroe give Federalists offices in his government. General Andrew Jackson wrote after the election that Monroe must use able men from both parties and in specific make Colonel William Drayton his secretary of war. A South Carolina Federalist, Drayton proved his loyalty in the War of 1812. Republican job seekers did not like the idea and Monroe predicted this to Jackson when the president-elect wrote. Monroe used Jackson's letter and his reply to influence Washington DC politicians. This proved an embarrassment when they were printed early in 1824. Jackson and Rufus King were offended. Jackson had used the correspondence, however, to gain the support of Tennessee Federalists. [3]

James Monroe, American statesman, army officer, diplomat, governor, and president, was born on April 28, 1758, in Westmoreland County, Virginia. His father was Spence Monroe and his mother was Elizabeth Jones Monroe, the sister of the prominent Judge Joseph Jones. His ancestor, Andrew Monroe, was a Scottish royalist who fought as a captain in the cause of Charles I. After the king was beheaded, Andrew emigrated to Virginia in 1650 to return ten years later when Charles II became ruler of Great Britain. He still owned land in Virginia where various branches of the family lived. His descendants lived in the colony. Young James attended the academy of Reverend Archibald Campbell which was noted throughout Virginia. His father died in 1774 and his uncle Jones sent him to William and Mary College. When war shut down the college, Monroe left for the military.

He entered the Revolutionary War as a cadet in the Third Virginia Regiment raised and led by Colonel Hugh Mercer. Shortly, Monroe was promoted to lieutenant. The first assignment of the regiment was to march to New York. They reached there after the Battle of Long Island. Meeting the British at Harlem, they checked them. However the British came up the Sound and there was another fight, this time in White Plains. Following orders, the regiment supported troops at Fort Lee in New Jersey. When this fort fell, the American army fell back with Monroe in its ranks.

In the vanguard of fifty men was Monroe in the attack at Trenton across the icy Delaware. His captain was wounded and Monroe took charge of the vanguard. Then he too was wounded. For his bravery and wound, he was promoted to captain. In July of 1777, American Major General Lord Stirling made young Monroe his aide-de-camp. He served through the next year and a half before trying to raise a regiment and failing.

Next, Monroe re-entered college and then studied law under Thomas Jefferson, governor of Virginia. While in this process, he took off time to do some intelligence work for the head of South Carolina's government and served in the militia which kept the British out of the interior of Virginia. In April of 1782, James was elected to the House of Delegates of his home state and became a member of the Council. From December of 1783 to November of 1786, he served in the Continental Congress.

Thomas Jefferson and James Monroe were planning to tour the frontier when Jefferson was tapped for a diplomatic post in Paris. Monroe had to go alone. He joined the negotiating party of Governor Clinton in New York state. On this trip, he met many of the chiefs of the Six Nations, including Colonel Brandt of the Mohawk tribe. Then he headed west by the Great Lakes to Detroit and returned by Montreal and Vermont. Monroe returned to his duties in Congress.

He retired from Congress and was a lawyer for a few months. Soon he was elected to the Virginia legislature and to the convention for the Constitutional ratification. He was to opposed the Constitution for the grant of power to level direct taxes and the absence of a bill of rights. The framework lacked the responsibility idea of the parliament and allowed the president to serve more than one term. For these two too, he voted against ratification. He served in Congress as an anti-Federalist.

In 1794, he was sent to Paris to serve as diplomatic minister. This was recognition of his abilities and due to his anti-English feeling which would be an asset in France. His friendship for that nation would help the strained relations between the United States and France. Because of Federalist criticism and a rocky time there, he was recalled. For four years he served as governor and then Jefferson sent him to Paris in time for the sale of Louisiana agreement to be clinched. No sooner was this done then he went to London as minister.

While in London, Monroe met Nicholas Biddle, whom we shall see again. The two started a close friendship of an old Monroe and a young Biddle. For awhile he went to Spain but did not accomplish much there. He negotiated a treaty with Great Britain but it did not please Jefferson and it was never sent to Congress or put into effect. In the ensuing years he was a legislator and governor again. Madison made him secretary of state, in which office he served as was seen in the previous book I wrote. [4]

When it came time for Monroe to chose a secretary of state, there were three main candidates: John Q. Adams, Clay, and Crawford. The last two were high in position in the party and it was logical that either one were high in position in the party and it was logical that either one of them would be accepted. Clay had had diplomatic experience and it would likely be him, but Crawford was also strong in Congress and even more prominent than Clay at the time. The secretary of state had been a stepping stone for Jefferson, Madison, and Monroe to the presidency presidential politics played a role. The appointment would be next president of the United States.

Both Clay and Crawford wanted to be president and each felt that they would be if they got the position. Because of this neither could accept the other in that post. They canceled each other out. Neither could be secretary of state. Adams on the other hand had no chance to become president, or so it was thought; if placed in the position this would leave both Clay and Crawford an opportunity to be president after Monroe fulfilled his two expected terms. And Adams had plenty of diplomatic experience. He had been out of the United States for eight years in such posts. So Monroe chose Adams and months later he was to be back home to serve in that place. As it turned out, Adams was to follow Monroe, but it was not to be an easy election for him. He was to have much competition, but this is left to the future and does not figure here. [5]

On January 6, 1817, Andrew Jackson ordered Edmund Pendleton Gaines to establish his headquarters at Fort Montgomery, Alabama, north from the Gulf of Mexico, near both Pensacola and Mobile. From there, he could protect those two points and march for the protection of New Orleans in case of a war with Spain, which was a distinct possibility after the election of Monroe whose inauguration was then two months away. On the way south to his new post, Gaines was feted at Richmond and was to share a dinner in honor of him and Winfield Scott had he not felt he must get to Fort Montgomery for his mission of protecting the Gulf coast against any enemy.

He was no sooner in Alabama when he heard word from Governor David Brydie Mitchell of Georgia that a certain George Woodbine was stirring up the Seminole. He was blamed for an incident in which a white man was killed in southern Georgia and his cattle driven off. However, Mitchell wanted the troublesome whites like Woodbine removed from Indian lands. The Indians would not understand anything but force, Gaines replied. On his way to Montgomery, he had seen the people of the barely settled frontier filled up by destitute people, poor and wretched for what were supposed to be a civilized people. Still corn had cost eight dollars a bushel.

At Fort Montgomery, he learned that a woman and two children had just been killed by Seminole, who were rumored to be preparing for war. The murder of some more whites terrorized the frontiersmen on the St. Tillas. Gaines ordered a new fort built. He heard of a settlement of French Napoleonists at White Bluff, which had to be abandoned. It was named Demopolis. Gaines soon was feeling that Alexander Arbuthnot was acting against American interests in Florida. Gaines thought that the British or Spaniards were secretly influencing the Seminole in Florida. Later, that year, he warned Jackson that the Seminole would not surrender murderers. [6]

The Bank of the United States began limited operations in January of 1817 and, within weeks, specie (gold and silver) payments resumed at all major banks. Whether this was cause and effect is unknown, but it probably helped matters, giving strength and encouragement to the banking industry. With a national bank on the scene, the bankers could well believe that stability was ahead. At the least, it helped fill a gap in the financial situation, which had caused the interruption of gold and silver resumption in the first place. Bankers could look ahead with more confidence and act accordingly. In the evolving economy, businessmen acted upon what the near future would hold and in this case they could be optimistic and not know that in two years, the economy would tailspin down. But then businessmen did not generally look that far ahead, even if it was evident. A powerful national bank could not change an economy that was too strong. It could however play a vital role in the economy. [7]

The year of 1817 was a year of false promise with a bank whose right to exist was little questioned. The greats who had opposed the Bank of the United States in the past were now its friends. The bank was recognized by the private banks and relied upon by the Treasury for the services it could provide for them. It had ended the suspension. In that same year, Canada had its first permanent bank. This was the Bank of Montreal. The American Bank of the United States had been justified by the experience of Americans after the dissolution of the first bank. The lack of a strong national bank had hurt the war effort. Finally the fact of the need chastened its opponents and many of them had been greatly converted to the advisability of the Bank being good for the economy. [8]

Merchants in Tennessee were unhappy about the banks in their states. The bank in Knoxville and in Nashville loaned money for speculation by the directors and their friends. These loans were dangerous and left out merchants. Only the controllers of the two banks benefited. The merchants wanted a bank where they could get commercial credit on solid prospects, a regular help in maintaining and expanding business. They wisely tried to get a branch of the Second Bank of the United States. Opposition leaders in the state championed the merchants and a bank was organized for their benefit, but it was a private bank and soon met the hostility of state leaders, the very speculators who control the banks originally mentioned. When the panic occurred, Tennesseans rose up and cried for relief and defeat for the special interests, speculative landowners. [9]

One of the notables who began a correspondence with Monroe was Nicholas Biddle, a nationalist, an egalitarian, and a supporter of government power for state and national improvement. He had recently been defeated in an election by his enemies. He was still a young man and had entered college as a boy to receive a great education, and he was already a marked man for talent. He was seeking employment, but Monroe had nothing for him. This did not stop Biddle from visiting the president at least twice a year and exchanging letters on a regular basis, just about once a month. Biddle encouraged Monroe to establish a system of federal governmental payment for internal improvements, such as roads and canals. Monroe had his doubts about the constitutionality of such programs. The president wanted a constitutional amendment for the use of federal funds for improvements. Biddle did not let this deter him and went on to support the president's statement on the independence movement of Hispanic America. He approved of the presidential kind words for the rebels allied with a strict neutrality followed by Madison.

Biddle was well informed and was a confidant of Spanish minister Chevalier de Onis. Both men were alarmed at the Russian advance down the west coast from Alaska. For the American and the Spaniard, the Russians were intruders and trespassers of a dangerous nature. Biddle was also in contact with revolutionary circles. Through the Spaniard and the South American, Biddle kept informed of the happenings to the regions of the Spanish conquest three centuries before. De Onis wanted to defend his country's possession of the lands and the revolutionary wanted free and independent governments for the provinces in the rest of the Americans south of the United States. [10]

On March 20, 1817, Edmund P. Gaines reported from Fort Montgomery in the south to the secretary of war that the danger to Pensacola was subsiding. Although the Creek Indians and the whites in the woods were invited by revolutionaries to cooperate with them, they did not do so. To the credit of the Indians and the whites, they did nothing although they were strongly disposed to see Pensacola change masters. They had suffered too much already in the recent war to embark upon another, especially against the will of their country in this instance.

General Gaines also wrote that he ordered supplies needed for Fort Crawford, within the limits of present day Brewton, to be shipped by water through Pensacola. There they were to be temporally deposited near the mouth of Escambia by coasting vessels and put on board the barges to interior points up the rivers of Canaka and Escambia. Gaines made arrangements for this with the Spanish governor of Florida to whom he emphasized the need for forage and provisions in the Mississippi Territory. [11]

[1]Ketcham, Ralph, *Presidents Above Party: The First American Presidency, 1789-1829*, Chapel Hill: University of North Carolina Press, 1984, pp. 124-127; Cresson, W.P., *James Monroe*, Chapel Hill: University of North Carolina Press, 1946, p. 282.

[2]Ammon, Harry, "James Monroe and the Era of Good Feelings," *Virginia Magazine of History and Biography*, LXVI (October 1958), 390, 397-398; Wait, Eugene M., "Mariano Moreno: Promoter of Enlightenment," *Hispanic American Historical Review*, XLV No. 2 (August 1965), 374.

[3]Ammon, "James Monroe," pp. 387-391.

[4]Monroe, James, *The Autobiography of James Monroe*, ed. Brown, Stuart Gerry, Syracuse University Press, 1959, passim.

[5]Lynch, William O., *Fifty Years of Party Warfare (1789-1837)*, Bobbs-Merrill, 1931 (1967 reprint), pp. 252-253.

[6]Silver, James W., *Edmund Pendleton Gaines: Frontier General*, Louisiana State University Press, 1949, pp. 66-70.

[7]Adams, Donald R. Jr., *Finance and Enterprise in Early America: A Study of Stephen Girard's Bank, 1812-1831*, Philadelphia: University of Pennsylvania Press, 1978, pp. 58-61.

[8]Bray Hammond, 1957, p. 251.

[9]Sellers, Charles G., Jr., "Banking and Politics in Jackson's Tennessee, 1817-1827," *Mississippi Valley Historical Review*, pp. 65-67.

[10]Govan, Thomas Payne, *Nicholas Biddle: Nationalist and Public Banker 1786-1844*, Chicago: University of Chicago Press, 1959, pp. 52-54.

[11]Carter, C.E., *Territorial Papers of the United States*, XVIII, 75.

Chapter II

SPAIN AND AMERICA

Spanish minister Onis was unhappy in Washington. His personal problems planted dissatisfaction. His wife was dying and he blamed the climate. His daughter seemed destined to follow her in the future. Onis asked to be relieved. Maryland seemed no place to live. He felt that any assignment would be preferable to Washington.

The former foreign minister, Pedro Cevallos "made the biggest blunder he could in transferring the negotiations here; for with these people it is impossible to do anything." Talks with them are disadvantageous since they "publish the notes they wish, and hide those which do not suit them; in addition to which you must understand that nothing but force can make them give up West Florida which they have occupied." Americans wanted a war with Spain, but such a war would ruin Spain. He did not say so, but Spain was too tied down in Hispanic America. Mrs. Onis died, but the daughter survived.

The Spanish diplomat had great trouble in arranging a treaty which would settle the territorial issues at hand. It was to remain difficult in the months ahead, especially when Adams arrived in Washington from overseas. Onis knew that Adams was able and indeed Onis himself was capable of great expertise at diplomacy, but Adams was to hold most of the cards. Spain's minister of foreign relations Jose Garcia Leon y Pizarro was demanding and took a strong stand, but matters were stronger for Adams. The first Spanish claim was for West Florida from New Orleans to the Perdido River. East Florida was to be kept in Leon's plan. [1]

Monroe made the decision in April of 1817 to send a special commissioner to South America. Because Joel Roberts Poinsett was well traveled in Europe and South America and had experience in stirring up the leaders of Argentina and Chile for independence, Monroe offered him the position. Poinsett, he correctly noted, had the best qualifications for the mission. If Poinsett accepted, Monroe would be greatly gratified and the South Carolinian would find the pay would be good. He planned to send him on a public ship to call at the capitals.

The proposed envoy's friends wanted him to accept and naval officer David Porter, who was busy with newspaper propaganda in favor of American recognition of the insurgents there, was particularly interested and eager for Poinsett to go. Porter feared that Great Britain was gaining all the power to influence the Hispanic Americans and would leave the United States out, politically and economically. However, Poinsett declined. Acting Secretary of State Richard Rush expressed regret and accepted the advice which Poinsett had offered. When it came to a decision, Monroe selected Caesar Rodney, John Graham, and Theodoric Bland to go in his stead. They were to sail on December 4th.

Adams asked Poinsett for more advice and Poinsett wrote a 25,000 word treatise to guide him in foreign affairs to the south based upon his opinion. He argued against the recognition of Argentina since that would encourage Buenos Aires to ask for aid, which the Americans were not prepared to send. Jealousy would prevent the leaders of South America from accepting American advice and guidance, much less any control of political and military affairs. Poinsett regarded the affairs of his own country to be more important than those of those emerging states. This was the opinion of most Americans; a situation which Britain exploited. The Hispanics to the south regarded the Britons as better friends than the Americans. This was to make Poinsett's later career in Mexico more difficult. Poinsett sent his letter off to Washington DC and turned to state and national politics which he thought needed his services. [2]

Early in 1817, an adventurous Scot, Gregor McGregor showed up in the United States to talk of his deeds in the army of Simon Bolivar with whom he had been in friendship in Gran Columbia. He had been in good graces until they had a quarrel with some fellow officers. He resigned at that time and came to North America to act against Spain once more. Talking of his future deeds too, he made free use of his connections with Bolivar, in whom the people of the United States were most interested. Many a man or woman asked him about the great liberator. He was their direct source and made the most of the popularity of the rebels, which transferred to McGregor.

At first he had indefinite plans; but he appealed to British minister Sir Charles Bagot to warn of the danger of American interest in Hispanic America and note what it would do to British commerce. He talked to Bagot of ideas for invasion and liberation.

However, Bagot distrusted McGregor and the Scotsman went to Richard Rush next. Rush was taken in by the idea of an expedition to Florida to seize that Spanish colony and enable his country to purchase this province lying to the south of the United States. However, Rush could do nothing and dismissed McGregor with sympathy but not aid or acceptance. So McGregor sought out Spanish exiles such as Vicente Pazos and Pedro Gual to take Amelia Island. The adventurer went to Charleston to promote his plan. He was feted and dined royalty, secured a brig and went to Savannah with men and ship. There he got more volunteers and money. He and his men seized Amelia Island, a base for smugglers, but McGregor got no further.

The early Spanish terms for the boundary were an insistence upon a Mississippi boundary at least up to the Missouri or even Arkansas. The first liberalization action for the Spanish was to cede part or all of the Floridas and then somewhat later to accept a Sabine boundary and the Spanish even considered giving up northern Texas. [3]

Jared Sparks became editor of the *North American Review* in May of 1817 and served for ten months, before seeking to become a minister. He was not particularly happy with the editorship; it was a heavy yoke to bear. Just before undertaking this responsibility, Sparks wrote a life-long friend, Miss Storrow, that "a certain number of our most distinguished gentlemen had associated themselves, and have agreed to furnish articles in their turn, and it is on this condition only that I would engage at all in the affair." Jared was going to make a trial of the job. He would not be required to do much writing, which was a relief to him. At any rate it was a step up from tutoring.

The *North American Review* was founded a number of years before, growing out of a club publication in Boston. The original publication was produced by a circle of highly cultivated and scholarly friends. Each article was about a book, hence the word Review, although each was an independent treatise about the subject of the book. Each article author contributed his own ideas, oftimes to the exclusion of the works being reviewed. The writing was better than average for that period. The object of the review was not to make money, but to promote the intellectual vigor of the nation.

As early as March, Sparks was preparing his first number, which was May, and again wrote Miss Storrow. The review and his tutorial duties required much time, and he wanted not to forego his theological training. He had in mind to become a minister before assuming his work on the *North American Review*. The new editor believed a man could do what the thinks he can do; and the ambitious Jared was not afraid to undertake responsible and demanding tasks. At first he emphasized articles of dark Africa, notably explorers and others with African experiences. One of them on the narrative of Robert Adams, a shipwrecked sailor on the west coast, detained in slavery by the Arabs and a resident of Timbuktu, was written by Sparks. During this time, he was influenced by Dr. William Ellery Channing and after his stint as editor became a Unitarian minister. He preached, but it too was a hard row to hoe. His first sermon caused him anxiety and pain. Soon, he was called to administer to people in Baltimore. [4]

In the summer of 1817, Monroe made a grand tour of the North, which was well received. He met many men and women, including the Pintard, we have met in the earlier book. Pintard had a friend in Governor De Witt Clinton of New York state and knew James Monroe, a relative of his, and was pleased to see both again when Monroe visited New York City on his tour. The president recognized John, although they had not seen each other in a long time Monroe's ability to remember faces and names stood him good stead throughout his life.

The editor of the leading Boston Federalist newspaper the *Columbian Sentinel*, hailed the Monroe presidency. Monroe, he wrote, was ushering an "era of good feeling." Benjamin Russell wished that the Federal party should be well treated as if there had never been any earlier differences. Many readers felt it was an effort to heal past differences. Monroe had made a peace gesture before this when he named John Quincy Adams to his first cabinet position in his power to grant.

On his grand tour of the country, Monroe had hoped to travel as a private citizen but when he reached Baltimore, he had to change that idea. He was received with enthusiasm although he arrived on a Sunday, which merited no little criticism in that age. He did attend church and he visited Fort McHenry. He gave patriotic and pleasant speeches and then continued northward. Crowded in Philadelphia, he went through Trenton. The citizens of New York City honored him and he was the guest of his vice-president Tompkins on Staten Island. There were cannon salutes, addresses, and parades. Veterans saluted him and visited.

There was warmth in New England. His greatest greeting was in Boston. There was a legislative resolution. He found escorts and parades. His headquarters at the Exchange Coffee House, America's largest, was the scene of addresses and replies. He meet the John Adams and Harrison Gray Otis gave him a fireworks display in celebration. The Dearborns gave him a grand ball. Only the Quakers were not to welcome him. Because of their austere religion, they were not allowed to enjoy such displays. [5]

On his tour, Monroe arrived at Concord. The people did not have much warning of his coming. Immediate arrangements followed the news. People set aside their party feelings and jealousies for the occasion. Monroe entered Concord with pomp and ceremony. The streets were crowded. Everyone wanted to see the president. There were ladies at every window to view the procession. People had come from the neighboring towns. The welcoming committee conducted Monroe to the stage. He was greeted and Thomas W. Thompson got up and gave a speech.

Editor Thompson said to "permit us, as the organ of the citizens of Concord, to express the high satisfaction we feel in beholding the President of the United States in our village, and in having an opportunity to present you our most respecting acknowledgments for this distinguished honor. All hearts, sir, bid you welcome." They enjoyed his inspection of the works of defense on Concord's extensive lines. Thompson talked of a new era dawning. They all hoped for a blessing upon the administration. Monroe rose and replied to the satisfaction of this editor of the *Maryland Gazette* who reported this occasion.

That evening, the committee conducted the president to the Meeting House. The whole hall was lighted and decorated to the taste and judgment of the ladies of Concord. They had special carpets laid down. Ladies and gentlemen filled the hall. Singers entertained Monroe and the people. On the next morning it was business. Monroe dinned with Thompson and his party of dignitaries. Afterwards they all went to the Canal and embarked. Monroe then went to other towns and attended church services. He received a grand welcome in a land which had opposed his predecessor in the War of 1812. There were more speeches as he toured New England and reached Kennebunk. The tour was a most happy occasion for all concerned. He then traveled other Northern states. [6]

A meeting had been held of free blacks in Philadelphia in January of 1817 aimed at remonstrating against the colonizing of parts of Africa with free blacks. James Forten presided. They resolved to remain in the United States, having contributed with sweat and blood to the cultivation of the nation. They resolved that they opposed the stigma of danger and useless placed upon them. They would not separate themselves from their brethren, the slaves of the South.

Another meeting was held to address the people of Philadelphia. They said they "relieved from the miseries of slavery, many of us by your aid, possessing the benefits which industry and integrity in this prosperous country assures to all its inhabitants of worshipping the only true God, under the light of Christianity, each of us according to his understanding; and having afforded to us and to our children the means of education and improvement; we have no wish to separate from our present homes, for any purpose whatever." [7]

African Americans took the colonization arguments as an insult. Besides the black idea that the society was a form of exile, it proclaimed that the African Americans were inferior and were innately incapable to be successful as a free man. They wrote that if free to do as they willed they would tend to be corrupt and depraved. They would be certain to fail. These ideas offended the African American. Blacks were particularly provoked because it is much harder to succeed if it is believed you can not. In 1818, they protested against African expatriation four times.

The New York weekly *Freedom's Journal* advised African Americans to stay with the ship of America, because if they did not they would not be saved. Lewis Woodson in Ohio, stated that blacks neither asked for nor wanted to move to Africa and would not go. Of course, many were to go in the years ahead, but the majority of freed African Americans did not, not to speak of the slaves to whom the United States was home. Whites were expected to render justice to African Americans wherever they were, and not ship them across the seas. Confirmed natives did not want to be treated as foreigners; of course they were Americans and wanted to be treated well. African Americans had paid with blood for independence.

Early abolitionists leaned over backwards to avoid offending the South and tried to win Southern support for gradual emancipation. They told them that slavery was a calamity and not a crime; they would gladly help Southerners to put an end to the burden of slavery. Southern slaveowners were assured that they would not interfere with property rights and would compensate them for freed slaves. Hesitant about supporting colonization, they turned toward the idea after a brief period of outright opposition because African Americans opposed it. Most African Americans were hostile to the idea of going off to Africa to solve the race problem. However, many were to go and often regretted it with death and hardship. [8]

The Colonization Society stimulated a renewal of anti-slavery activity and was the major idea of the early nineteenth century for a national appeal of antislavery. But there was a major problem aside from what we have already seen. Its constitution assured Southerners that the goal was to remove free blacks, that is to send them to Africa. The founders did expect this to increase voluntary manumissions. They wanted to convince "the Southern people that emancipation might be safe, practicable, replete with blessings, and full of honor." Those abolitionists were suspicious. Preachers overwhelmingly supported the colonization idea. There was a short range result in the increased interest in antislavery ideas in the South. Indeed, there was a large expansion in abolitionist societies in both slave and free states. It also increased the anger of slaveholders. [9]

Virginian aristocrat and successful criminal lawyer, Andrew Stevenson, later speaker of the national House of Representatives was in a race for the position of representative in his Richmond district. The election was to take place in April of 1817. The past January. Andrew had been appointed director of the Richmond branch of the Second United States Bank. Soon, he was running for Congress against the sitting representative John Tyler. The two men were Republicans and held the same beliefs. For this reason it was a popularity contest. An exciting and close race, it invigorated the friends of each. Stevenson carried Richmond by a large majority, but Tyler received an all but unanimous vote in his home county of Charles City. When the votes were counted, Tyler won by the narrow margin of about 100 votes. The key was described by Mrs. John Tyler, who later went with her husband to the White House as First Lady.

She was quoted as saying that "one time, in his contest with Mr. Stevenson, when it was thought the votes would count very close, old Mr. Minge took his horses and wagon, in a perfect fit of enthusiasm, and drove for three days over all the country, and collected the maimed, the halt, the blind, and those who never had voted for any one, and brought them to the polls, and Tyler had *a larger majority than there ever had been voters in the county before.* Was it not a pretty signal defeat for Mr. Stevenson?" So Stevenson went on to serve in the Richmond City Council for three years. [10]

On April 19, 1817, ex-president John Adams wrote Thomas Jefferson that he could not be a misanthrope, because he was a man. "I must hate myself before I can hate my Fellow Men; and that I cannot and will not do. No! I will not hate any of them, base, brutal and devilish as some of them have been to me."

He did not think well of his fellow men however, but he pitied them. He deprecated their universal credulity cause by fears of calamities in life and fears of punishment after death. The pain and death in life "do not seem to have so unconquerable a fear of what is to come hereafter." The elite were just as credulous as to the lowest grades of employees. Both believed in divine right. He scored the churches for their auto de fees and excommunications. Baptisms had been refused in Philadelphia. Adams was a religious man but organized religion was too criminal to suit the ex-president. Adams did believe in the devil. Freedom of religion was still debated in America in 1817, as denied even into the twenty-first century.

The days later, Abigail Adams, John's loving wife, wrote Jefferson in the interests of a young man going to Europe for his health. She noted that "Mr. Thomas Lyman, who possesses an ardent thirst for Literature, and whose father, is one of our most respectable characters for probity, honor, and wealth, this young gentleman has been much out of health, occasioned by too close application to his studies. He is now going abroad with the hopes of regaining it. He is desirous of getting an introduction to some gentlemen of letters in France." John had given him introductions to such as La Fayette, Marbois, and Gallatin. She wished more of a recent date from Jefferson. The young man knew French and had an uncle, Mr. Williams, who had been a consul in England, but who evidently could not help him as much as Adams and Jefferson. He had been to Europe and understood that only introductions could open doors there.

Having just received the letter of John in early May, Thomas Jefferson wrote that he had believed that the "last retreat of monkish darkness, bigotry, and abhorrence of those advances of the mind which had carried other states a century ahead of them. They seemed still to be exactly where their forefathers were when they schismatised from the Covenant of works, and to consider, a dangerous heresies, all innovations good or bad." He was happy that these dens of priesthood had been broken up in America. Jefferson's religion was based on Jesus. Shortly, Jefferson was to answer Agibail's letter in providing some introductions, but many that he knew had long since been given up to the guillotine. [11]

At Charlottesville, Virginia, a group of gentlemen met on May 5, 1817, to form an agricultural society. Their mission was to stimulate and improve agriculture with encouragement by various means including the offer of premiums, increasing yield per acre of staple crops, land reclamation of exhausted farms, crop rotation, experiment, improvement of farm implements in the days before tractors and farm machinery, and improvements of building and work programs.

On October 7th, the retired James Madison was elected president. Many aristocrats attended while Madison, Thomas Jefferson, James Barbour, and Andrew Stevenson, among others, voted by proxy. Stevenson was to attend all regular meetings and give money to the society for its work. Years later the society tried to establish a chair of agriculture at the University of Virginia when it was established. In the year of 1817, the college did not yet exist. The members of the society wrongfully blame the protective tariff for the current agricultural decline. They passed resolutions against high tariffs. [12]

On the celebrated holiday of the Fourth of July of 1817, Governor De Witt Clinton presided over the breaking of ground at Rome, New York, for the Erie Canal. The idea of a canal from the Hudson to Lake Erie had its birth with Governor Morris on the banks of the Niagara River when he wrote to a friend in European 1800. The statesman had been a patriot leader in the Revolutionary War and was a senator in Congress from 1800 to 1803. Morris was a Federalist and was soon to oppose the War of 1812.

It was his vision that hundreds of large ships would be sailing on the lakes. America would, he predicted, become much greater than any empire in Europe. Morris talked about his ideas and took part in many discussions in the first decade of the nineteenth century. Many Americans became interested in the idea. Then Thomas Jefferson recommended that federal surpluses be used to construct canals and turnpike roads. The New York legislature voted to build Morris' canal. Next, it was decided the idea would be practical. In 1810, the state senate established a committee for the project, which included Morris and De Witt Clinton. They estimated in their 1811 report that the canal would cost five million dollars which would be paid back by commercial success in the decades ahead. Six years later, in 1817, work was begun. [13]

---

[1]Brooks, Philip Coolidge, *Diplomacy and the Borderlands; The Adams-Onis Treaty of 1819*, Berkeley: University of California Press, 1939, pp. 78-80. Quotes on p. 78.

[2]Rippy, J. Fred, *Joel R. Poinsett, Versatile American*, Durham NC: Duke University Press, 1935, pp. 65-68.

[3]Griffin, Charles Carroll, *The United States and the Disruption of the Spanish Empire, 1810-1822*, New York: Columbia University Press, 1937, Rep: Ann Arbor: University Microfilms, 1963, pp. 86-96, 110-112.

[4]Adams, Herbert Baxter, *The Life and Writings of Jared Sparks*, 2 vols., Boston: Houghton, Mifflin, 1893, I, 98-112 (Quote on p. 99), and *North American Review*, various.

[5]Daniel, Clifton, *Chronicles of America*, New York: DK Publishers, 1997, p. 264; Morgan, George, *The Life of James Monroe*, Boston: Small, Maynard, 1921, 364-271.

[6]*Maryland Gazette and Political Intelligence*, August 7, 1817, p. 3, August 14, 1817, p. 3.

[7]Garrison, William Lloyd, *Thoughts on African Colonization*, Reprint 1968, Part 2, pp. 9-13.

[8]Quarles, Benjamin, *Black Abolitionists*, New York: Oxford University Press, 1969, pp. 6-7.

[9]Fogel, Robert William, *Without Consent or Contrast: The Rise and Fall of American Slavery*, New York: W.W. Norton, 1989, pp. 252-253.

[10]Wayland, Francis Fry, *Andrew Stevenson: Democrat and Diplomat, 1785-1857*, Philadelphia: University of Pennsylvania Press, 1949, pp. 39-40.

[11]*The Adams-Jefferson Letters*, ed. Cappon, Lester J., 2 vols., Chapel Hill: University of North Carolina Press, 1959, II, 509-514. Quotes pp. 509, 512.

[12]Wayland, *Stevenson*, p. 43.

[13]*America*, VI, 13-18.

Chapter III

WEBSTER

As early as March of 1816, Daniel Webster, a power in national councils, decided to retire from public life with no intent upon returning to the forefront of national politics. At thirty-four, he was already head of the New Hampshire bar and he wanted to return to his legal practice to earn some money. His income of two thousand a year, although high for the times, was insufficient. Webster had the desire for the life of the rich and well connected. His present situation was unhappy for him. He was to live beyond his means all of this life and be subsidized by wealthy men. But at this time, he had just lost all of his property in a fire and wanted to recover that and better himself. The fire had taken place in Portsmouth on December 22, 1813.

He did not want to remain in his native New Hampshire, but move to a big city and obtain the fruits that could only come from that kind of place of legal employment. The ambitious always had an interest in big cities where their talents could usually be better employed. Webster considered moving to Albany, New York City or Boston. One of the three would surely give him the opportunity to wealth that he craved. Public acclaim was not enough; money was his goal. Money was a means however and not an end. He wanted to live well and enjoy the living style of the rich. He was always to spend lavishly for a man of his position and never salted away money that could be spent.

Finally, he decided upon Boston, probably because he had connections there and it would be easier to start, a difficult task for independent lawyers. With his fame it would not take time to develop his practice, but the choice of Boston would give him a head start. The city was also in his New England and after all Boston was almost as good a place for being a lawyer as was New York City. While a senator, he had practiced law and loved the profession, evidently more than the more difficult task of serving the people in Washington DC.

In Boston, Webster was a success and in time the chief lawyers had to accept him as their equal. Biographer Frederic Austin Ogg wrote that "there had not yet come into his countenance that striking, even awe-inspiring, appearance of solemn majesty which in later years transfixed men who gazed upon him. But even now his presence was such that, by all accounts, when he so much as entered a room every eye was riveted upon him and voices were hushed." He soon gained the friendship of not only the outstanding lawyers in the city, but with the leadership in all callings.

Business so crowded upon him that his earnings went up ten times to upwards of twenty thousand dollars a year. He could be glad he was no longer in the government. Busy, he worked long hours, but still had a happy home life and was prominent in high social circles. He read and studied, pursued the items of his profession such as documents and court room performances. His chief interest was in British politics, reading all he could on that subject. However, in the evening, he rested, played, socialized, and spent time with his wife and family.

His biggest case was the Dartmouth College case which helped develop constitutional law. This had its beginnings in the attempts of some trustees to drive John Wheelock from the presidency of Dartmouth. There had been friction from this then hereditary college office. The trustees attacked and Wheelock counter-attacked. He hired Webster, but the man was to prove a weak reed for Wheelock and abandoned the president because he felt he had a poor case.

In 1815, Wheelock was dismissed. Wheelock and his friends went over to the new Republican governor William Plumer, who had left the Federalist party to run and win. With Plumber's help, they extended the college to a university and appointed additional trustees. Plumer wanted to model Dartmouth on the liberal and boring University of Virginia. Webster decided to defend the college. He won the case with a two-hour speech against Wheelock and his faction. The court validated the charter of 1816 and ruled that the college was a public and not a private institution since it was a corporation. Therefore, it was subject to the actions of the government.

Wheelock appealed to the Supreme Court of the United States. Webster pleaded the case in Washington DC and at the end of the argument, grew emotional. Soon Marshall and the justices were also in tears. The case was discussed further, but since the justices were so divided, the decision was delayed. Then came the time: Marshall ruled that contracts were sacred and the college was no exception. The legislature could not change this. Plumer's acts were unconstitutional. Five justices including Marshall had agreed upon this. One was absent and one was dissenting. Justice Story was not for the decision but he went along with the majority. There was a vote of five to one.

This decision was to have a great effect upon the laws of the land and upon government. Contracts were supported as binding and the state could not intervene. Webster was benefited by his performance in the case and went down in history as the deciding factor in the decision being such as it was. His renown was great and the business poured into his office as never before. Wheeler's contract with the college was approved and Dartmouth remained a Federal college until the end of that period of political parties.

But changes were to eventually come even to Dartmouth. Nineteenth century liberalism was a powerful force that was to win all campaigns if not all victories. At the time liberalism was not conservative, but in our day many of its principles have become the property of conservatives. Others have not and the liberalism of that century was to begin the groundwork for liberalism of today. That is, it looked ahead to the future and supported change that would bring benefits. But not all change, as the Communists of the twentieth century proved, was for the good. Liberalism also set the stage for radical movements, which had been ever present in the nineteenth century. [1]

At this time, in Florida, there was a British merchant named Arbuthnot who was licensed to trade in the Spanish colony. The friend of the Americans, Edmund Doyle, told the Americans that this trader was an illegal trader . Doyle had a bone to pick with Arbuthnot because he was a competitor. He claimed that Arbuthnot was an illegal merchant because Forbes and company had the exclusive right to control trade in Florida. It turned out not to be so exclusive because other licenses had been issued. This probably made Forbes even more friendly to the Americans.

It was true that Arbuthnot was favorably disposed to the Indians of the colony and his reasons are clear. There were profits to be made and a living to be earned. He wrote in his journal that "these men are children of nature, leave them in their forests to till their fields, and hung the stag, and graze the cattle, their ideas will extend no farther and the *honest* trader in supplying their moderate wants may make a handsome profit on them." He believed that the Indians were victims of ill treatment by his fellow British and cheated by the Americans and others. They sold them high priced goods in return for low cost peltry; an uneven proposition of unfair trade and greater profits.

The British had used the Indians against the Americans in the War of 1812 and now abandoned them to those same former enemies in the then recent conflict. Colonel Nicholls had laid down instructions for the Indians to conduct themselves by, but left them no guide. He placed himself in the position of legal spokesman for the natives, which stand engendered jealousy among the other traders and conflict with the American. The latter had their reasons to hateArbuthnot, stirred up by Doyle. Arbuthnot wanted the lands in Georgia returned to the Indians as provided for in the treaty of peace.

However, the peaceable Arbuthnot was not encouraging the Florida Indians to fight the Americans. When Jackson invaded Florida, he advised the Indians to retreat. There is no evidence that Arbuthnot arrival in Florida caused a hostile view to be undertaken by the Indians, however much it is claimed to the contrary. The natives were already hostile, as they had been for a long time. The presence of the escaped slaves was more likely to have more effect on the Indians as had the war fever of the border between the United States and Spanish America. The testimony of William Hamby and Peter Cook which led to the conviction of Arbuthnot was tainted since the Britisher was a commercial rivalry of Hamby and had fired Cook for stealing.

Arbuthnot had met Captain George Woodbine in Florida where Woodbine was trying to reaffirm Indian friendship and support for England. Arbuthnot considered Woodbine to be deceiving the naives. The pro-Indian Arbuthnot and pro-British Woodbine were on a collision course. He felt Woodbine to be overbearing and wishing to have everyone be subservient to him. Woodbine had as an assistant Robert Christie Ambrister, a noted liar. Woodbine had the position as the instigator of the Indians against the Americans in the war. According to accounts, everybody disliked Woodbine.

Woodbine did sympathize with the Indians and anti-slavery, but as an adventurer he did cause trouble.

The Spaniard and the Americans were soon met with trouble from another adventurer. With some support from Baltimore merchants and commissioners from New Granada and Mexico, Gregor MacGregor led two hundred men in June to Florida. They seized Amelia Island and drove out eighty or so Spanish soldiers on garrison duty there. Woodbine visited him and promised British disbanded soldiers would come from New Providence and Jamaica to aid him in conquering Florida. Woodbine was acting on his own initiative without British support. When MacGregor went with Woodbine to New Providence, Mexican filibuster Commodore Luis Aury moved in with his men and took Amelia Island, and most of MacGregor's men went over to him, giving Aury over three hundred men to hold the island. Woodbine was set to raise an army for MacGregor when Bahamian Governor Charles Cameron stepped in and quash the deal, thus preventing a Woodbine-MacGregor conquest of Florida which had been momentarily possible. [2]

The commanding officer of the 7th Infantry demolished Fort Montgomery (Alabama) and built it into a camp. He directed that on the site of the fort be built tolerably good barracks using round logs which would promote the health and comfort of his troops unlike the confines of the walls of the fort. Next to camp he built a large enough hospital under the able direction of Surgeon Thomas Lawson. The nearest fort was now Fort Crawford , fifty miles to the east and fifty miles to the south was the town of Pensacola in Spanish Florida. Fort Crawford was not yet finished by the last of April of 1817. It was a good defense against small arms. It was also a healthy location.

Provisions came from New Orleans on a wagon road, but Major General Gaines was still busy making arrangements for a supply route upriver from Pensacola. The Fourth Regiment had a cantonment called Montpelier seven miles from Camp Montgomery. Also there was Fort Gaines in the vicinity, supplied from Georgia. It was surrounded by rather hostile Indians, especially the Seminole who were being supplied with powder, lead, knives, tomahawks, drums by British agents according to reports received by the Americans.

The inspector sent out to report had this to say about the Seminole. He would not be astonished to see this tribe or tribes to carry out their threats. This was because of the large number of dissatisfied people among them. However, in case they do make trouble, it would take a twelve-month war to crush them. In the opinion of John M. Davis, the Seminoles and their party would always annoy the Americans until one gets possession of East Florida. He hoped this would not be too far distant.

As dangerous as Fort Gaines with its Seminole, Fort Scott was on the west bank of Flint River and a temporary work of logs, with a small magazine. The Fourth Regiment had been working on this fort when they received orders to go to Camp Montpelier. Seminoles were reported to have burn the unfinished work. Judging from the dangers of the Seminole, it might have been better to have finished and staffed Fort Scott strong enough to have kept them in hand. Fort Jackson was almost abandoned although it was a healthful situation for troops. Supplies could come up the Alabama River from New

Orleans. In Georgia was Fort Hawkins on the road from Milledgeville to St. Stephens in the Mississippi Territory. It was a regular built stockade. [3]

British Colonel Nicolls, harboring ill will toward the Americans, decided to encourage the Red Sticks to believe that Britain would help them regain the land lost to the Indians by the Treaty of Fort Jackson. At the end of the War of 1812, he took Hillis Hadjo or Francis the Prophet, leader of the Red Sticks rebels who had gone to Florida, with him back to England. The chief was well received by the Government and had an interview with George the Prince Regent. Francis was led to believe that the British would intervene militarily, when in fact they had no such notion. When Francis returned, he received the support of the Scotsman Alexander Arbuthnot, who also protested the treaty. He wanted to trade with the Indians and encouraged them for this reason. From his base in the Bahamas Islands, Arbuthnot established a trading store on the edge of Ochlockonee Sound.

Meanwhile, the whites and Indians were a loggers-head and there were killings on both sides. The settlers struck first and the Indians retaliated, trying to equal the score. Then Major General Edmund P. Gaines demanded that the Indians turned over the members of their tribe who had murdered a woman and two children near St. Mary's River. On September 11, 1817, Chief Kinhagee justified the Indians as merely seeking retaliation and stated the situation had not yet reached their satisfaction. They needed to kill three more men. Gaines responded by sending this letter and calling the Indians belligerent.

Monroe sent a large force to Fort Scott demanding retaliation and moving of the natives if they did not make reparations for what they had done. Gaines tried to begin talks with Chief Neamatha, but he refused. He wanted to have nothing more to do with the white man. When Gaines sent two successive forces to attack and kill a few Indians, the rest fled to the swamps. From what was found in one village, the British were implicated. Then Lieutenant Richard W. Scott and four others were killed in an Indian attack on a barge. They were ambushed along the Apalachicola River. Calhoun sent General Andrew Jackson in to destroy the Indians, at which missions he was good and could be counted upon to win.

Jackson marched some several hundred Tennesseans, Kentuckians, and regulars against the Indians. Nine hundred Georgian militiamen and fifteen hundred Lower Creek warriors joined Jackson. The Creek wished to establish their power over the renegade Creek Red Sticks. Jackson marched south of the border without opposition. Chief Okiakhija's Indian forces shattered before the Jackson army, which was formidable indeed. Needing a food supply, Jackson then marched to secure one. He ordered Lieutenant James Gadsden to build a fort at Prospect Bluff. After resting Jackson proceeded forth from Fort Gadsden. Major David E. Twiggs scouted the Indian town of Tallahassee in what he considered to excellent land, where the Indians had their fields of agricultural product. The hostile Indians were outnumbered by almost three to one. However, they fired upon the Americans and then retreated.

Jackson seized St. Marks from the protesting hands of Spanish commandant Francisco Caso y Luengo, who justly claimed that this was Spanish territory and that the Americans did not belong there. There was a running battle with Chief Peter McQueen with light Indian losses and even lighter American losses. The Indian chief fled to the swamps, and Francis escaped for the time being. Indian trader William Hambly turned against the Indians when captured and informed Jackson of the moves of the hostile Indians.

Francis was then tricked into a ship from which the Americans flew the British Union Jack flag. Jackson ordered Francis and a friend hanged. Francis, a humane man of wealth and virtues, died a brave man. Then Jackson put Arbuthnot and Richard C. Ambrister, a British Marine veteran to death. Hambly told of Spanish support of the hostile Indians at Pensacola, so Jackson marched there and took over the Spanish town, before returning to Nashville, Tennessee, happy with the results of his wolf hunt. Some of the soldiers of Jackson's army returned to this area to settle at a later time. [4]

It was election time in Missouri. Thomas Hart Benton was going to the polls on August 4, 1817, He stepped up to receive a ballot and saw an old enemy by the name of Charles Lucas, son of Judge John B.C. Lucas. The twenty-five year old Lucas challenged Benton's right to vote. He asked if he paid his taxes. Affronted. Benton turned to the election judges to say that he would answer any questions from them, but none from this "puppy." Charles felt insulted.

This was worthy of a challenge for a duel. When Benton would not withdraw his statement, it was a prelude to action. It was a matter of honor in the terms of the men of the day and arrangements were made. They had equal pistols in length and both smoothbore. The pair met on an island in the Mississippi, thirty feet apart. When it came time to fire, the word was given. The men pulled their triggers. Two reports were heard. Lucas fell from a throat wound and Benton had a slight contusion below his right knee. Dr. Garrit Quarles said there could be no second shots, but Lucas agreed to another meeting. Helped back to his boat, he fainted.

People talked about the duel and divided into pro-Benton and pro-Lucas factions. For the judge it was no longer a matter of honor, but a murder if Benton persisted in another encounter. Thomas' friends tried to convince him to forgo a second meeting, since it would seem like vengeance. Judge Lucas thought that Lucas honor would insist upon a second duel. Charles tried to avoid another meeting, but Benton, unhappy about rumors about his former experiences at the University of North Carolina, insisted.

The second encounter ended in a shot to Lucas' heart ; the young man forgave Benton and died. It was anguish for Benton, but even more pain for the judge. His son was dead and he published many attacks on Benton. The elder Lucas tried to arrange a boycott of Benton's law practice. He attacked Benton at every opportunity, but Benton held his peace. He told friends however that he wished it had never happened. Sin in haste and repent at leisure! The elder Lucas never forgave Benton to his dying day.[5]

After a trip of difficult and hard dimensions, Henry B. Fearon arrived at New York and formed a good impression of New York Bay, but a not-so-good opinion of the people of New York City. In hiring a boy to procure them two hackneys, he was upset somewhat by the boy's independence and dissatisfaction over what he was paid. John Quincy Adams was of the party and paid the boy a half-a-dollar, better than three times what Fearon was paying. Fearon noted this adventure in his letter to friends in England as a part of his mission in America. His goal was to seek out the land and report back on what he found, so Britons could determine whether they wished to emigrate there or not.

Fearon found the streets narrow and dirty and the people also lacked cleanliness. He saw a lot of tall, lean men, very few old people and women. The women, he was told, were at resorts. The chronicler wrote that the laboring men were better dressed than their counterparts in England. They were more erect and less care-worn in their countenances. The people did not worry about tomorrow and there were no beggars. Indeed due to the still scarcity of labor in America the working class were better paid and better treated than at most times in United States history, excepting the colonial times when labor was even more in demand. The contrast with England was great. There workers were poorer and in bad shape. However the status of the American working people was in a decline, which was to lead to labor unrest in the thirties.

Building contractors were very busy in the city, working for the most part by contract. The country was still in the midst of a boom. Houses had to be made of brick, except in the suburbs. There was a superior cabinet work in New York, being light and elegant. In all, Fearon found America in good economic shape. [6]

Acting Secretary of State Richard Rush wrote Richard M. Johnson on September 16, 1817, that he had received a second letter from the British Minister about the question of the release of prisoners. These had been held by the Indians in the Old Northwest. Rush wanted the killer of Tecumseh to know that the Department was trying to gain the freedom of those captives of previously warring Indians around Lake Huron. In Canada, Sir John Sherbroake was making efforts for the release of the people. [7]

In 1817, Thomas Lincoln hunted a lot and made a trip back to Kentucky to buy hogs. Nancy's aunt and uncle, Betsy and Thomas Sparrow, and her cousin Dennis Hanks joined them in Indiana. Lincoln had almost completed a cabin, which lacked a door, windows, or floor, and whose roof was unfinished. The male folk in the extended family spent their time mostly hunting, but managed to clear a space of six acres which they planted in corn and vegetables. [8]

The Lincolns found Indiana to be a wild land with bears, deer, and other wild animals. Thomas had settled in a land of forest and his priority after the dwelling was built was to clear land of the trees. Young Abe was large for eight and was given an axe to use for chopping down trees. This useful tool was used a lot by Abraham for the next fifteen years. He also helped plow and harvest. Hunting was a major source of food for a pioneer family bur Lincoln did not take to it. In February of 1817, Abe was in the log cabin when he saw a flock of wild turkey. He took his rifle and shot a turkey through a crack. Since this bag, he never shot at any larger game. [9]

Young Abe grew up to be strong like his father. He was well disciplined by Thomas. They were much alike, being friendly and endowed with a good sense of humor.

Moderate in their habits, both men were noted for patience and kindness. The pair had the same saying which was cherished. Thomas and Abraham would say that "if you make a bad bargain, hug it tighter." Childhood friend John Romine remembered that Lincoln loved to read and think even to the inclusion of his work. Romine hired him and thought him decidedly lazy because Lincoln preferred to tell jokes and stories. Lincoln told the employer that Thomas taught him to work but never to love it. Lincoln decided upon learning as much as possible. The young man was also a listener. [10]

[1]Ogg, Frederic Austin, *Daniel Webster*, Philadelphia: George W. Jacobs, 1914, pp. 110-126. Quote on pp. 111-112.

[2]Owsley, Frank L., Jr., "Ambrister And Arbuthnot: Adventurers of Martyrs for British Honor?," *Journal of the Early Republic*, V (1985), 289-308.

[3]Carter, *Territorial*, XVIII, 92-95.

[4]Paisley, Clifton, *The Red Hills of Florida, 1528-1865*, Tuscaloosa Fla.: University of Alabama Press, 1989, pp. 44-56.

[5]Chambers, William Nisbet, *Old Bullion Benton: Senator from the New West*, Boston: Little, Brown, 1956, pp. 72-76.

[6]Fearon, Henry B., *Sketches of America*, 2d ed., 1819, pp. 1-6, 9-10, 22-24.

[7]*Maryland Gazette and Political Intelligencer*, October 30, 1817, p. 4.

[8]Beveridge, Albert J., *Abraham Lincoln, 1809-1858*, 2 vols. Boston: Houghton Mifflin, 1928, I, 44-46.

[9]Pratt, H.E., *Lincoln 1809-1839*, 1941, p. 4.

[10]Strozier, Charles B., *Lincoln's Quest for Union: Public and Private Meanings*, New York: Basic Books, 1982, pp. 14, 20-22.

Chapter IV

LUNDY

Quaker Benjamin Lundy published his first anti-slavery essay on October 10, 1817, to establish himself as an early abolitionist of the nineteenth century school which wanted the total demolishment of slavery. This article came out in the *Philanthropist*, a Quaker newspaper at Mount Pleasant, Ohio. Lundy had been an only child, born on January 4, 1789, in Greensville, New Jersey. When he was four, his mother died and he was reared by a kind step-mother. He received little formal schooling and early worked on the farm. Benjamin worked so hard that he became ill and developed a deafness. Reared a Quaker, he was led in a path of distinction in that his faith set him apart from the usual life of a boy and of mistrust of worldly values.

Because of the humanitarian nature of his faith, Lundy was early adverse to slavery and this was to set the pattern that made him his important contribution to life in his times. New Jersey then was a slaver state, but when he was fifteen, its legislators provided for gradual emancipation for the black slaves. At age twenty, he left home to travel and see the world which he had been excluded from. He became a leather goods craftsman in Wheeling, West Virginia. There was freedom in the town, but Lundy kept his Quaker manners and conscience. He saw the coffees of chained and handcuffed slaves headed for new plantations down the Ohio and Mississippi Rivers, and was moved by the sight of his fellow sufferers. It was the shock of his life. Benjamin vowed he would break at least one link in the chain of slavery.

He was now dedicated to the anti-slavery movement. Soon he moved to Mount Pleasant, a few miles west of Wheeling. Lundy now paid attention to the opponents of the peculiar institution. The young man opened up his own saddle shop and married Esther Lewis of Mount Pleasant. They moved ten miles west to St. Clairsville. His wife was a Quaker girl and they were well matched in faith and character. Then he met Quaker minister Charles Osborn in the slavery society. His Union Humane Society was founded with friends in 1816. Osborn, who had been passing through, returned to Mount Pleasant and started publishing the *Philanthropist*. Lundy helped Osborn edit the paper in addition to working in his saddle shop. His life was set. [1]

On this date, November 28, 1817, a lady of about fifty by the name of Anne Newport Royall was taking her first long trip following the death of her rich husband. She wrote a series of letters on her trip which she later published. Later, when her money ran out, she made a career of her writing but was often in great poverty and resorted to powerful language and even abuse against religious and political opponents. This was usual in the newspapers and books of the period and is not unknown today, but the fact that she was a woman made it unusual and more subject to criticism. But she lived to be in her mid-eighties and wrote up until that time.

She was to reject religious organizations and people and attack politicians who did not contribute to her newspaper sales and buy her books of which there were ten in all. These politicians who included the great as well as the minor were greatly relieved when this ardent reformer died. She did act as a brake on and exposure of corruption and was much feared by those engaged in putting relatives on the public payroll and selling influence. She proved to be against anti-Masonry, especially because Masons had come to her rescue so many times, and against the Bank as well as clerics and churches in general.

She made herself known and is known today chiefly as a travel book author, at which she excelled. Her fiery nature led to her being abusive from time to time, but most people continued to be interviewed by her more or less willingly. If one includes her newspaper work, she outwrote everyone else in sight. And interested them and kept them in line as much as any single woman could do in a man's world.

This was all in the future, however, for at the time she was unknown and not yet strong in dipping her pen with strong portraits. She did record the true and stirring events of her time. On this night she was setting in for her writing with a Mr. Ladely, who was doing the same. They were in a tavern where two drunk friends were in their small family room and found them arguing politics most loudly and insistently. They had no concern for the peace of the others and soon turned to the scriptures about which they then proceeded to disagree about too. Anne objected to this since the scriptures in her views were meant to be practiced and not debated.

At this point Anne retired for the evening into a room for women in the tavern. She was not to say whether the argument which she observed continued. If they talked on, she could have heard the loud conversation through the walls. At any rate she did not appreciate the loudness of the quarrel, being reasonable in her age, as she was not always to be in her future. [2]

Calhoun was selected as Monroe's secretary of war after many men had turned down the office including Clay, Jackson, Governor Isaac Shelby of Kentucky and others. He was successful in the office and a reviewer of his life wrote that "fortune favored him again. Entering to office a long vacancy, and when it was filled with the unfinished business of the war--fifty million dollars of deferred claims, for one item,--he had the same early opportunity for distinction which a steward has who takes charge of an estate just out of chancery, and under a new proprietor who has plenty of money. The sweeping up of the dead leaves, in gathering of the fallen branches, and the weeding out of a path, changes the aspect of the place, and gives the passer-by a prodigious idea of the efficiency of the new broom. The country was alive, too, to the necessity of coast and frontier defenses, and there was much building of the forts during the seven years of Mr. Calhoun. Respecting the manner in which he discharged the multifarious and unusual duties of his office, we have heard anything but commendation. He was prompt, punctual, diligent, courtesy, and firm. The rules he drew up for the regulation of a War Department remained in force, like changed, until the magnitude of the late contest abolished or suspended all ancient method. The claims of the soldier were rapidly examined and passed upon." Calhoun gathered troops at forts for training. He took interest in Indian education. He reduced expenses, making things more effective and efficient. In total he was a great secretary of war. Quality will out. [3]

One of Calhoun problems was the Indians. The Seminoles of Florida and the white settlers were in conflict. Both raided the others livestock, burned each other's houses, and murdered each other. Gaines lectured Kinache and Bowlegs. He said the Seminole were very bad people, having murdered and stolen. They had harbored African American slaves at Suwannee River. "If you give me leave to go by you against them. I shall not hurt anything belonging to you."

Kinache replied that Gaines had charged him with murder, thievery, and burning., "While one American has been justly killed while in the act of stealing cattle, more than four Indians while hunting have been murdered by these lawless freebooters. I harbor no Negroes...I shall use force to stop any armed American from passing my towns or my lands." Red Stick Neamathla of Fowltown village near Fort Smith warned Major Davis E. Twiggs: "I warn you not to cross or cut a stick of wood in the east side of the Flint. That land is mine. I am directed by the power above and power below to protect and defend it. I shall do so."

Neamathla and his Seminole people were living within American territory and because they refused to turn over alleged murderers, Jackson authorized Major David E. Twiggs to remove them. Twiggs asked Neamathla for an interview, but when the Indian chief refused, Gaines ordered Twiggs to attack the village. Twiggs prepared his men and then moved out for a night march in an attempt to surprise the Indians with his 250 men. At daybreak on November 21, 1817, Twiggs attacked. Before the Indians could flee to a swamp, the Americans had killed four men and one woman. This began the First Seminole War.

Lieutenant Colonel Aruckle led his 300 men through the town and was attacked by sixty Seminole who then retreated with light losses. The Americans lost one killed and two wounded. The Indians lost six to eight men. The Seminole then moved to Lake Miccosukee to join with Kinache's villagers. Creek Indian agent David Mitchell was later critical of the whole episode, considering Naemathla and his fellows friendly to the whites.

Indians decided to take their revenge on the settlers as the war expanded. On November 30, 1817, a band ambushed an open boat, commanded by Lieutenant Robert W. Scott, on the Apalachcola. The large boat came close to the shore to avoid a strong current when the Indians fired upon its forty soldiers, seven women, and some children. Only thirteen survived. Soldiers who had plunged in the river and swam to the fort reported the massacre. A later convoy of three boats was attacked on the same river and stayed until rescued from the fort. It was unsafe on the waterway. There was another attack on a store and still other raids on American plantations for plunder and killing.

Washington reacted promptly. Calhoun directed Jackson to raise men and lead an expedition to protect Fort Scott which was running out of food. Jackson arrived in forty-six days and soon built another fort nearby called Fort Gadsen. Meanwhile, General William McIntosh and friendly whites moved in the area. They captured 53 warriors and 180 women and children, stealing Jackson's thunder. The also liberated a great store of corn. Colonel Edward Elliott arrived with more troops and soon the entire force under Jackson including McIntosh numbered 3,500 men. When Jackson advanced the Indians outnumbered ten to one had to flee for the swamps. Jackson then seized the fort at St. Mark's. Two Red Stick leaders were hung without a trial, a task congenial to Jackson. He did capture Englishman Alexander Arbuthnot, who had a trading post in Florida and who was suspected of stirring up the Indians against the Americans.

In an engagement between the Americans and Seminole, the latter were badly defeated with great loss of life and captives. The Americans also took 500 head of cattle plus many horses and large amounts of corn. There was a battle on April 16, 1818, in which freed blacks were soon forced to swim across the river to safety. Losses were light. Jackson also captured Robert Ambrister, who was trying to wrest Florida for Great Britain. Jackson executed the two men after unfair trials. [4]

The Seminole had raided American settlements encroaching upon their tribal lands in Florida and had caused losses among the whites. Calhoun was angry and demanded that the Seminole pay reparations. Monroe decided that if the Indians did not give payment that the Americans could cross the international line and strike the lands of the Indians. He would draw the line at attacking them if they found refuge in a Spanish fort. If this last was the case, General Edmund P. Gaines was to notify Calhoun. Monroe did not want war with Spain.

Andrew Jackson wrote from Nashville that the recent victory of the Americans over the Seminole at Fowltown might incline the Indians toward peace. If this peace was not reestablished than America must strike them in their den of Florida. Spanish territory would be no place of safety. The Seminole had murdered too many people to get away with punishing action. After all Spain was bound by treaty to keep the Indians at peace. [5]

Generals Andrew Jackson and Edmund P. Gaines wanted to march into Spanish Florida and clean out the Indians. Because Washington was deeply involved with Spanish-American negotiations, the administration did not think it to be a good idea. Then they contradicted themselves and informed the two men that it was their decision whether to act or not. On December 16, 1817, came firm orders. It was all right to chastise the Indians in Florida, except that they were not to attack the Seminole if they were camped beside a Spanish fort. Then came distinct orders from the secretary of war.

He directly ordered Jackson to take command and bring them under control. Calhoun felt that Jackson was the man to terminate the conflict with force.

Jackson did so, but before he arrived, the commanders at Fort Scott undertook the campaign. Their intelligence system told them that Capechimico, a Mikasuki chief, was generaling the hostile activities of the Seminole. The army marched to Fowltown. They reached the Indian town on January 4, 1818, and burn it to the ground. It had been deserted and there was not a shot fired. On March 9th Jackson arrived at Fort Scott. He was ready for action and marched 1,500 Americans and 2,000 Creeks into Florida. Of the white soldiers, five hundred were regulars and one thousand were militiamen, chiefly from Tennessee, Jackson's home state. The Indians opposed them with bows and arrows when the ammunition ran out. However, the Seminole were swiftly defeated and Jackson had his men burn the Mikasuki towns.

There was one hard fight. A band of over two hundred and maybe three hundred black Seminole, west of the Suwannee River, were in good spirits and fought a rear-guard action. These escaped slaves were outnumbered four to one, but they fought bravely. They had muskets to the American rifles, but nothing could daunt their fervor. When Jackson defeated them, the general moved on to the principal non-Mikasuki Seminole town and found the Indians had left before their arrival. He ordered the town robbed and burnt. It is possible that the blacks had delayed Jackson enough to allow the inhabitants to escape. Jackson's aggressive manner and leadership abilities bore fruit. This Florida action were to earn him enemies and a long lasting controversy. [6]

One frontiersman was in a position to discern the advantages of western settlement and English Prairie, Illinois. He was a prosperous farmer and settlement leader named Morris Birkbeck. Born in Yorkshire, England, on January 23, 1764, he grew up to be a prosperous farmer in Surrey. Still he did not own the land, only leased it, and this he deemed an disadvantage. He was credited with being the first breeder of merino sheep in England and was progressive in many farming ways, but was denied the vote because he did not hold his land and was a Quaker. Things were not good. Taxes and prices were too high. Agriculturally, the country was in trouble. His wife died. So Morris Brikbeck went to America following the advice of his friend George Flower.

In America, Birkbeck published two books. One was on his American trip. The other was on his settlement in Illinois. Birkbeck and Flowers bought up land for the settlement of Englishmen who wanted to farm in fertile and stout land. Each man founded a town. The land cost them two dollars per acre. Into this Eden came some trouble. Birkbeck's daughters had brought alone a young Englishman named Eliza Andrews. Birkbeck, a widower, was attracted to her and wanted to marry her. Then he discovered the young lady and Flowers had an understanding to marry. Birkbeck attended the wedding but thereafter the two men went their separate ways.

Two years later Birkbeck became president of Illinois' agricultural society and pioneered in raising cattle, scientific farming, and drainage. His farm was a model for all to see. He worked to save Illinois from slavery and briefly was secretary of state for the state. He died crossing a swollen river months later. The reason for choosing Illinois was that the good land was not yet taken there and was cheaper. Prices varied from low to high all depending on the items purchased.

The next day, he wrote that his outlay in Illinois required one half the capital that would be needed in England. The land was his and after fourteen years there was no lease to expire. At that time the land would have increased in value many fold. His house would be just as good as the one he had in England. He advised others not to be timid, but come and settle in Illinois. [7]

Settlement and colonization in the enormous Mississippi river system faced a harder danger than the relatively short-lived Indian menace in any particular frontier area or the temporary task of clearing the land. That problem was the ill-health caused by the great and almost universal attendant of fevers with no geographic exemption. The boundaries were the Appalachian Mountains in the east, the Rocky Mountains in the west and the southwestern dry region of mountains and deserts. Pioneers measured the valley's reputation for unhealthliness and made a regular topic of fevers and illnesses of various parts down to the locale.

Farmers soon learned that farming areas like western Virginia, in the mountain valleys, were poor, and they learned that where the soils were deep and fertile there was a price to pay in the lack of a healthy environment. And it was not the climate but the region that was the determining factor. This was realized, but they were not knowledgeable about the actual cause of disease. The people believed most commonly "in the early nineteenth century was that the fogs and vapors which hoved about stagnant waters, swamps, and muddy river bottoms, and the miasma and effluvia which arose from the decomposition of vegetable and animal matter were the chief causes of physical disorders."

Although the pioneers were well aware of the troublesome swarms of mosquitoes and other insects and animals, which could be found everywhere, they did not know of the connection between these pests and the spread of disease. Mosquitoes with their breeding grounds were nuisances and an abomination, but the insects' roles in transmitting disease was unknown. The early pioneers sought healthful locale but in time they recognized the great river system was overspread with bad health. Older frontiersmen were to warn prospective settlers not to construct homes near stagnant waters and bayous, with an unfortunate advise to deaf ears. [8]

North Carolina Governor William Miller, following his predecessors in urging a public school system for his state. His promotion of education went to the legislature in whose committee Archibald D. Murphey wrote as chairman a report for the democratic form of education. Thousands of children were raised in ignorance in the state. Strength lay in people and Murphey thought that the state could afford an expenditure of half of one million dollars, a very large sum for the time, for education. He presented his report in November of 1817. This was the dawn of a new era for North Carolina. The emphasis of the plan was primary education, which would be extended to all children. Murphey was to be called the father of North Carolina education. [9]

On the second day after Sam Houston became sub-agent of the Cherokee Nation, he was called upon to attend an important meeting of agents and Indians. He had been delayed by illness. When he arrived, Houston found the party unready. He was there when the agents exhibited plenty of provisions, which had just reached the store for the Indians. They were delighted at the abundance and readily agreed to withdraw blankets and other items for a long trail as emigrants to the west. Houston followed the advice of Governor Joseph McMinn and issued some second rate blankets. He recognized that the Cherokees would not have enough to make the journey tolerable. However, Sam believed that Monroe would have approved his action. This sustained Houston although he knew that he was skating on thin ice and did not entirely approve of his own actions. [10]

Federalist Louis McLane from Delaware found common political connections in the House of Representative. He joined a dining group, or mess, of the four Pennsylvania Federalists, the only remaining Federalists in their state. He became friends withJoseph Hopkinson and young John Sergeant of Philadelphia. The other two men were from villages. They were Isaac Darlington of West Chester and Levi Pauling of Norristown. McLane took a dislike to the Federalists from New England[11]

[1]Dillon, Merton L., *Benjamin Lundy and the Struggle for Negro Freedom*, Urbana: University of Illinois Press, 1966, pp. 1-23.

[2]Royall, Anne Newport, *Letters From Alabama, 1817-1822*, University, Ala: University of Alabama Press, 1969, pp. 15-79. This includes an article by Lucille Griffith on Anne Royal.

[3]"John C. Calhoun," *North American Review*, CI (Oct 1865), 400-401. Quote on pp. 400-401.

[4]Covington, *Seminoles*, pp. 41-47. Quote on p. 41.

[5]Calhoun, John C., *The Papers of John C. Calhoun*, Columbia, SC: University of South Carolina Press, 1959-, II, 20-21, 39-40.

[6]*Ibid.*; Mahon, John K., *History of the Second Seminole War, 1835-1842*, Gainesville, Fla.: University of Florida Press, 1967, Revised edition, 1985, pp. 24-26.

[7]Birkbeck, Morris, *Letter from Illinois*, Rep. 1970, *passim*.

[8]Jones, Billy M., *Health-Seekers in the Southwest, 1817-1900*, Norman: University of Oklahoma Press, 1967, pp. 3-8. Quote on pp. 5-6.

[9]Knight, Edgar Wallace, *Public Education in the South*, Boston: Ginn, 1922, pp. 146-148.

[10]Calhoun, *Papers*, II, 15-16.

[11]Munroe, John A., *Louis McLane: Federalist and Jacksonian*, New Brunswick, NJ: Rutgers University Press, 1973, p. 67.

Chapter V

ALBANY REGENCY

Drawing upon his past experience, Martin Van Buren of New York began the creation of a political machine in 1817 at a time when his political career was at a low ebb with the victory of De Witt Clinton. This organization was the famous Albany Regency which was to raise Van Buren to the pinnacle of state power and open the door to a position in national councils. He knew that a group of lieutenant with leadership abilities would be needed, would be vital to his plans and so he gathered around himself able men for New York's legislature.

The most effective of the Van Buren politicians was the state senator from Utica in his second term. Henry Seymour was born in Connecticut, but had come to upstate New York and settled at the frontier village then named Pompey Hill and later renamed Utica. He had made his way by his own efforts and was a wealthy man by 1817 with a gentility and political ability which was to serve Henry so well in the Albany Regency. Opponents of the machine called him a schemer because of his successful operations in the state legislature. Van Buren benefited from Seymour loyalty to Jeffersonian principles, the party, and Van Buren and also from his friendly and objective criticism.

Roger Skinner also came from the wilderness, representing Vermont emigrants on the northern frontier along the Saint Lawrence and Lake Ontario. De Witt's 1812 dealings with the Federalists had turned these patriotic frontiersmen against him and they also remembered Clinton's harsh treatment of the Green Mountain boys who had settled in eastern New York. These emigrants gave their loyalty to the impetuous Skinner and to the seasoned Van Buren.

Among the chief lieutenants were Samuel Young with important connections and a quick temper, the prosperous merchant from New York City named Walter Bowne and Van Buren's brother-in-law Moses J. Cantine. Young was a hard drinker and Bowne and Cantine were moderate Republicans. There were no great followers in Washington DC, but Van Buren had some influence with Vice-President Daniel D. Tompkins and Senator Nathan Sanford. Although he also had indirect contacts with Smith Thompson who was a personal friend of Monroe's and naval secretary, Van Buren's best hand in the national capital was a trump card. Monroe disliked Clinton. Still Clinton was too strong and popular in New York for Van Buren to oppose openly, but this was to change due to a series of flawed political judgments by Clinton and shrewd moves by Van Buren in personnel changes in the powerful council of appointment. [1]

Meanwhile, the negotiations continued with Spain. Minister Pizarro wanted them assumed in Madrid in a letter to Minister to Spain George W. Erving dated July 16, 1817. The Spaniard then had a plan of settlement. He promised that Spain would cede the Floridas in exchange for title of all the lands the Americans claimed or possessed west of the Mississippi from the Gulf to its source. This plan of August 17th, was immediately rejected by Erving. Within two weeks, Pizarro had return the scene of diplomatic action to Onis with new instructions. He had given concessions, but they were unacceptable. Erving wrote to Adams that the Spanish had an ancient policy of not conceding anything, but this was not quite accurate. He was right when he said the Spanish grandees were living in the times of Charles V when Spain was great.

In January 16, 1818, Adams was to present his own plan, conceived after some months in actual possession of his august office in the Monroe cabinet. Spain was to cede Florida and all land in northern Texas. The border line for Texas would be the Colorado River in the central part of the province. The boundary would go due north from its source to the border of the Louisiana Territory. The United States would then gain Oklahoma and the northern half of Texas along with Florida. Commissioners were to decide upon outstanding claims. The final decision was to be a compromise between this program and the Pizarro claims. [2]

Calhoun found the work in the War Department to be overwhelming and difficult. This was his first executive work and he found it troublesome. On December 14, 1817, he wrote Charles Jared Ingersoll that he was facing the task like a patriot. "If any labors in the War Department, which I find will be considerable, should tend in any degree to advance the growing prosperity of this Republic, I will find myself amply rewarded. The further I look into its concerns, the more I am impressed with the magnitude of its duties. I believe, I may say, little heretofore has been done to give exactness, economy, and dispatch to its moneyed transaction. This has risen from a variety of causes, many of which, I expect, will be found difficult to overcome. I cannot flatter myself that I will be more successful than my predecessors. I can only promise industry and, I think I may say firmness. I certainly have the strongest reason to exert myself, for none felt more deeply than myself that total want of preparation which preceded the last war, and which had nearly been succeeded by the most disastrous consequence." Calhoun began to meet the challenges and persevere like a man. In his letter, he was facing the realities of executive office and was to perform well. Calhoun had the talent. [3]

As secretary of war, Calhoun "strove to organize the War Department into efficient bureaus, maintaining a substantial standing army, construct roads adequate for rapid deployment, and remove the possibility of future collusion between the British and the Northwest Indians." He sent out the Yellowstone Expedition of 1819 and the Long Expedition. He was never able to have as much funding from Congress that he needed, especially with the economic crisis of 1818, but Calhoun was able to institute most of his program. His "surveys and patrols pushed farther up the tributaries of the Missouri and Mississippi Rivers, impressing the Indians and erecting fortifications, and throughout the country soldiers built military roads." In these peaceful years, Zachary Taylor wrote that "the axe, pick, saw and trowel, had become more the implement of the American soldier than the cannon, musket or sword." His department's study of the Indian problem recommended Indian removal. Calhoun supported a high tariff because it raised funds for internal improvements. Calhoun was very much of a nationalist at the time. [4]

Viewing Europe from afar, the Americans found much to deplore there. They were disgusted by and ridiculed the reaction they saw there. The editor of *Niles' Weekly Register* condemned the Congress of Vienna for its disregard of national sovereignty in drawing up the map of Europe. Months later the editor noted that Europe had rid itself of one tyrant, only to become the slaves of a group of despots. It seems that the Congress of Vienna had restored tyranny and called it peace. Editors attacked the idea of the divine right of kings. How could an idiot and madman like George III be seen as possessors of the right to rule rational men numbering in the manifold millions. Americans read in their press of the cruelty engaged in by monarchs to repress revolutionary movements. Later, in 1821, a St. Petersburg editor published his conclusion of the emperor of Austria that he did not want learned men in his country, only good and loyal subjects. Other editors called this remark to be an example of fanaticism.

When Americans learned of the formation of the Holy Alliance, they were suspicious and distrustful. Even the average conservative Americans had no confidence that the alliance would mean peace. How could there be peace with such large standing armies? The editor of the *National Intelligencer* wrote that it looked like an agency for territorial expansion than an organization for religious ideas. However, there were a few who had founded peace societies and jumped at the chance of a Europe meaning peace.

Most people thought that no good would come from the Holy Alliance. They were soon to learn how correct they were. The leaders of the American press kept their readers fully informed on what was happening in Europe. Americans had little good to say of nations which were ruled by kings. With this in mind it is easy to understand why Americans became isolationist in this period. They lost interest in what was happening in Europe. They often stopped subscribing to newspapers which carried so much news on Europe for that reason that they did not want to know events of the east side of the Atlantic.

At this time, the question arose of what Europe would do if the United States supported the independence of the Hispanic Americans to the south. Few people feared any interference. One editor wrote that it was impossible for anyone with any intelligence not to see that there was no danger in the actions the Americans might take to support the people they sympathized with. The Europeans could not and can not hurt America in such a cause. They had enough to do at home to suppress the spirit of freedom, and would not bother the champions of liberty in the New World. No nation had the courage of means to wage open war on America. Henry Clay, John C. Calhoun, and Andrew Jackson felt that there was no problem. [5]

The Reverend John Mason Brown, a Baptist missionary, went forth to preach in 1817. Born to a childhood of poverty on a Connecticut farm, he got his church license as a minister in 1811. Six years later, Brown and James Welch established on western missions in St. Louis. During the ensuing years he rode, reach, and preached throughout Indiana, Illinois, and Missouri. He also organized Baptist churches Brown distributed Baptist tracts and Christian Bibles and wrote down notes on the countryside and people. To train teachers and ministers, he helped found the Rock Spring Seminary. He wrote an emigrant's guide and gazette, dying in 1858. [6]

There appeared in the Alabama territorial capital of St. Stephens an itinerant preacher who proclaimed the gospel, but the people were so opposed to reform that they told him to shut up. But being a zealous religious, the preacher persisted. They told him that the town banned such preaching. Not needing any awakening and averse to freedom of religion, they put him on raft and forced to float down the river. He turned toward the town and cursed the town. He had come to them and they had not received him, so he consigned it to bats, snakes, and owls. Sure enough Cahaba was made the new capital and St. Stephens declined. Soon the last person left and the town became an abode of bats, snakes, and owls amid the tangled vegetation binding oaks to each other as they lined the once bustling streets. There were places in the young nation where preachers were not wanted, but none of them fell so rapidly upon a curse. [7]

A group of Quaker merchants formed a new departure in shipping. They soon founded a packet service called the Black Ball. Instead of sailing whenever they had full cargo holds and when the tide was favorable, they sailed between New York City and Liverpool at a set time. Whether they had a full cargo or not, whatever the sea weather. They carried both cargo and passengers and goods between other ports such as London and French ports. Also there was a beginning move to steamships on the high seas. Business increased at the port of New York City, which developed into even more of a import-export emporium. Unreliable shipping time schedules was an important contribution to this. Insurance, banking, and auctioning expanded. America broke the London monopoly of marine insurance, with a world-wide use of agents. [8]

Kentucky needed roads, and badly, but the Jeffersonian ideas of the government there precluded the state from doing any building of roads. The state legislators agreed that roads were not the responsibility of government. If Kentuckian roads they would have to construct them out of private funds. The state would not pay a nickel for their establishment. The exception was the widening of the Wilderness Road and the improvement of its fords in 1818.

Interested individuals formed corporations. One of these companies was established with a capital of $700,000 constructed and maintained roads in central Kentucky. They reserved to the state some $50,000 in stock, but the government was not interested. It was the investors concern; the legislators would not give a cent. There were two roads made by this company. The first was from Louisville to Lexington. The second connected with the roads of the national system with a road to Maysville. It proved to be a part of the national defense, but no money was forthcoming from Washington. In the twenties, there were to be local road companies connecting small towns, all raised by private capital and with only $1,000 to help construct a brazed trail from Lexington south to the Tennessee line. All of these levied tolls contributed to profits for the capitalists, large and small. Toward the end of the twenties, the state provided funds, in one case of $150,000.

Even with road improvements and construction, the roads were bad in rainy and in winter weather. Stagecoaches were hard to ride because of the potholes even in good weather conditions. Many people preferred to walk. Goods were especially expensive because of the high cost of tolls and expense of travel due to road conditions. There was none of the streamline travel of the twentieth century. It cost too much to transport coal for general use. Some of the roads were good, however, Some local companies put up log roads or plank roads. Others macadamized the roads they built. These were in the minority and well appreciated by those used to terrible roads. Even terrible roads were better than nothing and the money was well spent. [9]

Located in the southwestern corner of the Alabama Territory, the Tombigbee district was largely separated from civilization, being surrounded by Indians and the Spanish at Mobile. The leader of the communities was Harry Toulmin, the Scottish free-thinker seeking refuge from a hostile civilization. At this time he was the territorial judge. People there went through Toulmin for their relations with the outside world, being even more divorced from society than him, who after all had a commission to be judge. They trusted and relied upon him and peace reigned.

To the northern extreme was a more prosperous colony, this one from Georgia. Originally followers of General George Matthews of the Broad River area of Georgia, by this time intermarriage had inter-related them. They had had political power in Georgia and in northern Alabama formed a cohesive band of people who expected power to be theirs in Alabama. At this time they dominated what existed of the territory at this time although a small number in 1817, before others of their group emigrated in 1818. They became wealthy in Alabama and founded Huntsville. Leroy Pope, the founder of the town was to have a plantation outside the town. By this time the territory of Alabama began to grow. The Indians had just ceded the state and the emigrants moved in with large numbers. [10]

Irish-American James Workman returned to New Orleans late in 1817. He had been away for a number of years due to legal action against him. Workman was a London political reviewer for the powerful *Monthly Review* before he left to come to New Orleans before the nineteenth century. When Louisiana became American, he had the legal training and speaking ability for French, Spanish, and English. Because of this, he was appointed to the judgeship of the Superior Court of the Orleans Territory. He contributed to the culture and educational processes of the city. Shortly, he saw the territorial legislature pass an act for the establishment of academies and a university in New Orleans. They also started a library society of law. Workman had proposed these acts and was to become a regent of the university.

About this time, he and Governor W.C.C. Claiborne got into a quarrel and General James Wilkinson had him charged with taking part in the Burr schemes for an empire in the west. A grand jury indicted him and he was debarred. He reacted with returning the insult of the district attorney when he publicly declared the said Philip Grimes to be a coward for not dueling with him over the issue.

He left New Orleans for the better part of a decade and returned to be a force in the city with him temper under control. Elected Chairman of the Administration of the College of Orleans, he also dominated the Hibernian Societies in the next decade. His main interest was in promoting a youth library and a law library. He crusaded for a home for orphan boys and worked for it as president. He led in the charity work of the city. He was a director of banks and a canal company. Earning his living as a lawyer he became president of the New Orleans bar. He was truly a community leader and helped a multitude of people. Workman left no corpus of letters and papers but his life can be constructed through newspapers.

A business leader of the city, Maunsel White came down by flatboat in French Louisiana, soon after Workman, and worked his way up as a businessman in the commission business. Dealing in commodities and land speculation, he did well and soon became rich. He married well and became a militia officer and a friend of Andrew Jackson. White evidently played a role in the Battle of New Orleans. He had a fine home on Julia Street. He was an inspiration to immigrants who were like himself newcomers. [11]

[1] Niven, *Van Buren*, 1983, pp. 59-60, 65-68.

[2] Fuller, Hubert Bruce, *The Purchase of Florida: Its History and Diplomacy*, Cleveland: Burrows Brothers, 1906, pp. 275-277.

[3] Calhoun, *Papers*, II, 16-17. Quote on pp. 16-17.

[4] Fowler, Wilton B., "Calhoun, John C.," Lamar, *Reader's Encyclopedia*, p. 148. Quotes on p. 148.

[5] Tatum, Edward Howland Jr., *The United States and Europe 1815-1823: A Study of the Background of the Monroe Doctrine*, Berkeley: University of California Press, 1936, pp. 29-35, 46-50. Quote on pp. 46-47.

[6] Gabriel, Ralph H., "Baptists," Lamar, *Reader's Encyclopedia*, p. 73.

[7] Flynt, J. Wayne, "Alabama," Hill, Samuel S. ed., *Religion in the Southern States: A Historical Study*, Macon, GA: Mercer University Press, p. 5.

[8] Lankevich & Furer, *Brief*, pp. 76-78.

[9] Clark, *History of Kentucky*, pp. 181-183.

[10] Thorton, J. Mills, III, *Politics and Power in a Slave Society: Alabama, 1800-1860*, Baton Rouge: Louisiana State University Press, 1978, pp. 7-12.

[11] Niehaus, Earl F., *The Irish in New Orleans, 1800-1860*, Baton Rouge: Louisiana State University Press, 1965, Rep New York: Arno Press, 1976, pp. 8-10.

Chapter VI

CLEVELAND

Richard Jeffry Cleveland, American merchant and navigator, was born on December 19, 1773, in Salem, Massachusetts, the eldest child of Stephen Cleveland and his wife Margaret Jeffry. Stephen had been kidnapped and impressed into the British Navy from the streets of Boston. He had learned much while in the navy. In the Revolutionary War, Stephen used his knowledge to design and equip American privateers. The Continental Congress issued one of its first naval commissions to him. [1]

Son Richard reached the age of fourteen and went to work in the counting house of Elias Hasket Derby in Salem. Derby was an adventurous merchant who led the way in shipping and trading well in front of other American businessmen. He carried the American flag to the West Indies, the Cape of Good Hope, India, and China. There the people first viewed the flag of the already legendary Americans, a domestic nation in an array of monarchies and aristocracies. Richard benefited from the liberal hand of this successful merchant. Derby was noted for giving his employees a part of the profit they had helped him win at home and abroad.

Not being satisfied with a desk job in Salem, Cleveland longed for a voyage to these distant lands. In June of 1792, he boarded a Derby vessel commanded by Nathaniel Silsbee and served as a captain's clerk in business at port, and a foremast hand at sea. The long course of southerly winds made the progress slow and once Richard swam alongside the boat until a shark came up. So as not to alarm the young man the captain dropped his hat in the water and asked him to pick it up and bring it abroad. Richard did not know of his close call until he looked back while boarding and saw it where he had just picked up the hat. He came close to losing his life. Cargoes were sold and bought and the ship returned to Salem in September of the same year.

Silsbee shipped out on the new Derby ship and Richard went with him in the same capacity. The ship left Salem harbor on December 11, 1792. A gale struck them and the men suffered from cold, sea, wind, and exposure. A black cook was aboard and had frozen feet because of which the second mate had to amputate the cook's toes with a penknife and to dress the wound to the best of his ability. Once in port, a British naval surgeon examined, dressed, and left salves and medicines with directions for their use. Thus the cook's life was safeguarded.

On April 10, 1793, they reached the Cape of Good Hope delayed by long calms. There they obtained fresh provisions including vegetables, grapes, and other fruits. In those days produce soon ran out on the trip as did fresh meat and the cape stop was joyously greeted. They sold part of the cargo there and went to Port Louis on the Isle of France, arriving there on June 6, and learning on the way of the declaration of war by England against France. Delayed there by French fears that America would side with Britain, the American waited. French officials had decided America would be neutral and when word of this reached the port, they were allowed to go on their way. The delay was five months. They picked up coffee, later transferred to another ship, and next picked up produce at the Cape to be delivered to the French island. They also took wines for the trip to sell the French. Again, they were back, on March 13, 1794, and they made their way once again. Reaching Salem on July 10th, the ship's company was welcomed there with extra fondness because of their long absence.

Silsbee wanted Cleveland to serve as his chief mate on the next voyage, but Darby wanted the position for his nephew and Cleveland to go as second mate. This was unacceptable by Richard and he looked elsewhere for employment. A captain named Chapman named asked him to go with him as chief mate of the bark *Enterprise* belonging to Darby's son. Cleveland accepted and went with him on the ship to Bordeaux, where they were stranded by the severe winter of 1794-95. They sold their cargo of fish and bought wine and brandy for the returning March. Back in America, Cleveland was put them under. They escaped destruction and followed a little fishing vessel to safe harbor since he knew his way into Boston harbor.

In October of 1795, he captained his first ship. He had a mate and four men. They set sail from Havre on September 25, 1797, and no sooner out were subject to a near destruction along the coast. They were fortunate in avoiding rocky beaches on both sides of the calm beach they finally reached. During the next day, they set out and reached Havre and Cleveland's crew except for a black man, left the command of Cleveland. Finally men were hired and they set sail, to reach the Cape of Good Hope and sell the boat. Despite success, he broke even in profit.

After four months he was able to ship out again and was bound for Batavia in the East Indies. From there, he saw the Chinese at Canton and the extent of his traveling brought its own rewards. The trip continued when Richard learned about the preparation of ships in Boston for the northwest coast of America. Arranging for a ship and a motley crew, Cleveland set out of the coast of such fame from the Indies. They left on January 10, 1799. Along the way, he put down a mutiny with foresight and made his way with some contrite mutineers, leaving some of the worst behind on foreign shores. Cleveland and the rest reached the Northwest coast by mid-spring.

They met with the natives and took caution as they talked to the various tribes eager for mischief and having little to trade, to the probable disappointment of the Americans. This alertness on the part of the captain and his sailors saved them several times from being killed by the Indians who from time to time sought scalps and booty. The Americans had superiority in guns, ships, and position and they were of course safe with these advantages. One problem arose a few days from their arrival when they were outnumbered and had a calm sea, unable to escape for awhile. On the next morning they were able to sail. Out to sea they were momentarily stuck on a sunken ledge. Soon they ran out of goods for trading and left loaded with furs. They sailed to China and sold furs and ship. He paid off the crew and took the profits and sailed for Calcutta, escaping a pirate ship. At Calcutta, Richard rescued his man George who was in the progress of being impressed.

In May of 1800, Richard and George reached the Isle of France with ship and cargo for more sales of supplies needed by these Frenchmen. There was a good market for goods and ship. When a prize was brought into port, captured from Americans, Cleveland bought it an loaded it with coffee he got at a low price. Setting out from the islands, he undertook to avoid dangers by going to the south of the Cape of Good Hope to prevent contact with possibly hostile ships. They were in Denmark next.

Proceeding to Hamburg, Cleveland purchased a ship, and set about improving and repairing it. He was now in partnership with Mr. Shaler. Before they left the river, a storm hit and they now lost the vessel. They bought another and went off to sea on November 8, 1801. Heading for Rio de Janeiro, they stopped at the Canary Islands where they bought some supplies but because supplies were scarce, they bought only enough to last to Rio. Stopping by Rio and rounding Cape Horn, they were at Valparaiso, Chile, on February 24, 1802.

William Shaler and Cleveland found other American ships there. The suspicious Spaniards in Chile detained them and confiscated various ships for various reasons. Imprisoned for awhile, they were met with preparations for a battle and conflict between the ships and the land. The ship the *Hazard* being near Cleveland's ship was boarded by the Spaniards. A mob, used to take it, plundered the vessel and the governor was unable to stop the plundering. Cleveland's ship did not suffer any trouble, but had to sail away, leaving one of its crew imprisoned. Two and a half months had passed and it was now the sixth of May of 1802. They sailed northward and visited other Hispanic lands without seeing any vessels along the way. They traded off the coast of Mexico and left again for the broad seas after the new year began.

Next, they reached San Diego, California, still a young town commanded by Don Manuel Rodriquez, a pompous commandant. The official forbade them to enter the town, but they could land on a nearby beach. They accomplished some trading, but soon realized they must soon leave to avoid being plundered. Leaving San Diego with a trade of shots with the Spanish fort, they stopped again at another place or so. They left California bound for Hawaii, having gained pearls to trade and sell elsewhere. They left on May 28, 1802, headed for Hawaii, then called the Sandwich Islands.

Stopping briefly at the islands, they made their way to Guam, stopped to work on the ship, and reached Canton. Then Shaler and Cleveland made their parting, with Cleveland boarding a ship for Boston, where he had not been for years. There he rested and George acted as a domestic, dying at Roxbury, ending a long period of service to Cleveland. In New England, Richard could add up his gains and deduct his costs. It was a hard world for Cleveland: the excess goods were not sold profitably. He lost the money credited to the California missionaries, and Rouissillon died in Mexico. So Cleveland and his partner failed to recover the money trusted with him for credit in the United States. He still however preferred the large risks of his endeavor, which could return larger profits than the "common" voyages gave.

After a time, Shaler and Cleveland joined their fortunes for another trip to the corners of the earth. They purchased a schooner, the *Aspasia*, built in Baltimore and now in New York. Both men put their entire savings into the ship and its cargo, neither having amassed great capital. Shipping out in August of 1806, the seas were calm at first, but soon they suffered damage from a gale. Losing a foremast, they were in great danger, but one of the sailors managed to cut away the stay and keep further damage away. Arriving at Rio Janeiro in safety, they were allowed to make repairs, undertake a beef cargo for Havana and set out again. Along the way the British took control of vessel and cargo and the two partners were ruined. Cleveland shipped out for New York. It later sunk off North Carolina. He continued to trade as well as he could, faced with opportunity.

In late 1809, he headed for Italy and in particular Naples. Coming back from that peninsula, he stayed for awhile in London. Following this, he continued to trade in northern Europe for his profit before going to New York in late 1813. Riches and an independent wealth continued to allude him and his way continued hard. He did not seek an easier and smaller profit and so his services were not rewarded to the extent that it had to many American merchants, many of whom he knew. Cleveland chose the way though; it was at least helpful to purchasers and sellers of the supplies and cargo he bought. On a day to day basis, his life on the seas provided an existence and perhaps for him a sense of worth and of service in out of the way places. He also benefited others while traveling the world through. Sometimes there was money to be made, but Cleveland was soon to lose through poor investments.

Cleveland was hired out to captain a voyage to Tenerife and Batavia. He guided out of Salem on the ship *Exeter* late in July of 1815. The way had its problems and the way was slow. Nearly six months after their start, they were anchored in Batavia Roads. Taking on coffee and sugar, he tried to sell the cargo of wine from Tenerife. Unsuccessful, he hoped to sell it at the Isle of France. This was not to be for when he arrived it was not needed. Still he managed to trade it for produce and headed for Boston, making it in August of 1816.

Ever eager for trade in needed places, under strained circumstances, and where opportunity appeared, the captain sailed his ship forward on July 1, 1817. This time he guided his ship for Chile where there had been a revolution. His hopes were raised, but when he got there he found trouble instead of sales. In Chile, he fell into royalist hands and thus had much to worry about In his depressed state of existence, he planed to capture his Spanish captors and revolutionize the country with a nearby patriot force present and helpful. Then the plans were ruined by the arrival of the Spanish fleet from Lima, Peru. The Spaniard were over confident and were defeated by the Chileans.

Still in loyalist hands, Cleveland was taken to Lima for an interview with the viceroy. This did not favorably effect his release, but the existence to which he was stuck was now very pleasant and indeed enjoyable. The Spanish of Lima were nice to him and he made short trips comfortably. Finally, Cleveland returned to New York. [2]

---

[1]*Dictionary of American Biography*, II (2), 204-205.

[2]Cleveland, Richard Jeffry, *Voyages and Commercial Enterprises of the Sons of New England*, New York: 1857, Rep. New York: Burt Franklin, 1968, *passim*; *Who Was Who*, Hist Vol., p. 179.

Chapter VII

END OF 1817

Before the War of 1812, Philadelphia had been the leading port in North America, but after the war, it lost much of its luster. Released from wartime limitations, European shipping took the preeminent place of Philadelphia and other American centers' shipping. American ships no longer dominated the sea lanes. America had lost its place to Europe. And for American ports, Philadelphia lost the chief position to New York City. It was in that latter city that the state passed auction legislation that drew more British manufactures to its wharves. In addition and more importantly, New York established a line of regularly spaced packet ships. They did not have to wait for the Erie Canal to spur on business, although that canal added another impetus to the city's business. [1]

At this time in Illinois there was public disorder. Organized bands of robbers operated in the territory and were running free. They had the sheriffs on their side and public opinion tolerated their escapes, when arrested, from the slight jails of the frontier. In cases when brought to trial, they had smart lawyers and plenty of witnesses and got off from punishment through juries of their friends and associates. Judges were often in their favor also. It was a general mess. In order to protect the people, the latter formed regulator committees to work against the criminals and hold them at bay. Regulators were formed into military companies. They armed themselves and operated at night when the criminals were most busy. When they caught the varmints, they whipped them and banished them from the territory.

One gang managed to maintain its strength in this pro-law onslaught. This was the gang in Pope and Massac counties near the Ohio River. They built a fort and for more than a decade defied the government. Finally in 1831, the people armed themselves in great numbers and attacked the fort. They stormed the fort with one regulator killed and three outlaws killed. The rest of the men were captured and tried and got off with verdicts of not guilty. Later still, a gang was broken up in Edgar county. This was the end of organized mobs in Illinois until the Lovejoy incident where a mob destroyed an abolitionist press later that decade. [2]

Reverend Thomas H. Gallaudet was a pioneer of deaf-mute instruction in the United States. In 1807, when a child of Dr. Mason F. Gogswell became deaf and mute through the effects of a malignant fever, Thomas interested himself in giving the child instruction. He was partially successful. Seven men of Hartford then financed Gallaudet a trip to Europe to learn how to teach deaf and mute pupils. After several months of study, he came back with Laurent Clerc to teach. He was superintendent of the American Asylum at Hartford for the Education and Instruction of the Deaf and Dumb, founded in 1817 for him. Starting out with seven pupils, it grew to be quite sizable. In April of 1830, he left to become chaplain of the Retreat for the Insane at Hartford. He died on September 10, 1851.

David Bates Douglass was an American military engineer, professor, and explorer. He was born in 1790 in Pompton, New Jersey, the son of Nathaniel and Sarah Douglass and the nephew of famed engineer David Stanhope Bates. Young David was educated in New Jersey, Yale College, and in practical experience throughout his career. He had watched the course of the War of 1812 between the United States and Great Britain and now upon graduation this was the time for action.

So he quickly applied to General Joseph Swift at West Point for a place in the engineer corps of the American army. After approving this application, Swift suggested that David apply for a position from the secretary of war at Sackett's Harbor. Traveling there by himself, David told the secretary that he would like to serve as an engineer. Since there was a great demand for officers in that department, the secretary commissioned him within ten minutes. The new lieutenant was sent to West Point to prepare for the next year's campaign. Rising rapidly, he commanded a corps of sapper and mines and then the fort.

In June of 1814, having received his orders, Douglass took his men to the Niagara frontier and fought the British at Queenston Heights. Afterwards, they constructed defensive works and batteries for the defense of Fort Erie. Working long hours, day and night, David commanded the building by crews of workmen. Faced with this, the British retired and General Gaines commended the officer for his work. Further, Douglass was promoted to the rank of captain in September and sent to Castine, Maine, to serve there until peace and returned to West Point.

Staying in the army, David surveyed the fortifications at New Haven, New London, Stonington and Newport in April of 1815, and surveyed the eastern entrance of Long Island Sound in 1817. Meanwhile, he taught at West Point. The government appointed Douglass assistant professor of Natural Philosophy at West Point, a position in which he served for the next 15 years, with time off for official capacities in the Cass Expedition, which we shall see soon. He married Ann Ellicott, the daughter of Andrew Ellicott, professor of mathematics of the Military Academy. In Douglass, the Cass Expedition gained an able member.

Douglass wrote a journal about the expedition, telling of his observations along the way. His role was one of studying what was to be seen and to help out on portages and traveling of the expedition. Nothing startling came out of the expedition except the debunking of Copper Rock, which was nothing sensational as it had been reported by many explorers. They did not pioneer in new territory, neither did they see anything which had not already been seen, but the reports doubtless helped in the accumulation of information, although his journal did not become published until 149 years later. For the small cost, the expedition accomplished enough to make it worthy. Better maps could be made and many Indians had agreed to American authority.

Back at West Point, Douglass learned French to teach a new method of calculus which could come only from French texts. While there, he worked as an engineer for canal companies in the states of New York and New Jersey. In 1832, he began a one year later as the first professor of Natural Philosophy at New York University. Further, he surveyed the route of the Brooklyn and Jamaica Railroad on Long Island, designed buildings for New York University, drafted initial plans for the Croton aqueduct, investigated the coal region of the Upper Potomac, and created the Greenwood Cemetery on Long Island. Later, he was a short term president of Kenyon College in Gambier, Ohio. After a clash with trustees there, he practiced engineering. He taught mathematics at Hobert College in Geneva, New York, before a sudden death. [3]

In the first three decades after the American Revolution there were large numbers of manumissions or freeing of slaves by their owners. Also many former slaves made enough money to buy and free slaves up to almost two dozen in one case. Also many slaves simply left and were absorbed into the free African American population, notably in the cities or were hired by small farmers who were not slaveowners and needed the hired hands or were antagonistic to slavery in principle. Some slaveholders were alarmed at this and passed various restrictive laws against the freeing of slaves, but as a rule, they were generally repealed or did not stick or were ignored by the populace.

These were good days for manumission, but things slowed down in the 1810s when the free slave population increased by only 20% including those born to free African American families. This was the beginning of a negative change in attitudes and the spirit of the laws. The abolitionist impulse in the South began to dry up and there was a reaction by slaveowners and citizens of the South, and especially in the Deep South where except for New Orleans and a few other cities on the Gulf, there was a widespread objection to slaves being freed under any conditions. This reaction was to grow even stronger in the years and decades ahead. The spirit of the Revolution was being found lacking since although the Americans spoke of freedom just as much, it applied to whites only and only partially to free African Americans in the South. This racial feeling was not absent from the North, but not as strong.

Restriction increased as slavery grew and the South became more conservative and hide-bound. Rights of manumission were curtailed and liberalism lost out in popular opinion. Racism grew in the thought and actions of men and their families and there was more fear of the African Americans. Suppression became more and more pronounced. Legislation was supplemented by the courts. In three years, Maryland was to quash the use of hearsay evidence in cases where the slave petitioned for freedom on the ground that he had white blood in him or her. They began to refuse freedom even when the white owner stated that they should be allowed to make that choice. The illiberal feeling of the government began to be expressed and this was to increase. Courts in South Carolina opened up some, however, but the legislature slammed the door shut. Especially in the Deep South the law read that there was to be no more manumissions and there were shades of this, lessening the further north one went. Freeings of slaves were few in Alabama for instance. [4]

Baptist minister David Wood was blind when he moved from Georgia to Alabama to preach. He rose above his blindness and spoke out indefatigably. Using a rod for support, he was led about by a slave boy to his appointments. Wood preached the first sermon ever heard in Conecuh County. Later, the Bellville Baptist Church was built nearby. Shortly, a South Carolinian, young and sure came there. This was Alexander Travis. He rose above the fact that he had no formal education. His lack of such training did not keep Travis from being wise. He was also devote in spirit and gentle in disposition. Leading his brethren, he was able to establish two churches. Travis would walk up to forty miles to preach; a real pioneer preacher, he would not hesitate to swim the streams to get to where he was going. He was also subject to dangers from the Indians on these long walks, but no incident marred his life.

At the time, Baptists believed in predestination to such an extent that they did not support missionary work. It was needless, in their view; if they were not saved it was because it was God's decision. Because of this belief, they did not try to convert. Individual ministers did try to convert, believing if they did convert, it was in accord with God's will. However, the people had not yet divided into pro-missionary and anti-missionary factions. The general idea of the Baptists at that time and place was one of peace and harmony among themselves. After conversion and baptism, they did not seek the development of the people in the right ways as taught by Jesus. They were satisfied with giving an occasional sermon for edification and their own expression. The ministers studied the Bible zealously, but were not involved in church life. They were not paid salaries, considering to do so was unseemly. Church members were giving contributions toward pastoral needs, but this was uncertain money. [5]

The Baptists did not believed in theater going and would not have approved of the performance of a young lad of eleven years on the stage. In his native Philadelphia, Edwin Forrest was playing the part of a girl in his first appearance at the city's old Southwark Theater. The part was Rosalia de Borgia in the play *Rudolph, or the Robbers of Calabria*. One of his classmates recognized him in the dress and yelled: "The heels and the shoes! Hi yi! Look at the legs and the feet!" Forrest could not contain himself. He replied: "Look here chap, you wait till the play is over and I'll lick you like hell." The boy had a rejoinder when he bawled: "Oh, she swears! She swears!" The actors rushed Edwin off the stage and ended for the moment a brilliant career. [6]

One of the Bent children, Juliannah Bent went west from St. Louis with her new husband. At age sixteen, she had married Lilburn Boggs from Lexington, Kentucky. He had a new job as cashier of the new Bank of Missouri when he married, but he pulled up stakes for Boone's Lick's country up the Missouri to take advantage of the land boom there. Boggs started a store in Franklin, Missouri, which failed about the time his son was born. He might have returned to St. Louis, but the frontier had a hold on him. Hired as deputy factor and Indian agent at Fort Osage and New Harmony Mission, where he met the lank red-haired Bill Williams, who was to become known as an eccentric. Juliannah gave birth to a second son and moved to St. Louis to recover. He did not survive but died one month after that. Her brother Charles Bent soon became a fur trader.[7]

Rufus King was an American legislator, delegate to Congress and the Constitutional Convention, senator, diplomat, candidate for the presidency. He was born on March 24, 1755, in Scarborough, Maine, to merchant Richard King and his wife Isabella Bragdon of York, Maine, who died in 1759. She had given birth to Rufus and two daughters. They had a good upbringing and being on the frontier had plenty of pastures and woods to play in. There were farm animals and a pet deer. Being on the coast, three miles upstream from the mouth of the Scarborough River, they had a different area to explore also.

Rufus' father Richard was the son of John King, an English cutler and swordmaker who had emigrated to Boston, Massachusetts. John married there, and his first born moved to Maine for its opportunity. His sawmill helped construct ships and loaded them with Maine masts and lumber. He opened a large store and was a local official. Isabella's first cousin kept house and cared for the Kings. Richard soon married her. Mary Black King bore him six children. The Kings were very religious and were ruled by the basic biblical laws.

In 1766, some of his debtors got together drunk and attacked the King homestead, burning his private papers. During the next year, they burned his barn to the ground. Because he was a conservative property holder and a loyalist he incurred some enmity. On March 27, 1775, when Rufus King had just turned twenty, Richard King died. Having received an education in his hometown and at Dummer School in Byfield, Rufus was in his second year at Harvard University. It was there that he left the Congregational Church for the Episcopal Church.

When fighting erupted at Lexington and Concord, the Committee of Safety closed the college. In the fall of 1775, Harvard opened in Concord and King started his junior year, during which he took a special interest in history, public affairs, and oratory. He was a patriot. Graduating in 1777 at the head of his class back in Cambridge, King studied law under Theophilus Parsons in Newburyport. The town was prosperous and growing and King was faced with a cost of L 90 per year paid out of the estate of his father.

He served in the Revolutionary War, and became a lawyer, becoming a legislator and member of the Confederate Congress. After serving in the Constitutional Convention, King moved to New York and was a senator during most of Washington's administration. He was the minister to Great Britain from 1796 to 1803 and retired before becoming as senator. He gained renown as an orator. By this time he was retired and in 1819 was to be elected a senator still another time. Meanwhile he had run for vice-president twice and then president in 1816.[8]

At noon on October 19, 1817, General Mason brought in Manuel Hermenegildo Aguirre to see Adams. The Argentine gave the secretary of state a letter which contain the declaration of independence of that nation of the previous year. Enclosed were several statements by Supreme Director Puyerredon and Director O'Higgins of Chile across the Andes from Argentina. O'Higgins wanted to purchase war stores. On the next day, the Cabinet discussed South American matters, relations with Spain, and the pirates at Amelia Island and Galveston. The rest were hesitant, but Adams was for rooting the pirates out and this was decided.

They talked of dispatching commissioners and a frigate to Buenos Aires and Adams said it was not yet expedient to recognize Argentina. Regarding the situation with the Mexican insurgents and the French settlement on the Tombigbee, Adams had a talk with Lallemand. The French general said they would not join the Mexican rebels. Soon Adams learned that the idea of settling the war between Spain and the Hispanic America was for the king's brother Carlos to go to the hemisphere without troops and to become king of a free Latin America. On the day after Christmas, it was decided to act on the Amelia Island matter. [9]

[1]Richardson, Edgar P., "The Athens of America, 1800-1825," Weigley, Russell F., ed., *Philadelphia: A 300-Year History*, New York: W.W. Norton, 1982, pp. 214-215, 218.

[2]Ford, Thomas, *A History of Illinois: From Its Commencement as a State in 1818 to 1847*, Chicago: S.C. Griggs, 1854, Rep: Urbana, Ill: University of Illinois Press, 1995, pp. 160-161.

[3]Jackman, Sydney W., "Introduction," Douglass, David Bates, *American Voyageur: The Journal of David Bates Douglass*, Marquette, Mich.: Northern Michigan University Press, 1969, pp. xiv-xxii, 1-112.

[4]Berlin, Ira, *Slaves Without Masters: The Free Negro in the Ante-bellum South*, New York: Pantheon Books, 1974, pp. 51-141.

[5]Riley, B.F., *History of the Baptists of Alabama from the Time of Their First Occupation in Alabama in 1808, Until 1894*, Birmingham: Roberts and Son, 1896, pp. 29-36.

[6]Oberholtzer, Ellis Paxson, *Philadelphia: A History of the City and its People*, Philadelphia: S.J. Clarke, II, 42-43.

[7]Lavender, David, *Bent's Fort*, New York: Doubleday, 1954, Rep. Lincoln: University of Nebraska Press, 1972, pp. 25-26.

[8]Ernest, Robert, *Rufus King: American Federalist*, Chapel Hill: University of North Carolina Press, 1968, *passim*.

[9]Adams, John Quincy, *Memoirs of John Quincy Adams*, Adams, Charles Francis, ed., 1874-1877, Rep. Freeport NY: Books for Libraries Press, 1969, IV, 14-22, 30-32.

Chapter VIII

ECONOMICS

Great Britain was an economic giant and almost submerged the United States with her production. After the war, the British expanded and dominated in world trade. Her products flooded America and put great pressure upon American manufacturers. Her shipping soon forced a decline in American shipping and trade. American prosperity was in danger and the Americans responded with high tariffs. This did not please the South, but it was a matter of survival with the industrial and commerce sections of the North. Agricultural areas benefited in various sections of the country, but their food production was not needed as much as during the War of 1812. Still for the South there was such a demand for cotton with the resulting rise in cotton prices, that that region was prosperous and able to bear the high tariffs which made their living expenses high. This resulted in land speculation and migration to new lands to grow more cotton, which would eventually depress the market. [1]

The trading and shipping company of Brown and Ives began a long and gradual decline and decay. At first the fall was unrecognized as the company had only a fewer less ships to carry their trade. In the six years after Napoleon fell, Brown and Ives vessels were in Canton or Batavia for twenty-one times, over three visits a year. This trade was very profitable. Still the firm was faced with strong competition and even discrimination, in European ports. It was big business on an early nineteenth century scale and required long and sometimes difficult voyages. They benefited from the rise in the price of tea at the emporium in Amsterdam. Tea was a big product, but cotton and rice were also traded. Coffee and sugar were good products for the American trade.

One ship remained in Java in 1817 for the new crop of coffee to be ready for export. However, the coffee supply was not enough for the demand and it was hard to buy the product because of the speculators and traders in that tasty item for drinking. This ship left without coffee but took on a cargo of tea, sugar, and cassia elsewhere. The voyage was not as great success but it was profitable. There were further adventures in world markets for this ship, The year 1821 was a peak year for the Canton trade; it went downhill from that point on, after three decades of Asian adventures in Canton. The trade did continue. The Batavia trade declined also. International merchants were subject to price swings, which made trading no easy task. [2]

There were high prices in agricultural products after the War of 1812 and until 1819. They soared as never before hand, reaching prices never seen again until 1857. Cotton was twenty-five and thirty cents, sugar was nine cents. Tobacco was fourteen cents, and wheat was two dollars. These high prices were enough to inspire the men of the land to greed and they turned from a concentration of agriculture to land speculation. There was a scramble for land capable of producing these crops. Excitement was great on the part of petty and large capitalists. Here was a way to get rich quickly, that empheral dream of the centuries.

Land purchases and speculations were aided by the easing of credit restrictions and bank expansion. Bank circulation increased to double in the five years from 1812 to 1817 and the Second Bank of the United States had loaned $41 million dollars on real property and bank stock. For now this was a boom which was to last for many months. Men of hope seized the opportunity to borrow money for land and invested in soaring land prices. In those states of Mississippi and Alabama, there was a rush for land settlement and the price of land reached unusual heights. this land mania was most intense in Mississippi and Alabama, where production of cotton was almost to double during the post-war period.

Receiver John Brahan of the Huntsville office was the most grasping speculator, buying up tracts of any size in large numbers. He later claimed that he was trying to keep them out of the hands of large speculators, but he himself was one of them. Brahan took advantage of his position to acquire these lands. Going overboard, he soon was forced to default on government obligations. At this same time, General John Coffee used advance information from land surveys to buy up large amounts of land. Andrew Jackson himself speculated using insider information to gain the best of lands for himself. He arranged his military duties to enable him to buy up all of this good land. Also using inside information, William Bibb and Thomas Bibb bought up land in large quantities.

These speculators were like wild bulls in a china shop and did not hesitate to make their ruthless ways across the horizon. The small investor and farmer were left out of this advantage and had to make their usual hard way in the land market and pay excessive prices and go into such debt that they were to lose their lands when agricultural prices fell and the scramble for land was over. As we have seen the land speculation had eventually ruined speculators such as John Brahan. Jackson was more steady and solvent and did not make the mistakes of Brahan. [3]

In the Madison years, there had been many a textile mill constructed and put into operation in rural Massachusetts. Two such places were Dudley and Oxford. Some of them failed and went into bankruptcy. Those that survived combined with a number of commercial, handicraft, and nontextile manufacturing businesses which had been formed. There were local cotton and woolen mills. Being small concerns, the owners took the role of management and were at first close to their employees. They were after all neighbors and friends, but in time they were to grow apart in the normal course of events. After all there was a gulf between them in the social order of things and this gulf grew exceedingly from its origins in the community and state.

People who had known everyone in the rural towns grew to know only their class. This was inevitable since after all the owners were members of the upper class to begin with. They had money and other enterprises in the towns and countryside. That is where they got their investment funds to start the factories. Still at first they knew the people who worked for them. The differences grew as their position was aided by managers under them. They early hired others to help them manage.

Who worked in these factories? They were neighbors and close friends, mainly farm families. Although all manner of sons and daughters of farmers were soon at textile work, the work force was mostly to be made up of women between school age and marriage age. When family needs were greater than income, they continued to work for the textile plant owners after marriage especially to support children. Once the girls finished their schooling, they left the farms and went to work for a living. Younger children of the farm families took up their tasks on the farm and the cycle continued into times of present.

Other girls and women found work outside the factories, as seamstresses, milliners, and domestics in the larger cities in their area. Men found work in other pursuits as the women dominated the workforce in the factories. Some were to build lodging for the female workers, but not at first. Men went to work in boot and shoe shops and building textile machinery, leaving the women to work in the textile manufactories. All of these were smaller establishments than the cotton and woolen mills. Jobs were often let out to farmers and their families when possible and in increasing amounts. Life did get complicated. Many sons and daughters of farmers moved to more industrial towns and commercial centers like Boston, seeking the greater opportunity that smaller communities could not provide. There were not enough good paying jobs for them at home. This last has been the problem of towns to this day. They liked their home towns but had to leave for jobs or/and ambition. [4]

Thomas H. Benton informs that "the treasury notes could not be used as currency, neither legally, or in fact: they could only be used to obtain local bank paper--itself greatly depreciated bank notes. Loans were obtained with great difficulty--at large discounts--almost on the lenders's own terms; and still attainable only in depreciated local bank note." Coin, fell in value, subject to the vagaries of the market place. [5]

Lord Selkirk of Scotland was visiting America at this time. He was accompanied by his doctor, his secretary, and his servant on a mission to find a place or places of settlement for the poorer of his countrymen. He visited the western coast, the United States, and Canada in search for the best place for them to settle. He met Anne Royall in the wilds of western Virginia or eastern Kentucky riding ahead of his fellows with little protection from the bitter cold of the season. Selkirk had been traveling for three years when the two met ever so briefly. They both soon stopped at Mr. Clark's house where Anne learned of his identity. [6]

Thomas Jefferson and men interested in higher education for their state of Virginia were promoting a bill in the state legislature for the purchase of fifty acres near the center of their state and money for buildings and a library. Charles Fenton Mercer, chairman of the House of Delegates' finance committee drew up a good bill for that expenditure. Although it passed the delegates on February 8, 1817, it failed in the senate two days later. The state senators wanted to go home and thought that the large expenditure should be sent to the voters for a decision. This was voter participation; an idea which was strong at the time. However, before they adjourned, they appropriated money for education with the priority being funds for elementary schools, a needed item at the time when public education was not strongly placed in the South.

State Senator Joseph C. Cabell asked Jefferson to provide a plan for a university which could be used as a substitute. This suggested plan must be low enough in cost to conform with state resources. The whole undertaking must fail if it were too expensive for the tastes of legislators. Jefferson drafted another educational plan for primary schools, academies, and a university. This was a difficult task, but Jefferson soon had a plan, but it too was rejected. Samuel Taylor had introduced it and it was voted down on February 11, 1818. A Mr. Hill of King and Queen County had an amendment which passed. Hill wanted the educational appropriation to go only to schools for the poor. When the news reached Jefferson so intent upon a second university for his states, he was despondent.

The amended bill reached the state senate. Cabell acted and ignored his colleagues talk of a university being too expensive. He managed to get a bill passed providing money for the University of Virginia as well as lower levels of public education. The total sum was much less than the sum for a university presented and lost the previous year. Deeply interested in higher education, Jefferson was consoled and looked at the way from that start to be favorable. Jefferson was to play a big role in the building of the University of Virginia for the rest of his life. [7]

Federal land policy was imperfect because farmers were falling behind on payments when extended credits. This was soon to result in extension acts and other relief legislation. There was the same problem when states sold land. This happened even in Kentucky where land sold at from 20 cents to as low as five cents per acre. Many farmers had no capital for land anyway. Credit was given in Tennessee on farmland with payments extended ten years at low prices, but there would still be problems for some in paying even then. Credit arrangements created a source of trouble for the future.

In 1819, lands acquired in East Tennessee from the Cherokees were sold to the highest bidder, but not less than $2 per acre. Purchasers were to pay one fourth down and the rest of ten years every year. Limits were placed on the amount of land which could be bought. A parcel of 640 acres was allowed per person and 320 acres for each child in the family. By 1833, all of the land had been sold. Giving credit led to increased land speculation with harmful effects, especially beginning in 1819. [8]

There were about this time a group of Seminole African American former slaves who sought their freedom away from the United States. They were slaves in the South before escaping to Florida to live under and with the Seminole Indians as freemen subject to some control and peonage of a mild nature of the Seminoles. They felt much harassed by slave-catchers and moved on several occasions ever southward to find refuge from them. Some 150 to 200 of them reached Cape Florida, and heard an English sea captain tell of a land to the east where there was freedom. He was referring to the Bahamas, a group of British colonial islands in the Atlantic not far from Florida.

Indian doctor Scipio Bowlegs led them in dugout canoes eastward. They landed at Red Bay on the west coast of three main islands and many very small ones known as Andros Island. Others of the party landed on the Joulter Cays to the north, but moved to Red Bay with seeds of corn, peas, and pumpkins to plant. They lived apart from Negroes on the other side of the island, whose origin was unknown, but whose race was established. The African Americans from Florida had some Seminole blood in their veins. Perhaps they traded with the Seminole back in Florida, because those Indian tribes were known to travel long distances for commerce. The island had poor soil and the freedom loving Seminole African Americans lived in poverty, but they were free and were not noted for complaints. The Bahaman Indians on Andros had been few and there might not have been any there in the nineteenth century. [9]

[1]Hedges, James B., *The Browns of Providence Plantations: The Nineteenth Century*, Providence: Brown University Press, 1968, p. 135; North, Douglass C., *The Economic Growth of the United States: 1780-1860*, Englewood Cliffs: Prentice Hall, 1961, pp. 61-63; Channing, Steven A., *Kentucky: A Bicentennial History*, New York: W.W. Norton, 1977, pp. 78-79.

[2]Hedges, *Browns*, pp. 135-158.

[3]Gates, Paul W., *The Farmer's Age: Agriculture, 1815-1860*, New York: Holt, Rinehart and Winston, 1960, pp. 57-63.

[4]Prude, Jonathan, *The Coming of Industrial Order: Town and Factory Life in Rural Massachusetts, 1810-1860*, Cambridge: Cambridge University Press, 1983, *passim*.

[5]Benton, Thomas H., *Thirty Years' View*, New York: Appleton, 1854, I, 1. Quote on p. 1.

[6]Royall, *Letters*, pp. 79-81.

[7]Bruce, Philip Alexander, *History of the University of Virginia 1819-1919*, New York: Macmillan, 1920, I, 82-94.

[8]Gray, Lewis Cecil, *History of Agriculture in the Southern United States to 1860*, 2 vols., Washington DC: Carnegie Institution of Washington, 1932, II, 625-633.

[9]Goggin, John M., "An Anthropological Reconnaissance of Andros Island, Bahamas," *American Antiquity*, V (1939), 21-26.

Chapter IX

THE YEAR 1818

Transportation was a major problem during the third day under the Constitution and began to be a major effort of the various states. In 1808, Albert Gallatin spoke of the need for internal improvements and favored the building of canals as well as improved roads. The farmers in the interior were glad to see this proposal since better transportation would benefit them. Costs to transport agricultural products were excessive. The carrying of a bushel of wheat from Buffalo to New York City cost three times the original market value. For a bushel of corn, it cost six times the farm value to transport. Other products such as furniture from the east and manufactured supplies were payable at an increase. There was freight traffic to Pittsburgh and other western towns.

During this time, there were road improvements in New York and Pennsylvania with the states providing aid. The National Road was extended to Wheeling, Ohio, just across the river in 1818. Over one hundred miles of canals had been built by 1817 and the Erie was authorized in that year. The longest canal was less than 18 miles long. Also, in 1817, nationalist John C. Calhoun wanted to bind the Republic together with a system of roads and canals. There were dreamers in 1813, when Colonel John Stevens of Hoboken obtained the first steamship charter in American rivers and by the end of the decade they had increased in numbers. [1]

During the first week of 1818, there set sail a new concept. That was the ocean liner making a set trip to two or three ports. The Black Ball Line it was called, using square-rigged sailing packets and later steamboats. For the first time in American history, regular shipping was instituted on a large scale. Previously, the British government mail brigs had traveled as regularly as it was possible for a sailing ship to do, but the Black Ball Line was devoted to freight and passengers for the American nation with set fares and set courses. This was of course much appreciated.

There were four ships in the company line of Isaac Wright. The first, the *Pacific*, was built in 1807 for Isaac and became, all 384 tons, a very fast ship for the New York-Liverpool journey. William Wright became a partner in his father's concern as did Francis Thompson, another Quaker, who had come from Yorkshire to New York to sell woolens his father and brothers had made. Francis' nephew Jeremiah Thompson next joined. He had been an importer of woolens and an exporter of cotton from the South. Finally, Benjamin Marshall joined. He imported Lancashire cotton goods and exported raw cotton to England. In 1816, the company became owners of the *Amity* and the *Courier*. In 1817, they built the 424 ton *James Monroe*.

A small crowd gathered at the dock to see if the *James Monroe* would set sail upon the exact day and hour promised. That was lived up to. Although it had to leave headed into a snowstorm, punctuality was so important a concept that it was of great importance to live up to it. It left for Liverpool with a small cargo, without waiting for an adequate charge of freight. The sailors and the watching crowed must have been cold on the day due to the snowy weather. The people did go away satisfied. The name of the line was made. Its word was bond.

Future sailings were prompt although they had to rely on coal and salt as cargoes instead of the fine cargoes which would be more profitable. The year 1819 saw a recession and shipments were low for a few years, although the packet ships had gotten the best of cargo over the transient, non scheduled ships. As things got better in the 1820s, a new company, the Red Star came into being, giving competition. Regular schedules were the rule for the two lines. [2]

Virginia, home of the first five presidents save one, was wealthy and industrious, filling up towns and cities at a rapid rate, not being content with remaining an agricultural state. Although forests gave way to farmers in Virginia in the early years of the Republic, the new emphasis was on internal improvements. In 1785, the Potomac Company was established to build a canal connecting the Potomac with the Ohio River and the James River Company was founded to build a canal across the Allegheny Mountains connecting the James and Kanawha Rivers. Progress was slow and neither company finished their systems of canals, but they were soon outdated by the railroad. The new canals provided transportation for the coal of the Alleghenies and there was continuous river traffic for other finished and unfinished products both eastward and westward bound. Virginian efforts were insufficient for big success and other parts of the country passed her up, reaping the majority of the country's industrial development.

Pennsylvania's system was more successful, reaching all the way from Philadelphia to Pittsburgh, the industrial center of the West. The flaw in the Pennsylvania system was the necessity for the transfer in switching of goods from railroad to canal several times. The transportation system was to begin with a railroad west of Philadelphia to the Susquehanna River, followed by a long canal, with a portage railroad, and another long canal.

The most successful of the internal improvements was the system built by New York, providing water transportation between the Atlantic at New York City and the Great Lakes at Buffalo. The canal extended from Albany on the Hudson by the water level route to Buffalo. Finished in 1825, the canal was so profitable that it quickly paid off the original cost of construction with the tolls charged. Not only did this Erie Canal provide opportunity for the transportation of goods, but it opened up areas for settlement, areas which were more profitable because of the canal. In addition, all of the canals provided jobs in their construction and in their operation for an ever expanding population. These new jobs were particularly helpful to the emigrants who were once again flooding the country, especially from Ireland, where there were many discontented peasants and city dwellers, who chaffed under British rule.

In the same year that the Eire canal was completed, the government of Ohio embarked upon a canal building program. Federal land grants and loans from eastern capitalists provided the financing for the canal and Governor De Witt Clinton of New York was present at the start of construction at Licking Summit. A canal system from Cleveland to Portsmouth was finished in 1832, followed by the Cincinnati to Dayton canal, later extended to Toledo on the Lake Erie. Toll roads followed canal construction, built by private companies with state and local aid. Canals were later built in Indiana and Illinois.

Another means of transportation were the stagecoaches throughout the states. This had long been used and provided passenger moves to other towns. This was important for all states, but particularly so for Kentucky. The travelers were serviced by taverns along the roads and encouraged the building of toll roads in that state. It was not a static business because there were various great improvements. They could carry a certain amount of luggage. There were also freighters for the transport of commodities and products. They too happily paid the tolls and added the cost to the bills of lading. A leading manufacturer of stage coaches was Abbott-Downing Company of Concord, New Hampshire. They developed an improved coach in the Concord in 1827. [3]

The Federal Government was concerned at the opening of 1818 about the introduction, illegal transportation, of enslaved blacks into the South through Amelia Island in Florida and at Galveston in Spanish Texas near the mouth of the Trinity River. Authorities had sent a naval force to prevent this crime against the laws, not to say against humanity. A congressional committee reported on January 10, 1818, that freebooters and smugglers, renegades from several nations were operating out of Texas, a Spanish province claimed by the United States as it had been by the French who had sold Louisiana to the United States. This transfer included the claim and Monroe and other Americans felt they had the right to intervene to crush this slave trade, in a land which Spain was unable to police.

These freebooters were also pirates who plundered the seas, especially seizing Spanish ships. Often, these pirates would take slave ships and could only sell the blacks to the American South through the Texas wilderness. They flew a flag, claimed to be Mexican, in those days shortly before the Mexicans gained their independence under Iturbide. Force alone could destroy the pirates.

Monroe was authorized by a law of 1807 to employ naval force to end any importation of slaves into the United States. An 1811 joint resolution also gave the president the right to occupy Florida east of the Perdido River. West Florida had already been seized. The congressmen of the Committee on Foreign Relations clearly wished that Monroe would take action to take Amelia Island, to take this refuge from the pirates. They felt that the slave trade was repugnant to justice and to humanity.

Meanwhile, Monroe had acted and was able to announce on the 13th that he had suppressed the pirate establishment at Amelia Island. Pirate chieftain Aury claimed he had founded a nation in Florida and rejected the American demand to surrender Amelia. Naval Captain J.D. Henley and Major J. Bankhead, commanding the American force, replied that they would seize Amelia that day. Aury immediately replied that he would surrender the island. The Americans came ashore and raised the American flag without a shot being fired. The pirates respected superior force. The date was December 23, 1817.
4

The Creek were upset. They were increasingly hostile because of the other smugglers who were brining black slaves into Georgia from Florida. There were reported to be two considerable droves brought to the vicinity of the Creek agent to report such. Gaines promised action and also noted that the victims of the Seminole attacks were guilty of intruding upon public lands. Gaines also feared that the Georgian militia units would be late reaching Fort Scott. The general wrote Calhoun about the matter for his and Monroe's information. 5

The president is not above the law and indeed must respond like any citizen to a subpoena of the courts in any case involving him. Precedent number one was in the Burr treason trial when the chief justice of the time, John Marshall, ruled that the then president, Thomas Jefferson, must respond to a subpoena calling for his providing certain papers to the Court in Richmond. Burr made this request in his trial and shocked the court. This request was debated for four days before Marshall made his ruling.

A naval courts-martial involved the president in a legal action. The case set an additional precedent for a president to be served a subpoena. On the basis of Marshall's ruling in the Burr case, it was again ruled that such could happen in Dr. Barton's case in 1817/1818. Dr. William P.C. Barton was a surgeon in the U.S. naval hospital at Philadelphia. He had ousted Dr. Thomas Harris, trading positions which elevated Barton. In turn, Barton was accused of conduct unbecoming an officer and a gentleman. He had criticized the Philadelphia naval hospital as overcrowded and unsanitary, and soliciting the removal of Dr. Harris so he could have the position.

With a letter of introduction from former secretary of state Richard Rush, Barton had gotten to see Monroe and discussed the application of Barton for the job. Barton felt that this would start the ball rolling for the acceptance of his application for the job. Rush talked and Barton went back. Monroe, later, did not remember talking with the secretary of the Navy about the application afterwards.

The court issued a subpoena, requiring the president to testify in court about the Barton matter. Monroe was served with it and, in mid-January of 1818, the presidential advisers in the cabinet were consulted. Adams sent Attorney General William Wirt a copy of the subpoena and asked his advice. By coincidence, Wirt had been one of the prosecution attorneys at the Burr trial. It was true that the precedence was set. Wirt decided that indeed the president could be served with a subpoena, but that by stressing his need to be in Washington DC, he would not have to appear in person. Monroe then made an endorsement stating the facts involving him on the back of the subpoena. Ironically, it arrived too late, reaching in Philadelphia after the trial. [6]

On January 26, 1818, Philanthropist John Pintard wrote his daughter that the historical society in New York was "making rapid progress. We purchase not only American history, but rare and curious writers on European, especially English history. We bought last week the Byzantine historians in 30 folios and the Concilia about 20 more. Works extremely scarce and seldom to be obtained even in Europe--too voluminous to bear republication in this age of lighter reading of course of difficult attainment. It is our object to make our library one of research for all that is curious and valuable. A work of slow growth, but if persevered in will in the course of years be accomplished and may become like the extensive libraries of the Old World inestimably valuable to the erudite scholar. To have had a hand in the foundation and elevation of such a library will her hereafter, no small praise."

In order to solicit a grant of $1,000 for each of the three societies in the New York Institution for ten years from the state legislature, Pintard went to Albany on February of 1818. He would have the aid of Governor De Witt Clinton, who had planned for a week before, a speech to the cause of science and literature. Among the people he traveled with was Eleazur Williams, a half-breed Oneida Indian, well educated and in the process of preparing for the ministry. The Indian was undertaking a history of the native tribes. Pintard presented to Colden, a representative from the city, a copy of the memorial. He found considerable support from various legislators, but his errand proved abortive. He found hopes of success, but the legislators were always putting him off. One reason for failure was the backing of Clinton, for the legislators, for political aims, wished to confound Clinton's objects to keep his administration from being successful. Perhaps there was a little jealousy mixed with politics. [7]

In southern Arkansas, that part of the future state situated between the Arkansas and Red Rivers was to be Indian territory after the War of 1812. All of this tract was fertile land except for a beautiful range of mountains from the Washitas westward to the Canadian River. It was good cotton land with many rivers and creeks suitable for water machinery, springs of pure water, and salines, and medicinal springs. The Caddos, who were a dwindling tribe, and resided to the south of the Red River laid claim to the tribal lands of southern Arkansas. There were also the Quawpaws, who were another small tribe, lived on the southern banks of the Arkansas. They were a branch of the Osage nation and laid claim to a portion of the country, a claim to much of the Washitaw country, but the Osage proper had the best claim.

Stephen Harrison Long of New Hampshire, a graduate of Dartmouth College and one-time West Point instructor, set out to embark upon an expedition to the Rockies. The Osage had just ceded to the United States through Indian agent Mr. Lovely, who shortly died, great acreage. Long had information that William L. Lovely took advantage of the Osage chieftain Clermont since it was not the intention of the Indian people of that tribe to cede such a large territory in the negotiations. The Osage accepted this and wanted the whites to settle near them and teach the men to farm and the women to spin. They were chagrined to find that the Americans used the land to settle, the Cherokee being removed. The two Indian people were deadly enemies.

There were a number of new settlers moving into the territory who were without sufficient sustenance, having expending all that they had in getting to Arkansas. They had not been in Arkansas long enough to get in a crop. The military needed to keep peace between the Cherokees and the Osages and to keep the whites from trespassing upon Indian lands. The troops of Major William Bradford were assigned to Arkansas for these two peaceful purposes presented for their solution. [8]

Adams laid claim to territory to the Colorado River in Texas, while Onis agreed to use the then present established de facto line as the boundary. At this point, Great Britain offered to mediate. At a cabinet meeting on January 31, 1818, the American government decided to turn down the offer because public opinion in the United States would not support a third party interposition. [9]

Adams was feeling the political heat of his high office. He was performing well, but he was a sitting duck for those with presidential bugs who saw him a possible rival. He noted that it was "in the interests of all the partisans of the candidates for the next presidency...to decry me as much as possible in the public opinion." He named Secretary of the Treasury Crawford and Speaker Clay and Governor De Witt Clinton of New York. Clay especially was in position to oppose Monroe and to give "the tone to all his party in running me down." [10]

Onis protested the occupation of Amelia Island by the Americans on January 8th of 1818. There was a draft of a message withdrawing American troops, but the matter was undecided. The Cabinet was divided. Calhoun strongly urged retaining the island. Onis told Adams that Spain wished an alliance with the United States, at least a defensive one. Adams was favorable. He told the Spaniard that if America withdrew from Amelia Island, he needed guarantees that Spain would not allow the pirates to return to the island. Meanwhile, Clay was working in Congress to aid the South Americans in their revolution against Spain. He was in general opposition to the Administration.

When Adams was asked if he had determine to work for his secession to Monroe, Adams was somewhat affronted. He said he would not do a thing in that regard. He knew that the others would not be so scrupulous, but he would not stand on an equal footing with them. In other words, let them politic. He would not; it was his business to attend to the business of his office, to serve the public. Adams further said he had no interest in seeking public office and had expressed no wishes in obtaining the presidency or other office. Clay on the other hand was active in working for his bid for the presidency. [11]

[1]Stover, John F., *American Railroads*, Chicago: University of Chicago Press, 1961.
[2]Albion, Robert G., *The Rise of New York Port (1815-1860)*, New York: Charles Scribner's Sons, 1939, pp. 38-43, 44.
[3]Coleman, J. Winston, Jr., *Stage-Coach Days in the Bluegrass: Being an Account of Stage-Coach Travel and Tavern Days in Lexington and Central Kentucky, 1800-1900*, Louisville: Standard Press, 1935, *passim*.
[4]*American State Papers-Foreign Affairs*, IV, 132-144.
[5]Calhoun, *Papers*, 68.

[6]Stathis, Stephen W., "Dr. Barton's Case and the Monroe Precedent of 1818," *William and Mary Quarterly*, pp. 465-474.

[7]Pintard, John, *Letters from John Pintard to his daughter Eliza Noel Pintard Davidson, 1816-1833*, 4 vols., New York: New-York Historical Society, 1940, I, 106-111, 114.

[8]Carter, *Territorial*, XIX, 4-8.

[9]Marshall, *Louisiana Acquisition*, pp.. 53-70.

[10]Lynch, *Fifty Years*, p. 254. Quotes on p. 254.

[11]Adams, *Memoirs*, IV, 36-46, 64-72, 78.

Chapter X

MISSIONS

The territorial legislature of Illinois sent their delegate to Congress, Nathaniel Pope, a petition to ask for the admission of Illinois to the Union. Pope presented it to Congress in January of 1818. The press of congressional business delayed the action on the petition until April when Congress voted to admit Illinois to the Union with two amendments to extend the northern boundary of the state, and to use the three percent funds from public land sales for education instead of the usual road construction.

That summer a state constitutional convention was called and it, led largely by Elias K. Kane, a senator, established an agreeable constitution. Kane was born in New York state and was educated for the law profession. From there as an early youth he went to Tennessee and at twenty years old reached Illinois where he settled. He became secretary of state in the territory and then a legislator. The Reverend Mr. Wiley and his Convenanters in Randolph County petitioned the Convention to establish the laws of the Bible in faith and practice, placing Christ at the head of the government. The delegates paid no attention to this petition and thereafter the Covenanters refused to recognized the state government and refused to serve on juries or do road work and voted once only, to express their anti-slavery views in 1824. Slavery was the biggest debate of the Convention.

The people elected Shadrach Bond the first state governor. Bond was a farmer and early settler in Illinois, coming with his family. A native of Maryland, he was several times a legislator and was once a delegate to Congress. Thomas Ford wrote that "Bond was a substantial, farmerlike man, of strong, plain common sense, but with little pretensions to learning or general information. He was a well-made, well-set, sturdy gentleman, and what is remarkable for this day and place his first message to the legislature contains a strong recommendation in favor of the Illinois and Michigan canal." [1]

Congress by this time had acted on a number of bills. The House had voted down the soldiers' compensation bill by a vote of 82 to 80. This bill would give veterans $1 per acre in lieu of land grants for service, at his option. It was for the benefit of them. There were a number of new laws, but the bankruptcy bill was not one of them. However,

Congress had ended internal taxes. This was because of the large amounts of money in revenue from tariffs and other taxes flowing into the treasury. Congress was able to cut taxes to the relief of the consumers. There was a sinking fund for the retirement of the public debt now. Things were looking good; no one knew that a panic was just ahead. Pensions had been provided for veterans of the Revolutionary War. William Hendricks reported this and the fact that his state of Indiana was building a number of roads. He was a representative from a district of that state in the House. The movement of mails was improved in keeping with the steady progress of the state and nation. Also, the Indians were to be forced by diplomacy to give up more land.

Hendricks also wrote that "the cause of the patriots of South-America, although subject to the vicissitudes of all revolutionizing colonies, is still gaining strength. By degrees, and by exertions they have learned the art of war. By the same means, some provinces have long since vanquished the armies of the King, and others are marching forward, with a firm and steady pace, to liberty and independence." [2]

Lewis Williams also wrote of those patriots. Everyone in the United States were rooting for them; everyone wanted them to achieve their liberties and independence. However, the people who elected congressmen did not elect them to become involved in such matters or even to send diplomatic ministers to their new capitals. Williams thought that interference would lead Americans to war with Spain and even all Europe. Even with Spain alone, war would be disastrous. Spain would have the services of English privateers who would destroy American commerce on the high seas. They would oppose any form of action and expression of sympathies from the American government. American should not trade peace for war. [3]

Looking to the other countries, newly liberated, of the Americas, Henry Clay saw a certain American hegemony of ideas. In a March 24th speech in the House of Representatives, he spoke of the United States in the role of a great example to the Hispanic countries of the two continents of the western hemisphere. As the most knowledgeable congressman on the subject, he averred that the Latin American constantly speaks of his countrymen as of brothers with a similar origin and noted the adoption of American principles, institutions, and sentiments about liberty and liberalism. Clay's fellow citizens the legislator knew were ignorant of Hispanic American affairs and in this lack of knowledge believed their neighbors to the south were too ignorant and too superstitious to admit there was such a thing as free government. This was a monarchical claim he told his fellows. The United States had the greatest interest in the independence of the various countries of Hispanic America. They were different from Europeans and would have an American feeling.

Clay not only had a feeling of solidarity with the newly independent nations to the south, but he was anti-Spanish in the tradition of the Black Legend of Spanish cruelty, not that they were not cruel. Not only did Clay have a feeling of pan-Americanism, but he was envious of the position Adams held in the United States as secretary of state. This all colored his feeling about the treaty work between the United States and Spain. He openly criticized the work of Americans and Spanish on an agreement which would settle the boundary question. Had Clay managed the recognition of the Hispanic nations, he would have scuddled the treaty work with Spain. As it was, it was difficult enough to deal with the proud, suspicious, and dilatory Spanish. [4]

Monroe wanted an appropriation of $30,000 to help defray the expenses of the mission to South America. Henry Clay, eager for revenge upon Monroe for not naming him secretary of state instead of Adams, decided to oppose such an expenditure. The legislator charged that Monroe's action in naming the commissioners was unconstitutional and impolitic, because the Senate had not approved, prior to the appointments, the mission. The proud and able Clay had a substitute bill. He moved an appropriation of $18,000 for an outfit and one year's pay for a minister to Buenos Aires. In addition, he wanted a change in the neutrality law of the previous year to make aid to the revolutionaries of the south easier.

John Forsyth of Georgia defended Monroe's measure in a debate. Because Forsyth was, as Adams observed, "a man of mild, amiable disposition and good talents, but neither by weight of character, force of genius, nor keenness of spirit at all able to cope with Clay," he did not decided the outcome. His noble defense paid off to some degree. However, it was Clay's ignoble attack upon the administration that made the day against himself. Perhaps eager to stand up to Clay at least once, the members of the House of Representatives defeated the anti-Monroe motion by a vote of 115 to 45. They then granted the original $30,000. They provided a contingency fund for that amount. Clay kept quiet publicly, but privately, he attacked Monroe's Hispanic American programs violently. Monroe was kind and made excuses for Clay. Statemanship prevented the president from an more active program for the other Americas.[5]

In April of 1818, living in the national capital was still primitive. John Quincy Adams records that the earth streets were a terror. They were returning from a dinner when their carriage was upset and the harness broken. Getting home with difficulty, they were almost upset two times more, and at the Treasury office corner, they were obliged to get out in the mud. In time, they were home and happy that they all got home with their bones intact. This was undoubtedly a common condition for all residents and visitors in Washington. Many could tell similar experiences of traveling in the dust and mud of a rutty board streets of the city.[6]

John Tyler of Virginia was concerned about Great Britain. He wrote his constituents that "while we open our ports to her West Indies trade, receive her as a friend and evince towards her the most amicable disposition, she shuts us out from those possesses; and does not even permit an American merchant, factor or agent to reside there--and this too when the very same trade is open to the vessels of almost every nation of Europe. So long as we submit to this state of things, her policy will never change.' It is to England's best interests that we do not protest or take other action against this situation. Congress had spoken at last, the Americans would henceforth prohibit trade with British vessels from the West Indies. America was only dependent on the British West Indies for half of their rum. All else could be supplied by the other countries. [7]

On September 25, 1817, President James Monroe appointed William W. Bibb of Georgia governor in and over the Alabama Territory. Bibb received in mid-April of 1818 intelligence which prompted him to return to the territorial capital St. Stephens. He learned that the Indians who had committed recent murders in the vicinity of Manacks had been seen at Pensacola. Writing Secretary of War John C. Calhoun, Bibb, the governor noted that his situation was extremely unpleasant. He was without funds to protect the territory and had no information on the views of the government on the subject of Florida. The hostile party who were killing Americans operated two miles south of the Florida line on Yellow Water Creek. He did not, however, know what orders were issued to General Andrew Jackson.

The Indians again raided from across the Florida line a week after the previous raids. They killed the husband and wounded the wife and two daughters and stole all that could be carted or driven away. Again Bibb told Calhoun that he lacked funds to act and authority to cross the border. As long as they were protected by the border, they could attack with impunity. He believed that they must be attacked and at their place of refuge or such attacks by the Indians would occur again.

Calhoun received Bibb's first letter and wrote him to make "such arrangements and incur such expense as, in your judgment, the defense of the territory may require," and draw upon the department "to cover such disbursements as you may order." The secretary of war informed him that Jackson was "vested with full powers to conduct the war, in the manner which he may judge best." [8]

In May of 1818, Pastor Horace Holley came to Lexington, Kentucky, to interview for a job as president of the Transylvania University. The newly elected liberal trustees took a liking to him instantly and approved of his liberal ideas. They wanted to turn the school from its conservative Presbyterianism to the liberalism of the time and to the ways of the modern education of the time and place. The trustees sensed better times for the state and its university and Holley proved them right, for he soon brought the college to the threshold of greatness. They wished a progressive, rational, and evangelical leader and this is what they got in Holley. His attitude pleased them, the people of the state and city generally, and Henry Clay and Governor Gabriel Slaughter who greeted the New Englander. Holley had been pastor of the South End Church in Boston.

The churches in Lexington invited him to preach in their churches. Transylvania was primitive and ready to be formed. Holley did not need to change people and rules. The college had no organization or rules. He needed to buy books--there were few in the library. He had to buy apparatus--there were only two or three pieces. The new president and his wife came to Lexington permanently and he got to work. There was much to be done. He improved the course of study, set standards for admission, adopted the usual framework of collegiate life, remolded and enlarged the physical plant. He got funds from the legislature and the citizens of the city for books and salaries for additional professors. He purchased the finest scientific equipment he could obtain. The college boomed and Holley got the credit. His greatest success was in the medical department.

Holley did run into opposition from the Presbyterians. Their preachers called him an infidel. The newspapers, magazines, and pamphlets said he was an immoral, coarse, and dangerous man. He was accused of drinking and gambling. They criticized his visits to the theater. The opponents of the liberals labeled the trustees as very wicked men who embezzled college funds. All of this was false and he stood it well. In 1826, those opposed won over Governor Joseph Desha to their views and the latter criticized the college. As a result of this last measure, Holley resigned. The date was March 24, 1827. Without Holley, the college foundered, but recovered somewhat. The golden age of the school had ended. From that point on, Transylvania was noted for its medical school chiefly. In 1839, it became a municipal college until 1842. [9]

George Graham was born about 1772 in Dumfries, Virginia, a town founded by his father among others. Richard Graham was a Scotch merchant in Dumfries and provided his son with a college education at Columbia College, where the son studied law. George was admitted to the bar and practiced his profession in his home town. The people elected him to the Virginia Legislature. There he met Madison, Monroe, and others. After a number of years, George Graham moved to Fairfax County. With the coming of war in 1812, he raised and led the Fairfax Horse. Because of the failure of General John Armstrong to protect Washington DC from the British invasion, James Monroe became secretary of war. He was already secretary of state and the war portfolio was temporary. Monroe named George Graham to be chief clerk and for awhile George ran the War Department. He remained chief clerk under William H. Crawford and was in charge in the year between Crawford's departure and John C. Calhoun arrival on December 9, 1817. Crawford went on to become secretary of the Treasury.

While he was busy with his routine functions, he served the government in other tasks. In 1815, Graham was one of three members of a commission to negotiate with the British concerning the public and private property in British hands in Chesapeake Bay at the end of the war. Next, he was appointed to be an agent to treat with the Cherokees and then the Sacs. Indian relations proved to be one of his specialties. Outside the line of his usual work was the presidency of the Washington branch of the Bank of the United States. He was later to be an commissioner from 1823 until his death in August of 1830, in which he worked to see that the Indians got a square deal. He was influential with John Quincy Adams over federal land policy. In office he was noted for his sound judgment, rectitude, character, and industry.

In keeping with his character, Monroe selected him in 1818 to go and warn French exiles to desist from their attempted settlement in Texas at a time when the United States claimed Texas. The settlement of the exiles had its roots in European history. Four years earlier, the Allies exiled a defeated Napoleon Bonaparte to the Mediterranean island of Elba and proceeded to divide up the spoils and redress the map of Europe. Although Europe had not been fond of the Bonapartes, the people were restive over the return of the old regime and an opportune Napoleon set out to return to his power. Frenchmen reminded of their glory under the former emperor flocked to his banner and the Allies had to defeat him once again and send him to a further exile in the island of St. Helena in the South Atlantic. The Bourbons wished to punish his supporters this time and they fled to the United States as political refugees.

One of the refugees was Charles Lallemand who arrived in Boston from Smyrna in April of 1817. This general was born at Metz, France, on June 24, 1774. At eighteen, he was a volunteer among the masses to defend France in 1792. In time, he became an aide-de-camp to General Andoche Junot, a longtime general under the command of Napoleon. When young Charles showed merit in the 1806 battle of Jena, Napoleon made him a colonel. Five years later in Spain, Napoleon promoted Lallemand brigadier general. Lallemand served General Davout in the defense of Hamburg as Napoleon tried to hold Germany.

A forgiving Louis XVIII gave him a command, but when Lallemand deserted to Napoleon and fought at Waterloo, he forfeited his position after the fall of Napoleon, a general of division and a peer of France. When the British would not let him accompany Napoleon to his final exile, he went to Egypt condemned to death should he return to France. He sailed for America with the leadership of a group of French refugees. Later, he offered his services to the Spanish constitutionalists. He then directed a school until allowed to return to France by the July monarch, where he was made a peer of France once again. He served out the remainder of his years as a division commander and died on March 9, 1839. But in 1817, he was in America as one of the leading refugees.

Meanwhile, other refugees had received relief from Congress at their request in the form of a tract of land on the Tombigbee River in territorial Alabama. They were helped by friends and the leaders were received in the best of society. Late in October of 1817, his brother Henry married a niece of Stephen Girard of Philadelphia in a ceremony attended by Joseph Bonaparte, former king of Spain. General Lallemand introduced himself to John Quincy Adams and denied having been engaged in projects contrary to American law. He had declined an invitation to join McGregor's expedition to Amelia Island and other similar projects. In his interview, Charles expressed his ardent love of liberty and sympathy with Hispanic Americans. Should he be an object of uneasiness and suspicion to the American government, he would leave the United States.

Adams replied that he was not an object of uneasiness, but that he had received information on a project to raise American money for an expedition to join the Mexican insurgents in which Lallemand had been implicated. Joseph Bonaparte was to head that army. This was contrary to American laws of neutrality. The secretary of state had information that the idea had been abandoned. As long as Lallemand conformed to law, he would be allowed to remain in asylum in the United States.

In time, Lallemand saw the New Year of 1818 in and talked over their common prospects with other French refugees. Soon there were rumors that his party, for he headed it now, would not settle on this Tombigbee grant but settle at Spanish Galveston. The Spaniards, who claimed the island were alarmed as were the French because their nationals were involved. The Americans still claimed Texas and wished the refugees to stay out. French minister to the United States Hyde de Neuville visited Adams on March

18, 1818, and said the expedition of refugees were at New Orleans and some had landed at Galveston.

The French minister again contacted Adams on the last day in April. They met on Adams' walk to his office. Adams wrote in his diary that Neuville was anxious and alarmed that Lallemand and his friends had landed at Galveston. It might be part of a Bonapartist plot. When Adams referred him to Onis, Neuville said that Onis had protested that he knew nothing of the matter. Neuville knew that Onis was involved and had given Lallemand money and maybe a letter to the viceroy in Mexico City.

It was at this time that the Monroe administration decided to send an agent to go to Galveston and ascertain the French objects and warn them that they were on American territory illegally. Adams informed Graham that he should go for the government and within a few days Graham said that he would go as agent. He had been wanting to visit the Alabama Territory during the summer and perhaps he would settle there. This would be a good time for him to go. As it was, he saw Louisiana and took an interest in the state to the extent of buying an interest in a cotton plantation.

Meanwhile, the Lallemand party had 92,000 acres to work for the encouragement of the cultivation of the vine and olive, sold it at two dollars per acre due in fourteen years without interest. The grant was abused by speculation. Land was sold and the money used by the Lallemands to settle on the Trinity River about twelve miles from its mouth with 120 people. They erected military works with mounted cannon, supposedly to farm plantations and raise cattle in the vacant land. It had been an empty land except for Indians, and the Frenchmen claimed no hostile intentions. They would be peaceful, active, and laborious or so they told the world. It would be a colony for agricultural and commercial purposes, but militarily organized for the colony's preservation, divided into cohorts. No time was spent on agriculture or commerce, but in gathering volunteers and training, with talk of striking out for the liberation of Mexico.

Adams was not fooled by the talk of agriculture. Rumor had it that the French colonists were contemplating an invasion of Mexico. The administration decided that this was true, but recognized that it might not be effected. President Monroe wished Graham to proceed rapidly to the banks of the Trinity or wherever the Frenchmen might go, without taking any risk of being captured by the Spanish. He would show to the chief of the French expedition his authority and express surprise that the French should be there without the authority of the American government which claimed Texas. Graham was ordered to ascertain their national authority they professed and their precise and real object for being there. He should also find out their numbers, sources of financing, and contact with the viceroy if any. The United States would pay Graham five dollars a day plus reasonable expenses.

Envoy Graham left Washington on the sixth of June for Galveston, but when he reached the Natchez, he learned that the French were inland, so he went to Natchitoches. There he learned that they had left their fort for Galveston. He went southward and went on a smuggler's ship to the town on the Gulf, where he waited on Lallemand. Graham told the general what he was instructed to say. The general said he had occupied empty land and had acted under authority of a treaty with the Mexican revolutionary Congress. The Spanish had attempted to use the Indians to cut off his supplies so he took this colony back to Galveston. He had planned to march upon San Antonio for the patriot cause. His finances had come from English and American mercantile houses who hoped for favors from the Mexican Congress. The general admitted to smuggling and privateering against the Spaniards. He asked for American authority to settle the Trinity, which Graham could not grant because the settlement could not be protected by American troops. [10]

[1]Ford, Thomas, *A History of Illinois: From Its Commencement as a State in 1818 to 1847*, Urbana: University of Illinois Press, 1995, pp. 7, 10-13.

[2]Cunningham, Noble E., Jr., ed., *Circular Letters of Congressmen to Their Constituents, 1789-1829*, 3 vols., Chapel Hill, NC: University of North Carolina Press, 1978, III, 1015-1016.

[3]*Ibid.*, 1021-1022.

[4]Perkins, Dexter, *A History of the Monroe Doctrine*, Boston: Little, Brown, 1963, pp. 3-4; Poage, G.R., *Clay*, 1936, p. 4.

[5]Cresson, *Monroe*, pp. 300-301. Quote.

[6]Beveridge, Albert J., *The Life of Marshall*, III, 5.

[7]*Circular Letters*, III, 1034-1035. Quote on pp. 1034-1035.

[8]Carter, *Territorial*, XVIII, 161, 303-304, 317-318, 325-326. Quotes on pp. 303-304, 325, 326.

[9]Davenport, F. Garvin, *Ante-Bellum Kentucky: A Social History, 1800-1860*, Oxford, Ohio: Mississippi Valley Press, 1943, pp. 40-47.

[10]Prichard, Walter ed., "George Graham's Mission to Galveston in 1818: Two Important Documents Bearing Upon Louisiana History," *Louisiana Historical Quarterly*, XX (1937), 619-638.

Chapter XI

JACKSON I

Onis wrote Adams, on June 17, 1818, a protest of the Jacksonian action in Florida. What Jackson did was not the proper course to take. Adams should have sought redress for any injuries done the harmful culprit should be turned over to American authorities. Of course, Spain could not have taken any physical action because of her weakness and this was recognized in certain circles in the United States. Onis then stated that these facts of the capture of the Spanish forts needed no comment for they were notorious and spoke for themselves. The enormity of the actions created wonder and surprise in the United States. They would astonish the world. Jackson could have no pretext or subterfuge for invading Florida. It was pure aggression. Onis demanded the return of the captured places to Spain with all they had possessed and restitution for the damage Jackson had done to Florida.

In his reply, Adams defended Jackson and noted the harm the Indians had done in Georgia. The action was the normal pursuit of an enemy. Spain had been bound to restrain the Seminole and had failed. Adams took the offensive and asked for the punishment of Spanish officers. Onis answered with complaints that have been done to the Indians by the Americans in the past. He asked that Jackson be punished. The war of words was to continue. [1]

General Andrew Jackson's seizure of Ft. Marks and Pensacola caused a furor in the Monroe cabinet. Jackson had not been authorized to do this and when Monroe learned of the action, he was in Norfolk touring the fortifications. Monroe immediately cut his inspections short. Reaching Washington DC, he found out that Jackson's official reports are not yet arrived, so he went to his country home. John Quincy Adams thought he would have stayed in the capital because people and press were denouncing the Jackson seizure. The other members of the cabinet had been summoned from their summer homes so there was nothing that could be done despite Adams' worries. There was an advantage for Monroe being in Loudoun County, Virginia. Away from the White House, he did not have to deal with Spanish ministerial presentations. When the Jacksonian dispatches arrived, he and his cabinet met.

There was a division of opinions. One factor that made the issue of such importance for the secretaries who were intent upon running for the presidency was the factor that Jackson was a contender for the position. Not only was it a diplomatic and state matter, but it was a political issue. In a position to hurt their rival all of the secretaries wanted Jackson reprimanded for exceeding his order. Only Adams was against this. The secretary of state wanted Jackson approved and the places kept. He said it was not an act of war. Monroe took a neutral stand, a middle ground to retain advantages and let Jackson off the hook.

Finally the matter was settled for stating that Jackson had had to seize the towns on the basis of information that he had at hand. The president had the posts returned to Spain and wrote Jackson and had Attorney General William Wirt write an administration editorial for the Washington *National Intelligencer* newspaper, the administration organ. Monroe won a majority in Congress for his stand and the matter was allowed to die without grave damage to anyone. The public went on to other happenings and Jackson was off the hook. Meanwhile, Adams had begun negotiations over Florida cession with the Spanish Government. [2]

Benjamin O'Fallen led twelve hundred Americans through St. Louis to join three hundred others at La Bellafontaine, a large spring south of the town of present day Waterloo. His object was to invade New Mexico in concert with forces at the mouth of Yellowstone River into the Missouri River, almost a thousand miles north of Santa Fe. The force at the Yellowstone was commanded by Lieutenant Colonel Talbot Chambers.

Viceroy Venadito of Mexico wrote at Santa Fe that Colonel "Melgares stated that because of the above mentioned distances, as well as because of the great obstacle which the deserts of that country and the mountain range, which serves as a barrier for New Mexico, present, he believed it very difficult for the Anglo-Americans to penetrate into the said province but that nevertheless he was taking proper measures to impede them and was maintaining spies and confidential agents who would communicate news of the movements of the foreigners. He was inclined to believe that the object of the Anglo-Americans in that expedition was to take away from the English of Canada the commerce in pelts which they have with barbarous tribes; concerning this point, the office of the vice-consul of St. Louis also speaks."

The twenty-four braves and four squaws of the Arapahoe tribe who had come to Santa Fe from the north country knew nothing about a congregation of whites at the Yellowstone. The Spanish at that time had been in the area much earlier and knew of the existence of the Yellowstone and where it was. Venadito knew, being informed of intelligence regarding any excursion in the province of New Mexico.

Venadito was also interested in the Long expedition whose mission was to invade Texas and take it for the United States. General James Long was an adventurer such as was O'Fallen. Again Venadito relates that Consul Fatio stated "that the first body composed of more than three thousand men has already crossed the Sabine River, that it is being augmented daily by recruits whom they receive from all parts of those states; that they are also relying on a party of Spanish rebel commanders, which is considerable, under the revolutionary leader Bernardo Gutierrez who was in Nacogdoches. Considering the people of Louisiana who have taken part in the enterprise and favor it, he states that he must believe that the Anglo-American government had not only willfully countenance it but that it will supply the assistance which it has always given those rebels in defiance of law and good faith whenever it suits their selfishness and particular purposes." Long was soon defeated and lost his life. Texas and New Mexico remained Spanish and then Mexican for a long time. [3]

Calhoun wrote from the department of war that he had received a letter from Henry Hitchcock, Alabama territorial secretary, in the absence of Governor Bibb, informing him that he had drawn upon that department for military disbursements put in the field for territorial defense. John C. Calhoun promised that the bill would be paid when presented and gave instructions. He said the measures that Jackson had done would give security to the southern frontier. If there was any more danger, Bibb was to apply to Gaines for regular troops. Should Gaines be unable to supply troops, Bibb was to continue to employ militia. However the shortage of funds meant that it was important to avoid using militia services. Calhoun hoped that Gaines might be called upon for regulars. Calhoun was able to provide enough troops to work on the road, but insufficient troops to help Indian agent David B. Mitchell with the Creeks. [4]

Sam Houston rode into Nashville, Tennessee, seeking a new beginning of age twenty-five. He looked up a lawyer friend Judge James Trimble, whom he knew slightly and asked if he could study law under him in the time honored fashion in the young United States. The judge prescribed an 18 month study, but Sam said he could do it in six months. Beginning his studies in June of 1818, he read and memorized with an easy stride. There was time for a social life. The aspiring young man made prominent friends in the fashionable Dramatic Cub of Nashville. He played several roles and met John H. Eaton, future secretary of war under Jackson. Soon six months were up and he took and passed the searching test with ease.

Seeking opportunity, Houston decided to move thirty miles to the east in the county seat town of Lebanon. Starting from scratch, he was fortunate in meeting and making friends with the postmaster and merchant Isaac Golladay. In those days postmasters were political leaders in the communities. Golladay was one of the leading citizens of Lebanon. Since Houston had no funds, his new friend lent him money to buy a new law library and suitable clothes as well as renting him a room as an office. Golladay introduced him to people who might use and pay for his services. Houston did not forget old friends and made frequent visits to General Andrew Jackson. This reintroduced him to Joseph McMinn, who was then governor of the state. McMinn made him a militia colonel and adjutant general. Jackson endorsed him for a state district attorney position and he moved to Nashville again. He became known as a trial lawyer of great force. His fellow officers elected him militia major general in 1821. [5]

Abraham Camp wrote the American Colonization Society from Lamott, in Illinois territory. Under date of July 13, 1818, he informed the society that he was "a free man of color, have a family and a large connection of free people residing on the Wabash, who are all willing to leave America whenever the way shall be opened. We loved this country and its liberties, if we could share an equal right in them; but our freedom is partial, and we have no hope that it ever will be otherwise, here; therefore we had rather be gone, though we should suffer hunger and nakedness for years. Your honor may be assured that nothing shall be lacking on our part in complying with whatever provision shall be made by the United States, whether it is to go to Africa or some other place; we shall hold ourselves in readiness, praying that God (who made men free in the beginning, and who by his kind providence has broken the yoke from every white American) would inspire to hear of every true son of liberty with zeal and pity, to open the door of freedom for us also." [6]

In the summer of 1818, Jacob Gruber, who was a Methodist minister from Pennsylvania, went to a Methodist camp meeting at Hagerstown, Maryland. When it became his turn, Gruber preached strongly against the institution of slavery and compared Maryland and Pennsylvania unfavorably. There were some twenty-six hundred white people before the stand and some four hundred African Americans behind it. After preaching against infidelity, intemperance, and profanity, Jacob hit the practice of holding slaves. Telling his listeners that Americans lived in a free country, he cited the Declaration of Independence proclamation that "all men were created equal, and certain inalienable rights, such as life, liberty, and the pursuit of happiness." This was inconsistent, grossly inconsistent, to hold this and wield a bloody whip of slavery in the other hand. Even the most humane slaveholder and upholder of the rights of free blacks among the audience wanted no such doctrines preached before them and the African Americans behind the preacher.

At the next grand jury meeting, members of the community brought forth charges against Gruber. They incited him for attempting to incite the slaves into open rebellion against their masters. Lawyer and councilor for the society to protect free African Americans, Beene S. Pigman secured fellow councilor Roger B. Taney to secure Gruber. A change of tenure was obtained to move the trial to Frederick, Maryland. Taney made the appeal to the jurors on the grounds of free speech under Maryland laws. Under these laws, "no man could be punished for preaching the articles of his religious creed unless they were immoral and calculated to disturb the peace and order of society" To convict, it was necessary to prove that his doctrines were dangerous and also that he intended to disturb the peace. This was hard to prove. Taney noted that peaceful abolition was a tenet of his church and that Methodists were accustomed to preaching that slavery was unjust and oppressive. Furthermore, the slaves came to the meeting and Gruber did not go to the slaves. They could not have come without the consent of their masters. There was no law against speaking of slavery in any manner the public wished to hear. The jury found Gruber not guilty. [7]

Monroe had departed on a trip out of Washington and left a tranquil season behind him. There was little of interest in the affairs of state, but Calhoun promised Monroe that he would quickly inform the president of any occurrence that merited his attention. Calhoun as the only high official at work in Washington in August, was virtually in

charge of the executive government. War Secretary Calhoun thought the public would approve of Monroe's action over the issue of Pensacola and he himself believed it to be highly prudent and correct. He was glad to hear of the improvement of Mrs. Monroe's health and her health should be reinstated with the enjoyment of the fine country air of Albemarle in North Carolina. Calhoun's letter to these effects was dated August 1, 1818.
8

On August 1, 1818, as aide-de-camp to Jackson, Captain James Gadsden reported to the general on the defenses of Florida. It was written concerning three forts. These were Fort Carlos de Barrancas at Pensacola Bay, Fort Gadsden on the Appalachicola River twenty plus miles upstream, and Fort St. Marks, not far from the Bay of Apalachee.

He wrote about Fort Carlos de Barrancas that it was well-selected because it had command of the bay's entrance and could be well fortified as protection against any enemy. He proposed a battery on the opposite side of Rose's Island as being indispensable. He would have a fort on the hill above. The existing fort was a temporary one. "The entrance between the island and main exceeds one mile and a quarter, and the largest vessels may approach either shore." This was a natural harbor and was an important one to defend if that were ever required.

Fort Gadsden was also on a well selected location. He wrote that "being the lowest bluff on the Appalachiocola River to which a land communication could be obtained, and near enough its mouth to ensure a safe and certain navigation to and from the ocean, it becomes invaluable as a depot for an army operating in the Floridas, and dependent for supplies from the granaries of the Gulf. Its vicinity to Fort Scott and St. Marks and the facility with which the land communications between these points could be maintained, enhances its importance as within a chain a cordon of posts, which it became necessary to fortify in giving security to our southern frontier." It was "at such distances as to enable the garrison to concentrate at will for any operations against marauding parties of Indians that might assemble." Fort Gadsden was also temporary in construction. The fort could not last long. He proposed a new work to replace it like the new work required by the needs of the Barrancas position.

The third fort, St. Marks, was also in a well selected place. This fortress was incomplete and required enlargement and permanency. He suggested for Florida a well established and active military presence. Florida was still vulnerable. In his report, Gadsen went into the recent history of the war there to prove that statement of weakness. After these statements, he went into the need for strong defenses in Florida. He ended his report on the subject of strategy and closed his engineering report with respect. [9]

There were the usual numbers of escaped slaves from the South and from house slaves of Southerners living in the north at this time. One of the masters who lost a slave was John C. Calhoun. He had lost a domestic named Hector, who sometimes called himself Johnson or might be able to conceal himself by another name. In order to secure Hector, he wrote Charles J. Ingersoll of Philadelphia where Hector was headed according to Calhoun's information. He had left Calhoun in Washington while the secretary was on a trip to South Carolina. The slave left without provocation, probably under the advise and aid of free African Americans near the Calhoun residence in Washington.

He hated to give Ingersoll trouble in the matter, but the secretary had been advised that he should not advertise, but to gain the services of an active constable or agent who had experience in regaining escaped slaves for their masters. Calhoun informed Ingersoll that Hector had been gone for twenty-six days and was about 25 years old. He was very black and a bit short, of a compact form, and spoke slowly with a feeble voice. His upper eye lids drooping over his eyes gave him a sleepy look. Hector was not found as can be determined in the records. Since he was easily recognized by Calhoun's description, he probably went to another community where he was safe. [10]

The people of New York State and because of this the government of the state and federal government wanted to move the Iroquois out of their land for white settlement. They would move them to the Arkansas River area but when Calhoun wrote New York's Representative David A. Ogden on May 14th, Calhoun got a letter of August 4th from Olden. The New Yorker said that the Iroquois were opposed to this particular movement, but said that they would emigrate to the Fox River valley, west of Lake Michigan.

Soon after this, Calhoun wrote Luis Ass at Detroit and ordered him to ascertain whether the Indians of this northwestern area were willing to grant the Iroquois any lands in their vicinity and would allow them to reside there. Days later Calhoun wrote Ogden about the desirability of the Arkansas lands and said that should the Iroquois agree, he would not ask Cass to talk to the Indians at the Fox River about that locale. Calhoun made it clear that the Arkansas lands would be preferable for the Federal government, whom he claimed were the best friends of the Iroquois. He also claimed that the individuals who were trying to turn the Iroquois away to the Fox were their worst enemies.

Of course Calhoun was wrong. The Iroquois had no best friends in the federal government and certainly not the likes of Jackson and Calhoun. Even the pro-Indian Houston had to bend to white interests for it was not the Indians best interest to move them to the Arkansas but that of the white settlers, who wanted more and more of the land and would not stop for the ensuing century.

Shortly Cass wrote that the Iroquois would not receive land in Illinois and Indiana. These Indians decided not to emigrate at all and Calhoun took the next steps of bringing an Indian delegation to Washington in order that they might be convinced of the truth of his statements and the need of their going to the Arkansas River valley to settle. This would open New York land as Calhoun and the white settlers wished. Months later Cass reported that the Iroquois would be welcome in Ohio for settlement on reservations. [11]

Still active, Pintard and a few friends were founding a literary club which would meet over dinner and ale and wine. There they talked of matters of literature and politics. It would be weekly. They listened to Lancaster give a lecture on education and the teaching of younger students by the older students. Pintard was introduced to Lancaster, which he enjoyed. He had expected a scholarly man, but found a rosy full blown Briton. Lancaster was a Quaker, polished and very pleasant. An active man, he visited an

Lancaster school in Albany with Clinton. Next he went to see Niagara Falls, the greatest sight in the north. He planned on his return to give an education course. At this time, Charles Picton arrived. He was to take charge of Lancasterian schools in the city. There were by this point three and a fourth was underway. An idea was to educate the young men to become teachers to go to other parts of the United States. The principle victorious was that the children learn faster and more delightedly than they did under the old educational philosophy. [12]

[1]Fuller, *Purchase*, pp. 282-292. Quote on p. 282.

[2]Ammon, Harry, "Executive Leadership in the Monroe Administration," Boles, John B., *America: The Middle Period, Essays in Honor of Bernard Mayo*, Charlottesville:; University Press of Virginia, 1973, pp. 122-124.

[3]Thomas, Alfred B., "The Yellowstone River, James Long and Spanish Reaction to American Intrusion into Spanish Dominions 1818-1819," *West Texas Historical Yearbook*, IV (June 1928), 3-15. Quotes on pp. 9,11.

[4]Carter, *Territorial*, XVIII, 373-374.

[5]Hopewell, C., *Sam Houston*, 1987, pp. 39-42.

[6]Woodson, Carter G., *The Mind of the Negro As Reflected in Letters Written During the Crisis, 1800-1860*, Washington DC: The Association for the Study of Negro Life and History, 1926, pp. 2-3. Quote on pp. 2-3.

[7]Swisher, Carl Brent, *Roger B. Taney*, 1935, Rep. Hamden, CT: Archon Books, 1961, pp. 95-98. Quote on p. 96.

[8]Calhoun, *Papers*, III, 4-5.

[9]James Gadsden to Andrew Jackson, August 1, 1818, in "The Defenses of the Floridas," *Florida Historical Quarterly*, 15 (1937), 242-248.

[10]Calhoun, *Papers*, III, 9.

[11]*Ibid.*, III, 11, 42-43, 56-57, 90, 188, 255, 336, 670.

[12]Pintard, p. 141. See pp. 143-144.

Chapter XII

CALHOUN

Calhoun wrote Jackson on September 8, 1818, that he concurred in the view that Jackson had taken "in relation to the importance of Florida to the effectual peace and security of our Southern frontier, and such, I believe, is the opinion of every member of the administration." Calhoun noted that "St. Marks will be retained till Spain shall be ready to garrison it with sufficient force, and Fort Gadsden and any other position in East or West Florida within the Indian Country, which may be deemed eligible, will be retained so long as there is any danger; which, it is hoped, will afford the desired security."

Timid measures were out, but caution was in. A war solely with Spain would be nothing, however Americans needed time to fortify and enlarge one's navy, to replenish depots and pay debts off. Especially since a Spanish war would escalate into an English war. And indeed Calhoun thought it would in a few years. He then discussed the fortification of Baton Rouge for which Congress made appropriated a considerable sum for a military depot and barracks. Work should soon begin there. [1]

A band of hostile Creeks returned to Alabama, finding that they could no longer find safety in Florida, entered into U.S. territory. They numbered seventy warriors and large numbers of women and children. They applied to Chickasaw tribesmen for land to settle on. They denied this land to the hostiles and he latter crossed the Alabama and Cahabia Rivers. On the way the hostiles killed two white men and three Choctaw; further, at Cornwall's Settlements they murdered and pillaged. Major Samuel Taylor led a force following their trail. They proceeded to a point eight miles from the falls.

The major marched his men in cane breaks and through swamps, becoming separated from Captain Bacon. The Indians were in a good position when the Americans reached them with a thick cane break on the right and a high bluff on the left. When they saw the whites, they gave their war whoop and were attacked by the whites. Eight or ten warriors were killed. With the loss of two whites, the force retreated, but was reinforced by Bacon. In the ensuing fight, six or eight more Indians were killed, but the whites retreated once again. There was the possibility of some more fighting, but before this was undertaken, the Indians fled. The battle took place on the sixteenth of September with an engagement of thirty-two men and officers. The place was near the Black Warrior River. [2]

There were the usual wars between Indian tribes in the backwoods. One such took place at this time. The Western Cherokees, having just removed west to the Arkansas River, allied themselves with the Delawares, Shawnees, Quapaws, and the number of Americans for a raid against the Osage on the Verdigris. They found Clermont's village in the absence of its warriors and killed over 80 old men, women, and children and captured over 100. They fired the town and destroyed what provisions were there. The Osage did not seek vengeance but signed a peace treaty with Cherokees and their allies and the Big and Little Osages for amity on October 6, 1818. It was soon broken and hostilities resumed. These wars lasted until 1822.

Meanwhile, the Pawnees had attacked the Osages, some 400 Pawnee ambushed a party of Osages close to the Arkansas River by 50 or 60 miles. Only one of the 48 warrior party escaped to tell the tale. An expedition of hunting Spaniards moved into the territory of the United States in the search of game. Pawnees Loups killed them, taking a ten-year-old Spanish boy captive. He was destined for a sacrificial rite when a trader ransomed the boy and sold him to Manuel Lisa. The lad was lucky to have survived and come into the hands of Lisa. At this time William Clark signed treaties with the Pawnees and the Osages. [3]

On or about the first of October, there landed at Baltimore an immigrant family, the Mellons with their five year old boy Thomas Mellon, later to found Mellon Bank in Pittsburgh. They had just come from Ireland where the head of the household was a small farmer. They came seeking economic development and were to find it in America. Andrew Mellon hired a Conestaga wagon and team for a journey to backwoods Pennsylvania. The long tedious trip was over very bad roads muddy and torturous to travel. Orchards were numerous along the way. The luscious fruit and vegetation were so bountiful that it seemed to young Thomas to be a paradise they were passing through. With another wagon of people with them, they stopped at nights to make a campfire and prepare their evening meal. They neared their destination where they had friends and relatives. His uncles Samuel and Archibald Mellon were directing the turnpike construction of the area of which two miles they had undertaken to construct, anxious to better themselves financially.

Thomas enjoyed the gathering of the apple and corn harvest and was plagued by the burs and Spanish needles. He also ate for the first time Indian corn prepared in a mush and other concoctions. He always remembered the sensation of the peculiarly wild favor or taste when he first tasted it. He soon became very fond of the mush. He had never before seen such storms and lighting; greater than that he had known in Ireland. He also avoided the snakes of which there were none in his former homeland. [4]

The engaging Abbe Jose Francisco Correia called upon the able John Quincy Adams at the State Department. The minister from Portugal did not get to the point at first. There were many interests to talk over between the two widely educated men. Correia was one of the few men whom Adams had a high respect for in Washington DC. The

Portuguese envoy was interested in many things and could be an expert at several as far as Adams was concerned. A scientist, Correia was the co-founder of the Royal Academy of Science in Lisbon, but was no pedant.

His diplomacy was so able that he had single-handedly arranged a change in American neutrality laws some time before though his influence upon Monroe. Now he was to take advantage of that change in asking Adams to stop a preparation of a privateer against Portuguese shipping then underway in Maryland on the Putuxant. The ship was being commissioned by Jose Artigas, the Uruguayan leader and gaucho against both Spain and Buenos Aires. Adams told Correia that it was a matter for the American courts, but Correia did not trust the American courts but Adams brought up the matter with Monroe.

Attorney General William Wirt was instructed to act against the outfitting of the privateer. Wirt gave orders to a district attorney in the matter as a matter of advice, since he had no jurisdiction over the federal district attorneys, surprising to relate. Wirt then turned around and told Monroe and the cabinet that the prosecution would not succeed. The president then suggested that Wirt follow a cautious policy in the matter. Meanwhile, Wirt had been offered a bribe by the Abbe. Wirt then went to Baltimore to press the case.

In the confusion on the matter, action was being taken. It was what was being done and not what was being said that mattered. Abbe next wanted the privateers declared pirates. Soon the Portuguese government took up the situation with the powers of Europe, who then rebuked the United States. The French minister to the United States came calling upon Adams. Hyde de Neuville stated his government's policy and Adams went to Monroe, who was not concerned and brushed Adams off on the subject. Soon the question was sifted to the American slave traders on the prowl. [5]

In October of 1818, Zachary Taylor had built Fort Howard at Green Bay, and now was assigned to the task of recruiting once again at Louisville. During the next June, he breakfasted with President James Monroe and Major General Andrew Jackson on their visit to Frankfort, Kentucky, in the hills. He went with Monroe to visit Colonel Richard M. Johnson. By this time, he was promoted to the rank of lieutenant colonel and soon joined a unit building a road in the Old Southwest. In the early fall of 1820, tragedy struck the Taylor family. All contracted a bilious fever and their two youngest girls died. This decided him against buying a plantation in the area of Louisiana. Taylor survived the peacetime cuts and assumed command of the post at Natchitoches on the Red River as ordered. His men built Fort Selden at Shield's Spring, twenty-two miles from the town. It was on a ridge between the Red and Sabine basins. They next constructed Cantonment Jesup. Later, he was assigned to Cantonment Robertson at Baton Rouge as its commander until March of 1824. He was to support the Monroe Doctrine. [6]

Adams publicly defended Jackson on his Florida expedition controversy. He said that if the Spanish could not rule its Florida colony, Spain should cede it to the United States. He then told Spanish Minister Luis de Onis that Jackson's action was against the Seminole and not the Spanish. Onis had wanted Jackson punished severely and the town returned. Adams replied that if Spain could not control its Florida Indian population, the United States must assume control of Florida. Although Monroe would neither censure or punish Jackson, the general faced a congressional inquiry. Jackson said that Monroe had indirectly authorized the invasion through Congressman J. Rhes of Tennessee. Later the House voted 107 to 63 not to censure Jackson as Clay wanted. [7]

There was a pirate loose in Charles Gibbs at this time. He operated from 1818 to 1824, capturing more than twenty vessels and killing their crews. An officer on the *Chesapeake* under Captain James Lawrence, Gibbs had been captured and spent time in England's Dartmoor Prison for prisoners of war in the naval warfare of the War of 1812. After the war, he joined an Argentine privateer operation against the Spanish. From this, he graduated into a full time pirate, raiding and plundering. In time, the British raided his base near Cape San Antonio in Cuba.

In November of 1821, the Maine brig *Cobbosseecontee* sailed for Cuba. Four miles out, she was attacked by a pirate and plundered; the captain and mate captured and dealt with severely. With its New England cargo of fish, lumber, and provisions, the schooner *Exertion* sailed forth and was caught and plundered at Key Largo. The men were marooned. Only a few survived. Finally, the pirates were wiped out by American and British forces by 1825. There was a trade in loot and also in slaves in the area of the Caribbean and Atlantic. This last activity did not die out until the Civil War. [8]

At this time on December 13, 1818, in Lexington, Kentucky, Mary Todd was born into a favored family of culture and bearing in contrast to the close to the earth Lincoln family. Family ties linked Mary to leading families in Kentucky, Illinois, and Pennsylvania. The fun loving Mary had a good childhood marred by the death of her mother and remarriage of the father she adored. There were three men in her life that she looked up to. Besides her father, Robert Smith Todd, there was Henry Clay and later Lincoln. She came into contact with Henry Clay while she was a girl. Todd was a southern Whig whose ties to Clay were close. Mary was well cared for, enjoying the attentions of many servants. The Todds had come to America in the eighteenth century to escape from religious persecution in Scotland. Her great-grandfather was a friend of George Washington.

Robert Smith Todd saw to it that his daughters were educated. Mary took to books and became interested in the issues of her day. She had a fine memory and loved to recite poetry. Next the girl learned the graces at Madame Mentelle's boarding school in 1832. The older sister of Mary's, Elizabeth Todd, fell in love with Ninian Wirt Edwards at Transylvania College. The student was the son of the governor of Illinois. They got married and moved to Springfield. While Mary was in finishing school and Elizabeth was settling in Illinois, Abe Lincoln lived in New Salem and was just getting by. Mary learned fluent French which never left her and conversation and letter writing as well as other subjects. She knew Henry Clay and paid close attention to politics being with important leaders who came to talk with her father.

In 1837, she went to live at the Edwards in Springfield to find a husband. She then returned to Lexington for some more education and was back in Illinois in 1839, soon to meet Lincoln. Mary had many suitors of important and upcoming standards in the community including Douglas. However, she was drawn to Lincoln and he was drawn to her. Her family disapproved of Abe and worked to get her married off to a seemingly better suitor. They were concerned about the social gap. [9]

On December 14, 1818, New York intellectual John Pintard wrote his daughter, who lived at New Orleans, that there was little stirring outside of congressional debates. Public sentiment was against her hero Jackson in the Arbuthnot and Ambrister incident. Allowances were being made for the situating the southern states faced. But Jackson had showed his famous temper. Jackson should have referred the matter to the president. He did wish to deter others by the example. How superior was the character of George Washington. His successors did not match him. Even in war, he never forgot justice and humanity. Washington was very much the better of Jackson as Pintard relates. There was other strong opinion on the matter. [10]

Ritchie spoke out against the Jacksonian invasion of Florida and against popular support for the seizure of Florida. America's honor was at stake. It had international duties and could not act like a bandit. He distrusted the military and believed in negotiations in order to gain Florida. He was to be right, but Jackson resented it when Ritchie editorialized about Jackson's failure in his military record as governor of Louisiana. He demanded that Jackson be subjected to a court of inquiry for his actions in Florida. However, he did not question his patriotism or his good intentions He accepted that Spain had not lived up to its treaty obligations but required his country to do so.

Extension of national territory was not sufficient reason for such action of whims and passions. He thought reasonably and clearly, but to Jackson it was an affront and Jackson, who never forgave, was to ignore Ritchie and his talents when Jackson became president. Ritchie had to speak his piece and he took his stand without recourse to lying statements or passion. The press of the lower South supported Jackson and made violent and false attacks upon Ritchie. These editors did not consider his actual views, but in anger wrote a series of lies against him. His talk, they wrote about national honor was a scam, they wrongfully said. Ritchie ignored such editorials, but answered when they accused him of being a minion of Federalists or the agent of one of Jackson's Washington enemies. They also said his support of Monroe was a measure to enhance Monroe's popularity.

They could not see Ritchie's honest opinions and his right to them. It was a personal matter and they reacted strongly. Ritchie stuck to his peace policy and peace was maintained by the efforts of more important men than Ritchie, but with his influence. He wanted both Florida and Cuba in the United States, but honorably by negotiations or purchase. The goal was the same, but the means were different. [11]

Destined to play a role in American diplomatic history when be became president of Mexico. a ragged little Indian boy of twelve ran away from his Mexican Oaxacan village on December 17, 1818, to seek his fortune. This boy, Benito Juarez, was a Zapotec Indian and therefore born in poverty. His birth took place on March 21, 1806, in the small San Pablo Guelatan. His parents died when he was three and he was left in the care of his uncle Bernardino Juarez, who treated him carelessly and without much thought. Both uncle and nephew worked very hard, the boy herded sheep and kept them clear of the fenceless patches of corn and beans.

The uncle tried to teach him to read Spanish. The only way out of poverty for young Benito was to study for the priesthood and his uncle pressed him to learn what he could not teach him. The boy wanted the education that his uncle wished for him. Because he wanted an education and his uncle could not take him to the city of Oaxaca, he had to go there himself. There was no school nearby and the only way to get an education was to either work in the capital of the Mexican state or in the homes of the well-to-do while a servant. Because he was at work most of the time, he had little time for learning in his hometown. He walked the whole way down from the mountains onto a life during which he was to meet Lincoln. There was a bond between the two back in Civil War days.

Juarez found work, for his board, until he got a job with a bookbinder, who offered to send him to school. This pious bookbinder of the Third Order of St. Francis loved the works of Feijoo and St. Paul's letters. Three weeks had passed and Juarez was settled in to a chance at education and association with youths. He earned not only his keep but their friendship. Benito showed an interest in books and what they taught. Oaxaca had the population of 24,400 or so in 1792, of which 88% were pure-blooded Mixtecs and Zapotecs. Many of these knew only their native tongues so Juarez was at home. Oaxaca was a religious city with many monasteries and churches, which made the hard way of life an easier one. Juarez had been bought up in the church so he was at home early in the fabulous world, he found there so different from his little village in the mountains. [12]

[1]Calhoun, *Papers*, pp. 110-111. Quotes on p. 110.

[2]Carter, *Territorial*, XVIII, 419-420, 430-431.

[3]Barry, *Beginnings*, pp. 78-79.

[4]Mellon, Thomas, *Thomas Mellon and His Times*, Pittsburgh: University of Pittsburgh Press, 1994, pp. 16-19. Quote on p. 19.

[5]Noonan, John T., Jr., *The Antelope: The Ordeal of the Recaptured Africans in the Administrations of James Monroe and John Quincy Adams*, Berkeley: University of California Press, 1977, pp. 2-13.

[6]Bauer, K. Jack, *Zachary Taylor: Soldier, Planter, Statesman of the Old Southwest*, Baton Rouge: Louisiana State University Press, 1985, pp. 34-43.

[7]Daniel, *Chronicles*, pp. 266, 268, 273.

[8]Duncan, Roger F., *Coastal Maine: A Maritime History*, New York: W.W. Norton, 1992, pp. 285-287.

[9]Ross, Ishbel, *The President's Wife: Mary Todd Lincoln: A Biography*, New York: G.P. Putnam's Sons, 1973, pp. 14-23, 27-41.

[10]Pintard, *Letters*, p. 160. See p. 168.

[11]Ambler, Charles Henry, *Thomas Ritchie: A Study in Virginia Politics*, Richmond: Bell, Book and Stationery, 1913, pp. 68-71.

[12]Smart, Charles Allen, *Viva Juarez*, Philadelphia: J.B. Lippincott, 1963, pp. 27-38.

Chapter XIII

LINCOLNS

At the death of Nancy Lincoln, the woman told little Abe to be kind and good to his father and sister. Both he and Sarah were to be good to one another. They should love their kin and worship God. Nancy passed away and left the children to their dreary life, poorly protected through later in the winter Parson Elkin gave a funeral sermon over her grave.

One day in his tenth year, he took a family horse to the mill to grind corn. Abe was driving the horse forward to get the most out of the process where the horse provided motive force. He yelled, "Come on" when the horse kicked him unconscious. Taken home he was in a coma until the next day. Coming to, "he automatically finished his yell: "you old Hussy." [1]

Abraham and his sister Sarah went to the school of Andrew Crawford during most of the school year of 1818-1819. Nat Grigsby later was to remember this Indiana schooling with Lincoln. Five years later, the future president went to school under the institution of Azel Dorsey for six months. Two or so years passed and then he was taught by a Mr. Sweeney. This third Indiana school lasted six months, but Lincoln was not there all of the time. In these schools, he learned writing, spelling, and arithmetic. Nat remembered Lincoln to be studious and the leading scholar. Crawford taught manners and preached against cruelty to animals. When the boys would turn terrapin turtle on their backs, Lincoln would tell them this was wrong and then write about this. He wrote poetry on his own. Remembering Lincoln as kindly disposed, Grigsby stated he rarely quarreled and he was prompt and honorable. The students wore buckskin pants and linsey-woolsey hunting coats with low shoes and short socks. Lincoln's britches were generally too short for him.

While other boys were wasting their time, Lincoln would be at home studying. Sitting by the light of the fire, Lincoln would cipher on boards and wooden fire shovels when he did not have a slate. In order to rescue the boards, he would shine them bright and cipher on them. Then he would dirty them and reshave them for later use. [2]

One year passed after Nancy's death due to milk sickness. Thomas remarried to Mrs. Sarah Bush Johnston, a widow with three children. The twelve year old Elizabeth, the widow's first born soon married Dennis Hanks at the age of twelve. The girls and parents slept downstairs and the boys slept in the loft. The gentle Sarah filled in the place of mother for Abraham and he was always to have the highest regard for the stepmother. She became a strong force in her life and he said he owned much to her of what he became. [3]

Four percent of the inhabitants of neighboring Illinois were French descended, many of them a mixed French-Indian origin. These lived on common acreage farms in the French peasant style and were attended by good-hearted priests. They did not make improvements on their land and disdained the improvement ideas of their Anglo neighbors. But they lived closely to the soil and endured bad crops and bad weather, and celebrated good crops, marriages and births. And mourned the dead.

For the Protestants there were educated ministers, but many of the preachers were not educated but sprang from the people with their studies of the Scriptures and religious upbringing to excel as regards to their talents at preaching and advising and directing their people in the life of salvation. Many read such books as Young's *Night Thoughts*, Watts' hymns, Milton's *Paradise Lost*, and Hervey's *Meditations* which raised their talents into poetics and flowery language. They had strong convictions and often entered into religious controversy. They taught justice and sound morals. They taught reward in Heaven and punishment in Hell.

American pursuits were largely agricultural. They bought the few necessities from the few merchants that they could not produce on the farm. They seldom used coffee and tea. Raising sheep for wool, their womenfolk made it into garments. They did the same with flax and cotton, all farmers' crops. Taking the bark of the trees to make dyes, they used the colors to look good to family, friends, and beaus and belles. Raccoons provided fur for hats and caps. Shoes or moccasins provided by animal hides, were not added to by factory made boots which they rarely bought. They made almost everything else they needed including the simple farm equipments, One of their chief joys was land speculation. Money paid to militiamen found its way into land purchases for sale at higher prices. Soon Illinois had a state bank to provide credit mostly for land sales. [4]

Reformer and woman's rights advocate Lucretia Coffin Mott was born in Massachusetts' Nantucket on January 3, 1793, to Thomas and Anna Folger Coffin. She learned good work habits as a child, doing chores and went to school. After leaving the school house, she helped her mother in her shop and learned sewing arts. Lucretia also became adept at cooking. Theodore Parker expressed his view of the latter Mrs. Mott as "the most distinguished preacher, a woman who adorns her domestic calling as housekeeper, wife, and mother, with the same womanly dignity and sweetness which mark her present deportment." He was to write this in 1853.

The girl was the foundation for the woman. Thomas Coffin moved his family to Boston in 1804 and founded a merchandise store and limited banking place. He was successful and moved his family to a new brick house, costing $5,600, a considerable sum. Lucretia continued her education in one of Boston's Free Schools. She did so well that Thomas sent his daughter to Nine Partners Boarding School, a Quaker academy in southeastern New York. The friends school was conducted on principles of enlightened education of the times. Harsh methods of education such as threats, scoldings, and arbitrary punishment were rejected. Instead they learned as they read of the natural resources, economic order, and social life of the world so they could appreciate the comforts civilization and parents provided them. Principles of ethics and example of were interwoven in the conversations of an imaginary family of Harcourts.

Lucretia also learned of the murderous middle passage of slave ships and pleas for the abolition of the slave trade which were already underway. Her teachers stressed the fundamentals of education. After two years, the principal made the advanced Lucretia an assistant teacher without pay. About this time, there was an attraction between her and the blond Quaker instructor of the school, James Mott, Jr., who was second only to the school's superintendent. Also the family moved to Philadelphia with Lucretia in tow. James followed her there and wooed her and got a job with her father's firm of commission merchants. They got married and Mott became a partner of Thomas Coffin.

After a time, following the War of 1812 and enmeshed in the pursuing depression, the two families struggled along. Thomas tried Ohio, but had to come back to Philadelphia. James worked in his uncle's cotton mill, worked as a New York bank clerk, before establishing a Philadelphia business in foreign and domestic staples. Lucretia taught school. With her husband's success and a third child, Lucretia now devoted herself full time to the tasks of being a wife, mother, and housewife. She also found time for reading; especially the study of the Bible. Of significance in her center table was Mary Wollstonecraft's *Vindication of the Rights of Woman*, which was first published in 1792, a book which enjoyed an enlarged education for women. Women must be equipped with means of weighing assistant values and focusing their understanding of the issues of right and wrong. [5]

In the Quaker church silence was maintained in religious gatherings until some one felt moved to state, pray, or preach. One day, Lucretia Mott felt so moved and for the first time made a public speech in a prayer that "as all our efforts to resist temptation, and overcome the world prove fruitless, unless aided by the Holy Spirit, enable us to approach preservation from all evil, that we may be wholly devoted to Thee and Thy glorious cause." From the prayer to God forward Mrs. Mott played an increasing role in the Friends or Quakers. Benefactress Sarah Zane made religious tours of the area as far as Winchester, Virginia, from Philadelphia, giving land there for a French meeting house and money for a volunteer fire company.

In 1818, Zane took Mott with her to Wincester. Lucretia Mott enjoyed the scenery and was affected by the condition of the slaves, who seemed content. Virginians told her that the slave's contentment was the result of the tolerance of Virginian slaveholders. It was the nature of the African Americans to be cheerful whatever their condition, free or slave; of course, the better the treatment of the black and the tolerance of the slaveowner would have its effect. No one said how many slaves had escaped to the North from the countryside of Winchester and no one knew what the enslaved person thought of slavery, but given the nature of men and women, they preferred freedom. Slaveholders, however, would not admit this last, contending that the enslaved persons were happy being cared for in slavery. [6]

The issue of slavery was an old one in the United States, an even older one in the world. Arguments on its rights date back to the ancients. To the Greeks and the Romans it was justified in law and nature. The early fathers of the Church sanctioned slavery and it continued throughout the Middle Ages. Spanish conquerors made slaves of the Indians they found in the New World. When they discovered that the natives made poor slaves and died off rapidly, they eagerly adopted the Las Casas suggestion that blacks be imported as slaves. Las Casas had wanted to protect the Indians, but when he comprehended the evils of black slavery, he was to regret the idea. It was too late then. The Spanish were happy with slaves. Slavery was early introduced in the English colonies about one century later. Both sides of the argument drew upon sources from the ancients and medieval writers.

Black slaves were imported into Virginia in 1619 and the Puritans made slaves of captured Indians in 1637 during the Pequot War. Shortly, they brought in black slaves, legally recognized in 1641. Large numbers of slaves were put to work in the South, but there were limited numbers in the North. Roger Williams and John Eliot spoke out for better treatment of the slaves. Warwick in Rhode Island granted slaves their freedom in law after a service of ten years. However, there is no record they actually freed slaves. Decades later, Samuel Sewell espoused anti-slavery and was answered by John Saffin who defended slavery. Both men used religious arguments in their pamphlets. Saffin argued that God made the different orders in life. Some were to be subjects and slaves. He denied that all men had equal rights to liberty. His opinion prevailed.

The Quakers and Mennonites were the first religious groups to take an abolitionist stand, believing in liberty of conscience and body. Many Quakers wrote on the subject. Benjamin Franklin published one of these tracts in 1729. As the century progressed, John Woolman and Antony Benezet led in writing against slavery. George Washington and Patrick Henry read the works of Benezet. All of them believed that all men had equal rights. Early abolitionists argued their cases based upon Jesus' Golden Rule of doing to others as you would have them do to you. Itinerant Methodist preachers took up the refrain at the time.

Slaveholders and their defenders were active too in this contest for the minds of men. They answered the arguments of the abolitionists, using Mosaic law and Calvinistic beliefs. Saffin had argued that men were naturally unequal in the order of God's universe. Defenders of slavery relied upon historic sanction and Biblical sanction. They argued with passages of the prophets' curse on Cannan, the Levitical ordinance, and Paul's view of the duty of slaves and masters. To them, the black was inferior and even a separate species. Slaves in America were better off than the peasants in Europe. Defenders drew upon Montesquieu, Pufendorf, Aristotle, and Grotius. George Whitefield, Methodist divine, stated that since blacks could work in hot countries while whites could not, slavery was right.

One of the questions debated was the religious instruction of the slave. Most slaveholders did not want their property taught Christian precepts and doctrine. They argued that the African American slaves did not have souls and were not of the human species. Some feared that religious instruction would turn the slaves to thought that could be dangerous of the institution. They would learn such things as the Golden Rule and salvation for the world. They also feared that the knowledge of Christianity would elevate the blacks to their position. In short, they should remain property and not be thinking soul-filled persons.

In 1818, several anti-slavery Senators spoke out in the Senate. William Smith of South Carolina replied. He countered that the senators had been slaveholders and having sold their slaves and put the money in bank stock, they now attacked the institution. New England had lately transported slaves from Africa. Further, they were employing free African Americans in hard work on better terms than they had as masters. These critics knew nothing about the condition of the slaves. He used the Biblical argument that the Africans descended from Cannanites and were prophesied to be hewers and drawers of water, slaves to the other races in keeping with the curse. This was nonsense since the Africans had not ancestors in the Cannanites, while many had ancestors in the slaveowners of this time and past. However, he did hit a weak point in talking about New England treatment of Africans in the middle passage. [7]

There were slaves who fled through Wilmington, North Carolina, by sea for freedom in New England. Wilmington was the largest and finest town and harbor on the coast of the state. It had a reputation for being a secret asylum for escaped slaves, because it was located close to the mouth of the Cape Fear River and its steady sea traffic. Many of the ships leaving Wilmington harbor traveled to New England and fleeing slaves could be smuggled abroad to go to freedom there. In addition it had a large African American population, who were in the majority and who most willing sheltered and interceded for the escapees.

There was a flow to the town along the various rivers moving east to the coast. They fled from the rice and turpentine plantations in southeastern North Carolina. Other came from further away from as far inland as Kingston with its cotton and tobacco fields. They also came from timber camps and herring fisheries. Some arrived at Wilmington from the Virginia boundary with the state of North Carolina for the wharves and ships. The Great Dismal Swamp was a great way-station, protective and passable for the slaves, to the coast and freedom. [8]

Having been born on November 29, 1799, on a farm near the crossroads Spindle Hill, Connecticut, whose occupation was farming, Amos Branson Alcott was to become adverse to work other than philosophizing. He was different from his father who worked hard and long. The elder Alcott could do many things well and ran a self-sufficient farm with profit from and use for his family. Among the many things he sold were farm tools, furniture, barrels, timber, shoes, wool, rye, wheat, oats, corn, apples, pears, vegetables, and the products from cows, swine, and fowls. He was also a mechanic and blacksmith.

Joseph Alcott worked long hours and every day. When it was too wintry outside, he made boxes and baskets. With a beginning education, Bronson was sent to Cheshire Academy which his uncle the Reverend Tillotson Bronson. Soon, he was homesick and returned home. The boy and his cousin William began studies the next year with Pastor John Keys of Wolcott Hill. Branson learned grammar and composition, but never learned to write well. Throughout his life, his style was puffy and inexact, using classicians and the passive voice.

For about one year, Amos Bronson Alcott, went to work in the Seth Thomas clock factory in Plymouth, Connecticut, two miles away. Despite his farm success, Joseph had no money to send Bronson to Yale, so the growing boy began to peddle northern goods in New England and New York. He wanted to see the South, but his father had him wait and he worked on his grandfather's farm. In late 1818, Alcott went to Norfolk, Virginia. Unable to find a teaching job, he went door to door selling trinkets and almanacs. He took to Southern graciousness and manners. This trip was such a success that Bronson was able to give his father $80 to help build a new house, there being nine Alcotts. He and his brother Chatfield Alcott sold door-to-door in 1819-1820. The peddlers in the South were making such sales of fifty cent tin lanterns as silver at the price of forty dollars. No wonder such operations were to give New Englanders a bad name in the South, not to be erased for generations and known to history. [9]

Edmund P. Gaines, the general, did not relish taking of life in battle, but he felt it a necessary part of life. He was mainly fighting against the Indians, whom he felt must be forced to put down the scalping knife and turn to the ways of civilization. He did not write that civilization had its great number of wars too, but the Indians must be made to do what was right. It did not dawn on him that this meant that the whites would decided what was correct, which was to complacently move out of the way of the white expansion whenever demanded. But this did mean an end of the killing of whites by Indians. Still whites would kill Indians.

He would, he wrote Calhoun, prefer to lead the Indian to the lights of civilization, but he felt that his task was necessary. Reason alone was not enough. Justice must be reinforced and crimes punished. The Indian must be taught and compelled to do the things that were right. He would make the best impression on the savages with the least loss of life which was possible. Gaines wrote of the transgressions of the native against the Indians. That did not enter into the thinking of the whites. It was all one sided. However, this letter was indicative of Gaines' thinking and of the statements of many whites. As a final word, at least Gaines wanted the Indians to be civilized, while the frontiersmen often wanted them exterminated. [10]

Disappointment had set in as John Tyler wrote to Dr. Curtis from Philadelphia. He wrote that their "wise men flatter us into the adoption of the banking system under the idea that boundless wealth would result from the adoption." They dreamed of canals, industry, and enterprise. The banks were to turn all of this into bounty. The dream was now over, "instead of riches, penury walks the streets of our towns, and bankruptcy knocks at every man's door. They promised us blessings, and have given us sorrows; for the substance they have given the shadow; for gold and silver, rags and papers." [11]

In the South as elsewhere, commodity prices were falling. At the beginning of 1819, cotton sold for 33 cents a pound. By June the price was 20 cents and that fall had fallen to from fourteen to eighteen cents. Tobacco prices fall even further, continuing a terrible fall beginning in some months following the war. In June the overall drop was ninety five percent. During the nine months of 1819 bank stocks slumped significantly, but they were the first to recover. Southern planters in cotton had overproduced and when the buying binge ended in early 1819, the market dried up, leaving depressed prices. They found it very difficult to reduce expenses because their slaves still had to be fed and mortgage loans aid. It was neither the first nor the last time when high prices induced farmers to buy more land and slaves and make improvement. Facing ruin, planters and farmers worked to get debt relief from state governments and the Federal land office.

Bankers faced dire dangers and acute distress. Capital was not sufficient as it was in the southern states and now it was particularly short. Because money had been so short, the banks, including the Bank of the United States, had overextended its credit. From July of 1818, they called for loan repayment which was one of the direct causes of the distress of 1819. Soon banks began to suspend specie payments, a result and cause of credit problems. Atlantic coast banks were the most stable, but even they were in trouble in 1819. A deep gloom descended upon the young nation. Rents dropped and real estate prices collapsed in the mortgage crisis.

There was a lot of discussion about the panic. Men of every political and economic philosophies had their own prescription for the cure, but the situation was not well understood. Officials were generally careful to avoid fanning the public discontent with ill-chosen command. Many suggested that that the nation must have patience. People must practice economy and let the economic problems work their way out. Conservative wanted the people to be quiet and humble and turn from their ways of wickedness. Faced with collapse, men of great debt worked with politicians eager to solve the problems at hand by putting a cap of six percent on interest rates and create state banks with plenty of paper money to lend, backed by the value of state owned lands. In the South and the West, there was a great deal of hostility to the East, the Bank of the United States, and Yankee peddlers who took money out of these actions. [12]

---

[1]Herndon, William H., *Life of Lincoln*, 1936 edition, pp. 26-27.
[2]Pratt, *Lincoln*, p. 5; Hertz, Enamel, *The Hidden*, pp. 354-355.
[3]Stonier, C. B., *Quest*, 1982, pp.. 22-24.
[4]Ford, *Illinois*, pp. 18-27.
[5]Crumble, Atelier, *Lucretia Mott*, Cambridge, Mass.: Harvard University Press, 1958, Rep. New York: Russell & Russell, 1971, pp. 3-14.
[6]*Ibid.*, pp. 30-31. Quote on p. 30.
[7]Jerkins, William Summer, *Pro-Slavery Thought in the Old South*, Chapel Hill: University of North Carolina Press, 1935, Rep: Gloucester, Mass: Peter Smith, 1960, pp. 1-22, 39, 56-58.

[8]Cecelski, David S., "The Shores of Freedom: The Maritime Underground Railroad in North Carolina, 1800-1861," *The North Carolina Historical Review*, LXXI No. 2 (April 1994), p. 177.

[9]Saxton, Martha, *Louisa May. A Modern Biography of Louise May Alcott*, Boston: Houghton Mifflin, 1977, pp. 17-21.

[10]Calhoun, *Papers*, III, 339.

[11]Tyler, Lyon G., *The Letters and Times of the Tylers*, 3 vols., I, 303.

[12]Sydnor, C.S., *Sectionalism*, 1948, pp. 104-113.

Chapter XIV

VAN BUREN MACHINE

Agriculture was the key to the economy and farmers and planters were wasting away the soil. They were exhausting the lands. A number were experimenting with soil conservation measures. Some were neighbors in the Virginia of John Taylor. He watched them at work and approved of their measures. In his newspaper *The Arator*, Taylor wrote that "when the future historian of our republic shall search for acts of patriotism, and matter for biography, the contrast between the heroes (wise farmers) who created , and the politicians who have ruined a nation will afford him ample room for exhausting the strongest phases of eulogy and censure." However, there was little crop rotation. In Virginia the soil was being leached by tobacco plants of that vile weed whose effects on the soil were being discovered and whose effects on the health were for the far distant future to be known.

In the year of 1818, the notable work on agricultural was that of the newly formed--that year--Fredricksburg Agricultural Society. The great agriculturist, James M. Garnett was president. He was to serve in this office for twenty years. Garnett made speeches extolling soil reform, tariff reduction, and internal improvement. Prominent among his associates were John Taliaferro, W.F. Gray, and Robert Semple. Their society declared that "agriculture should avail herself of this improvement to keep pace with the progress of society; and to make such regulations as may favor the general communication of knowledge and the acquisition of improvements from abroad, in the vegetable and animal kingdom." [1]

New York Democrats were divided into the Bucktails and the Clintonians. The chief difference was the personality of Governor De Witt Clinton, born in New York in 1769, a scion of an English family earlier settled in Ireland before coming to America. An educated lawyer, Clinton spent his early years chiefly in land speculation and then as private secretary to his uncle. In 1787 he was against the new constitution and later opposed President Adams and Governor Jay. He was in the state assembly and senate and gained the power of the state to replace state officers, then Federals, with Republicans. Serving briefly in the U.S. Senate, Clinton became mayor of the New York City and the most powerful politician in the state.

De Witt worked hard as mayor and accomplished a lot for better and more public services. He dictated the choice of two governors and then reached the national stage when he ran for president against Madison with Federalist and anti-war Republican backing. He lost and because of his new ties with Federalists was repudiated by New York Republicans and ousted from office as mayor.

Promoting the canal project, he gained support for the governorship and won it despite Tammany opposition. His gubernatorial stand for constructive leadership and active government won him the support of many old Federalists. For this, he was branded as a Federalist by Martin Van Buren, now leading the Tammany Society. This lost him great support but Van Buren's ability as a political organizer undermined him more. Part of the reason for the division was pro-southern policies and beliefs of the Bucktails and the opposition of the Clintonians to what was called the Virginia influence or southern rules.

Anti-southern sentiment in New York was tapped by Clinton, but it was New Yorker Gideon Granger, postmaster-general Madison, who in 1810 attempted to lead a revolt against southern influence in the national capital. In secret, Granger wrote Clinton and urged him for the presidency against Madison. In 1811, Granger wrote the speaker of the Pennsylvania house against slave representation and the subservience of Pennsylvania to Virginia. To Granger's delight Clinton ran in 1812 and saw the issue of southern domination as a major issue. In 1816, the New York legislature passed resolutions warning against the election of another Virginian to the presidency, but Monroe ran and won. In 1819, there was definite hostility toward the south in New York. Although Monroe was exempted, the rest of his administration was denounced as hostile to New York and its Republican prosperity. [2]

In New York politics, the Martin Van Buren machine moved slowly and carefully against Governor De Witt Clinton. Martin did not use his influence in the lower house to appoint an opposition council of appointments. The Bucktails wished to revenge themselves upon Clinton for their defeat in opposition to the Erie Canal and would have gladly used Van Buren for these aims, but the able politician knew the price would be to gain a public image of being a revengeful politician against a folk hero, the governor. His success would turn into a rout when these appointments were reversed and the state would suffer from the lack of wise and judicious decisions. Still a Clintonian council would be a blow to Van Buren's Albany Regency. He wanted a stable council with a majority of neutral members, neither opposed to nor controlled by Clinton.

When Clinton suggested Jabez Hammond, a state senator, for the council, Van Buren saw a great opportunity. The senator was honest and a Clintonian, but he had promised to be a politically ineffectual politician so far and would not pose a challenge. Even better, Van Buren was able to gain a Bucktail, his own man, on the council in return for the Hammond appointment. This anti-Clintonian was a highly partisan politician and could be counted upon. His name was Peter R. Livingston and he was most outspoken. The next selection was Henry Yates who though a De Witt Clinton supporter, could be counted upon to be independently minded because of well placed relatives including a brother, Joseph Yates, who wanted to be governor. He also disliked Clintonian Ambrose Spencer. Once again, Clinton's judgment was defective and he did not suspect the division until Yates came out publicly against Spencer.

Meanwhile, Van Buren used a bitter rivalry between two Clintonians wanting a place on the council to get his lieutenant Seymour in the council. Things had gone better than expected and Van Buren controlled the council. Clinton was to make more mistakes in the coming months. Concerned with grand projects and dreams, he neglected the exercise of politics. With an unruly council, the governor turned further away and allowed Van Buren to consolidate his machine and establish it as the regular organization in the state.

Van Buren decided upon the young lawyer, William Thompson, for the speakership because he could not be managed. Instead of choosing a candidate acceptable to the Republican party, Clinton selected Obadiaih German, who had been one of the congressman who voted against the War of 1812. Once again, Van Buren had an opportunity of linking Clinton to the peace Federalists. On January 4, 1819, the Republicans in the New York house nominated Van Buren's Thompson to be speaker. The Clintonians bolted and with the help of Federalists elected German speaker. Once again, Van Buren's organization was cast as the regular faction of the party.

Since the Bucktail Republicans in New York acknowledged Van Buren to be their leader, they were persuaded by him to run Samuel Young for the United States Senate. Newspapers lead by Van Buren's *Albany Argus* and Tammany's *Advocate* in New York City gave fulsome backing for Young. They felt he was the best man for the job while Clinton's John C. Spencer, then in his first congressional term was unsuitable and nepotic. He was Ambrose's son. Because of his tense spirit, lack of humor, dislike for small talk, and his inability to work with others, young John was unpopular with politicians and his support of the Eire Canal was insufficient to win him enough popular support to make up for his negative personality traits.

Meanwhile, the governor continued to stress his great project of the great waterway. His weakness in political maneuver did not touch his prestige. Van Buren's quiet political success was a foundation of a newer order, but Clinton himself was as much a symbol for progress as his great work itself. The people of this state were enthusiastic when Clinton prophesied that New York State would lead the nation. The state would become the richest and most powerful state in the Union. It would be the most advanced of the states. New York's canal promoted a feeling of optimism, of accomplishment, and of expansion which was a part of the times, marred only by the coming of a temporary panic.

In detail, Clinton issued reports which told of a regular progress of new machinery and tolls from the finished parts of the canal interspersed with information on route, geology, fauna, and flora which the people must have felt were marks of learning reflecting the governor's greatness. Also, in his addresses, Clinton noted foreign and domestic events, while recommending reforms. Education, taxation, fiscal matters, prisons, and insane asylums must be reformed and improved. His coldness and arrogance did not come through and even those who knew him had a great respect for his statesmanship. The canal was definitely popular and the people took pride in their governor as well as his great contribution. He would not allow the voters to forget this. The Van Buren Bucktails were in the minority and their Young was facing an uphill but not hopeless battle.

Van Buren's wife was gravely ill. Her tuberculosis was in an advanced stage. While a distressed Martin stayed with his wife, his lieutenants carried ably forth in a caucus. There, the Bucktails loudly baited German and counted upon the speaker to lose control and engage in a hot tempered shouting match. German was known as a most argumentative man. They were able to raise tempers and the caucus fell apart in wrangling until adjournment. Clinton forces lost the opportunity to push the nomination of young Spencer through the meeting. Then the two factions met separately and nominated their respective choices.

In a February 3d vote neither Young nor Spencer nor the Federalist's King won a majority. Two days later, Hannah Van Buren died. Then the Federalists joined Clinton in gaining a Clintonian council, which got rid of all Bucktails in office except for Attorney General Van Buren, who lasted until summer. There was a general call for party harmony, but Clinton wanted Van Buren's capitulation, especially when Van Buren swung around his Bucktails to a support of the canal and garnered some of the waterway's popularity for themselves. Van Buren had long ago supported the Eire Canal.

Then John A. King led the Federalists in a key election on the canal commission to support Van Buren's candidate Henry Seymour. The leading Albany Regency lieutenant won by one vote and the Bucktails now controlled Clinton's political power base. Tammany ceased being a vociferous critic of the canal. The governor had been warned by Jabez Hammond of the dangers, but because of his dislike for root politics he had not acted. Now he was furious and his council removed Van Buren from his lucrative public office. Van Buren later helped secure Rufus King's reelection to the United State Senate in February of 1820. [3]

As Monroe's secretary of war, John C. Calhoun laid a plan of internal improvements before Congress on January 14, 1819. He wrote that "a judicious system of roads and canals, constructed of the convenience of commerce and the transportation of the mail only, without any reference to military operations, in itself one on the most efficient means for 'the more complete defense of the United States,' without averting to the fact that the roads and canals where such a system would require are, with few exceptions, precisely those which would require for the operation of war, such a system, by consolidating our Union, and increasing our wealth and fiscal capacity, would add greatly to our resources in war."

Calhoun later wrote about the Indians, that there was needed a radical change in Indian relations. Preparation was the adoption of a system of education. Education for the Indian was the foundation of all other improvements. They needed a simple and plain system of laws and government for all of them, like that that the Cherokees were enjoying. He wanted a contraction of their settlements and a division of the Indian lands for their private ownership. He would introduce them into a state of intelligence, industry, and civilization which would lead to power of the American laws over the Indians. Calhoun did not add: their excess lands would belong to the whites. [4]

Tallmadge of New York made his amendment to end slavery in Missouri and the slavery issue became important for the first time in the nation's history. A revolutionary feeling for the freedom of slaves in the South was ended earlier. The cotton gin had long made cotton culture very profitable in the South. The price of slaves trebled and slave breeding was more profitable. All slaves were useful for the economy of the South and did the work in the fields which formed the great profitability of cotton growing. The slaveowners came to the conclusion that slavery was not so hurtful and wicked as their revolutionary fathers thought. They look upon the revolutionary sentiment of equality as a thing which should be erased from the memories of mankind. Northerners still thought slavery was wrong. They had abolished slavery in their home states and felt it would be ended elsewhere as well. They were surprised by the vehemence its raising in the South caused. [5]

The Spanish Government appealed for help. Spanish ministers wanted the power to guarantee that Spain keep Florida and recover the Louisiana territory. When England was discussing peace terms at Ghent, they wanted her to help. Later, at the Congress of Vienna, they talked to the European nations about such aid. Europe had no more energy after Waterloo and they did nothing. Onis and Adams talked. Onis wanted the Mississippi as the boundary and Adams insisted upon the Rio Grande. Spain fell back to compromise positions when it was clear that no other European nation would help. Great Britain wanted peace. [6]

Finally a treaty was reached on February 22, 1819. Reading the Washington newspapers, Thomas Hart Benton kept abreast of the progress of the treaty with Spain. He was shocked at the American cession of Texas and the boundary in the southwest. Feeling that the entire network of the Mississippi River valley should belong to the United States, he took to the press his dislike of a treaty which lost Texas and dismembered the valley of the Mississippi and mutilated the noble rivers of the Red and the Arkansas. Both rivers lost their upstream courses of Spain. He objected to a treaty which established a western wilderness between Missouri and New Mexico which hurt the trade his constituents so earnestly wanted with that Spanish province.

He expressed himself in no uncertain terms by denouncing the treaties authors and supporters and those who would continue to support it. His efforts were to be to no avail since he was almost a sole voice in the protests. It was his belief that the treaty was drawn up as it was because the Spanish authorities offered the United States more than we accepted. This was not true but Benton believed it. He blamed northern men and Adams and was later to learn that the southerners were the enemies he had to contend with. Thus he was buffeted by false beliefs and he was never enlightened by the actual fact of the case in a clear manner. Later historians were able to have the documentation and the lack of bias to bring out the story as it happened. Benton became mortified because no newspaper at the time backed his views. [7]

The Bank of the United States in Ohio with its two branches was unpopular. Early in this period the legislature, newspapers, and the people talked about a tax upon the bank, not to raise revenue but to drive it out of the state with its western dislike of banks. When the Bank contracted its loans the summer of 1818, the people got more angry. Some of the people thought it would be against the constitution for a state to tax a federal agency. Others thought the agency or bank itself was unconstitutional. Marshall decision to uphold corporations against the states was objectionable in Ohio and some thought the bank demolished state sovereignty.

In February of 1819, there was a tax bill taxing the bank. The bill passed and the state government seized the tax money from one of the branches. Public opinion in Ohio supported this move. Most of the men in the fight against the bank were supporters of the tariff and internal improvements, but they were out to protect the states' rights of their state and protect its common economic interests. They disliked banks on principle. That was the way of most westerners. [8]

Once again, there was a controversy over the Bank of the United States; this time going into the Supreme Court. In a case argued in February and March of 1819 by a vote of 7 to 0, the Court decided that such a bank was constitutional. It was neither the beginning nor the end of a long debate. When several other states taxed its branches, the Baltimore branch would not pay and the case went up through the courts. Finally, the Supreme Court decided that the Maryland tax was not constitutional.

Supreme Court Chief Justice John Marshall studied the issue and decided that the Constitution was derived from the people. This was the position carried down in United States history beginning with this momentous decision of *McCullough v. Maryland*. Contrary to the Jeffersonian view of the compact of the states, Marshall's view was populist. Governmental powers are granted by the people to be exercised directly on them and for the benefit of the people. Marshall followed the example of Alexander Hamilton in his expansionist interpretation. Despite any limitation of powers, the government was supreme within its sphere of action. Nothing is excluded on the issue in the Constitution. The government had all the powers necessary to carry out its given powers. Thereby the Bank was constitutional. On the taxation of the Bank, Marshall ruled that the state governments could not tax the Bank or other agencies. [9]

Most Virginians opposed the Marshall decision on the case of *McCulloch v. Maryland*. Under the influence of Judge Spencer Roane, Stevenson of the House of Delegate committee for courts of justice, resolved a protest against the doctrine of implied powers as was given in the case decision. A strict constructionist, Stevenson thought the Marshall action undermined the pillars of the Constitution and the rights of the states. If his ideas prevailed it would lead to consolidation or great government powers. On that, Stevenson was right, but without it the United States would have been a third rate power in the Twentieth Century and a pawn of Hitler or Stalin.

However, to the states' righters of the time it was dangerous beyond recall. It would lead to terrible powers and laws for the central government. Stevenson said the Constitution was for a weak and limited government. He denied that the decision was binding upon the states. This was the first use of nullification in the arguments which were to occupy Americans for the next four decades. These arguments were to crop up for the next century and a half. The Court was making itself the final arbiter, which is exactly what the Founding Fathers wanted. But they could not anticipate the powers to which it was to ascend.

Indeed, they did not see ahead enough to envision the powerful government which was to follow upon the demands of the majority of the people. Indeed, even today there are people who want a very limited federal government or no government at all. The Founding Fathers wanted protection from external and internal foes and they plotted a Constitution which they felt would meet the needs of the nation. No one could have seen the extent that these needs were to go.

Stevenson wanted a special court to decide upon the constitutionality of congressional laws and executive acts in relation to state power, in which the states would have an equal say. He next struck at the U.S. Bank. According to Stevenson, the Congress would be denied the power to create banks except for the District of Columbia. All of this fitted the wishes of Virginians but to the people of all of the states. [10]

[1]Turner, Charles W., "Virginia Agricultural Reform, 1815-1860," *Agricultural History*, XXVI (July 1952), 80-81.
[2]Moore, Glover, 1967, pp. 16ff; *Dictionary of American Biography*, II (2) 221.
[3]Niven, *Van Buren*, pp. 67-75, 80-81.
[4]Von Holst, *Calhoun*, pp. 38-39, 41-44, 46-48. Quote on p. 39.
[5]Schurz, Carl, *Henry Clay*, 1887, I, 172-175.
[6]Bemis, S.F., *A Diplomatic History*, 4th ed., 1955, pp. 188-190.
[7]Benton, *Thirty Years*, I, 14-15.
[8]Buley, R. Carlyle, *The Old Northwest: Pioneer Period, 815-1840*, 2 vols., Indianapolis: Indiana Historical Society, 1950, II, 9-10.
[9]Ellis, Richard E., "McCulloch v. Maryland," Hall, Kermit L. ed., *The Oxford Companion to the Supreme Court of the United States*, New York: Oxford University Press, 1992, pp. 356-338.
[10]Wayland, *Stevenson*, pp. 47-48.

Chapter XV

SPRING OF 1819

On Thursdays, the 18th and 25th of March of 1819, Pintard attended the semi-annual examinations of the first and second free schools school of New York City. The improvement of the discipline and educational progress over the previous year was almost incredible. During the summer of 1818, John gave strict attention to the free school as trustee and had he not known the actual state of affairs at the school, he would not have realized the great advancement that had been made.

He favorably compared it to his youth and lauded modern education. The girls at the girl school were first rate in the pieces they gave as regards to the speaking arts. The instructress had been educated there and appeared to be still in her late teens. For that reason it was even the more amazing. This was good education which included moral and religious training. There must be great benefits in all of this to society. To sum it up, he praised the school highly and went away in a happy frame of mind. Advances were being made under the aegis of good education for the education of the masses in New York City. The boys were equally being well taught in the classes of the sexes separated.
1

The new president of the U.S. Bank was an able and highly regarded individual. An attorney from South Carolina, Langdon Cheves had served in the Congress as a Republican and obtained the speakership of the House. Earlier, Cheves had turned down an offer of secretary of the Treasury from Madison and now he undertook a more difficult task. When Langdon went to Philadelphia, he knew that the bank personnel lacked talent. He had read of the troubles faced by the bank and the scandal of its Baltimore branch, doubtless, but in his own words he found the state on the Bank on close examination to be badly managed and defrauded. The millions in specie borrowed abroad had been entirely exhausted and were yet to be paid for. The Bank was about to have to stop payments when he arrived to take charge.

By March of 1819, when Cheves took control the directors had made some changes, but Langdon made more. Initiating investigations, he soon brought many men to court and dismissed some. Drastic retrenchments in salaries and other expenses were made. Conservative officers and directors replaced the speculative ones. Business was curtailed at the southern and western offices and a two million dollar loan was obtained from London.

James McCulloch, who had been building an empire of his own in Baltimore, was in trouble. As cashier McCulloch had lent himself a half million dollars and now economic conditions and probably mismanagement had McCulloch over a barrel. Cheves removed McCulloch. The Baltimore papers complained about the removal for a few days, concerned about the related failure of one of the greatest commercial establishments in the United States. This was S. Smith and Buchanan. One of the firm's main businesses was exporting specie to India. [2]

Abram Blanding wrote Calhoun for a Doctor Elias Marks of Columbia, South Carolina, who wanted an official position in Pensacola in the revenue department in case the Spanish treaty be ratified. Evidently Blanding and Calhoun knew one another, which is why Marks had Blanding write. At any rate Blanding wanted to promote Marks interests. Marks had talent and standing as a physician and needed a place where the climate was congenital for his health. At Columbia, the climate and his work as a doctor was bad on his health. Should he have a good government position in Pensacola, he could work at a post which was harmful for that health. He had two valuable assets for the place. He spoke perfect French and tolerable Spanish useful in the place where there were not many Frenchmen and Spaniards.

Marks was not the only one who wished a position in Florida. Wilson Lumpkin was conversant and a participant in the arrangements in Florida. He requested an appointment in Florida, realizing that for every position there were many applicants. Calhoun had been helpful before and he wished a position with the Treasury Department there. He like Marks preferred Pensacola as a working and living place, being a port and chief town in the area. He did not ask it of Crawford since both were of the same area in Georgia, Lumpkin resided in Madison, Georgia. Crawford was acquainted with him and knew his talents and abilities, so he had good reason for a successful outcome. Lumpkin and Calhoun had corresponded before and were to correspond later. The applicant was a surveyor of Indian reservations lands in Florida and Lumpkin had written about that and would do so again. [3]

The first newspaper west of the Mississippi was published on April 23, 1819, in Franklin. This settlement was founded in 1817 on the north bank of the Missouri some 150 miles west of the Mississippi. Two years passed and the town of Boonville was established opposite on the south bank. Nathaniel Patten Jr. from Massachusetts joined in a partnership with Benjamin Holliday Jr., who had been born in Virginia. Patten was a printer in Boston before moving to the western country. This four page newspaper was printed on a Ramage press and entitled the *Missouri Intelligencer and Boon's Lick Advertiser* and opened with one hundred subscribers. In time, Patten began publishing such local news as the rising of the river in floodtime. He did little writing, and the newspapers were filled with short articles taken from St. Louis newspapers, which had been clipped from the eastern press. The paper contained poetry among other items. Shortly there were newspapers in Jackson and St. Charles. St. Louis had two presses. [4]

In April of 1819, there appeared in Baltimore a new magazine. The concept was new; it was the first agricultural journal in the United States. The title was the *American Farmer*. It began a long move upward in improving agriculture in the Middle Atlantic states. It was not until 1833 that a journal edited by Edmund Ruffin was started in Virginia. This was the *Farmers' Register*, which had a life of ten years. Ruffin did what he could with methodical efforts to organize Virginian agriculture. Even before the arrival of these magazines, there were agricultural societies.

In Virginia there was an Agricultural Convention in Richmond on January 11, 1836; it was adjourned without undertaking any substantial effort to improve farming, but individual farmers petitioned for the establishment of a board of agriculture for the state. Years later the Virginia legislature established one, but it was short-lived. James Barbour served as president and Edmund Ruffin was secretary. The society formed in 1845 for farmers did little. For awhile in the sixties, there was a general fair to supplement the county fairs which had existed for ten years. Ruffin continued to serve the farming interest, but with lack of support for agricultural improvement, nothing was done on the state level. [5]

Monroe entered the city of Charleston on April 26, 1819. A large and tumultuous crowd turned out to meet him. In it were many dignitaries who rivaled the president and Monroe passed through the crowd unobserved by the many. Among those who were able to see the president was English traveler W. Faux who was seated near Monroe in the Scottish church on the following Sunday, May 2nd. Faux described Monroe as "an amiable, mild-looking gentleman, of about 60, dressed in a common hat, plain blue coat with gilt buttons, yellow kerseymere waistcoat, drab breeches and white silk stockings, and a little powder in his hair, just a sober grey. His eyes beam with an expansive kindness, gentleness, and liberality, not often seen in persons of his elevated station, and his physiognomy, viewed as a whole, announces a noble , well-judging, and generous mind." [6]

Meanwhile, across the Atlantic in rural Kensington Palace, a daughter to be named Victoria was born to the Duke and Duchess of Kent, to be second in line to the British throne. It was 4:15 AM, Monday 24, 1819, and to the relief of the British people, the infant girl was plump and healthy. In Indiana it was night and Lincoln was probably asleep, having turned in for the night having perhaps read by the fireside a little before. One was born to power and position, while Lincoln was frontier bred. Victoria gave her name to an age and Lincoln was to be immortalized for eternity after his death. There was another destiny. Months later, on August 26,1819, Prince Albert was born. It was decided at this time that the two cousins should marry. Months passed and on January 23, 1820, the duke died and Victoria became third in line for the British throne. [7]

Change was swift in Jackson's Tennessee when the Panic of 1819 hit the state and swept away old contentment. The cotton market broke. Prices fell for the product upon which much of the South depended. Banks had a run on their small supply of specie or gold and silver coin to pay eastern and European creditors. Banks had to call in their loans, forcing Nashville merchants to call in debts owed by country merchants, who dunned their customers. There was real fear of forced sales of property and the entire credit system failed.

Banks had built up a credit system by making loans on their bank notes, backed by only a small amount of specie and that was draining away. These bank notes had made a boom until trouble came and now they were the economy's downfall. There was a call of the suspension of specie payments to protect banks and economy. Bank directors gladly complied. This relieved some pressure but there were more problems. People sought the answer in their law making bodies and in politics.

Blounts' political machine was led by lawyer John Overton of Nashville. He was a rich planter, bank president, and of course a land speculator. The men's brother-in-law Hugh Lawson White of Knoxville was sub-chief there. Governor Joseph McMinn, Senator John H. Easton, and Andrew Jackson were members of this faction. Andrew Erwin, a planter and land speculator, led the opposing faction with a following of Senator John Williams of Knoxville, and Representative Newton Cannon. Almost all of its members had quarreled with Jackson. Felix Grundy stood aloof for awhile, but in 1819 he ran for the state legislature on the program of debt relief.

Grundy channeled voter discontent into dominance for himself and the Erwin faction. He worked for the satisfaction of land claims in the last land grant of Tennessee. Establishing a state bank to loan to debtors in the state proved a popular measure, but was hampered when Grundy put it into conservative hands. It was thus a restrictive measure. There was no relief for the masses and the people turned from Grundy's leadership.

The Erwin faction found a new popular leader in General William Carroll, a hero in the New Orleans battle. Carroll had been a wealthy Nashville merchant before being ruined in the panic. He now ran as a poor man. Jackson's faction, the Overton, presented the voters with wealthy planter Colonel Edward Ward, Jackson's neighbor and friend. Carroll was anti-bank, but Ward was considered a friend of bank directors. The Erwin men found popularity for their anti-bank stand and Carroll was elected. The Overton faction were now on the outs, but this was not to fail Jackson in a later move for the presidency. [8]

The chief of the Caddo Indians was unhappy about the settlement of the whites above the Raft on Red River. He claimed land in both sides of the river and threatened to drive the Americans out. John Fowler suggested to Thomas L. McKenney that since the chief had always been a mischievous Indian, he thought it would be right to withdraw his American commission to be chief and displace him according to their wishes. By this means there would be peace on this part of the frontier. He would be prevented from coercing the selection of a replacement by the stoppage of rations and services to the Caddos.

The Caddo had been guilty of many crimes and this chief was especially inimical to the Americans and visited the Spaniard. They commissioned him colonel. The Indians draw rations, presents, and had their arms repaired at Natchitoches in Spanish territory. Indian agents from the United States could use judicious powers to control these natives and obviously should. In contrast, showing what could be done, Fowler noted the settlement of Delaware Indians with good stock. This had its drawbacks because the Delaware were driven off. The Americans seized what they wished and the Indians had to bear the injustice as nothing was done against even the greatest of plunders on the frontier, notably a man named Music and one named Williams. Generally, they used liquor to trade for the more valuable cows. Stock was driven against the scattered Choctaws, who were wronged on a regular basis. One can only wonder of the Caddo chief's dissatisfaction with the United States settlers, given their treatment of the Indians. [9]

A reviewer in the *North American Review* wrote in June of the book on New Netherlands by Dutch author N.C. Lambrechtsen, a member of the school of scholars and historians who came to the front in the Dutch renaissance at the end of Napoleon's domination. Lambrechtsen added little to the history, but his work was well written and deserved comment by the unnamed reviewer. The people of Holland wished to revive their old culture and this was one of the efforts in this regard.

The author was president of the Academy of Science in the province of Zealand and wrote in Dutch, once again the language of choice by writers of Netherlands. He gave a summary of the history and he was more accurate than Smith or Dr. Trumbull. The reviewer stated that the book was "animated throughout by a fine spirit of nationality and a patriotic exultation in the long departed glories of his native country. He enters heartily and honestly into the controversies of Governors Kieft and Stuyvesant with the commissioners of the English colonies, mourns over the loss of the province as if it had been an event of yesterday." [10]

The American reviewer wrote that "we are so little accustomed to see any portion of our company treated in this manner by foreign writers, that the good feeling and hearty warmth of this worthy Dutchman towards us are really quite refreshing; and we feel sincerely disposed to reciprocate all his kindly sympathies, and as far as is in one power to participate in the enthusiasm with which he looks back upon the heroic achievements and bold adventures of his ancestors, and to listen with a willing ear while he descants on the bright and glorious epochs of the history of his 'Father-land.'" [11]

Lambrechtsen said that the archives of the Dutch West India company were weak on their colony. He saw what he could of papers and books, but notes the things he did not see in writing the work. The author corrected the mistake of Smith and others that Hudson traveled under English auspices when he discovered the Hudson and later sold the claim. Actually Henry Hudson was an Englishman sailing for the Dutch and the Hudson and its vicinity belonged to the Dutch. He thought Hudson was the first discoverer of the river, but did not think that an earlier discovery by the Florentine Verrazzano was ruled out. There was no definite proof either way in his opinion.

It was the idea of the government and trading company that the land must be bought, and purchased it was, but Lambrechtsen thought that the Dutch almost never tricked the Indians. Modern research proves that many people in the colony did trick and maltreat the Indians. However, this was not government policy and was deprecated by the government back home and in New York. The historian wrote that "negotiations were opened with the Indians to obtain the cession of different districts and islands, and these were fairly purchased on certain stipulated, though perhaps advantageous terms." He wrote of the controversy of whether the Dutch or the English were intruders on the other lands. That can not be definitely settled, but it was probably the case of both being guilty. He did not however come to this conclusion. [12]

The savings bank he had been working for, opened its doors on the evening of July 3, 1819. It was planned to hold its doors open for a few hours every Monday and Saturday. Pintard hoped that it would take in one thousand dollars on the first day and more once it became better known and appreciated, but he was pleasantly surprised when $2,807 was deposited on the first day and this in bad financial times. There were 80 depositors in all for an average of a little over $35 each. Further upon the second day some $1,269 was deposited. More money came in until the first four days, they had nearly $20,000, much more than they expected. Substantial amounts came in in succeeding days. It was a success to Pintard's gratification. The money rolled and before the end of August they had some $52,000 or so, which they expect to take a year to gain. Further growth followed despite a conflagration of yellow fever until mid-September when whole deposit exceeded $80,000. [13]

---

[1]Pintard, I, 176.

[2]Hammond, Bray, 1957, pp. 261-264.

[3]Calhoun, *Papers*, IV, 3-7, 371, 583.

[4]Dary, David, *Red Blood Black Ink: Journalism in the Old West*, New York: Alfred A. Knopf, 1998, pp. 9-10.

[5]Morrison, A.J., "Note on the Organization of Virginia Agriculture," *William & Mary Quarterly*, lst series, XXVI (July 1917), 169-173.

[6]Faux, W., *Memorable Days In America*, 1813, Rep. in vols. XI and XII of *Twaites' Early Western Travels, 1748-1846*, 1905, XI, 68-70. Quote on p. 69-70.

[7]Woodham-Smith, Cecil, *Queen Victoria: From Her Birth to the Death of the Prince Consort*, New York: Alfred A. Knopf, 1972, pp. 29, 37, 44.

[8]Sellers, Charles Grier, Jr., *James K. Polk: Jacksonian 1795-1843*, 1957, pp. 66-71. 87-92.

[9]Carter, *Territorial*, XIX, 73-77, 85.

[10]"Lambrechtsen's New Netherlands," *North American Review*, June 1819, pp. 77-82. Quote on p. 82.

[11]*Ibid.*, p. 82. Quote on p. 82.

[12]*Ibid.*, pp. 82-87. Quote on p. 85.

[13]Pintard, pp. 202, 205-206, 208, 212, 219.

Chapter XVI

NEW YORK

The bulletin of the tenth of September revealed no additional cases of Yellow Fever. New York City's board of health had ordered infected houses at the Old Ship to be evacuated. This was done. They kept the streets clean and purified all dwellings. A northwesterly wind blew in on the tenth and kept up is refreshing airs on the eleventh, giving the people hope that every seed of contagion would be dissipated. Panic subsided. On Sunday, the eleventh, three new cases were reported and one death due to the fever was reported. Health officer Doctor De Witt died and was promptly buried.

Pintard wrote his daughter in New Orleans of the occurrence of Yellow Fever in New York City. In his letter of Friday, September 10, 1819, in the midst of a financial panic which should induce economy, John wrote of the health hazard. "Perhaps," he wrote, "my dearest daughter will have experienced some solicitude on account of the health and safety of her parents and sister, which thank God, remain as yet in perfect security, in consequence of the bulletins of our Board of Health, announcing the existence of *Yellow Fever* in this city. After a lapse of many years 10 or 12, except a few sporadic cases which always have occurred, we have till the present season, been free from all of this desolating disease, which was ascribed, under Providence, to the vigilance of our Quarantine officers. The post, and indeed 'till yesterday, the last of the Dog Days, and present season had been unusually hot, beyond all former experience within the recollection of the oldest livers. A great drought has also prevailed, along the Atlantic states. The same causes must produce the same effects, and if the tropical heats endanger yellow fever, we have shared an abundance of such heat, without the refreshing sea breeze."

Danger appeared on the fifth of September at the Old Slip and Water Street, upon which the Board of Health recommended evacuation and purification in that part of the city. Feeling that the airs caused the fever he could hope that removal would snuff out the malady.. "Whatever determent may arise to our foreign commerce, direct benefit will result to our city, as the alarm being general, great attention is paid to ventilation and purification. The old inhabitants require not such inducements, but the multitude of newcomers, amongst whom are a large portion of the lowest offscourings of Europe, who live in low damp dwellings crowded to excess, unaccustomed to our changeable climate, and extreme heat, improvident, careless and filthy, it would be a miracle if fevers when they appear should not be of the highest type." There was a measure of panic in the excitement and the yellow fever was the most discussed topic in the city, although confined to one quarter. All infected areas and houses were to be abandoned. [1]

The New Englander had acquired an odious hostility in the rest of the country by 1819. Although there were always sectional differences, the New Englanders were learning a special dislike in the country. This was based in large part on the aristocratic stands of the Federalists and particularly in the War of 1812, their pro-British sentiments. The New Englanders, called "damned Yankees" were accused of treason and allegedly had signaled American shipping information to the British navy. Many Yankee peddlers in the southern and western states acted as sharp and crafty traders and by their high prices and inferior merchandise earned the dislike of the people, although not all Yankee traders and according to modern scholarship, perhaps most of them were as honest as the people to whom they sold goods. [2]

In 1817, the people of Missouri began to petition in favor of statehood for the territory and in 1818 movements were put underway for its admission to the Union, followed by a movement to prohibit slavery in any states to be admitted. Because of the presence of many slaveholders in Missouri, everyone expected Missourians to want to come in as a slave states and so some northerners felt it necessary to prohibit all slavery in new states by constitutional amendment to include Missouri. In November of 1818, Representative James Tallmadge Jr. of New York opposed a resolution for statehood for Illinois because the state did not sufficiently prohibit slavery. He gained thirty-three northern votes and one from Maryland, but this was not enough and the resolution passed.

December of 1818 saw Speaker Henry Clay introduced a Missourian memorial that Missourians be permitted to adopt a constitution and form a state government and a meeting in Philadelphia of antislavery societies. The abolitionists formed a committee to prepare a memorial to prevent slavery in all new territories and states. When in February of 1819 the House met as a committee of the whole to consider a bill for the statehood of Missouri and Alabama, Tallmadge moved to amend it to prohibit slavery in Missouri.

Representative John W. Taylor, a Democrat from Saratoga County in New York, spoke first, declaring that if slavery were allowed in Missouri, it would inherit all of the west. He stated that since Congress had the power to prohibit slavery in the new states, the Tallmadge amendment was constitutional. If Congress allowed slavery to exist in the west, more slaves would be imported from Africa. As for the charge that this amendment would decrease the value of southern slave property, he asserted that this was not planned but incidental. The charge that it would discourage southern immigration to Missouri was untrue, said Taylor.

The South, maintained Taylor, degraded the working man since labor in the slaves states was considered disgraceful. Only slaveholders were allowed to fill public offices in the South. Slavery would reduce the value of farm property in Missouri because southern lands were less cultivated than northern lands. The boundary between Pennsylvania and Maryland was well marked by the highly cultivated farms on the north side and weed covered fields on the south side. Pennsylvania had stone barns and stone bridges and Maryland had stalk cribs and no bridges.

Representative Timothy Fuller of Massachusetts demanded the exclusion of slavery in the new states. When he stated that slavery was a departure from republican principles and cited the Declaration of Independence, Fuller was interrupted by several congressmen. Colston of Virginia stated it was improper to smear southern states as not republican. Fuller explained. He did not question the established slave states' right to own slaves. Although the Constitution was republican, an exception existed in the early slave states of the southeastern United States. But this did not apply to the new states. Congress must require every new state to have the pure state, which must mean they had to be free. Fuller was followed by Arthur Livermore of New Hampshire, a fellow Democrat, who spoke of the cruelty and immorality of slavery.

We do not have Clay's speech defending the southland, but we do know that his chief argument was that the slaves would be happier and better fed in west than concentrated all in a few states to the east. Philip P. Barbour, representative from Virginia, spoke up protesting that the people of Missouri had the sovereign right to decide upon the slavery question for themselves. Even it Congress could constitutionally restrict slavery in Missouri, it should not do so for reasons of humanity, justice, and sound policy.

Because Southerners were personally attached to their slaves and considered them valued and favored property, they would not move to Missouri if slavery was forbidden in Missouri and this would close the right of westward migration to southerners. Although there was no chance of slave insurrections at that time, future slave insurrections could be controlled if slaves were dispersed throughout the west. This argument was not attacked, but the future was to prove that slave populations would not decrease in the older south merely because slaves were moved westward. At the time there was an influx of slave importations into the United States although this was illegal.

After the House as a committee of the whole voted 79 to 67 to accept the Tallmadge amendment, the bill was reported out to the House. John Scott, Missouri's territorial delegate to Congress, spoke out stressing that according to the 1803 treaty with Louisiana by which Louisiana was acquired, Missourians and other people in the Louisiana purchase territory had their rights to liberty, property, and religion and slaves were rightful property. After this address, the House members heard an acrimonious debate by several members in which Thomas W. Cobb of Georgia talked of a dissolution of the Union if the Northerners persisted. Edward Colston attacked Livermore. Tallmadge spoke out against the moral iniquity of slavery and stated that more slaves would be illicitly smuggled into the country if slavery was allowed in the western territories.

House members voted separately upon the two clauses in the Tallamadge amendment and both won by narrow votes. Southerners almost unanimously voted against joined by various Northerners. The bill was voted upon and passed to the Senate by a vote of 97 to 56. In the Senate all southern senators opposed the bill with the Tallmadge amendment. They had a majority when Jesse B. Thomas of Illinois and Ninian Edwards of Illinois and other northern senators joined them. The clauses were struck out in the Senate by sizable votes. On March 2, 1819, the Senate voted for the Missouri bill without the anti-slavery amendment. The House immediately considered the changes in the bill and voted twice against concurring with the Senate. When on the next day Congress adjourned, the Missouri statehood issue was at an impasse.

There was little interest in the country over the Missouri controversy. The apathy was so great it was commented upon at a private dinner of Boston notables. On May 20th, the editor of the Boston *Yankee* commented that they did not conceive that this was the greatest matter facing the American people at that time. It did not command the attention of a British royalty birthday or what a Bonaparte was doing in the world at that moment. Political affairs were not important at a time when the panic of earlier months was turning into a depression.

The Panic of 1819 disturbed the manufacturers and their laborers. Economic bad times and the flow of goods from England threatened American industrialization and urban prosperity. The only salvation the people of these areas could see were higher protective tariffs which the southern delegations opposed. Southerner congressmen found some support from about half of the New England congressmen and congressmen from the middle states lost all hope for protection. The protectionists attacked the South in the newspapers when the South needed their votes to admit Missouri as a state. A New Jersey journalist wrote about the system of dependence upon English manufacturers in April of 1819. He said that if the South persisted they would be driven into a state of worst than colonial servitude. [3]

Hard times affected the newly arrived foreigners to a high degree. When Ludwig Gall visited New York City in late July, he attracted several young men who wanted him to take them with him to western parts. There were difficulties for them in this land of opportunities. Things were bad. Seeking betterment in America, eight had been mercantile clerks in Europe and could not find like-work in the city. Two were ex-officers in the German army and had fought against Napoleon.

One of these sought a university post to teach European languages, but had to give French lessons in the city after his work required only a few hours a day and pay accordingly. One of the clerks was in the same position. One sudden young man found work as a copyist with the low pay, requiring him to live at one of the cheapest boarding houses, which cost $2.75 a week. Another was doing well. When he learned that nobody wanted his penmanship, he became a barber and earned from $20 to $25 a week. He was saving enough to either return to Europe or go into the interior. [4]

The War Department was making plans to found a fort on the upper Missouri in what is now Montana. The fort's mission was to help police the Indians and keep the British fur traders out. Stephen H. Long was selected to head an expedition in preparation for the decision of where to put the fort and what to further do to secure the American west safe to Americans from the British and the Indians. Long had his instructions to explore and made additional scientific studies in the region.

Long had instructions for the expedition which read that "the object of the expedition is to acquire as thorough and accurate knowledge as may be practicable of a portion of the country which is daily becoming more interesting but which is as yet imperfectly known." Long was to enter in his "journal everything interesting in relation to soil, face of the country, water courses and productions, whether animal, vegetable, or mineral." [5]

Having gone on his expedition, Long was to agree with what Pike wrote and provide great amounts of information on all phases of the territory. The explorer wrote that about this extensive land, he did not hesitate to give the opinion, "that it is almost wholly unfit for cultivation, and of course uninhabitable by a people depending on agriculture for their subsistence. Although tracts of fertile land considerably extensive are occasionally to be met with, yet the scarcity of wood and water, almost uniformly prevalent, will prove an insuperable obstacle in the way of settling the country."

It could prove of value in serving as a barrier against enemies and to prevent too many people from moving west. It was before dry farming proved its own and the lack of substantial rainfall made the area seem unsuitable for agriculture. Also it was in a day when the East still worried about the migration westward which was sapping their labor supply. For most of America's history until more modern times, there were shortages of laboring men and women still worked almost always in the home. Eastern people feared the loss of population and its effect on their growth and operations. The idea being that only a small nation was vital for democracy, many Americans feared the country was getting too large and feared that the West might some day break away from the Union, as they talked of doing almost three decades before. The threat of the South breaking away was not yet on the horizon and it was the West that the East feared. Long's statements hit home and the maps were to label the Plains the "Great American Desert."

Also Americans in general felt that the "desert" was a good place for the Indians to live, away from danger to and from the whites. They envisioned the region to be a giant reservation as it were, where the Indians could live permanently. They did not worry about it being a barrier to civilization. Public opinion tended to think of the trans-Mississippi being a place where one need not worry about, although settlers were in Missouri and moving into Arkansas and there were scattered whites in the Plains from time to time. [6]

On September 29, 1819, a group of twenty-eight Seminoles arrived at Nassau, New Providence. They had traveled from the coast of Florida in a wrecking vessel. Their mission was to seek assistance. They told to the commander-in-chief of the British troops at Nassau and told him that they were completely destitute, having been robbed and driven from their homes in Florida. The commander gave them food and lodged them in the barracks. Then the Seminoles disappeared from the view of history. No one now knows what happened to them, but they probably settled in the islands of the Bahamas. [7]

Sam Houston was elected to the office of state attorney general and had to move to Nashville from Lebanon, Tennessee, where he had a law office, a popular business and personal life and had been appointed Tennessee adjutant general by Governor Joseph McMinn. In Nashville, he was serving as a prosecuting attorney when he became a member of the Tennessee Antiquarian Society. This, the first learned association in the region, was devoted to education, general literature, antiquities and history. When he became president of Texas decades later, Houston was elected to be a honorary member of the Copenhagen Antiquarian Society.

Since his state legal position did not pay very much money, Houston resigned to open a private practice in Nashville. He spent his time in his office, the court, and at the inn, where he associated with militia offices and became a major general. Jackson was pleased with Houston's progress and wrote of his expectation that Houston would be elected to Congress. Houston supported Jackson in Tennessee and in his desire to become president. To Houston, Jackson was the people's choice. Houston himself was his district's choice and he won election without opposition to the national House. When he went to Washington, he worked for a Jackson presidency and spoke out for Greek Independence and its recognition by the United States. He also worked for the use of the convention in the place of the sold caucus system of selecting presidential candidates. [8]

Adams wrote on July 5, 1819, that "the slave drivers, as usual, whenever this topic is brought up, bluster and bully, talk of the white slaves of the eastern states and the dissolution of the union, and oceans of blood; and the northern man, as usual, pocket all this hectoring, sit down in quiet, and submit to the slave scourging republicanism of the planters. Crawford, who sees how this affair will ultimately go, and who relies upon the support of the slave drivers, is determined to show them he is on their side." [9]

Sarah Bush Johnston had lost her husband at about the same time that Thomas had lost his wife. They had great needs of each other and were married on December 2, 1819. Abraham's new stepmother was born on December 13, 1788, in Hardin county, Kentucky, to Christopher Bush and his wife. She married young, on March 13, 1806, to county jailer, Daniel Johnston. He died in October of 1818, leaving her with a house full of furniture, three small children and heavy debts. Thomas came back to Kentucky to court her and since she was unwilling to marry and leave her debts behind her, he paid off the debts and borrowed a wagon from his brother-in-law for transportation. He took her property and three children to their new home. They had been married in Elizabethtown on December 21, 1819, by Reverend George L. Rogers, a Methodist minister. Everyone in both families benefited from the new marriage. [10]

[1]Pintard, I, 216-219. Quote on pp. 216, 217. See I, 220-221.
[2]Moore, Glover, *The Missouri Controversy, 1819-1821*, 1967, pp. 12-15.
[3]*Ibid.*, 18-19, 33-35, 41-55, 59, 65-66.
[4]"New York, Through German Eyes: The Travels of Ludwig Gall, 1819," Trans. Trautmann, Frederic, *New York History*, LXII No. 4 (Oct 1981), 445-446.
[5]Richmond, Robert W., *Kansas: A Land of Contrasts*, Saint Charles, Mo: Forum Press, 1974, p. 21. Quote on p.21.
[6]*Ibid.*, pp. 22-24. Quote on pp. 22-23.

[7]Goggin, John M., "The Seminole Negroes of Andros Island, Bahamas," *Florida Historical Quarterly*, XXIV (1945), 203.

[8]Friend, *Sam Houston*, pp. 9-10.

[9]Shipp. J.E.D., *Giant Days or the Life and Times of William H. Crawford*, Americus GA: Southern Printers, 1909, p. 155. Quote on p. 155.

[10]Barton, William E., *The Lineage of Lincoln*, Indianapolis: Bobbs-Merrill, 1929, pp. 86-87; Pratt, *Lincoln*, p. 5.

Chapter XVII

AUTUMN OF 1819

There were a number of the citizens of Burlington, New Jersey, who wanted to prohibit slavery in Missouri. They expressed their opinions to each other and agreed to hold a meeting on August 30, 1819, presided over by Elias Boudinot, a retired man who was known as a philanthropist, a founder of the American Bible Society, and an official at the time of the Revolutionary War. When Boudinot represented New Jersey in the first three Congresses, he became one of the first to attack slave representation whereby collective white southerners gained extra seats in Congress because of the non-voting and non-represented slaves in their states. He led in debates and introduced many bills.

In 1793, he defended Hamilton and in 1795, Elias became director of the United States Mint which he reorganized with energy and ability. An author of four books, Boudinot was a lifelong Federalist. As chairman, Boudinot was aided by the Quaker elder William Newbold, a compassionate man who played a major role in organizing the meeting. The group in Burlington decided upon and promoted a state-wide meeting to be held in Trenton on the 19th of October of 1819.

Boudinot was absent at the Trenton meeting because of age and indisposition, but the governor and most of the legislature was there and the well known Federalist Joseph Hopkinson gave the main speech. The resolutions presented by Hopkinson were unanimously adopted. One read that the meeting "would view, with unspeakable pain and mortification, any measure adopted by the *federal legislature*, tending to extend and perpetuate *slavery* among us; and holding out encouragement and temptation to the dealers in human flesh to continue their infamous trade, in defiance of the laws of the lands, and the more sacred will of Heaven." The people there decided to expand their protest and call upon the aid of other Americans to co-operate in their opposition to slavery in Missouri. They appointed a correspondence committee was formed which included Boudinot. This committee sent out many circulars.

When John Jay received one of the circulars, he wrote Boudinot, blessing the committee's work and regretting that his health prevented him from taking an active part in the movement. Boudinot gave the letter from Jay to the press and it was published widely, venerated in the north and feared in the south. This publicity coup did much to stimulate the movement and create interest. Rufus King, who had been working to gather support for anti-slave action in Congress and who tried to create home state pressure against senators who voted with the South, was a natural ally. Another New Yorker, Timothy Dwight played a greater role in advertising anti-slavery sentiment since he had a newspaper to use as a weapon in the fight.

In his New York *Daily Advertiser*, Dwight wrote against cruelty toward minorities and had conducted a campaign against the illegal African slave trade. During the spring, the editor endorsed the Tallmadge amendment prohibiting slavery in Missouri. He wrote about the sin of slavery and the destruction of free state influence that would result if slavery was allowed in the west. Although he was a political conservative, he was a reforming humanitarian and kept writing editorials about the injustice and cruelty of slavery which were republished in other newspapers. He gained support from the Federalists in the North, but Democrats in the North still remembered his participation in the Hartford Convention.

The Trenton meeting was followed by one in New York on November 16, 1819, at which two thousand people gathered in the City Hotel. Many of the leading city philanthropists and reformers were there and John's son Peter Jay spoke of slavery's injustice and inhumanity. It was immoral and irreligious in character and tendency. Washington Irving's brother John T. Irving spoke of the abhorrent character of slavery. The citizens formed a large correspondence committee to stir up the north. They issued a printed circular which they sent to communities from Maine to Cincinnati.

Many other meetings were held. James Buchanan helped to write the resolutions in Lancaster. Meetings were called in West Chester, Hartford, Boston, Salem, Albany, Providence, Newport, New Haven, and Cincinnati. They were an endless chain since they corresponded and multiplied. They spread to the west and a St. Louis newspaper noted that the meetings were held in every town and blacksmith's village in the North.

Although conservatives led this humanitarian crusade against slavery, there was some liberal interest and participation. The Democrats whose liberalism should have been arrayed against slavery had their political ties to the South which allied them to slaveholders. The Federalists had nothing to lose by attacking slavery so they did so, but their humanitarianism ended when their own interests were concerned. At this very time they were opposing the granting of the vote to non-property holders, a minority which was growing larger as immigration increased and towns grew, as opportunity began to lessen, but a minority which would dilute their power if giving the right to vote and one which might endanger their wealth. Self interest limited their liberalism. Even the philanthropist Boudinot was for restricting the freedom of slave, indentured servant, or apprentice although he spoke against slavery. [1]

A reviewer in the *North American Review* in January 1820 expressed his view of slavery. He wrote that "slavery although a great and acknowledged evil, must be regarded, to a certain extent, as a necessary one, too deeply interwoven in the texture of society to be wholly or speedily eradicated. It is a subject therefore, whatever careless or superficial persons may imagine, which neither can nor ought to be passed over by contemptuous sneers or bitter reproaches upon those who are possessors of slaves, or by animated appeals to the passions of those who are not. It should be approached with great calmness and good temper, with great firmness of purpose, with pure, enlightened, and benevolent feeling; but at the same time with that sober and discriminating benevolence, which regards not merely absolute right, but attainable good, and which in the eager pursuit of a desirable end. will not blindly overlook the only practicable means of arriving at it."

There was a general rule that it was wrong for one portion of the population to hold another part in slavery. However there were exceptions. One was self-defense. "In states where slavery has long continued and extensively prevailed, a sudden, violent, or general emancipation would be productive of greater evils than the continuance of slavery. It would shake if not subvert the foundation of society. It would be at once the cause of misery to the slaves, and of ruin to the community." Self defense therefore requires that slavery should not be ended quickly.

The condition of slavery must be ameliorated. The evils of slavery did not always rest with the problems of the slave. Society too suffered from the peculiar institution. It was not a privileged to hold slaves. It was to be deplored. A state could not be stable with the existence of slavery. [2]

A British traveler, W. Faux, found the western country a hard place of little comfort with impovished people, but he also saw many of good condition, especially Harmony village. It was hard to get a start. Land must be cleared and swamps and undulated land were common. Some of the frontiersmen were able and strong, while many had great difficulties. Faux continued to look negatively, born as he was to British society and economic advancements.

People nearby recognized the religious people, the Harmonites, as successful workers. Harmony lands were fields of great size with finer and thicker wheat. Faux noted that the fields lay in a vale of richness. They had a comfortable brick tavern, the finest and cleanest in Indiana. The beef was bad and bread good, but the charges were high.

Services held by George Rapp commenced at ten o'clock with bells pealing across the village and fields. The people filed in with the men and women separately seated. Rapp, now about eighty, strode in with his adopted son Frederick behind him from his fine home. Three times a day were religious services conducted. Rapp, in Faux's words, "professes to govern them only by the Bible, and they certainly seem the perfection of obedience and morality." He taught that "his way is the only way to Heaven. He does much by signs, and by an impressive manner, stretching out his arm, which, he says, is the arm of God, and that they must obey it; and that when he dies, his spirit will descend unto his son Fred."

Modesty was required. The people wore working clothes. Women wore their hair swept back in a severe and an unattractive manner with a head cloth holding it down. Everyone was dressed alike, each unto his sex.

Faux rode around the village. Rapp's was the only finished house in Harmony. The rest were log buildings, each with a cow house. Each family had a cow and garden. Everything else is held in common. Faux noted that their "horses cattle, and sheep, are all in one stable; herds and flocks are folded every night, in comfortable sheds, particularly an immensely large flock of Merino sheep; and so secured from the wolves." Vineyards are everywhere. Large and fertile orchards provide plenty for the Harmonites.

They had a large granary with big barns and barnyards. There were cloth manufactures since the people bought nothing outside which they could not make in the town. They sold much and could not make shoes fast enough for the market. All business is done in Frederick Rapp's name and the land is in his name. Harmony was five years old when Faux was there and had a policy of buying out neighbors to extend their domain. [3]

A botanist and ornithologist by the name of Thomas Nuttall went on his travels up the Arkansas River to Fort Smith, Arkansas. He examined the flowers and plants which he was to report on in a book published in Philadelphia in 1821. His travels took him to southeastern Oklahoma from Fort Smith over land and he reached back at the beginning of summer. Then he traveled up the Arkansas, reaching the trading houses of Joseph Bougie and Nathaniel Pryor located at the mouth of the Verdigris, where he talked to Osage Indians. He explored the Osage salt works up the Grand River and went to the Cimarron River in late summer. He contracted the fever and regained his health at Fort Smith, before going to the Mississippi and then down to New Orleans. This was his second journey in the West, having gone up the Missouri in 1811 and he made a third trip with N.J. Wyeth's second expedition. [4]

In a cabinet meeting at this time, Adams said that the world must be "familiarized with the idea of considering our proper dominion to be the continent of North America. From the time when we became an independent people, it was as much a law of nature that this should become our pretension as that the Mississippi should flow to the sea. Spain had possessions upon our southern and Great Britain upon our northern border It was impossible that centuries should elapse without finding them annexed to the United States." This broad claim was later, in January of 1821, expressed in a heated colloquy with the British minister, Strafford Canning. On the part of the Northwest there was as much of a potential conflict with Great Britain as with Russia. The point in dispute was the mouth of the Columbia River, now between Oregon and Washington state. [5]

On January 31, 1819, Nicholas Biddle had written to James Monroe that the "truth is, that with all its faults, the Bank is of vital importance to the finances of the government and an object of great interest to the community. That it has been perverted to selfish purposes cannot be doubted--that it may--and must--be renovated is equally certain. But they who undertake to reform abuses and particularly of that description, must encounter much hostility and submit to much labor. To these, the hope of being useful can alone reconcile me--and if it should undertake the task I shall endeavor to persevere till the character of the institution is reestablished." Biddle soon accepted the job of one of the directorships of the Bank of the United States and began his course to improve and direct the national bank to a success in operation which benefited the economy. [6]

The Sixteenth Congress met on December 6, 1819. Illinois voters had earlier defeated John McLean, a supporter of the South, and voted in Daniel Pope Cook, a strong opponent of slavery expansion in the west. Antislavery meetings and debates had convinced some Northerners who had voted against the Tallmadge amendments to vote against and work against the slave interests. The Federalist Senator Harrison Gray Otis of Massachusetts changed his mind and worked with those who wanted to restrict slavery to the old South.

Early in the session, Tallmadge's friend John W. Taylor made an attempt to arrange a compromise without success. The committee appointed to consider Taylor's proposals could not agree upon boundaries or restrictions. At this point the petitions of Maine, then a part of Massachusetts, to ask for admission as a state led Speaker Clay to make a stand against its admission unless Missouri was admitted without slavery restrictions. From that point forward the question of Maine and Missouri were entwined.

On February 3, 1820, Jesse B. Thomas of Illinois introduced a proposal which would amend the statehood bill by prohibiting slavery in the unorganized Louisiana Purchase north of 36o 30', the basis for the Missouri Compromise. The idea was acceptable to most southern senators, but was regarded as a southern measure by Northerners. Massachusetts congressman John Holmes wrote William King on the 29th that "the South have made offers of a compromise which the North and even Maine reject," but the Senate had already passed the Thomas' amendment by a vote of 34 to 10, which meant that many Northerners voted for it, and passed the Maine-Missouri statehood bill. The House rejected all of the Senate amendments by large margins and turned to its own bill. Congress was deadlocked, while many Blacks in the capital flocked to hear the debates, aware that it was their future that was being discussed.

During the debates, there was a rash of talk about civil war and disunion from the members. Some described the awesome bloodletting that the nation would suffer. Although he wanted to see the end of slavery, Henry Clay took the southern position that slavery was a state and local matter. Clay appealed to northern congressmen in an effort to affect a compromise, using charm, persuasion, power, and parliamentary trick and subterfuge. He managed to gain support for three different compromises.

In time, the House turned its attention to the Thomas proviso and approved it by a vote of 134 to 42. Over half of the southern congressmen voted for the proviso, Virginians being the most opposed. Only five northern congressmen voted against it. Clay promoted and protected the compromise. It went to the Senate where that body voted on the third of March of 1820 to admit Maine and on the sixth to allow Missouri to form a state government without the slavery restriction, but when the state constitution was published, it was attacked by anti-slavery groups. We will go more on the events of 1820 on the matter soon. [7]

Liberals like Thomas Jefferson believed that the panic and its pains was God's just punishment for the sins of the American people who had been extravagant and greedy.

God was, in their view, displeased with the recent course of American society. It was a just punishment. Responsibility rested with the Bank of the United States and an independent judiciary which supported the bank. Smooth talking lawyers, shifty creditors, and Federalist aristocrats had controlled the judges and now America was being punished. God required that Americans abolish the Bank and the Court. In their view, majority rule must be returned to the United States. Jefferson spoke as an agrarian with little understanding of economics; not that there was a whole lot of wisdom on the matter at the time. [8]

There was a bright new male star in the theater of America at the time. British actor Edmund Simpson discovered him for the States, having long been member of the New York Park company since 1808. He was on a recruiting trip to England. The find was James William Wallack. The twenty-four year old Wallack was handsome, versatile, ambitious and talented. His New York debut, when brought from England, was as Macbeth, on September 7, 1818. He was a success and acted in America for many years, with a number of trips back to England. He finally settled in New York City were he was the leading actor-manager of the times.

At this time there was a young featured player who was popular. The beautiful Ellen Johnson was the daughter of the long reigning actress Mrs. Elizabeth Johnson whose acting career was on the wan. She was a better actress than her daughter, but theater goers wanted new faces. Ellen was a fine singer whose rendition of "Home Sweet Home" was beautiful and tender and captured theatric hearts. She was greatly loved but never made the success that Elizabeth had had. [9]

---

[1]Moore, *Missouri*, pp. 67-83.

[2]"Slavery and the Missouri Question," *North American Review*, January 1820, pp. 138, 143-144. Quote on p. 138.

[3]Faux, *Memorable, passim.* Notably pp. 248-251. Quotes on pp. 248, 250.

[4]Barry, *Beginnings*, p. 81.

[5]Perkins, Dexter, *The Monroe Doctrine, 1823-1826*, Cambridge Mass: Harvard University Press, 1927, pp. 9-10. Quote on p. 9.

[6]Biddle, Nicholas, *Correspondence*, 1919, p. 12.

[7]Moore, *Missouri*, pp. 84-95, 101-103, 136.

[8]Fackler, Stephen W., "John Rowan and the Demise of Jeffersonian Republicanism in Kentucky, 1819-1831," *Register of the Kentucky Historical Society*, LXXVIII No. 1 (Winter 1980), 1-3.

[9]Hughes, Glenn, *A History of the American Theatre, 1700-1950*, London: Samuel French, 1951, pp. 102, 108-109.

Chapter XVIII

KENDALL

In his book on Amos Kendall, William Stickney, his son-in-law, wrote in a concise language that "on the 6th of December, 1819, the legislature of Kentucky met at Frankfort. The acting governor in his message earnestly recommended the establishment of a school-fund and common schools, and devoted a large portion of the document to the Bank of the United States, denouncing it as unconstitutional and dangerous, and contesting the principles laid down by the Supreme Court; and concluding by proposing a correspondence with the other states, to the end of securing amendments to the Constitution. On the third day of that month, the Court of Appeals had given their decision, so that in December, 1819, the executive, judicial, and legislative departments of Kentucky concurred with almost perfect unanimity in the opinion that the bank was unconstitutional, and its establishment a dangerous usurpation."

The cry for relief was by now overwhelming and legislators were intent upon finding a way to answer that requirement, but there was a diversity of solutions available. When they chose one, it was vetoed as unconstitutional. That was "an act suspending for sixty days all sales under executions issued on judgments, decrees, and replene lands." The General Assembly promptly passed the bill over the governor's veto. Various of there measures were passed, but the people were to be dissatisfied with the new laws as insufficient to relieve their dire needs and circumstances.

Amos Kendall, American politician and public official, was born on August 16, 1789, near New Ipswich, New Hampshire, on his father's farm. His father was Zebedee Kendall. As a farm boy he learned the hard work of his class. This Kendall farm was made up of bog meadows, pine plains, and oak hills, with a brook running through it. They raised some cattle and some sheep. Hay was made on the meadows to feed the cattle during the long cold winters. In the better section of the pine plains near the hills were two four acre plots alternating in crops of corn and rye. Once in five or six years the upland meadows were cultivated in potatoes or corn. Further, horses, oxen, and milk cows found pasturage in the rougher, uncultivated uplands, where crops could not be raised.

The parents were very religious and very strict. Both were Congregationalists and Zebedee was a deacon in the church. On Sundays, they went to church, read the Bible and sung a hymn, accompanied by the bass-vial, played by the eldest son of the family while he was living at home. On weekdays, they had morning and evening prayers, and said grace before meals and thanks after meals. They rested on Sundays except for preparing meals. No recreation was allowed on the holy day and no dancing, playing cards, and such entertainments were permitted at any time. Nor could the sons go to places where such things were done. Children did such behind their parents backs.

"The early education of Amos," according to his autobiography "was in the free schools of Massachusetts and New Hampshire. The boundary line between these states ran through his father's farm, who paid a school tax in both states, and had the privilege of sending his children to school in both. The summer schools were taught by women, and were in general attended only by children who were not old enough to assist their parents in their daily labors. They were generally kept from two to three months in each summer. The winter schools were usually kept by men, and lasted from six weeks to two months in each year. They were open to children of all ages from infancy to manhood." Fortunately for Amos, his parents believed in education and the schools were close at hand, being one or two miles from the farm, one on each side. [1]

Since the parents had five children, with Amos the youngest, Zebedee hired a woman teacher one winter and started a season's school at home for the siblings and one niece. Although he was the youngest, Amos took to education and own first distinction in the family school. He particularly excelled in spelling and most liked arithmetic. He lagged only in penmanship. No sooner did his father promised a new Bible to an older brother if he would read through one year, than Amos asked if he could earn a Bible the same way. The wise father Kendall said yes. Although he could barely read at the time, he advanced fast and read it in the same year, by which time he was an accomplished reader. Instead of playing games, Amos read and soon had read all of the books in the small township library in Dunstable. In the free schools, he was only exceeded in spelling by Sally Wright, whom he eventually bested.

Amos also had mechanical ability, which he expressed in various ways including the discovery of Archimede's screw invention. He did not already know that it had already been invented. The boys trapped minks and muskrats in the neighborhood and cultivated a small tobacco patch. They also fished with the rod and spear. Election day provided them with a holiday to play games; collecting birds' eggs to be counted to determine a winner and thrashing with shut eyes. Farmers encouraged this to cut down upon the number of birds in the neighborhood, which were eating grain grown in the area.

When Amos became eleven years old, he went to live at his grandfather's house, twenty rods from his father's. Besides doing farm work for his father along side his brothers, he took care of his grandparents by cutting the wood, making fires, looking after a few cattle, and helping them by doing jobs and running errands. After this period, the eldest boy had gone out on his own and Amos Kendall had to do all of the male work on the farm. His father was disabled by rheumatism.

Amos had time only for two or three weeks of school during the years of 1803 and 1804. This was not satisfactory to Mr. Kendall because he wanted to see his youngest son get a liberal education. Amos himself wanted more learning so it was decided he would go to work for the parson in return for tutoring by the preacher. This did not work well because the parson was indolent and did not live up to his part of the bargain and tried to extract the maximum of labor for the least of instruction. The minister lacked a Christian character and personality and treated badly a girl in his keeping. Amos befriended her. The father sent him to the academy at New Ipswich for eleven weeks paid by Amos' work on brother Samuel's farm. This was soon continued for the rest of the year. He next taught school and saved his money for a future education at the Groton academy. He went to Dartmouth College.

While at school, he was admitted to a secret club devoted to self-improvement with thirteen other Dartmouth students. Kendall and one of the boys visited Kendall's aunt, uncle, and cousins. They climbed a mountain with the cousins with great difficulty and trouble, having elected to walk the entire distance and partaking of some rum. On a latter visit, the party tried a gold dining rod and captured a porcupine. In July of 1809, Amos joined the college's Handel Society devoted to sacred music. Then he passed on to the sophomore class during which class year, he taught school, kept up his studies, and in the spring, re-entered his class. This pattern continued for the next year.

In April of 1810, Kendall joined the college literary club upon invitation in time for frolics. The pranks pulled were of a rural nature and once the students had to pay damages. After another year, he graduated from Dartmouth, having attended to his studies and chapel. His father had paid for a little over one half of his education for four years, while his teaching earned him about that.

On the first of September of 1811, he reached home with only a vague thought as to what he must do now as a graduate. Amos did not feel the inward call for the ministry. His parents were hopeful that he would become a parson. He was not interested in medicine or surgery. This left him with law, which profession he was not really interested in. He would have preferred philosophical studies and mechanical arts, but they did not pay. He decided to teach and study law. Lawyer William Merchant Richardson of Groton said he should study law full time and offered generous terms. This was accepted.

When the War of 1812 broke out, he was faced with a point of decision. Kendall was a Jeffersonian Republican and was hostile to the Federalist view of the war. The events stirred his patriotism while those around him were losing theirs. When the Federalist Boston *Repertory* advised the people of Massachusetts to withdraw from the Union and not to engage in war, he thought that this was madness. Concerned about the clergy's anti-administration stands and anticipating harsh words from the preachers on the upcoming National days, proclaimed by Madison upon the recommendation of Congress, concern was shown in Kendall's views. The young man was dismayed at the expected mockery that New England clergymen would display. They lacked common prudence. They forgot the maxim of charity of the faith and were treating the mass of their fellow citizens as outcasts and ministers of Satan. His feelings came true, for the pastors denounced the war and sowed dragon teeth. [2]

In October of 1812, Kendall mustered twice with his militia company but decided this was not for him. Despite his pro-Madison views on the war, he decided that military combat was not for him. When it came time for the regimental muster, he opted out and wrote of the events of that day in his journey such as was very revealing of the young Amos, to wit, that instead of his military duties, he took two young ladies to the field in a chaise. They watched the staged fight. Firing stop and a man was shot. Kendall was shocked to see the wounded man near the chaise. The sight of blood made him faint. Indeed, Amos was not fitted for mortal combat.

Kendall visited Boston in late January of 1813. His classmate Jonathan Fowle lived there and Amos stayed at his house. On the twenty-seventh, he visited the Massachusetts legislature and listened to the message of the governor. Neither session or the message impressed the young Kendall. He found no majesty, no reverence, and no merit. Since the Democratic membership of the Senate had gotten control through Gerrymandering, or the division of senatorial districts in odd shapes to enable about one third of the people to elect a majority in the senate, Kendall considered it an injustice and villainy. Truly Kendall did not have the greatest respect for the Massachusetts government.

Expressing his father's distaste for the theater when he visited one, Kendall was disgusted although moved by the love scenes. It was a new experience for the young man and he was momentarily lost, but the illusion of the acts faded fast and he saw nothing but the fiction. The actor Holman did not impress him because of his harsh voice, indistinct articulation, and excessive loudness as well as the stark nature of the theater, which required that an illusion be maintained. Kendall was biased and remained biased, but his criticism might well have had some basis because he thought that the after piece was better. He was captivated by the scenery and the acting of this play. The first play was "Alexander, or the Rival Queen," and the second was the "Forty Thieves."

While in Boston, he attended various churches, notably a Catholic church, whose ornaments displeased him. He liked the sermon but disliked the music and ceremonies. Next, he went to the Unitarian church of Mr. Holley's where he thought well of the eloquence and talents of that pastor's, but felt that the beliefs were of no religion. The evening sermon of the Congregational church by D.D. Griffin was Holley's equal in eloquence, but much more suited to Kendall's beliefs.

On the 5th of February of 1813, Amos returned to Groton with the idea of writing a tragedy based upon the fall of Switzerland to the French, but when he wrote it he was soon dissatisfied with the same and decided he was no playwright and never undertook another. He continued his study of law, did the office work and voted in March in the election for governor. Richardson took ill in May and came close to death and Kendall himself became ill with the fever, nursed by his mother until well. After recovering, Kendall took part in a sham battle as an Indian for the edification of the soldiers in a battalion muster. This was his only military achievement.

Having finished his law studies, Kendall decided to escape the poor business conditions of New England, which had been caused by the war and move to the south or west. Although the elder Kendall did not approve, he loaned him two hundred dollars to make the trip to new lands. Bidding his family farewell, Amos went to Boston to say his good-bye there. At nine o'clock on February 21, 1814, he took a stage from that capital on his trip to the national capital toward the west and south. Because the stage was full, Kendall rode beside the driver and enjoyed the scenery in this by far the longest trip he had ever made. He noticed the poorness of the soil and the mixed nature of the woods to the west of Boston. It was one o'clock in the morning when they arrived at Ashford for four hours sleep. Again he rode with the driver, this time because he preferred it to the interior. He could see the scenery better in that position. The soil improve. They passed through Connecticut until a night rest at New Haven. On the twenty-third, they went to Rye where horrible roads forced them to make a stop until morning.

After a brief stop in New York City, they crossed the ferry to Paul's Hook in a steamboat with high winds and waves. On land once again, the travelers passed through northeastern New Jersey over level land. At Elizabethtown, they saw many soldiers and were told that recruiting was successful. Because of the poor roads, the passengers had to walk many miles beside the stagecoach. Kendall viewed Philadelphia, Havre de Grace, and Baltimore with interest and got to know his fellows. When he reached Washington, he called upon Richardson, and met General Varmun, the president and his wife.

On March 3, 1814, General Varmun took the young lawyer to the senate chamber and introduced him to a senator from Ohio and one from Louisiana and to Mr. Bledsoe of Lexington, Kentucky. Kendall was told that Ohio was crowded with lawyers and Kentucky had enough lawyers, hardly encouraging to the young man. When Amos said his best plan would be to introduce himself as an instructor to some family's children, Bledsoe thought that he might want someone as a tutor to his children. At this point the Kentuckian was called away. Meanwhile Kendall visited the navy yard and southern parts of the city. He heard an old army chaplain speak, who subject was hostility toward England, and thought the preacher's sermon was suitable for the army, but not for an enlightened audience. Bledsoe, on the next day, hired him to tutor his children.

After a visit to the patent office, Amos set out on his journey to Lexington. He had the company of Governor Lewis Cass and Major Trimble, a native of Kentucky, who thought well of Bledsoe and his wife. Cass struck Kendall as a Republican in politics with a contempt for religion and religious men and Yankees, of whom Cass ironically was one. Kendall was delayed by illness, but was soon on the way again on the stagecoach, making a friend of an elderly German. The traveler stopped in Pittsburgh, which interested and drew Kendall to its positive aspects. The natural scenery was marred by coal-dust in the air. He saw troops there on the way to the frontier.

Kendall and a friend decided to purchase a skiff and go down the Ohio to Cincinnati from Pittsburgh. This done, they bought a buffalo robe and stories. At this point in time, they met Major William T. Barry of Lexington, Kentucky, who had a boat, thirty feet long with three rooms, in which to take his wife, servants, horses and carriages to

Maysville for the road to Lexington. Barry invited them to join him and soon the skiff came along side them for their common use. They did so. On March 25, 1814, all set out down river from Pittsburgh on the lovely trip. Kendall was expecting to see fields and felt disappointed with the miserable villages of a few log cabins and the hilly wilderness, unsuited to agriculture.

He and his friend made a side trip on the skiff to visit a coal mine on the bank. The miners would sell their coal in Cincinnati, a month's work, some 1,500 bushels for 32 1/2 cents per bushel. On the afternoon of that day, the 27th, the Barrys and their fellows passed Steubenville on the right bank, a growing place with some elegant buildings. They passed Charleston, Virginia, and Wheeling before, on the next day, visiting the Indian mounds, which Kendall called an astonishing pile. There were smaller ones nearby and a regular fortification.

They passed the days going down the river with a thunderstorm one night and a high wind on the following day. On the first of April of 1814, they entered Kentucky. At Maysville on the third, they parted with Barry, who led his wife and servants overland to Lexington. Kendall had a good impression of the pair. Proceeding down river, they ran into a harsh windstorm. Forced to land, they stopped at a tavern. It snowed that night. Reaching Cincinnati, the group parted company and Kendall headed overland to Lexington, reaching there on the 12th.

There he found that Bledsoe snubbed him, but fortunately, Mrs. Henry Clay hired him to teach five of their seven children. He had gained the intercession of Mrs. Hart with whom he boarded. Mrs. Clay gave him board, three hundred dollars a year, and the use of Henry's library. He accepted expecting to gain Clay's friendship and advice. The children were nearly ungovernable, but except for the eldest had fine minds. He used mild firmness and had the support of Mrs. Clay and soon had a successful career in teaching. The children improved in temper and manners. He was well treated and got to know people in the Clay social circle. [3]

[1]Kendall, Amos, *Autobiography*, 1872, Rep. New York: Peter Smith, 1949, pp. 1-4, 227-229. Quote on pp. 3, 227.
[2]*Ibid.*, pp. 4-73.
[3]*Ibid.*, pp. 73-116.

Chapter XIX

LEXINGTON

News reached Lexington that Paris was in possession of the allies. It was May 28, 1814, in the Kentucky town. Kendall lamented this because he would have France strong, probably as a counter-weight to England which was still at war with the United States and it people. He had no respect for Napoleon's character, but when in mid-June word arrived of Bonaparte's abdication, he expressed his view that Napoleon was great because his talents were great. Even more important, it left Britain free to concentrate upon its war with America. Britain could destroy all of our external commerce. This shock must bring the Americans to pray to God for unity and honor.

One month later it was learned that a requisition had been made on Kentucky for 5,500 militiamen to be readied for New Orleans to defend the country to that point. While uncertain about his prospects in service, Kendall read law and a history of Russia. With the set date, he went with the rest for the muster ground. The men with which he was surrounded talked with dread about the draft and took the starch out of Kendall. This was followed by another, a temporary muster. He noted that the men were filled with a want of subordination and the officers were ignorant and lacked energy. On September 2d, word reached Lexington that Washington DC had been burnt by the British. The war seemed to go very badly for the Americans, and a new effort was required.

Good news reached Lexington on the 30th of September and the first of October. Mail telling of McDonough's victory on Lake Champlain and the British repulse at Plattsburg brought celebration in the town with an array of light throughout the town. Jackson had won a victory at Mobile and twenty guns announced the news. Again, the town was lighted. Everyone lighted as many candles as they could. A procession, headed by drum and fife broke all windows without lights, not many in number and mostly in shops. Pictures were displayed and muskets were fired. Men and women filled the streets. Kendall was there also and in a few days went to a dinner.

Kendall went to Frankfort and applied for a license for the Court of Appeals, the highest court in the state. The judges questioned him at length. Dissatisfied with some of his answers, Amos was unsure of his success. The judges were satisfied and he won admittance to legal practices and all without help. Barry was to introduce him, but he did not show up until too late. Now, he was a lawyer, but without a clear or busy connection. He considered going into business or founding a settlement in Indiana, or leaving Lexington to take up his law career. The months passed and Kendall learned the signing of a peace treaty. He felt a heart felt job, but many were dissatisfied with the terms.

On June 8, 1815, Kendall was presented an opportunity which would shape his life. Colonel R.M. Johnson and Mr. Chambers proposed that Kendall buy out the Lexington print shop and become editor of the *Minera*. They would loan him money which would enable him to buy it and he could pay out the purpose price out of the profits, Saying he would consider the proposition, he left and talked to friends, one of whom advised to buy it and one who advised against it. The negative friend feared he would lose his independence to Johnson, a man prominent in politics. In time he came to an agreement with Johnson by which, he, Amos, was to assume the editorial business of the newspaper: edit, keeping accounts, and making such collections as were convenient. He would also fold papers and such tasks. In order to save money, he agreed to board schoolmaster Arnold in return for which he would help Arnold with his studies and become deputy of the post office.

His plans to promote an emigration company in Indiana Territory gained headway. It would be made up of residents and non-residents. Non residents would purchase $190,000 worth of Georgia scrip from holders in New England and advance $61,000 for purchasing 100,000 acres of land. They would make up among themselves the board of directors for the settler company. Now residing in nearby Georgetown, Kendall made agreements to buy the print shop and to become postmaster at Georgetown; also, he finished a case defending a man of voluntary manslaughter. The *Minerva Press* came out under his name. Around Christmas, his commission as postmaster came through. Kendall began publication of a bi-monthly religious paper. He seemed to be on the way to success. Attempting to sell the operation, but continuing editing the paper, the would-be buyer thought that Kendall was losing money. Amos did some figuring and found out that he was right. Soon after the first of 1816, Kendall issued the last number of the *Minerva Press*. [1]

Kendall soon got back into the newspaper business. Colonel James Johnson and Mr. Wood established a journal named the Georgetown *Patriot*. The colonel paid Amos $150 a year for editing the paper. The first issue came out on the twentieth of April of 1816. Three days later, Amos went to attend the wedding of Samuel Theobald, over in Fayette County. By the end of the month, Kendall knew that the *Patriot* was popular. They had fifty subscribers from the small town and its environs. Rather than printing political writings for either side of a contest, the editor decided to allow each pay for the printing of handbills which would be distributed with the newspaper. Kendall bought some 12,000 copies of an almanac printed for $200 to be sold for Kendall's profit. He hoped to make some $100 or more selling them for about 2 1/2 cents each.

Visiting the agreeable Clay in Lexington and an equally agreeable widow, he went on a trip to visit Indiana. He saw several Swiss vineyards and drank American wine. Finding the flavor not so fine as that of the imported, he also discovered it had more spirit. In America, the Swiss farmers got one and a half dollars per gallon, while in Switzerland the price of thirty-three cents. He found them growing rich and having fine houses and plantations. There was a pleasant old Frenchman, a refugee from post-Napoleonic France. In France he had been a well-to-do professor of mathematics, but he was now poor at nearly fifty as a gardener. He was happy in America and Kendall left him with feelings of pity, admiration, and esteem.

The hero of this story, went through Madison, New London, Jeffersonville, Louisville, and Versailles to Alexandria before returning to Georgetown, Kentucky. He was involved in political discussions, heated and less, but avoiding quarrels as best he could, during the electioneering contests swirling about him. It was not a popular stand, but Kendall avoided worst bitterness than he had taken a partisan stand for one of the fractions over another.

Kendall wrote a series of articles in his Georgetown paper on the currency question, taking a popular stand for resumptions as if that could have been obtained against economic realities. Not only did he express the public feeling, but the officers of the Bank of Kentucky favored it. Of course the bank wanted economic recovery and a resumption, but they did nothing for it since they knew that they could do nothing for resumption. On top of his success, while in Frankfort, he was pressed to take the editorship and part ownership of the state newspaper, the *Argus of Western America*. Since this meant that he would be busy as a editor and politician instead of a mixture including law, he hesitated. Dissatisfied with a law case which took quit-claim land for eight settlers with children they wished to educate, he swung in favor of that literary career. On September 30, 1816, he bought out half interest in the *Argus*. William Gerard remained as one of the editors and was Kendall's new partner.

At length Amos found a wife, one he could love and be loved by. He sought a woman of solid accomplishments, an amiable woman. In October of 1818, he married at her father's house in a small village in Jefferson County, Mary Bullard, now Mary Bullard Kendall. She was cherished and devoted. They lived five years together before her death on October 13, 1823. They had four children. Amos responded to his wife's passing by working all the harder at his editorial duties. Her father was a plain and honest farmer and she was country bred, but with a polite education and good at the useful arts of a wife. Mary did not affect fashionable dress. Mary planned to raise her sons with home instruction to precede public education and her daughter to be able to undertake household tasks. [2]

The economic situation was bad in Tennessee. Farmers and merchants were in desperate plights. Most of them operated on a small scale. They did not have the backing. The average producer was unable to ship his cotton to New Orleans and await the return. He needed to sell immediately and gain the financing for the next crop and living expenses. He sold to the local merchant who used the banks to handle paper for their large profit. Even worst, at this time debts were large and the banks were in deep trouble. Where had the money gone? The answer was that it had been spent on high living of the days of prosperity.

Little had been done to save for hard times. Some had to sell their property to pay off creditors who were pressed for payment and would no longer take bank notes. No one wanted that shaky money, which put hardship upon debtors and creditors alike. The debtor class turned to their legislature for relief. They wanted payments of their debts to be legally suspended. They found a leader in the newly elected Felix Grundy. This was especially important for the cotton growing middle because that is where overexpansion took place.

Who was Grundy? He was a well educated son of a Kentucky planter who had chosen law for a career. He early took part in politics and government and was an important member of a constitutional convention in Kentucky. Soon, Felix was a rising politician having taken a popular forefront on many issues. Grundy was very much anti-bank. Becoming state chief justice, he grew weary of the limited income for his growing family and moved to Tennessee. He was elected to Congress by the time of the War of 1812. A war leader in Congress, he played a major role in legislation. Almost elected speaker, in time, he returned home to become a major trial lawyer. [3]

Mississippi Baptists were concerned about the need for good treatment of the slaves by the masters. They were in favor of using pressure against abusive slaveholders by churchmen and members of their individual churches. In some cases, they were to expel Baptist members of their churches for such bad behavior, but this was rare; usually a few stern words with the masters would suffice. Peer pressure was not to be dealt with lightly. If their neighbors disapproved then they must change. Specific disputes were avoided since the church members did not want to impinge upon property rights in slavery. However, there were enough cases of pressure to help protect the slaves from excessive bad treatment.

In 1819, the Mississippi Baptist Association authorized a long circular record which they titled "Duty of Masters and Servants." The leaders of the association sent this message to their preachers. In it they promoted the ideas that slavery was right and good, being divinely ordained. Some people were born to have a lordly role in life. The letter instructed slaves to be obedient, because God had a grander purpose in mind. He allowed slavery to exist for a reason. Slavery is good and wise, according to the Baptists of the time. Good servants were to be rewarded with Heaven. However, masters must be kind and forbearing because they had a master in Heaven. Masters should provide the slaves with physical necessities.

Even more important, masters must give their slaves the spiritual necessities of life. Later, the Church defended the right of slaves to have their own African American ministers. Baptists worked with Methodists to get the law of 1822, which declared that the African American churches have only white ministers, voted off the books. During their session of the next year, the Mississippi legislature rescinded that law. The Baptists of that state promoted the idea that all slaves be instructed in the Christian religion which idea was contrary to the opinion of others that religious learning would be subversive. In 1819, there were but two all-black congregations in the association. [4]

The actor James Wallack played the lead role in the long-time popular *Marmion*. According to drama historians, *Marmion* deserved it's standing with the public. The playwright James Nelson Barker, born in Philadelphia on June 17, 1784, to General John Barker, who was served as mayor of that city in 1808 and 1809, adapted the poem by Scott, and used the same chronicle Shakespeare used for information for characters and plot. Barker wrote quality and created ten good dramas. At the time, Wallack acted the part of Marmion, he was himself mayor of Philadelphia. Ten years later, he was connected with the Treasury Department for the rest of his life. Barker generally wrote his dramas on American themes. One of his themes was the romance of Rolfe and Pocahontas. *Marmion* was written in 1812. [5]

[1]Kendall, *Autobiography*, pp. 117-164.

[2]*Ibid.*, pp. 165-267.

[3]Parks, Joseph Howard, *Felix Grundy: Champion of Democracy*, Louisiana State University Press, 1940, pp. 1-117.

[4]Crowther, Edward R., "Mississippi Baptists, Slavery, and Secession, 1806-1861," *Journal of Mississippi History*, LVI (1944), 132-135.

[5]Quinn, Arthur Hobson, *A History of the American Drama From the Beginning to the Civil War*, New York: F.S. Crofts, 1943, pp. 136-142.

Chapter XX

THE WEST

In 1819, Americans established the Union Mission among the Osage Indians in Indian Territory. It was the first mission in what was later to become known as Oklahoma. Within two years missionaries had built a school there. They were especially selected people noted for their intelligence and culture, for their spiritual attainment and strength of character, and for their skills and physical stamina. These men proved successful in their message and the women proved successful in domestic skills, teaching of the Indian children, and care of the sick. By teaching and example, the women gave an education in English, refinement, moral and religious principles, and housekeeping skills.

Many women teachers came to Oklahoma from the east, unmarried and tied by their eastern culture and fashions. Still they managed to use their own resources to meet the major and minor challenges of the west. They taught the Indian girls various female attainments such as knitting and needlework. These teachers had a quality education back east and dispensed quality education to the girls. The domestic curriculum was an essential part of the education since the young ladies needed the advances which American women had brought with them. Domestic education was important for better living and practiced in their youth and married lives. This was the same domestic arts and academic education that the teachers had in their schools. [1]

It was the winter of 1819-1820 that Cherokee Chief Bowles, led sixty of his men and their families into Texas Caddo land. They first lived at the Three Forks of the Trinity (Dallas), until the fierce Prairie Indians forced them to move to settled areas. He established his village about fifty miles north of Nacogdoches. There the Cherokee hunted and farmed. They had a peach orchard, mined and smelted lead. Bowles carried this lead to Shreveport, Louisiana, by pack train to sell. They had found a new home in Texas in an area where there were few white men. [2]

Rumors had percolated to the Indians that the United States was to have Florida from Spain. Remembering what the Americans had done to them during the War of 1812 and Jackson's campaign earlier that year, the Seminole were fearful and worried. The invidious white speculators, ever eager to steal from another, told the Indians that

Jackson was coming with a large army to destroy them. This scared the natives into selling slaves and cattle at low prices and to head for the interior. The two invasions and the scare tactics also broke the Seminole prosperity. While once they had large herds on extensive lands, now they lived in poor straits. [3]

The South of 1819 was at peace and generally satisfied. Their major problem was the economy, and the upcoming conflict over slavery was unimagined. Politically Southerners had a big say in government. The president, half of cabinet ministers, and the Speaker of the House were from southern states. Government was not a major concern since most Americans were wrapped up in their private affairs, economic and social. It was in these areas that the South suffered most from the North and from themselves. However the differences had yet to create any sectional difficulties. One half of the states were slave and one half were free. Southern states had less population but more slaves than the northern states. In the former one third of the people were black slaves and in the North only two percent were African American, almost all of which were free. The population was more homogeneous in the South if one does not count the blacks. Maryland, Virginia, and North Carolina were the most populated states in the South. About one half of all southerners lived in these three combined. Indians occupied much of the states of Georgia, Alabama, and Mississippi.

Ninety percent of the Southern population who worked were busy with farming and herding, while the percentage was 77 in the North. Most of the produce of the South was staple crops for export or to feed southerners. Food flowed from the northwest to the South too, because the South produced so much cotton instead of food. The income was spent for goods from England and the northeast in addition to the northwest. Besides the cotton and tobacco the South sold to Europe, Southerners raised corn, hogs, sweet potatoes, cowpeas, chickens, and cows. They grew fruit trees, grapevines, and had vegetable gardens. Further, they raised grains in the Upper South for local needs and sale abroad of flour and whiskey. This area also provided various flocks and herds. One could find sheep mostly in the Upper South. Rice was by its nature limited to the east coast region of South Carolina and sugar cultivation was confined to the Lower Mississippi River. In both areas slaves outnumbered the whites. [4]

Ralph Krume, who was Thomas Lincoln's brother-in-law, transported the pair and her goods to Indiana. She had quite a selection of furniture and household goods. One walnut bureau was valued at fifty dollars. The children were glad to see their father again and doubtless were open-eyed at the furniture, utensils, and good bedding she bought with her. They met her three children, their new kindred. Sarah Bush brought joy once again to their lives. First, she reclothed the children and made her husband put a floor in the cabin and add doors and windows. Thomas plastered the cracks between the logs and provide a clothes-press. Meanwhile, Abe and his sister enjoyed the luxury of a feather bed. She proved gentle, affectionate, industrious, and thrifty. A tall and straight woman, she had good looks, pride, and an ability to talk.

In his adult years, Lincoln used to tell the story of his yellow dog Joe and his fate. The dog always gave the alarm when the boys would slip out at night for a coon hunt.

One night, Abe, John Johnston and the other boys of the neighborhood, took the dog with them for a coon hunt. It was a success. They killed their coon and sewed the hide on the dog. Released Joe headed straight for home. Along the way, other dogs were attracted to the smell of coon and attacked and killed the Lincoln dog. Thomas Lincoln discovered the dead dog in the yard on the next morning. [5]

In Hanover, Germany, lived philanthropist Ferdinand Ernst, who came to the United States to find land for some thirty German families wishing to emigrate. Coming to Illinois in 1819, he reached Edwardsville, Illinois, northeast of St. Louis late on July 27th. The town was a pretty town, several miles from the Mississippi bluffs. The land was fertile with its fine farms. Ferdinand found maize from 12 to 15 feet high. There were many peach and other fruit trees. It took only four years from planting to the first harvest. Almost always the trees bore fruit in the falls of the years. The trees were so full that their branches had to be propped. People enjoyed peach brandy and dried peaches.

There were apples, plums, and large melons. Pumpkins reached the size of three feet diameter. Brown and red cabbage were important crops. Ernst found the ground too rich for potatoes and other growths. Potatoes never thrived when planted early, but they could be planted in July for a harvest. Farmers grew plentiful maize, wheat, and oats. They did not plant barley and rye.

Frederich Hollmann, who owned a store in Vandalia with Ernst later, rode to Illinois with Ferdinand Ernst. He was also an early member of the village board of trustees. Hollmann crossed the Wabash with ten others. They were on horseback entering the state of Illinois. He praised the great prairies and little wooded districts. He decided the scarcity of wood would prevent their cultivation. They reached the tavern full of travelers. Despite the numbers, each one was served well enough and their horses were well cared for. However the lodgings were poor and each one had to prepare his own bed.

In the prairies, there were no trees nor houses to shelter one from the intense heat of sun. Hollmann had bad times when the axle of his wagon broke. He wrote that his "mounted traveling companions could not help me and had to leave me; but two pedestrians, who had made the journey afoot from Baltimore in this manner, proved friends in need. They went back three miles to get a tree trunk which we had seen lying there by the road. With great difficulty, we then took the wagon to the next house. These honest Americans repaid me evil with good. They had been in our company for some time, and at the crossing of the river, I did not wish to permit them to take a place in my wagon." He had the services of a wheelwright.

The next tavern keeper was a Quaker and prayed and sung while they were there. They reached Edwardsville, where they found a camp of Kickapoo Indians who were there to give up their lands on the Sangamon and Vermilion valleys and the rest of Illinois. Ernst and Hollmann went to the farm of Burensbach and asked him to show them the lands which were to be sold at public auction upon the first of August. They decided to wait after seeing the lands until Vandalia was founded and settled there, buying neighboring lands afterwards. They were impressed with the lands of the

Sangamon. Ernst and settlers from Germany later took up land there, but most of the colonists died within a year of their arrival.

John Woods, well-to-do English farmer, settled on the English Prairie in 1819. Birkbeck and Flower quarreled and the settlement was divided into towns of Albion and Wanborough, northwest of Harmony, Indiana. Woods wrote of his arrival in Illinois. He saw three flat boats with their loads of flour, bacon, whiskey, tobacco, horses, and pine and cherry planks. They were headed for the New Orleans market. Because of the state of the water levels, it had taken 24 days for them to be transported from the Falls of Louisville to that place. They themselves had covered only nine miles on that day.

By the evening of the fifteenth, they moved off Shawneetown, Illinois, a town subject to floods which retarded its growth. It was in the neighborhood of the salt works, with its production of 300,000 bushels of salt per year. There was a land office there for southeastern Illinois, which extended almost one hundred miles to the north. Shawneetown was a brisk place, with the Bank of Illinois, many stores, and several taverns. Mr. Hobson, who came from the north of England, kept the largest, the Steamboat Hotel. The jail and about 80 houses were made of wood. The town was unhealthy with low land all around.

There were other towns. Wansborough had 25 cabins with a tavern, a couple of stores, several lodging houses, and a number of carpenters, bricklayers, brick-makers, smiths, wheelwrights, and sawyers, plus a tailor and butcher. Men were busy building a horse or ox mill and digging wells. Mr. Birkbeck had found a tolerably good spring, but his wells had little water in them. The building lots were sizable and laid out in squares. They were in woods but a number were being cleared. Two miles east of Wanborough was Flower's Albion in a woods north of the English Prairie, with its 20 cabins, church, market house, two taverns, two stores, a surgeon, several carpenters, brick-makers, bricklayers, wheelwrights, smiths, sawyers, and a shoemaker. There too were a number of wells but little water.

Woods found that most Americans were well acquainted with the law and quite fond of the subject. Law suits were many and often minor. Men were oftentimes drunk and when so were always quarreling. They could be industrious and idle, and were jacks-of-all-trades. Their need of many skills was a result of the primitive nature of their lives. He found them independent and well versed in politics. The subject was most interesting to them. All were independent from the poorest to the richest. He discovered that most of them were from the South and retained their prejudices. African Americans were held in the utmost contempt. For them the Indians and African Americans were inferior and treated as such. [6]

[1]Schrems, Suzanne H., "Teaching School on the Western Frontier," *Montana: The Magazine of Western History*, XXXVII No. 3 (Summer 1987), 58-59.
[2]Clarke, Mary Whatly, *Chief Bowles and the Texas Cherokee*, Norman: University of Oklahoma Press, 1971, pp. 14-17.
[3]Mahon, John K., "The Treaty of Moultrie Creek, 1823," *Florida Historical Quarterly*, XL (1940), 350-351.

[4]Sydnor, Charles S., *The Development of Southern Sectionalism, 1819-1848*, Baton Rouge: Louisiana State University Press, 1948, pp. 1-6, 11.
[5]Herndon, *Life*, 23, 28-29.
[6]Angle, 1968, pp. 68ff.

Chapter XXI

THE CASS EXPEDITION

The idea of an expedition along Lakes Huron, Michigan, and Superior in the wilderness was the idea of Lewis Cass, one soon shared with John Calhoun. This land was little known by the Americans, a land transversed by fur traders since the trips of Frenchmen, notably Pierre Esprit Radisson, in the seventeenth century, about one hundred and fifty years earlier. Anxious to search out the land himself, Cass wrote a letter to Secretary of War John C. Calhoun on November 18, 1819, asking his authorization and support to undertake the trip. The little that Americans knew of the area came from the reports of the Indian traders, and Cass wished to amend that knowledge. Cass was an explorer who knew that the roads were sketchy and there was no correct topographical delineation of the land.

Cass wanted to examine the area's animal, vegetable, and mineral kingdoms and its facilities for water communication as well as to draw its natural objects and determine present and future in value to the American nation. Michigan Territorial delegate William Woodbridge carried the letter, ready to support the idea which was so vital to his territory and his responsibility. Cass and the delegate were good friends and the governor could count upon him to explain and push the idea and plans of the proposed trip. Cass wanted to lead the expedition himself.

There were six political aims of the expedition. It was first of all a fact finding examination. Then as Cass wrote that "a personal examination of the different Indian tribes who occupy the country; of their moral and social conditions; of their feelings towards the United States; of their numerical strength; and of the various objects connected with them, of which humanity and sound policy require that the government should possess an intimate knowledge" was important. Cass expected that the knowledge to be gained would be beneficial, probably on both sides. He included extracts showing how little America knew of these natives of which much would have to be known.

Second, wanting title to Indian lands in the vicinity of the Straits of St. Mary's, Prairie du Chien, and Green Bay because of their strategic qualities in communication and travel, Cass thought that possession was essential and should be obtained for the considerable population of Prairie du Chien and Green Bay and the few families at the straits. It was important to have Indian cessions of land for immediate settlement. This would be highly important in case of difficulties with the Indians. He would have secured title at the Saginaw treaty for land in the vicinity, but he was not authorized to do so.

Third, there was profit to be made in the interior, the extent of which was unknown, but the Americans had samples of copper ore which was taken from the vicinity of Lake Superior. Cass wanted to search out the source. Such supplies of ore might be taken to the seacoast and used to hull ships. There were more rumored deposits in the country which the governor wanted to examine.

The next three advantages dealt with the Indians. Cass wanted to know the views of natives near Chicago concerning the removal of the Iroquois to their country. He wanted to explain governmental views to the British at Malden concerning relations between the British and Indians. Cass wanted to order the Indians to cease visits there. Ever since the Revolution this had been a sore point with American authorities. He also wanted to determine the status of the British-Canadian fur trade there in American territory.

When Cass suggested using some $1,000 to $1,500 of Indian funds assigned to Michigan, Calhoun and his superior James Monroe approved. There would be no additional funds needed and the plan fitted in with the larger plans of the two officials to secure the dominance of the American republic in the northwest territory beyond Michigan. The government had already sent some expeditions into the region, but this subsequent one seemed as necessary as the others. Before receiving his orders, Cass began preparing for the expedition, ordering canoes constructed, interviewing woodsmen, and seeking out guides and pilots for the journey. He wrote to secure essential scientific equipment. He sought personnel for the trip. Approving of the Cass Expedition, Calhoun suggested that Henry Rowe Schoolcraft be the mineralogist. This was done. [1]

Lewis Cass was born in Exeter, New Hampshire, on October 9, 1782 and studied law in Marietta, Ohio, on the frontier. Admitted to the bar, he took up the practice of law at Zanesville. Elected a state representative, he served in the War of 1812, and was appointed governor of Michigan Territory in 1813. Helping with the defense of Michigan during the war years, Cass learned about the Indians and politics. He played a major role in drawing up the laws of the territory from among those of established states and supervised Indian affairs from his appointment in 1813 to the end of his governorship in 1831.

After the war, he had the difficult task of securing the respect of the Indians in his territory. He had to overcome the distrust and suspicions of the native tribes. They were tired of the incessant demands of the whites for more land. Cass was kept busy keeping the peace and arranging for ever more cessions. There was no end to the need as settlers poured into the western lands and set up farms and towns. He was successful and in his biggest haul, Cass arranged for the transfer of four million acres in Ohio, Indiana, and Michigan. This removed the barrier between the settlements of Ohio and Michigan and gave the whites good communications between the state and territory. The way was clear for increased business and settlement. This was followed by his 1819 treaty with the Indians for six million acres and the need for exploration and preparation for more settlements and mineral exploitation for a growing nation.

Mineralogist for the expedition, Henry Rowe Schoolcraft became best known as an explorer and even more an ethnologist; a study of the Indians brought him future fame and a certain amount of respect in later times. At the time of his trip, he was very little known but the Cass journey was to open doors and provide opportunities, taken when he published a book on the trip the year afterwards.

He had just published a competent work, *A View of the Lead Mines of Missouri*, which established him as a competent geologist, a necessary ingredient for the Cass Expedition which sought among other things to discover copper and other metal ores in the area to be tracked through by Cass and his men. Still a young man, Schoolcraft had been born on March 28, 1793, in Albany County, New York. His father was a glassmaker and he studied this industry and started a book on glass making, after graduating from Union College and attending Middlebury College. At school, he specialized in geology and mineralogy, also taking languages and other natural sciences. He was already a rising young man when he went on this expedition. [2]

After the Cass expedition and Schoolcraft's publication of his *Narrative Journal of Travels through the Northwestern Regions of the United States ... to the Sources of the Mississippi River* in 1821, authorities thought he was well versed in knowledge of the natives and their problems and named him Indian agent for the tribes of Lake Superior. Schoolcraft became much interested in and had a predilection for the Algonquian tribes in the forests of Superior. One year later in 1823, Henry married a quarter-blood Chippewa girl Jane Johnston. She was educated in Europe but preferred primitive Indian culture and served a good tie between the Indians and the agent. [3]

Henry immersed himself in Indian life and soon a great governmental demand developed for his knowledge. After long service, he was promoted to the office of Superintendent of Indian Affairs for Michigan in 1836. Greed for more land for the whites, led him to negotiate several treaties with the Chippewa, obtaining title to the northern third of the lower peninsula and the eastern half of the upper peninsula of Michigan. Schoolcraft wrote very literary works on the Indians, mostly popular in nature, including one on Indian mental characteristics, Indian history and prospects, his personal memoirs about life among the Indians, and in 1851-1857, his opus magnus, the large six volume *Historical and Statistical Information Respecting the History, Condition, and Prospects of the Indian Tribes of the United States* with the help of others. Honors came his way. His first wife died in 1842 and in 1847, he married Mary Howard of Beaufort District, North Carolina. He died on December 10, 1864, toward the end of the Civil War. [4]

The official journalist for the expedition was Doty. With an acute mind, James Duane Doty had just become a lawyer one year earlier and was seen to be a fast riser in territorial affairs. He was clerk of the supreme court of the Michigan Territory and a clerk in the territorial council when he accompanied the Cass Expedition. A very young man, Doty was born on November 5, 1799, when John Adams was president in war threatening times, in which Adams was unpopular, but did prevent a war with France. Doty was not yet twenty-one when Cass picked him, so he was showing great promise for one that young. His promise was to be fulfilled.

After the expedition returned home, in 1823, he became judge of the then large Northern Michigan judicial district, a frontier and wilderness area. On April 14, 1823, James married Sarah Collins at Whitestown, New York, his home state. They settled at Green Bay, then in Michigan Territory, from which base, he traveled extensively. His duties required courage, keenness, and diplomacy and brought him in daily contact with Indians, settlers, rivermen, hunters, soldiers, and traders. Doty made friends among the trading firm men which helped his rise faster. There were some bumps for he resigned his judgeship in 1832 and explored the west, notably Wisconsin.

Doty mapped the area and selected sites for such as towns, mils, and wharves, which he planned to buy as soon as the surveying was completed. He obviously hoped to get rich quick by speculating in western lands. This followed the same path as George Washington, but Washington was the surveyor and not the mapper of lands he then bought. This land buying had made Washington the richest American of his day and Doty was on the way to wealth in real estate.

On the heels of this activity, the War Department commissioned Doty to survey military roads in Wisconsin in 1832 and he was elected to the legislative council of Michigan from the western territory west of Lake Michigan in the north. His friendships among the settlers and other people in the area paid off in political preferment and Doty opened up a whole new career in politics and government. Next, Doty served as Wisconsin's delegate in Congress from 1839 to 1841, when President Tyler named him governor of Wisconsin Territory. While in these high positions, he served his own self-interest rather than the public good and engaged broadly in political fights and intrigues.

He continued to rise rapidly in government. Obviously he knew how to politic as well as how to gain support and serve his own interests. Further positions were conquered. He was a delegate to Wisconsin's first constitutional convention, and a representative in Congress from 1849 to 1853. He was successively a Democrat, a Whig, and a Republican as each suited his position. In 1861, Lincoln appointed Doty superintendent of Indian Affairs at Salt Lake City and in 1863, the great president named him governor of Utah Territory.

Soon after Lincoln was assassinated, Doty died on June 13, 1865, another one of Cass successes in picking talented men for his expedition. Both Schoolcraft and Doty played important roles in the area in which they first entered in 1819 as members of the exploration of Lewis Cass, who himself went on to new heights as a negotiator in Indian treaties, in which the Indians lost title to their once vast lands, and as secretary of war in Jackson's administration, in which he managed the removal of the Southern Indians. He was then minister to France, a senator in Washington DC, a presidential candidate, and a secretary of state, an able man for the nineteenth century in America. Talent dwelled in the expedition.

With an uncle of Douglass' being the celebrated engineer David Stanhope Bates, it is not surprising to see young David Bates Douglass becoming an engineering officer in the United States Army and taking part on the Niagara frontier, defending Fort Eire. He learned command positions, taught at West Point, and made important surveys in the East. Born in 1790 in Pompton, New Jersey, he married Ann Ellicott, whose father was also a professor at the Military Academy at West Point. After traveling with Cass as topographer, David returned to West Point with the highest commendations of Lewis Cass written to John Calhoun. His father-in-law had died and David had family obligations, plus the need to learn French to teach the new method of calculus described in French texts. These pressing concerns and future disputes with Schoolcraft about publications keep Douglass from publishing his accounts or diary. It was not until 1869 that the Douglass diary was printed, with Schoolcraft immediate publications on the result of his trip. [5]

Subsequently, Douglass taught at West Point, worked as an engineer for canal companies in New York and New Jersey, and from 1832 to 1833, taught natural philosophy at New York University, followed by teaching engineering and architecture there also. A busy man, Douglass surveyed the route for the Brooklyn and Jamaica Railroad on Long Island, designated buildings for the university, drafted plans and supervised the building of the Croton aqueduct, investigated coal regions on the Potomac, and created Greenwood Cemetery on Long Island. As president of Kenyon College in Gambier, Ohio, from 1841 to 1844, he had a controversy with various trustees of the school. From 1844 to 1848, he worked as an engineer in New York. In 1848, he held a professorship of mathematics at Robart College in Geneva, New York, dying the following year with little warning.

Douglass had to travel from West Point to Detroit to undertake his position in the Cass Expedition. On April 20, 1820, he joined the steamship from New York City to Albany at eleven at night at West Point on the landing there. The ship arrived at Albany the next afternoon. There he took time to cash the draft of General Peter Buel Porter, a soldier of the republic, who had fought like Douglass in the War of 1812 and who was awarded a gold medal for bravery. A member of the U.S. House of Representatives from New York, Porter had also served as a member of the Boundary Commission of 1818. It was Porter who had prepared and introduced the famous report which recommended war against Great Britain in December of 1811. It was Porter who had been one of the earliest projectors of the Erie Canal. Later, he was to serve for a time as John Quincy Adams' secretary of war.

There was no explanation of the draft in Douglass' account, but it was to the amount of $500. Half of the amount, Douglass sent to his wife. He settled a few accounts, including one with bookseller James E. Eastburn of 108 Broadway in New York City for $15. Douglass evidently liked his books. His check was good for the trip of the time, seeing that he paid for $5,25 for a seat from Schenectady from Albany and fifty cents for the extra baggage Douglass needed for his trip to the wilds of Lake Superior including paper notebooks to write down such information including this trip to Detroit. [6]

From Albany westward he went by stagecoach over what he considered to be good roads. The snow then on the ground had receded to patches by the roadside and under some of the fences. Weather was inclined to be wet and three were already great quantities of grain planted in the fields, especially good towards Utica. This date of April 27th, he noted in his journals, was the last date of the bitter contest for the State of New York's governorship, between Martin Van Buren's man and Governor De Witt Clinton.

Clinton early had sponsored the Erie Canal. His support was strong since he was a powerful man in New York. He was a leader in his party and had been a legislator, United States senator and mayor in his early years and then a lieutenant governor. First elected governor of the state in 1817, he was running for reelection in 1820. The state's leader was very popular because he had promoted the Erie Canal, which was in the process of being built, owing more to Clinton than to any other man. Despite his popularity, the opposition was getting stronger and he was losing ground. He did win a second term as governor on April 28, 1820. Van Buren was a spoilsman who became the eighth president of the United States much later. At this point in time, Van Buren was a state senator but gaining political power a virtual "Little Magician," soon to be U.S. senator.

The stop at Utica was short, Douglass having left there at two o'clock in the dark morning for a muddy and rough ride as far as Manlius. In the daylight on a foggy early half of the day, he could see fifteen inch high wheat at Vernon. Further on the route, he noticed the broken terrain with its high hills and deep valleys and the progress of the canal in the area. Once near Skansatales, the countryside became more regular. The trip remained one of wee hours embarkation's.

On the next day at four in the morning they left for Canadaigua and breakfasted at Cayuga Bridge. Douglass saw the Eire Steamboat Company's vessel "Walk-in-the-Water," to transport people via the lake connecting Newburg and Geneva. The country was being developed and he saw many fine farms. At Canadaigua the passengers learned that their stagecoach ended there and that they should have to wait until Monday for the three-times-a-week. Douglass and others paid high prices to hire a cab to take them westward. Douglass' part came to seven dollars. It went to Batavia. He noticed the country's soft black slate and wrote about the fine lands.

Traveling toward the west from Batavia through rich and highly cultivated lands, Douglass learned about one township which did not even have forty acres in cultivation at the end of the War of 1812, had in 1819 eleven hundred acres of land in wheat. Further Genesee County had produced 800,000 bushels of wheat in 1819. Because of the Panic farms were cheap and the land company was the butt of attack. He found various corals along the route.

At Buffalo, on May 1, 1820, Douglass found the lake clogged with ice and was delayed. He spent the time collecting samples of plant life in the vicinity in the fields swept by a constant wind from the north. In Buffalo, on the third, he met Schoolcraft for the first time. They talked and waited the arrival of the steamship to come up to her wharf. The same south wind kept it from proceeding up the rapids.

Douglass met General Porter and sold him a chronometer, which David had purchased in New York City from the Demill Brothers of 239 Pearl Street, according to Jackman and Freeman. It cost $250 and Porter paid twenty dollars in cash and a draft on Albany's Farmers and Mechanics Bank. David sent the draft to a Mr. Gannett. With this done, Douglass turned to his study of the natural establishment of the countryside. Douglass wrote that he saw "a fine specimen of tremolite said to have found here, but presume it was part of a solitary rock as it was contained in quartz, whereas all the country is shell limestone." It rained, but oxen pulled up the boat up the rapids and they were soon underway up Lake Erie.

The towns along the way, Grand River, Cleveland, and Sandusky were said to be unhealthy. Slopes on the banks of the Ohio gradual with woods and fine farms alternating. Sandusky was then thinly inhabited. Strawberries and May apple were in blossom. He noted flowers and types of trees and passed up into Detroit about eleven at night. [7]

---

[1]Jackman, Sydney and Freeman, John F. (eds.), *American Voyageur: The Journal of David Bates Douglass*, Marquette, Mich: Northern Michigan University Press, 1969, pp. xiv, 114-117. Quote on pp. 114-115.

[2]*Dictionary of American Biography*, VIII, 456-457.

[3]*Ibid.*; Jackman, *American*, p. 5.

[4]*Dictionary of American Biography*, VIII, 457.

[5]*Ibid.*, III, 390-391; Jackman, *American*, pp. xiv-xxi.

[6]Jackman, *American*, pp. 1-2; *Encyclopedia Britannica* (1911), VI, 528.

[7]Jackman, *American*, pp. 2-3, 5-6. Quote on p. 5.

Chapter XXII

MOSES AUSTIN

On May 9, 1820, Douglass dined with Governor Cass, a doctor, and another man from Zanesville's coal mines. The canoes were not ready so the party was delayed. Douglas looked around the countryside of Detroit, looking at Bloody Bridge and Pontiac. There was wind, rain, and chilly weather. He walked the three miles to Springwells to gather flowers on its sandy hills, perhaps sixty feet above water, on the fourteenth. The next day, he rode there with General Alexander Macomb, who was born in Detroit in 1782, graduated from West Point, and defeated the British at the Battle of Plattsburg during the War of 1812. Macomb was an engineer officer for much of his military service. They could see Detroit from the elevation. When the subject of the Indian antiquities supposedly found there came up, the general said this was not so. Also, the hills were sand hills and not tumuli formed in congealed lavaflows, as was sometimes thought.

Douglass did note that the soil was as rich as elsewhere, but the farms looked fine. He remarked the case of Captain Stanton's 200 acres, which cost him $6,000 or thirty dollars an acre, on which there were 300 apple trees for the making of one hundred barrels of cider, a liquor made from apple juice worth some $7 a barrel, for a total of $700, a return of over eleven percent on the cost of the farm from this income alone. There were other revenues such as a fishery and produce, making almost as much combined, for a return of 20% on the original cost. In the vicinity were Mitchella repens or partridge berries.

The professor-on-leave called upon a Lieutenant Clark at the request of Cass about the matter of the use of his waiter as a member of the expedition. It was deemed that the waiter-soldier would serve ably on the trip, and what was never said, but likely at a position other than waiter. Clark did not want to give him up on the grounds that he made a good waiter. He finally said he would allow him to leave only at the command of General Macomb. This was not forthcoming and Douglass noted in his diary that Clark would rather keep the man although he was needed and would be "of the highest value to us in the performance of a national and most important enterprise." Also a lieutenant in the commissary department was not entitled to the services of an enlisted man as a waiter. [1]

In 1820, Detroit had about 1,200 inhabitants. One half of these were French, mostly Catholics, and they were in the process of building a large Catholic cathedral, some 116 feet in length, sixty feet in width, and 110 feet high with two steeples, an imposing building for a town the size of Detroit. However, it served a wider area than the town itself. The Catholics had purchased an organ built in Ohio. This organ was said to be a very fine organ. The cathedral was a stone building, while the Presbyterian church was made of painted wood. The stone came from nearby Stoney Island, white stone, and with copes of Cleveland Stone, albite stone. Methodists in Detroit met in the Council House, a public building made of stone, 50 feet by 17 feet, and on weekdays housing the town, territorial, and Indian department business. There were three schools, two regular and one Lancasterian, where the older students taught the younger pupils.

In 1820, David Bates Douglass of the Cass Expedition visited these places and wrote down his impressions of Grosse Isle-Grosse Point. On May 22d, he looked at the quarry of Grosse Isle. There, he took examples of the sulph of strontian and specimens of plants. He found a litiaceous plant, a small flowered species of Solomon's Seal, a small white flower, and some others.

Packing up on the twenty-fourth, they prepared to go without their canoes, but these arrived about ten in the morning and they had to load them up and were not able to depart until four in the afternoon. Most of the gentlemen set out on horseback for a nine mile ride to Grosse Point north of Detroit, with other citizens and the families of Governor Cass and General Macomb. They had fine weather that day, but it was cold the next day, getting colder, from 46 o in the morning to 43 o in the afternoon. The wind blew against them and they could not make progress on Lake St. Clair before then. Farms stretched back from the shore for a mile and there were pebble beaches along the shore of a siliceous nature.

The governor went back to Detroit and returned when the winds became favorable and the expedition headed out into the waterways. They could make sail for awhile. Passing a flatter land little elevated above the lake, they soon stopped to take refreshment. They took an arm of the lake and soon had the wind blowing against them once again no matter how hard the soldiers and Indians paddled. Mackey, Schoolcraft, and Douglass had to help paddle and got a little wet with the shallow St. Clair lake water. Nearing the river channel, they stopped off on the left (west) on what was then Mrs. Lauton's Island, now called Dickinson Island. There they made camp for the night.

On May 27, 1820, they got an early start and passed the islands and the main shore with its walnut and maple trees. They headed up the St. Clair River for Lake Huron. They saw timberland and huts. A strong wind came up and the expedition made sail at a rapid rate of fifteen miles on the wide river. To the left was St. Clair settlement, where there were many farms of long standing and plenty of fruit. On the right (east) there was the prewar site of an old Indian village and a little later Bell River on the left. It was about ten or twelve miles wide at its mouth. They were soon to reach Fort Gratiot near Lake Huron.

Fort Gratiot had a harbor in a bay of Lake Huron. The fort was on sort of a second bank a little distance from the southern shore. There is a flat of and from a second bank. One could see, wrote Douglass an ancient bank behind the one in 1820. Major Alexander Cummings at the fort extended them his help and hospitality. From him they got provisions and were underway at 8:30 in the morning of the 28th.

There was plenty of timberland and Douglass noted spruce, hemlock, cedar, white pine, birch, beech, poplar, and maple among the trees of lesser numbers. He saw new plants, four or five which he had not seen already. On the twenty-ninth of May, they passed an Indian hunting party of five canoes whose appearance seemed such superior to Indian tribespeople in the state of New York. One Indian had a captive bald eagle some seven feet from tip to tip in the wings. Douglass spent his spare time studying the plants and minerals of the region. He found more samples of plants than he had seen before on the expedition plus some currants and gooseberries. There was also a plant which was said to cure rattlesnake bite. Of course, no such plant exists and that specimen was not such a one.

Subsequent searches on a windy day past the march, Douglass found a species of Solomon's Seal with a purple bell-shaped flower and husky and fibrous root. Among rocks he found some mica slate and hornblende rock and later loose sandstone with parts of embedded remains. Among the trees already seen, Douglass named the sycamore, cherry, elders, and willows. [2]

Businessman Moses Austin was an American born, Spanish subject who was a mining entrepreneur in Spanish Missouri with an earlier background in business. He had a son, Stephen F. Austin and in 1819, he talked to him about settling people from the United States in the Mexican province of Texas beyond Louisiana. This was the first to be known that he had the idea. Moses opened up a farm on the Red River in Louisiana which he wished to use as a resting place for any emigrants for Texas. Later, he had to abandon this particular idea as being on an inconvenient route.

Moses was born into a fine family and lost his parents while a youth. He went into business with his brother-in-law. In 1783, he opened a dry goods store in Philadelphia, and in the next year entered into a partnership to import dry goods from England. This was followed by a wholesale business. Austin opened a branch in Richmond and moved there to supervise this part of his affairs of commerce. A brother Stephen was involved in the partnership. Moses later made his Richmond operation independent and stayed there to run it. He married into a prominent merchant family of Philadelphia. He leased or purchased lead mines in southwestern Virginia, introducing himself into an industry which was to be paramount later. Austin then went into manufacturing of lead products. [3]

In Spanish Louisiana, Governor Baron Carondelet was eager to settle Americans in his province and emphasized Spanish liberality of land grants compared to American requirements for money per acre. Carondelet was interested in settling his area. He was well acquainted with Americans who came down the Mississippi to trade and overland from Kentucky and Tennessee. His idea of the Americans was expressed in a statement by Carondelet quoted by historian Eugene C. Barker.

He wrote that "a carbine and a little cornmeal in a sack is sufficient for an American to range the forests alone for a month. With his carbine, he kills wild cattle and deer for food, and protects himself from the savages. Having dampened the cornmeal, it serves in lieu of bread. He erects a house by laying some tree trunks across others in the form of a square and even a fort impregnable to savages by building a story crosswise above the ground floor. The cold does not frighten him, and when a family grows tired of one place, it moves to another, and establishes itself there with the same ease." [4]

Moses Austin settled in Spanish Missouri in John Adams' day with other Americans. He took the oath of allegiance and became a Spanish subject. Prospering, he was again in the United States when the Louisiana Purchase took place and was joined by many more Americans like the hunters described by Carondelet. He sent his son Stephen to school back in New England. The boy remained three years at Boston Academy for a good education. It was there that he met many preceptors and fellow students and left a good record of himself. Afterwards, he studied at Transylvania College in Lexington, Kentucky, and this ended his schooling. He returned to Missouri to serve in the territorial legislature. [5]

This brings us down to October of 1820 when Moses met with Stephen at Little Rock and proceeded on this overland journey to San Antonio to meet with officials there. Mexico was soon to become independent but it was a Spanish governor that he met in the Texas city. He had grand hopes of a liberal grant, but found hostility instead of the open arms of a Carondolet. There was a prejudice against Americans in San Antonio. He was viewed as a suspicious stranger, an intruder and threat. Ordered to leave immediately, Moses instead went to see the governor Antonio Martinez for an interview. [6]

Under questioning by Martinez, Austin said he was a Catholic and a former subject of the king of Spain. He showed the governor his passport of 1797. He wished to settle with his family and raise corn, cotton, and sugar. There were no goods to sell. Austin stated that "he was moved by the re-establishment liberal constitution in Spain to request permission to settle in the empire, and that he represented three hundred families who also desired to carry out the same object and thereby fulfill the King's intention at the time of the sale of Louisiana to allow his subjects to move to any part of his dominions."[7]

Martinez told Austin to leave the city and domains immediately. A disappointed Austin left the governor's house and crossed the public square. There he was uplifted by meeting an old friend, the Baron of Bastrop. The Baron was now a magistrate in San Antonio and asked about what Austin was doing there. Bastrop listened to his tale and with possession of "both sagacity to appreciate the project and influence to aid its author, volunteered to bring the proposal under official cognizance, with an expressed conviction that it would be favorably entertained."

Austin returned to his lodgings. That evening he was to beset by a fever and because he was too ill to travel, "the order for his immediate expulsion was suspended. In the course of a week, when recovering from an illness, he learned that his friend the Baron had interposed successfully with the Governor." Since Martinez did not have the authority to grant Austin's petition, he referred the matter to his superior at Monterey. Austin returned home with Bastrop's promise he would act as his agent. [8]

The journey back to the United States was troubled and life threatening. He traveled with men who robbed and deserted him and his African-American servant Richmond. This left the two alone on the prairie without assess to any settlement since even Nacogdoches had been deserted by the Spanish in 1819. There was nothing between San Antonio and Louisiana on the road but acorns and pecan nuts for a meager survival. This return lasted eight days as the two went forward as fast as they could go. The weather was harsh and the streams and rivers difficult to cross. Finally, they reached a farm near the Sabine. This trip wreaked his health and Moses soon died, leaving to his son, the plans he had undertaken. [9]

Virginians led by Jefferson and Monroe were very much interested in public education in their state. While private institutions and churches might provide education for grade school education, higher forms of learning were up to the state to provide for the required learning of citizens alert to what was happening in government so they could play a role in governing themselves. This lead, in 1818. to the establishment of a commission to explain the locale selection for the University of Virginia that Jefferson was working to build. Conservative limited government forces wanted to quash state supported education. They wanted it to be a private matter with private funding. However, Jefferson knew that government help was essential if a university was to be founded in Virginia. The pro-government group felt good education led to worker productivity. One writer suggested individual contribution by all citizens to support education. [10]

---

[1]Jackman, *American*, pp. 7-9.

[2]*Ibid.*, pp. 11-15, 18-23.

[3]Barker, Eugene C., *The Life of Stephen F. Austin: Founder of Texas, 1793-1836: A Chapter in the Western Movement of the Anglo-American People*, Austin TX: Texas State Historical Association, 1949, pp. 4-7, 23-24.

[4]*Ibid.*, pp. 7-8. Quote on p. 8.

[5]*Ibid.*, pp. 7-22.

[6]*Ibid.*, pp. 22-23; Kennedy, William, *Texas: The Rise, Progress, and Prospects of the Republic of Texas*, London: 1841 (1925 Rep of Molyneaux Craftsmen), pp. 304-305.

[7]Barker, *Austin*, p. 24.

[8]Kennedy, *Texas*, pp. 305-306. Quotes on p. 305.

[9]*Ibid.*, pp. 306-307.

[10]Hodges, Wiley E., "Pro-Governmentism in Virginia, 1789-1836: A Pragmatic Liberal Pattern in Political Heritage," *Journal of Politics*, XXV (May 1963), 335-336.

Chapter XXIII

RUFUS KING

On January 10, 1820, Andrew Stevenson submitted several resolutions on the subject of the Missouri Compromise to the Virginia House of Delegates. Stevenson strongly denied the right of Congress to impose upon Missouri any restrictions of slavery as a price of admission to the Union. Such actions were contrary to the Federal Constitution and the principles of the Louisiana cession treaty of 1803. He wanted the General Assembly of Virginia to support the people of Missouri in the matter.

He urged upon his fellow delegates instructions from them to their congressmen to oppose slavery restrictions and qualify Missouri for admission on their own terms. Both houses of the legislature approved them on February the first. Virginians protested the Jesse B. Thomas amendment to the Maine-Missouri bill of the third. This was the famous compromise of 1820. Stevenson was opposed to all compromise as was Adams on the other side. Both of his state's Senators and 17 of the 21 representatives voted against the Thomas amendment. Only eight other Senators voted against it and only fifteen more representatives voted negative. [1]

One of the last of the Federalists, Rufus King led the force of Senators who wished to exclude slavery from Missouri against odds with which they must have realized that they could not contend successfully. Still they set forth the mission and politics to act upon their principles. King's stand earned him praise on his side of the aisle and denouncement on the other. Abner Lacock, who had been a Senator from Pennsylvania wrote Monroe that King was not his usual prudent and correct nature, but had brought upon himself the decision to dissolve the Union before he would allow slave states to be established on the west side of the Mississippi.

King was born in 1755 in Scarborough, Maine, and had excepted slavery to be natural. His landed merchant father held at least six slaves for much of his life. When he died, he had only four slaves, a couple and their two children. Rufus did not inherit them; perhaps his mother did. They might have been freed when Massachusetts outlawed slavery in the state shortly upon the ending of the Revolutionary War. He attended Harvard College and was a legislator, a delegate to the Confederation Congress, and a member of the Constitutional Convention of 1787. He settled in New York City and was one of the first two senators from that state in 1789.

With the rise of anti-slavery in the state, he remained neutral. He married Mary Alsop, daughter of the rich John Alsop, who owned slaves at one time. He never saw the harshness of slavery as it existed in the South in general. His associates became abolitionists, but he remained neutral. Serving as minister to England for seven years, King formed a friendship with William Wilberforce, advocate of the end of the African slave trade, but he was not moved. He would rid the United States of African Americans and send them to be free in Africa. In keeping with this belief, he freed a young woman.

His views extended to prohibiting slavery in the Northwest, but he would not deny the South the legal right to hold property. In time, King came to vote against the recovery of escaped slaves, the domestic slave trade, and slavery in Arkansas. In February of 1819, he spoke twice against allowing slavery to exist in Missouri. He did not use moral arguments but stressed that slavery was harmful to free labor and that the representation clause in the Constitution gave too much power to the southern states. Slavery impaired the productivity and power of the American nation. The institution harmed a free people's attempts to protect America. King put his views in a pamphlet used to whipping sentiment against allowing slavery to exist in Missouri. The lines were drawn and the fat was in the fire.[2]

The congressmen of the Sixteenth Congress were not popular anywhere in the nation. People viewed the concern of Congress with slavery in Missouri, congressional pompous and redundant speeches, and lack of interest with the realities facing the people. The *American Watchman* of Wilmington, Delaware, noted the debate on the Missouri bill as wasteful. Congress would not expend much time on that issue and sacrifice other measures such as those for economic relief for millions of suffering families. All classes were suffering and congressmen were satisfying their own vanity by making long speeches.

On February 3, 1820, the editor of the New York *Columbian* wrote that it was distressed that most important business should give way to a heated discussion which would profit the citizens not. Opinion in many other papers were hostile to Congress and the anti-slavery and pro-slavery interest which it represented on the respective sides of the Mason-Dixon line. One newspaper wondered about the feasibility of having two congresses, one devoted to debating and the other one devoted to the business of the nation, which at this point was rescuing the nation from depression. A minority in the country crusaded for and against slavery, mostly in the newspapers. The Missourians were especially agitated, believing that slavery restriction was an eastern plot to restrict the growth of the west.[3]

In the midst of the Missouri debates, Henry Meigs of New York City presented a condemnation of slavery and the idea of paying slaveowners for freeing their slaves from public land sale moneys. New representative Daniel Pope Cook of Illinois believed this to be a good idea since slavery was a deplorable evil. There was a massive rejection from northern congressmen as well as southern congressmen and the Meigs resolution was tabled and shelved. The New Yorker tried again twice, but soon had to give up. In this idea the freed slaves would be colonized in Africa, with the land sales money from the west.

This idea was not a new one. That sympathetic Englishman, once governor of Massachusetts, Thomas Pownell had suggested in 1783 that the new nation compensate slaveowners for freed slaves. Elbridge Gerry took up the plan in 1790. Ten years later, George Thacher made the proposal and he was followed by others. Then in 1819, James Madison took up the idea, following Jefferson, who wanted to avoid the explosion he had just seen in the Missouri debates in 1820. Americans considered the idea in later years but only a small minority in the nation thought it was a good plan. It was not considered a viable solution even by abolitionists. Certainly the planters did not wish to give up their workforce to Africa, so this hope was not viable.[4]

On February 11, 1820, King made a two hour speech for the prohibition of slavery in Missouri. In reply, Smith of South Carolina made a three hours speech in favor of establishing slavery in Missouri. Lloyd of Maryland spoke against King for one hour. On the twelfth, William Pinckney of Maryland made such an able and impassioned defense of slavery, that he became known as the chief proslavery orator in the Senate. Four days passed before King made another anti-slavery speech. Six speakers responded. John Adams Dix of New York, later a secretary of the treasury, general, and governor thought King was a great old Roman senator wrapped in the quiet dignity of the rulers of the Romans and masters of an empire long ago master in the world. King said that all men were born free, and should have life, liberty, and freedom of pursuing happiness.[5]

On February 14, 1821, Adams wrote that the conduct of Monroe and his cabinet "has been, upon the whole, wise, honest and patriotic; and it has been blessed with good fortune for which I can never be sufficiently grateful. Its great trials are, however, reserved for its ensuing term of four years. Its dangers are in its internal divisions, which have hitherto disguised and concealed, and which a happy current of events has overborne. They are now becoming manifest and assuming a formidable aspect. May an overruling Providence turn them eventually to the welfare of the country and the improvement of public happiness and virtue!"[6]

Virginian James M. Garnett and others were deeply concerned about the 1820 debate in their institution as related to territory. New Yorker James Tallmadge's amendment to the Missouri bill to restrict or gradually end slavery in Missouri internally was going too far in the view of Southerners. Garnett was so alarmed that he wrote on February 10, 1820, "that it would seem as if all the devils incarnate, both in the Eastern and Northern states, are in league against us." Comfortless Southerners achieved a concert in the threat at hand. Alabamian Charles Tait declared that on May 20th that "hereafter the North can expect no act of liberality on this subject from the South. Touching on this matter the sword had been drawn in the scabbard and thrown away."[7]

On February 24, 1820, John Quincy Adams wrote in his diary about a conversation with Calhoun "on the slave question, pending in Congress. He said he did not think it would produce a dissolution of the Union, but if it should, the South would be for necessity compelled to form an alliance, offensive or defensive with Great Britain.

Adams said they would turn the South back to the colonial state. Calhoun replied that this was true "pretty much, but it would be forced upon them." The issue of slavery so vital to Southern hearts was already beginning to turn Calhoun from a nationalist to a sectionalist. His loyalty was changing. It was aggravated by the tariff of 1828, eight years away. The economic situation of the South in slavery and tariffs were shaping Calhoun in the twenties. His political ideas were to follow. He would soon be a state's rights man instead of a nationalist. This started in 1820.[8]

Benton took a small role in the controversy swirling around the admission of Missouri as a state. Being equally opposed to both slavery agitation and slavery extension, Thomas favored the compromise and forwarded the prohibition of any change within his state. He was the instigator of a cause in the Missouri constitution forbidding the legislature from interfering with slavery in the state. It would require a change in the constitution to meddle with the institution. This would virtually prevent any successful agitation from taking steps to protect the slavery he deemed necessary for his state, without doing anything to prevent expansion of the vile institution. His influence was being felt and his career was just beginning to take off.

A similar harsh clause forbade the emigration of free black people into Missouri and this caused a strong reaction. Benton was of the opinion that this violated the constitutional provision for the protection of all of the citizens of the country. The denial of the right of free travel was a error counter to the Constitution. When the Missouri constitution with this anti-emigration clause was placed before the Congress, a select committee approved, but the House rejected the resolution for admission by a vote of 79 in favor to 83 opposed. Favorable resolutions passed the Senate but failed in the House of Representatives. Proponents for admission agreed to a declaration by the state in its constitution to protect any rights under the constitution granted by the federal constitution and the rights of free African Americans were protected if they were citizens, which then excluded the mass. But which was voted favorably as an exceptional compromise. Missouri was soon admitted into the Union as a state.[9]

John Quincy Adams privately wrote his opinion on the Compromise. So it was on the third that he scored the compromise. It was now "a law for perpetuating slavery in Missouri, and perhaps in North America "which has been smuggled through both houses of Congress." The result of the controversy was what he expected as a politician. He blamed the Constitution because it "has sanctioned a dishonorable compromise with slavery. There is henceforth no remedy for it but a new organization of the Union, to effect which a concert of all the white States is indispensable. Whether that can ever be accomplished is doubtful. It is a contemplation not very credible to human nature that the cement of the common interest produced by slavery is stronger and more stolid than that of the unmingled freedom." The South won because it stuck together.[10]

On February 8, 1820, William Tecumseh Sherman was born to lawyer Charles R. Sherman and his wife. Charles had established the family at Lancaster, Ohio, in 1811, just in time for the dangers of being close to the western theater in the War of 1812. The Indians had still offered a possible force in Ohio, which might sweep the west clean, but fortunately they did not go on the offensive. Charles was a commissary in the American army and the Perry victory on Lake Erie and Harrison victory in Canada safeguarded the Americans in the west. Ohioans could rest easy. With peace, Charles R. Sherman could return to his law profession.

Early in the next decade, Sherman was appointed a supreme court judge for Ohio which lasted until his death in 1829. Sherman friends gave the family generous care and assistance. Thomas Ewing took William into his family as his own son and he continued his education at the local academy, studying Latin, Greek, and French. He worked many months on a surveying party for a canal. As soon as he was sixteen, Sherman entered West Point in which he graduated in 1840, sixth in the class of forty-three.[11]

Andrew Stevenson promoted a bill to authorize the visitors of the University of Virginia to borrow up to $60,000 from any bank, corporation, or person in the state. The money was to be used to construct buildings for the college. The bill was passed. One year later, the legislature authorized another loan of a like amount from the educational Literary Fund or another agency to finish the construction. Stevenson helped gain the passage. He was on the standing committee on schools and colleges, and was a devote of education. Stevenson had attended William and Mary College, but it is not known whether he graduated or not. At any rate as an educated lawyer, he knew the value of education and was eager to promote it in a state where education was not stressed for all but a comparatively few aristocrats.[12]

William Jenkins Worth was born in Hudson, New York, in 1794, a descendent of William Worth (1640-1724) of Nantucket. His mother was Abigail Jenkins of Albany. When the War of 1812 broke out, Worth joined as a private and rose rapidly in rank to become major and serve on the staff of Brigadier General Winfield Scott with whom he was good friends until their argument during the Mexican War. Wounded at the 1812 battle of Lundy Lane, Worth convalesced a year. Once recovered, he was assigned to the Second Infantry serving in New York state as an officer and a recruiter. In 1818, Worth married an Albany girl, Margaret Stafford. In March of 1820, Worth began a long tour as commandant of cadets, the second position at the Military Academy at West Point. He was there for eight years, and inaugurated high standards of military bearing and precision in drill. He was later to take charge of the Seminole War and helped suppressed the Nat Turner slave rebellion.[13]

When Salmon Portland Chase, in time Lincoln's secretary of the treasury, was born the year before Lincoln, he lived in a comfortable standard of existence. While, Abraham lost a mother early on, Salmon lost a father at age nine, plunging the family in poverty. However, Chase had good educational opportunities that Lincoln on the frontier did not have, and by doing without Mrs. Chase was able to see her son through three more years of schooling. Then, his Episcopal priest uncle Philander Chase offered to take care of twelve year old Salmon in Ohio. Salmon journeyed from New Hampshire to Ohio in the spring of 1820 with an older brother Alexander by stagecoach and steamer.

The boy did farm chores and helped with planting and sowing on the uncle's farm. He continued his classical education at an academy, which his cousin directed. Because his uncle was so domineering, harsh, and severe, Salmon was soon eager to leave. Philander could also be kind and a delightful companion and laid a basis in the boy for a Christian strength in the future. Then the bishop moved to become president of the new and struggling Cincinnati College and enrolled Salmon there in 1822. It was an easy college and he did two years work in one without a devotion to study. When Philander went to England to find funding to establish Kenyon College, Salmon returned home to the New Hampshire community where he was born.

Chase taught in Roxbury before being asked to resign when he hit a student on the head in the pedagogical method of strict discipline. Next, he studied at Royalton Academy in Vermont and was soon able to join the junior class of Dartmouth. In 1826, Chase graduated eighth in his class of thirty-six. Afterwards, he went to Washington DC to establish a school and finance legal studies. This plan failed when only one student showed up. Another schoolmaster gave Chase the boys in his school and kept the girls who were easily taught. Chase taught and disciplined the boys with a sharp temper. One of the boys was a son of Attorney General William Writ and the official started him on his legal education and established a son-father relationship with Chase. At the age of manhood, Chase was in love with Elizabeth Writ, but the Wirts returned to Baltimore. He thought Jackson was an ignorant, rash, and violent soldier and his conservative views compelled Chase to move back of Cincinnati. By this time, he took an interest in antislavery and helped a Quaker prepare a petition to Congress for gradual abolition of slavery.[14]

One of the most controversial of the immigrants who arrived on our shores was Dr. Thomas Cooper. He came in 1793 and was involved in many controversies until near his death in 1840. Thomas Jefferson came to his assistance in 1820, obtaining for Cooper a professorship at the University of Virginia. When Cooper's radical beliefs on the subjects of religion and politics proved too much for the state; there was a debate on academic freedom.

Jefferson wrote that the most serious of the enemies of the university he was founding at Charlottesville, Virginia, was not the existing College of William and Mary, but the priests of sects and their spells. They claimed that he was a monotheist and not a Trinitarian. "Although the various sects disagree upon other points, they maintain a united front against those who believe in a single God and only one God." He found the Presbyterians to be the most intolerant and loudest in the attack. They would light the fires of burnings in the New World as Calvin had against the poor Servetus.[15]

Savannah was beset with a great fire on the morning of January 11, 1820, which ruined many in the city. The once beautiful city was devastated. This information opened up the first issue of *The American Critic and General Review* on April 1, 1820. The editor went on to present an article on South America which continent the writer found astonishing. The people there were most happy and mostly independent, but unknown to the writer their problems were just beginning. He noted the caution of the American government in recognition for them because it would have led the United States to war with Spain. Americans had been apathetic for this reason. However, the mass of the

American people had the most generous sentiment for the people and their struggle. Hispanic Americans realized all of this according to the anonymous writer.[16]

With presidential ambitions showing, Clay expressed an interest in being the vice-presidential nominee on Monroe's second ticket. When he was told it would not do to place him on the second half of the ticket, he became angry. This had an influence upon his criticism of the cautious foreign policy of Monroe. He was especially critical of the Spanish or Adams-Onis treaty. Clay wished to establish his own anti-Spanish policy.

Shortly, Clay was involved with the question of Missouri. His position was early one of compromise in order to mitigate sectional strife and preserve the Union. The Clay role in the First Missouri Compromise was not decisive, but during the Second Missouri Compromise of 1821, it was. While in 1820 he was not good enough in the party's view for the second position, in 1821 he was an important contender for the presidency.[17]

General Andrew Jackson was very popular in Mississippi. He was a military hero who was loved by his soldiers and the general populace. His officers and men had returned home after his campaign to talk of the great feats of their leader and his men. When westerners went to New Orleans, they visited the battleground of his great 1815 victory. At the site, they felt the rush of warm blood as they recollected the events that promoted Jackson's fame and America's glory. They were frontiersmen in Mississippi and delighted to take pride in one of their own. Jackson was a frontiersman and they found a common bond in there. He was a neighbor and had often been in the territory and the state. Having been in Natchez in 1790 for the first time of many and having married Rachel Donelson Robards in Greenville, he was almost a native son. He was a citizen of Tennessee to the north. Further, he held their views on Indian policy, all hating the Indian, and other issues close to the interests of the frontier.

Representative George Poindexter became an early supporter of Jackson in the national capital. In Congress, he spoke for Mississippi and Alabama in thanking Old Hickory publicly for protecting the new states from the Indians and driving them out of coveted lands. Shortly, the delegation from Mississippi unanimously supported the appointment of Jackson to negotiate more cessions of Choctaw territory to the settlers in their state. Senator Thomas Hill Williams wrote Jackson on March 19, 1819, that the people of his state believed that only he could convince the Choctaws.[18]

---

[1]Wayland, *Stevenson*, pp. 48-49.
[2]Ernst, Robert, "Rufus King, Slavery, and the Missouri Crisis," *The New-York Historical Society Quarterly*, XLVI No. 4 (October 1962), 357-368.
[3]Moore, *Missouri*, pp. 173-287.
[4]Fladeland, Betty L., "Compensated Emancipation: A Rejected Alternative," *Journal of Southern History*, XLII No. 2 (May 1976), 170-174, 176-186.
[5]Ernst, "Rufus King," 368-370.
[6]Lynch, *Fifty Years*, p. 274. Quote on p. 274.
[7]Heilder, David, *Pulling the Temple Down: The Fire-Eaters and the Destruction of the Union*, Mechanicsburg Pa: Stackpole, 1994, pp. 3-4. Quote on p. 4.
[8]Holst, *Calhoun*, pp. 73-75ff.
[9]Benton, *Thirty*, I, 8-10.

[10]Adams, *Memoirs*, V, 4. Quote on p. 4.

[11]Sherman, William Tecumseh, *Memoirs of Gen. W.T. Sherman, Written by Himself*, 4th ed., New York: Charles L. Webster, 1892, I, 11-17.

[12]Wayland, *Stevenson*, pp. 45-46.

[13]*Southwestern Historical Quarterly*, 1950, pp. 159-168; Holmes, *Ancestral Heads*, 1964, p. cclxxii.

[14]Blue, Frederick J., *Salmon P. Chase: A Life in Politics*, Kent, Ohio: Kent State University Press, 1987, pp. 1-13.

[15]Cousin, Norman ed., "'*In God We Trust': The Religious Beliefs and Ideas of the American Founding Fathers*, New York: Harper & Bros., 1958, pp. 131-133, 151, 155.

[16]*The American Critic and General Review*, April 1, 1820, pp. 1-8.

[17]Seger, R, II, *Register of the Kentucky Historical Society*, (1984), 7-8.

[18]Miles, Edwin Arthur, *Jacksonian Democracy in Mississippi*, Chapel Hill: University of North Carolina Press, 1930, Rep New York: Da Capo Press, 1970, pp. 3-6.

Chapter XXIV

SUMMER OF 1820

It was the fourth of July of 1820, in the small town of Little Satilla Neck, Georgia. The town was also called Hazzard's Neck and was a community ten miles due south of Brunswick, Georgia. Nearby was the plantation of Rural Felicity which was owned by Major John Hardee who had been a state senator from Camden County since 1808 and was the logical choice for the community's leadership of the festivities. As the president of the assemblage, he rose and made the initial toast. He rang out "Let the commerce of our country suffer its worst by a war than submit to further negotiations with the government of Spain." There were three guns and three cheers, and the toasting continued. Meanwhile, Hardee made his way though the populace and greeted his fellow planters and other he had known through the years. He was a tall and fat man, having the respect of the people.

The biographer of his son described his plantation as a comfortable home amid the giant cypress trees draped with Spanish moss. It was a wooden home of cypress or oak planking. There was a piazza or roofed porch on the northern and the southern side of the two storied house. From this point one could view the marshlands. There was a central breezeway which cooled the house. There was fine furniture inside dominated by a majestic grandfather clock at the first bend of the stairway.[1]

Dr. Jedidiah Morse was interested in missionary work among the Indians of the West for a Scotland missionary society and the Northern Missionary Society of New York State. He offered his services to the government of the United States and was accepted. He started by taking a tour to Green Bay. He started out in the summer of 1820. Going from New Haven for Michigan on an over one hundred day journey, he traveled two thirds of the time. Later in the summer of 1821, Morse went to New York, in upper Canada, to talk to Governor Sir Peregrine Maitland there about missions.

A review of the resulting book said that "it seems to be agreed, on all hands, that barbarous tribes have but a partial and imperfect right in the soil, that they cannot allege a prior occupancy of the forests and plains, which they do not in any civilized sense occupy. If this be so, a civilized company of emigrants have a right, to land and settle on a savage coast. It certainly had a right to do so, if as in most cases in our country, had a regular agreement and treaty with the natives, by which they transfer their rights, perfect or imperfect, to newcomers."

It was true that cutting down the forests would mean the extinction of the Indians. Besides the Indians were destroyed by liquor directly and indirectly. It poisoned his system and lead to quarrels and violence. European diseases had the result of killing the Indians in great numbers. He wrote that for their part the Indians had killed many whites, and the reviewer decided that this balanced things right. He further excused all of this that the Indians had possession of the land by the right of conquest on their part. He claimed that none of the tribes were aborigines. He did not say that Europeans were aboriginal in Europe either and nothing was said about the Golden Rule. That had been pretty well forgotten in Christianity since Jesus.

Morse wanted a change in the policy leading to the calamity. The step he envisioned was Christianizing the Indians. The reviewer expressed the idea that an Indian would have died anyway. Death was inevitable, to be followed by the birth of new generations. As if that made everything right and would not also apply to the whites. The reviewer also goes on to say that the two peoples could not co-exist with each other. Morse felt that at least they could go to Heaven to live forever after they died. The reviewer agreed with Morse. In the face of expected extinction, Morse felt that religion of what was left would be the right idea. The reviewer could see no future for the Indians except for them to be Christians. They could not be preserved among the whites. It was the idea of Christianizing them and then killing them. Meanwhile, forget Indians language, the native must learn English.[2]

Founder of the Missouri Fur Company, Manuel Lisa died on August 12, 1820, short of his half century mark. The competent Joshua Pilcher saw his successor, "a firmly wedded to the river as Lisa had been." In South Dakota, his men built a square stockade with a tower for a cannon. They named it Fort Recovery in commemoration of a rebound from a fifteen thousand dollars fire which several months before destroyed furs from this fort, Veteran trappers Robert Jones and Michael Immell led some other troopers to the mouth of the Yellowstone. They did not come into contact with the less than friendly Blackfeet but traded thirty packs of beaver from the Crow. Private enterprise was to be aided by the end of the government factory system in 1822, to the detriment of the Indians. There was a scramble for fur traders.[3]

An abolitionist magazine, *The African Intelligencer*, come out in July of 1820, to support the American Society for colonizing the Free People of Color of the United States. Judging from the contents of the periodical, the Society cooperated in providing information to the magazine. Indeed, in their prospectus, they stated that they made arrangements to insert colonization addresses, correspondence, and papers of general interest.

The editor wrote a discussion of the African continent. He stated that the inhabitants originated from the sons of Noah, a land was settled after the confusion of the tongues. Referring to the slave trade of African's western coast, the editor called it a detested commerce. For three centuries, this scourge of Europe and America had hurt the other continents scarcely less than Africa herself.

There were those who fought against slavery even at this date. Captain Trenchard of the U.S. warship *Cyane* cleared the coast of every slaver he could find in the spring of 1820. Since most of the ships had Spanish papers, he had to let them go. He did take off all Americans and manned four prizes he sent to New York City. However, one correspondent stated in a private of the notorious nature of the port which armed slavers. These ships go to Cuba to get their papers and carry forth with Spaniards, having a Spanish captain to trade in the human traffic. Next they go to Africa to trade their goods for slaves.

Communications from Africa were encouraging for the Colonization Society. Man killing diseases were little written about. Nothing was said about the dozens of re-capturing and much was written about the security and the welcoming Sherbo people. They wrote about the security they found. A lot was said about the needs of funds for the settlements. They were encouraged about the successes they found, but still funds were much needed. Evidently, they could not sustain themselves. American clergymen were asked to raise money from their congregations. Money was needed to give presents to the neighboring blacks from the settling African Americans, much as was being done from Americans to the Indians. The chief idea was for the blacks to settle on farms. The land was richer and produced a wide variety of fruits. The weather was comfortably warm.

An American agent wrote that it was necessary for the Society to obtain a footing on African shores. The poor African must be weaned away gradually. The articles of trade were palm oil, rice, ivory, cam wood, bee's wax, honey, gold-dust, and leopard skins. The society would have few whites by deliberation. They would need for starters to go to Sierra Leon to buy rum, tobacco, and trade-gun for the use of natives. Indeed, this reminds one of events in early American colonial history. This was the first and only issue. [4]

New Hampshire's retired governor was the only elector to vote against Monroe. William Plumer, Sr., was a long time political leader of his state and governor from 1812 to 1813 and 1816 to 1819 as a Republican. However, he began his political career as a Federalist and only left when the Federalists took a strong stand against Jefferson's foreign policy. Ill health forced his retirement in 1819. On February 7, 1819, he resolved never to return to politics unless the state of public affairs demanded this. His only diversion from that was when he allowed himself to be placed at the head of the electoral ticket for the presidential selection process. Plumer could not deny his party this simple service. The leading Republican newspaper in the state noted that universal sentiment in the state would dictate that its electors vote for Monroe and Tompkins. No one could be so degenerate as to vote for anyone else. No one would forget his national benefactors, Monroe and Tompkins.

Plumer, however, had for the past two years a negative view of Monroe's presidential performance and also that of his Congress. In the winter of 1818, Plumer compared the national legislature to "a rich young heir, who not having experienced the difficulty of acquiring wealth, dissipates the estate rather than improves it." Still, he hoped "a prospect of want will produce reform" and that they would no longer consider a public debt a blessing, but an evil which ought to be discharged as soon as possible." Soon, Congress met the problem, not by reform, but by authorizing treasury notes to raise money to meet the annual deficit. He was critical of this move. Then Monroe gave a message to Congress in which he ignored the issue of providing ways and means of meeting the deficit. Again, Plumer made his views known. He was not alone and on December 28,, 1819, his son wrote that "not a day passes, in which some abuse is not detected and some attacks made upon the administration."

Politicians and others were even more critical of Vice-President Daniel D. Tompkins. Fourteen electoral votes were soon cast against him. The complaint was that he did not attend the Senate (most of the time), being intoxicated on occasion when he did show up, and being more interested in New York politics than national affairs. Webster was a leader in the opposition to Tompkins. He decided to rally around John Quincy Adams for the second position. Since Jeremiah Mason was a good friend of Plumer's, Webster sent him to sound out the ex-governor on the matter in mid-November of 1820.

Those opposed to Tompkins did not expect to oust the vice-president, but Plumer wished to prepare Adams for the presidency in 1824, and he made this idea known to the secretary of state. Adams was opposed and said he wished for both Monroe and Tompkins to be re-elected unanimously. His idealism showed through in this position, but practically, John Quincy Adams did not want to alienate Tompkins' home state New York. The letters on Adam's opposition did not reach Plumer before he left for the state capital to vote. There he told the other New Hampshire electors of his decision to vote for Adams instead of Monroe to soften the blow. Plumer did not try to influence their votes, nor did they try to change his plan. On the next day, he voted for Adams and Richard Rush. The act occasioned little press comment. [5]

Because American literary works were so despised, often with good reason, and because the readers and other citizens of the United States thought British writers were the models and benefactors for and of Americans, there was no great American literature which was established before James Fenimore Cooper wrote his first successful novel. Cooper himself followed the British models for his first novel, published in New York on November 10, 1820, and entitled *Precaution*. The novel of parents and the marrying off of their daughters in the manner of Jane Austen, was an anonymous publication with the inference that it was written by an Englishman or woman. English reviewers were favorable because it was so like their usual publications of fiction. This gave Cooper, who was working on a second: *The Spy*. Writers in the early nineteenth century were careless writers who did not polish their works. A manuscript was a finished project and not a draft for a thorough rewriting. Coming out at the end of December of 1821, *The Spy* was an immediate success. This was an American book in the manner of Scott, a skillful adventure story.

The new writer was an well educated man with youthful naval experience and an inheritance and marriage which gave him great advantages in the America of the early Republic. He was a man of decided opinions with a number of contradictions. A true American liberal, he could and did espouse views which were not liberal but determined by bias as a member of the upper class. For instance, Cooper was to take the side of the New York landlords in the Anti-Rent War later in the century. No reformer, he was influenced by his class membership. His father, William, was a land developer and leader in upper-state New York, whose direction of his rural countryside at Otsego was manorial in character and molded James' views and life. He saw the manorial landlords as a group of distinguished individuals who would protect society.

William Cooper married an heiress and founded a settlement on the southern shore of Otsego Lake called by him Cooperstown. He sold the land in portions to settlers who desired to own their own farms and in time served them as a judge and congressman. Interested in mutual benefits, the men built roads and bridges. A Federalist, he once put a veteran in irons for circulating petitions attacking the Alien and Sedition laws which soon did irreparable harm to the Federalist party in the state. Born a Quaker, he eventually left that society. In 1803, William sent his son James to Yale, but James was expelled for mischief in his junior year. The judge sent his son James to sea for training to enter the navy. William died almost two years after his son became a midshipman. With an inheritance, James left the navy and married Susan Augusta De Lancey of the political family of De Lancey of New York City, a royalist family which returned after the Revolutionary War to live on a family estate. [6]

The author of *The Spy* set the place, one of the little valleys of Westchester (outside of New York City), and the time, the close of the year of 1780, in his first sentence. Interest was riveted in mention of a solitary traveler pursuing his way and the approach of a violent storm with the traveler seeking shelter. "Cooper whits the interest, discusses themes and background, and whits the appetite for the reader to discover who the man was and what role he played in the conflict of loyalties which bedeviled the people of the neutral ground. The stranger stopped at a dwelling which he learned was that of Harvey Birch who was never at home. Directed to the Wharton's better lodging, the horseman goes there, giving his name as Harper. The reader is introduced to the Whartons, who are divided in politics and loyalties. Center stage is left to the Whartons joined by Birch with his peddler goods and news of military events carefully given. The day was over."

On the following day, American cavalrymen came searching for Birch and Harper. Their captain claimed that Harvey Birch was a spy for King George III. They soon caught him, but with the aid of a mysterious woman, he escaped. Throughout the novel, Birch appears suddenly and without fanfare. His most moving appearance was while his father was on the deathbed. With this, the reader begins to sympathize with peddler although the reader has read Harvey Birth was a spy in the pay of the king's general in New York City. This sympathy must grow with his treatment by the Skinners, bandits living on the troubled conflict. They burnt the house and took the spy to the American major. More adventures are related, which warrants reading.

There is plenty of action and many dangerous escapes. Harvey Birch is always showing up for various rescues and troubles, a man of disguises and nerve. Others are endangered by the marauding Skinners, who also show up at sudden moments. There is readable excitement and strange turns of events. Cooper's dialogues are excellent and character is defined and personality expressed. The characters are many and there is still unity in time and place.

The author gives the spy Birch an exciting life, a sad life, and the most interesting and sad events involved him. He is the most interesting character, but the life of the Whartons play a major role in this novel. Cooper handles them well and produced a work which transcends the ages. This then is literature and it deserves its popularity. He excels in description as well as plot and dialogue and the readers of 1820 promoted a success, which made possible a long line of works. [7]

Benton wrote of this period that "distress was the cry of the day; relief the general demand. State legislatures were occupied in devising measures of local relief; Congress in granting it to national debtors. Among these was the great and prominent class of the public land purchasers. The credit system then prevailed, and the debt to the government had accumulated to twenty-three millions of dollars--a large sum in itself, but enormous when considered in reference to the payers, only a small proportion of the population, and they chiefly the inhabitants of the new States and territories, whose resources were few. Their situation was deplorable." [8]

When it became obvious that there needed to be a treaty with the United States giving over Florida to the Americans, Fernando of Spain decided to solve the problem of the demands of certain Spanish grandees to favored from the throne. He gave land grants in Florida to them, in the hopes that the Americans would honor them after annexation. His subject grandees Ferdinando de la Maza Arredondo did not rest his grant on hopes alone, but acted to benefit from that granted land.

He sold Moses Levy a tract and the enterprising Levy hired two Americans in Florida, Edward W. Wanton and Horatio S. Dexter to fund a colony. These two men were picked because they were friendly and friends with the Alachus Indians in whose territory the land was located. In November of 1820, the two established a colony, and founded the town of Micanopy, named after the head chief of tribe, the first in the interior of Florida which was not near the abundant waterways of that then territory. This settlement was in the center of fine limestone land in the future state. [9]

The Missouri Compromise was a reprieve. Thoughtful men such as Thomas Jefferson and John Quincy Adams believed it to be temporary. The issue of slavery was not resolved by this agreement. It festered like an unhealed wound. To Jefferson the settlement was like a fire bell in the night. There would continue to be a struggle, breaking out from time to time. It would change history and effect the young Lincoln and John Q. Adams and radically alter their lives. To Adams the compromise was a mere preamble. He saw that it would turn out to be a tragic volume.

There appeared at this time in Ohio at Mount Pleasant an irregular newspaper entitled *The Genius of Universal Emancipation* which preached against slavery. Its editor was a saddle-maker by the name Benjamin Lundy. Born of Quaker parentage at Hardwick, New Jersey, on January 4, 1789, months before George Washington became president, young Ben worked on his father's farm. From 1808 to 1812, he was apprenticed to a Wheeling, Virginia, saddler. One of the businesses of this later West Virginia town was an interstate slave trade. He decided that slavery was wrong and decided to devote his life to abolition. Married, Lundy took his wife to a town in Ohio, where he called on the people to found an anti-slavery organization. The Union Humane Society lasted a short while with little accomplished.

Life is a hard place. Lundy found it so and had to take on saddle making jobs while he tried to raise subscriptions. He had trouble finding printers because some were fearful of taking on the newspaper printing job since its subject matter angered so many people. Abolitionists were in a small minority at the time. In 1821, he lived for while in Tennessee where the Tennessee Manumission Society printed the newspaper. Although he did not rouse up dangerous hostility in that slave state, Lundy moved to Baltimore, where he felt he would make a bigger impact and could get more subscribers in that mountain village in the South. In Baltimore in 1824, he was so successful that he could support the family in comfort with profits from the crusading *Genius*. His object was to convince Southerners to abolish slavery because it was unprofitable and inefficient. Lundy had little impact on the slaveowners who controlled state governments in the South. He was more successful in raising national conscienceless about slavery and his belief that African Americans should be free, educated, and have political and economic rights so essential for their well-being. [10]

In New York state Clinton was faced with a weakening of his newspaper support. The Bucktail papers were winning subscriber circulation. An able editor Thurlow Weed went out of business with his Clinton paper so weak was the opportunity. Weed was offered a Bucktail press, but he turned down this idea. He bought and published the *Manlius Republican*, but competition soon forced him out because Bucktail presses sprung up around the state. He had problems with his powerful opponents and "a Bucktail victory deprived him of the sheriff's patronage, which had been secured through his continued support of Clinton." [11]

---

[1]Hughes, Nathaniel Cheairs, Jr., *General William J. Hardee: Old Reliable*, Louisiana State University Press, 1965, Wilmington, NC: Broadfoot Publishing, 1987, rep. pp. 3-4.

[2]*North American Review*, XVI, 30-45.

[3]Lavender, *Bent's Fort*, pp. 29-30. Quote on p. 29.

[4]*The African Intelligencer*, I, No. 1 (July 1820), 1-32.

[5]Turner, Lynn W., "The Electoral Vote against Monroe in 1820. An American Legend," *Mississippi Valley Historical Review*, XLII (September 1955), pp. 251-263. Quotes on pp. 253, 254.

[6]Grossman, James, *James Fenimore Cooper*, William Sloane Associates, 1949, pp. 5-24.

[7]Cooper, James Fenimore, *The Spy*, various editions, *passim*.

[8]Benton, *Thirty*, I, 11-12. Quote on pp. 11-12.

[9]Mahon, *History*, p. 33.

[10]Lacy, Dan, *The Abolitionists*, New York: McGraw Hill, 1978, pp. 12-17.

[11]Van Deusen, Glyndon G., *Thurlow Weed: Wizard of the Lobby*, Boston: Little, Brown, 1947, pp. 16-20. Quote on p. 20.

Chapter XXV

ELECTION TIME

About ten years after the American Declaration of Independence, Joseph Bays was born to Scots-Irish noncomformist parents in North Carolina. A few years later, in 1794, his family moved to Kentucky. Growing up in that new state, young Joe met Daniel Boone and learned the tales of that wild frontier. He also learned woodlore and how to survive in the wilderness. His mother taught him to read and write. He memorized the Bible and turned early to preaching. At age sixteen, he led in public worship and preached. Jefferson was then president. His father died and Joseph moved to Missouri. At eighteen, he married Roseina Wicher. His brothers John, Peter, and Isaac went with him, while his mother and her triplet brothers, Shadrach, Meshach, and Abednego remained behind in Kentucky, which was increasing in population and culture. Missouri satisfied Joseph for a time.

In Missouri, he met Moses Austin and was enthusiastic about Moses' colonization ideas for Texas. He also met adventurers from filibustering expeditions west of the Sabine during 1818 and 1819. Then in 1820, before Moses had set out for Mexico, he went with thirty-two families heading for Texas. They traveled through Arkansas into Louisiana, a mountainous journey. On June 30, 1820, they reached Pendleton's Ferry, where they waited for word from Austin. Meanwhile, he preached. In Texas about eighteen miles from San Augustine Mission lived Joseph Hinds and family in a large two-story home. Hinds invited Joseph Bays to visit and preach. This he did until some Texans opposed it. This was the first record of Baptist services on Texas soil. [1]

Westward expansion was not only going to Texas by dribbles, but Oregon was beginning to get interesting. Thomas Hart Benton saw great possibilities in Oregon for the United States. In 1818, he was a practicing attorney in St. Louis and wrote that the way to India for American trade would prove to be by way of the Missouri and Columbia Rivers. A great entreport would rise out of the soil at the mouth of the Columbia River. In 1820, he was in Congress and worked with John Floyd of Virginia to insure that Oregon belong to the United States. Both men expected great results for trade and settlement in Oregon.

Interested in steamboats, they dreamed of the steamboats plying the Missouri and Columbia Rivers with a canal between them. Most Americans laughed at their dreams and said communications never could be established over the expanse of the continent. Easterners had other plans. They wanted to establish the Indians across mid-America in perpetuity. Among those supporting an Indian frontier were James Monroe, John C. Calhoun, John Quincy Adams, and Andrew Jackson. [2]

Some of the Astor partners knew Representative John Floyd of Virginia in the national capital. They talked about Oregon and the adventurers of the fur trappers. Floyd listened to them eagerly and decided the country would be a valuable acquisition for the United States. He knew of the trip of Lewis and Clark and envisioned that someday Americans would develop to reach the shores of the Pacific and settle the Oregon country. Then on December 20, 1820, he stated in Congress his interest in the situation of settlements in that country on the Pacific Ocean and asked about the expediency of occupying the Columbia River.

This did not arouse much interest but one month later as a committeeman, he made a report stating American rights west of the Rockies. Many months later, he introduced a bill on the subject and soon had a debate going. His bill which was not passed was a bill to establish an American territorial government in Oregon. He was ahead of his times. Floyd said that the Americans should have the fur trade that was mostly in British hands. There needed to be a safe port for American whalers. Indeed Oregon should be American. The representative did not go beyond this in order not to be considered foolish. An Oregon colony would help the China trade.

Other people wanted an American fort there and Bailies of Massachusetts spoke of a canal between oceans which would bind the eastern coast to Oregon. Practical Tracy of New York spoke; there was no need for such a colony. Floyd and Bailie could not prove their contentions. People on the two coasts were too far apart to create one nation. There were natural limits and deserts and mountains would intervene. Tracy soon had 100 votes to Floyd's 61 and the bill failed. The ball was carried forward by Benton of Missouri in succeeding years. [3]

The Indians of Indiana were being pushed back treaty by treaty. The natives had three choices: they could retreat, fight, or become like the white man and joined the pioneer society. A resistance of battle was doomed so that it boiled down to two viable solutions. The Indians were divided, some were for moving further west which would mean fighting anyway. This choice would lead to conflict with Indians in those lands they would move to. Some were for trying to join the white society. Those who felt this way flocked to the white missions. There were missionaries who were eager to convert the Indians to Christianity and culture. In one case, Kentucky Baptist Isaac McCoy had twenty students in his Fort Wayne mission school in 1820. But preachers had a way of alienating the redman. Instead of a mass conversion of the tribes, McCoy and others had to settle for persuading only a part, a minority of the Indians.

Most of the natives did not want the white religion. They wished to have the material things such as superior cloth, blankets, hats, combs, ribbons, and cookware. The Indians did not want to farm. They looked not to the Anglo-Americans but the French fur trader as a model. And the most successful accultural Indian was the half-breed Jean-Baptiste Richardville who survived by outsmarting the white man and gaining private land for his kin. They adapted. Richardville prospered until he was rich by the then standards. [4]

Simmering trouble broke out in an incident between Osage and Cherokee on the Arkansas frontier. In February of 1820, a party of Osage hunters came across three Cherokees whom they robbed and killed. When the Cherokees wanted to go to war against the Osage tribe, Reuben Lewis, the Cherokee agent asked them to wait until the U.S. government had been informed of the incident. They would not do so, but they would await the notification of Governor James Miller of Arkansas with reluctance. Lewis set out to see Miller whom he found upriver. The two officials talked. The governor said he would meet with the Cherokees on April 20th, which would give them time to be assembled.

Mlller told the assembled Indians that the murders might been the acts of some unruly bad men without official sanction. He expected that the Osage nation would be willing to give up the murderers to satisfy the demands of the Cherokees. War would be "attended with distress and if the Osages were willing to do them justice without war it would be much better for both parties than to engage in it." Miller told the Cherokees that if they would wait, he would demand the murderers. Should the Osage chiefs not give them up, they would be free to act. There was also the possibility the Osage had grievances.

Four Osage chiefs went with Miller, invested with power to act for the nation. They were received by the Osage who said that they would give up any of their men who killed the Cherokees. The men involved were bad men they said. But they had some grievances of their own. According to a peace treaty at St. Louis in 1818, the Cherokee had promised to give up prisoners of war and had since refused to do so. Confessing that this was so, the Cherokee said there were four prisoners not returned, but two were at school in Tennessee, one with the Old Nation, and one child who did not wish to go back. Miller said that these four would have to be returned before the Cherokee could have the murderers. Although the Cherokee wanted the murderers then, they had to set an exchange date on October the first. Stolen horses on both sides would have to be returned. Miller returned with them to find Tick-a-toke ready for war, but the governor made him and his Cherokees, Caddos, and Choctows return home. [5]

When the House met again on November 13, 1820, its first task was the election of a new speaker. There were several candidates, but the majority of the representatives settled upon John W. Taylor of New York. Since Taylor had led the abolitionist restrictors of slavery in Missouri, it was expected that he would support the movement against the admission of Missouri, but Taylor bent over backwards to be impartial, so much so that he gave advantage to the south. A Federalist from Philadelphia, John Sergeant, played the role of leader of the anti-slavery party.

While the Senate voted in favor of the admission of Missouri, the House voting on almost exact sectional lines to reject it. This last decision informed everyone that the

Missouri controversy was still alive and that Missouri might not be ever admitted to the Union. Hostility developed between northern and southern members and opposing congressmen would barely speak to one another. Compromise was rejected.

At this point, Henry Clay arranged a committee of twenty-three to confer with a Senate committee about the issue. Clay chose moderates and men who might waver. Then he presented the resolution to the two committees who would break the deadlock. The vote was favorable in both committees although the compromise was scant. With the support of these men, the compromise bill passed the House by a vote of 87 to 81. Victory was achieved by Clay's wise use of tactics. The Senate then voted 18 to 14 to admit Missouri on the basis of the compromise, Clay received the praises of many for the compromise which he affected. [6]

On September 5, 1820, at a meeting of the Oneida, New York, Medical Society, Anson Jones, future president of the Republic of Texas, passed his examinations for a career in medicine. Jones then took up his practice in Bainbridge, New York, amid the enthusiastic pride of his siblings. Since he was competing with an established practitioner of the profession, his patients were not many and he made little money. He left Bainbridge and went to Norwich to open up a drug store. His landlord of apprentice days cut short that opportunity by suing Jones for his past debts. The sheriff seized his goods, but they were bought by F.A. De Zeng and enabled him to settle with the plaintiff, but he still had debts to the loaners who had set him up in business.

He sought to travel to western Virginia to practice medicine, but at Philadelphia, he was stopped by a creditor who took away his watch and last dollar. He could not proceed further and took up medicine in Philadelphia which was unfortunate because the city on the Delaware had no need of physicians at that point in time. However, fate once again intervened. He did not receive enough patients, being lost in the city where he was unknown. He seized another opportunity by going to Caracas, Venezuela, where doctors of training were in great demand. There he was paid in cash and his opinions listened to by the people who came to see him and with whom he was associated.

Caracas was then a leading city, near the sea, of Great Columbia stretching from Ecuador to Venezuela, inclusive. The people had declared their independence in 1810, and lead by Simon Bolivar had achieved this after much hardship and hard marching in the mountains of northern South America. Bolivar had ranged wide over the region and established independence in Peru as well to meet San Martin of Argentina who had achieved the independence of Argentina in 1816 and defeated like Bolivar Spanish armies and obtaining San Martin's acquiescence with freeing Peru and Bolivia.

Feuds had erupted in Great Columbia but this did not bother Jones, whose services as a healer were in great demand. He doubtless met with the American fortune seekers who were in Caracas and when he got ahead, he sent some money to America with great confidence which was lacking when he had gone to Caracas many months before. He returned to Philadelphia to set up his practice there once again.

Jones had been born the thirteenth child near Great Barrington on January 20, 1798. Settled by the Dutch in 1730, it was now mostly English descended and was close to where New York, Massachusetts, and Connecticut met. His father was a tenant farmer and a tanner who never quite made it in the world and had to move from farm to farm to cultivate a difficult soil and subject to all the vissitudes of farming life in the early nineteenth century. He had a good education to the academy level and read a lot, but there was always work around the farms they were engaged in cultivating.

He read medicine with a physician. He made money to support himself and pay debts by teaching and clerking in a brother's store. His first exemplar was not sufficient to teach Jones what he wanted to know, but when he came under the tutelage of Dr. Amos Gould Hull, he began to blossom in education. Hull also sold mineral water, a hernial struss he invented, and practiced electricity and galvanizing operations. The short doctor was kind ands had much to teach Jones. Finally, he was able to take his examinations to get his license. [7]

At the Missouri constitutional convention, one of the major formers of that document was David Barton, a North Carolinian who was college educated at Greenville College when his county had been a part of Tennessee. He then migrated with two lawyer brothers and settled in St. Charles, Missouri, right before the War of 1812. During the war David served as an Indian ranger, and then moved to St. Louis by 1813. Barton became a territorial attorney general. In 1815, he was working as the first judge of the St. Louis circuit court. In 1818, he resigned to become a legislator and the house speaker. He was a very popular man. After the constitution was adopted, the legislature elected him United States senator. Supporting Clay, he went against instructions to support Jackson after Clay by urging lost popularity to Thomas Hart Benton, because of his effort for Adams. Anti-Jackson, Barton retired from the Senate in 1830 and served as a judge for a number of years. He died in his mid-fifties seven years later. [8]

Thurlow Weed, American journalist and political leader, was born on November 15, 1797, the eldest child of Joel and Mary Ells Weed in a log cabin near a turnpike between Cairo and Acre in Greene County, New York, with the first name of Edward. Within two years the Weeds moved to Catskill on the Hudson, where Joel went into the caring business. Joel was faced with hard luck and frequently found himself in debtor' prison.

Thurlow as he came to be called enjoyed a boyhood amidst shipyards and hills. He sometimes went with men with hunts for Captain Kidd's treasure and fought with his peers against the sons of the prosperous. He listened to veterans tell of Revolutionary War fights, serious and oftime permanent unlike the youthful fist fights. One day, he and others swamped out to an island in the Hudson to better watch the passage of the first steamship Catskill had seen and one day, he watched Sickel's puppet show for the sixpence that his father thought he could spare. His favorite spot was about the office of the *Catskill Recorder*.

After some small schooling, he took the job at eight years old worked as bellows blower at a tavern until it was sold at sheriff's sale. For two years, he was cabin boy on a river ship, but dizzy spells on the masts ended dreams of becoming a sailor. In the winter of 1808,, when Thurlow was eleven, the family moved further west to Cincinnatus in central New York. It was a primitive life in which Thrulow worked as a farm hand. He went to some schooling and learned the love of reading. When Thomas C. Fay set up the *Lynx* at Onondaga Valley in December of 1811, Thurlow became his apprentice. In 1812, he tried to enter the army, but he was too young. When Fay abandoned his paper and family, Weed became a part time soldier and at one point rose to quartermaster sergeant of the Fortieth Regiment, New York State Militia.

Weed boarded in Cooperstown and fell in love with sixteen year old Catherine Ostrander whom he later married on April 26, 1818. He then went east to Albany where he found work in two different newspapers and indulged a newly acquired fondness for the theater. When work slackened off Weed without a job drifted down to New York City when he formed a journeyman printer's job. He was happy in the city, but a job offer as foreman on the *Albany Register* was too good a turn in fortune to pass by. Editor Isreali W. Clark allowed him to write editorial paragraphs.

His future was foreshadowed when he lobbied for the incorporation of the New York Typographical Society. Unfortunately, the state senate cut out the union functions, leaving a benevolent society. Clark and his friends managed to arrange the purchase of the *Norwich Journal* for Weed to edit. It was renamed the *Republican Agriculturist* and joined its fortune to those of Governor Clinton, who made Weed a commissioner of deeds in good time. However, competition and lack of political support among the people of the area who were in the opposite camp forced Weed to sell out in early September of 1820. Hard times followed. At one time, Weed, his wife and daughter were forced to live on bread, butter, and water for eight days.

A fortunate turn came when Weed became printer and junior editor of the *Rochester Telegraph* at $400 a year under Everard Peck. It was the beginning of his long line of successful years. Peck recognized Weed's talents and within a month, Thurlow was in charge of editorials. He early sounded a note for the liberation of the Greeks, denounced the invasion of Spain, and stated that the Holy Alliance had designs upon American freedom. He wrote against drunkenness, gambling, debauchery, and slavery. Alarmed over the Bucktail now called Albany Regency party in power with Yates as governor and Van Buren as senator, Weed praised Clinton and hailed John Quincy Adams as the logical choice for president. Van Buren was castigated. A newspaper war ensued between Weed and the opposition press with Weed called a liar, whiskey guzzler, and vagrant. Weed pelted his opponents with stronger words.

The world of a child in the post War of 1812, America was a much different place than that of a century plus later United States. There were few toys, still fewer manufactured toys, and no commercial entertainment. However, it was a world of wonder and awe, of adventure and knowledge, and of play and chores. In most parts, boys could hunt and fish and girls and boys alike had tales told them by their elders. Books designed for children were not common, but there were interesting and edifying adult books to read including the Bible. Harriet Beecher, for instance, took delight in a filched book of *Arabian Nights* and the usual religious tracts and works. Like many of the pastoral class, books on Christianity were numerous. Also there was the most interesting world of nature and cats and dogs to play with. And there was music which is the delight of young and old alike. [9]

[1]Ferguson, Dan, "Forerunners of Baylor," *Southwestern Historical Review*, XLIX No. 1 (July 1945), 36-37.

[2]Russel, Robert R., *Improvement of Communication with the Pacific Coast as an Issue in American Politics, 1783-1864*, Cedar Rapids, IA.: The Torch Press, 1948, pp. 4-5.

[3]Schafer, Joseph, *A History of the Pacific Northwest*, New York: Macmillan, 1938, pp. 96-101.

[4]Clayton, Andrew R.L., *Frontier Indiana*, Bloomington: Indiana University Press, 1996, pp. 262-263.

[5]Carter, *Territorial*, pp. 191-193. Quote on pp. 192.

[6]Moore, *Missouri*, pp. 139-141, 144-160.

[7]Gambrell, Herbert, *Anson Jones: The Last President of Texas*, Garden City, N.Y.: Doubleday, 1948, pp. 3-13.

[8]Parriah, William E., "Barton, David," Lamar, *Reader's Encyclopedia,* p. 77.

[9]Wilson, Forrest, *Crusader*, 1941, pp. 51-54.

Chapter XXVI

IN THE WILDERNESS

On June 1, 1820, the Cass Expedition set forth from Point Peninsula soon after sunrise, but the way was made difficult by loose rocks peppering the floor of the lakes to a great distance. There were some hazardous departures and one canoe at least had to be repaired near Elm Point. Stopped there, the Indians with the expedition took off on orders to hunt and fish; two of them wounded bears and the fishermen caught no fish on the course of the Black River. This was twice as far as they thought, twelve miles instead of six miles. After 3:15 PM, the lake became calm and they shoved out to pass Black River at a point where the rocks disappeared and the bottom looked like stratified rock lined up horizontally. That night, they camped two miles beyond Point aux Barques at a sandy cove, twenty-five miles in a day.

Early the next morning, they left the cove towards the traverse of Saginaw Bay, refreshing themselves at Point aux Cheves. The banks were higher in this section of Lake Huron and the Indians reported there were marshes inland. Large chequer berries were found in limestone country. Schoolcraft picked up chalcedony quartz and bronze yellow hepatic iron ore with mercury globules on an island near the shore, which Douglass thought maybe foreign to the Island. They passed Whitestone Point with sand soil and evergreen trees. After a sixty mile trip on that day, they reached the mouth of Sables River and encamped there, getting some fresh sturgeon for supper from a small camp of Chippewas. Nearby was yellow and white pine tamaroc, the North American larch. It looks like a pine but it is not.

The travelers made quick time on the third from Sables River at sunrise to Little Sturgeon Bar near Middle Island and pass Thunder Bay, which they calculated at seventy miles, still in limestone country. On the way, they found an Indian altar or manitou with offering of tobacco, vermilion, and other gifts on it. That night at Little Sturgeon Bar, Schoolcraft and Douglass made copious collections and saw balsam trees. A storm forced them to find shelter. It rained for awhile. When it let up, they went a short distance further and then to seek shelter once again. On subsequent days, they reached Michilimackinac Island.

On the seventh, Douglass walked all over the island and wrote down his observations. The country was generally flat but the area on the hill of the fort was lifted by natural forces over the surrounding water with a table on top. It was clearly a natural fortress. There was a fort, Fort Michilimackinac and a town. The two men examined the geology of the area and wrote their findings up. On the island were some 200-300 cattle and three or four farms. The rest of the area was owned by the government. Supplies came inland from Ohio and beef was 10 cents a pound and flour less than five dollars per barrel. The water teamed in white fish and lake trout. A revenue cutter took them to nearby St. Martin's and found gypsum there. The flats were muddy with little vegetation.

On the ninth, he visited Captain Benjamin Kendrick who was brother-in-law to Franklin Pierce, later president. After collecting mineral specimens about Fort Holes on the tenth, Douglass rode around the island with Cass and Pierce. He found human bones in Scull Rock cave. He noted the various trees. Grain did not flourish on the island but its people grew potatoes and garden vegetables.

Douglass and others dined with Robert Stuart, a mid-thirties fur trader, then a partner of John Jacob Astor, head of the American Fur Company, for the Upper Great Lakes from 1820 to 1834. Born in Scotland, he early came to the United States and soon was Astor's partner. Operating out of Detroit, he gave a dinner for the chief members of the expedition. The entertainment was equal to that of New York or Philadelphia. Stuart was a good host. He prospered and in 1840-1841, he served as treasurer of the state of Michigan and went to Chicago later where he worked as secretary of the Michigan Canal Corporation. His ability showed throughout the days of his life.

Lieutenant John Sullivan Pierce gave them twenty men to serve as a guard through the ever-increasing wilds and they all set out on June 13, 1820. It was twelve miles to Goose Island and though the thousand islands to St. Vital's and then northward between the mainland and Drummond Island. They could still see Michillimackinac Island. They next followed the boat channel. St. Joseph Island was soon on the right (east). One of the canoes in these waters was damaged and had to be overhauled. At one point, there were attacked by swarms of mosquitoes attempting to land, reaching Sault St. Marie soon afterwards. There they visited Mrs. Charlotte Kallarwahide Ermontinger, the daughter of Chippawas chief Broken Tooth, and the Johnson family headed by half-breed Jane Johnson who at twenty years old had children, three in number. Because of hostile natives, being pro-British in part, the members of the expedition needed to be alert and careful of their safety. Arms were kept close by sleeping men and guards were prepared for the worse. [1]

On one afternoon, Douglass went to see the Grand Medicine Indian dance performed. This was done when any Indian became a member of the secret Grand Mediciner mystical society. He described it as follows: "The party, to the numbers of perhaps thirty, were in a wigwam uncovered at the top, and on the poles of which some bits of stored and other things, intended, as I was informed, by way of offering, were hung. Round the circle were Indian men and women, highly ornamented and painted and in the center two persons were holding a long kind of drum on which one of them beat while the other shook in the same measured time a kind of gourd shell rattle. Around them and in the circle, seven of eight persons were moving with a solemn measured step which however they sometime quickened to a run."

The rest of the group kept time in moving around the circle. There were "voices in a low murmuring tone sometimes swelling out with much emphasis. The old man who shook the gourd, in particular, uttered small animal sounds such as an ermine, otter, and weasel etc., and on occasion the squeaking of an animal was heard." He could not tell whether it came from a real animal, or was but an initiation of such. At times, the group became frenzied. "Their motions were quickened, their chanting more emphasized, and all their exertions redoubled while their eye balls seemed almost bursting from their sockets." There was people who from time to time fell and got up again, when directed. More fell down for a minute of two and got up, until half of the Indians were down at one time. In this manner the dance was done until its conclusion. [2]

Governor Cass counseled with the Indians on the morning of the sixteen of June, telling them of the American claims to the territory of Upper Michigan. It had been successively French, British, and American, by means of treaties and a change of allegiance. Now it was American, seconded by an Indian American treaty, that of Treaty of Greenville, after General Anthony Wayne had defeated them in the 1794 battle of Fallen Timbers. He warned them that now was the time to gain such rights as fishing at the Sault. When the solders arrived it would be too late, there would not be time enough for negotiations. They must act now. The Americans were not here to ask their permission to establish a post, because a post could justly and surely be established in American territory in their area. When they agreed to cede land he was instrumental to give them presents he had bought for this purpose. If they declined them, this would not change the matter of the fort and American sovereignty, but merely cancel out the benefits being promoted them for the agreement.

The Count, or Sassaba, an eccentric chief of the Chippewa Indian tribe, who was especially hostile, did most of the speaking. He and his kinsmen denied that they had given away any land to the French, but conceded that they were offered a position on Sugar Bush Island near the Little Rapid to Americans General William Hull. They did not, he said, want a fort because the guns would scare away the fish and lead to conflict when drunken braves might kill dogs or cattle and give way to disputes arriving out of this. Shingwakouse spoke up, replying to the Count, and the council was soon ended. Sassaba was very insolent, striking the ground with his hatchet and kicking the tobacco on the ground. He would scarcely offer his hand to the governor.

Walking out during the closing of the council, Douglass saw a British flag flying over the Count's wigwam and soon told Cass about it. The governor reacted strongly by ordering the troops under arms and setting forth with the expedition interpreter for the flag. The two men went alone, but the Indians, knowing something was up, gathered in front of their teepees to watch Cass pull down the British flag and throw it upon the ground. They would fire upon them, if they ever attempted such a thing again. Indian women and children withdrew for safety sake, but nothing happen to endanger anyone.

This consternation among the Indians led to another council meeting in which none of the Indians wore their parts of British uniforms so often worn. Apologizing, the natives agreed to the boundary of the United States claim. The flag incident closed with a victory for the Cass Expedition.

On June 17, 1820, in mid-morning, the men of the expedition began to transport their goods pass the rapids, pushing the loads upstream with poles between the islands. The return was engineered to keep the boats steady and avoid the rocks. Once done, the expedition went to the edge of Whitefish Bay, encamping near Pointaux Pins. Douglass noted the land had more productive soil than any land since the St. Clair near Detroit. Trees in the area were mainly elm, birch, sugar maple, pines, and cedars. Fruits of the region were wild plum and the red currant.

The next day, they left their camp on the British side and came within sight of the British Gros Cap and the American Point Iroquois, two bold capes of sloping land, some three hundred feet in height. Thunder and rain led the Americans to seek shelter on the American side of this passage early in the morning. By noon, the rain was passed and they were soon in the bay. At nightfall, they made camp near the mouth of the Shelldrake River, near Betsy River. There they found a French fur trader of the American Fur Company, one of William Morrison's men.

One day later, they were joined by Morrison himself, who gave them advice on the route saying that the Grand Portage was no longer used by the company. It would take six days overland from Sandy Lake to the Mississippi. Upon the base of this information, the leader of the Cass Expedition decided not to visit the Lake of the Woods since it would require an extra month which would extend them into colder weather. With this information in mind, they proceeded forth and Douglass noted the thin growth of evergreens and small birches, pink moccasin flowers, and black iron sand.

Upon their way once again on the twentieth, they had left behind a man and recovering him found him sick. He was carried abroad. Douglass wrote in his journal about the high sand bank and then the swampland with its dead pines. They passed the Grand Marais and the curious Grand Sables, reaching into the air with a slope of 40 degrees topped by a perpendicular rise. Next there was sandstone country and a windy storms, blowing down the governor's tent as they prepared to spend the night near Hurricane River and wind was to delay them on the next day for several hours.

They reached the perpendicular Pictured Rocks "which were colored a multitude of hues by a discharge of metallic matter from the fissures and natural joints." This was followed on the trip by a beautiful waterfall of a height of seventy feet into a smooth green lake as Lake Superior was. Further, there was a little bay with a sloping shore and a fine natural arch known loyally as the Doric Arch. It was to collapse in 1906, less than a century away. Already a magnificent earlier structure had ended existence. What was even greater was the cape of more Painted Rocks and a sublime height of dizzy height. More sights were to be seen. Douglass described what he had seen in his diary. He was clearly impressed.

Soon they found a place to encamp. They entered Grand Island Sound and then Murray Bay, providing an excellent harbor. The water was deep and was landlocked. They found some Chippewas nearby, who had come from Sandy Lake on the Mississippi and were going to Sault. They danced for their whiskey and tobacco. Although they recounted their wars, they asked Governor Cass to talk to the Sioux about a peace between Sioux and Chippawas.

At five o'clock on the morning of June 22, 1820, the Cass Expedition was underway, proceeding out of the sound. Up the shore, they passed an island now named Au Train Island, but Douglass named it Red Stone Island because of its bluffs of red sandstone. At eleven they stopped at Laughing Fish River, now named Laughing White Fish River, for a break and generally westward once again and then a short trip north to Presque Isle, a rocky bluff island made up an irregular mass of basalt trap, a dark colored volcanic rock and hornblend rock. It was connected by an isthmus of sandstone and graywacke. Nearly parallel with the shore, he found a ridge of high land, "at a distance of three or four miles from it, except only some spurs which came to the water's edge."[3]

Up early and well underway, they looked to cloudy skies and expected rain. Noting sandstone bluffs with alternative bays, Douglass thought the soil to be the best they had seen since Detroit. The bluffs were topped by sugar maple and the bays were generally surrounded by pines, and by other trees. Rain forced them to quit at four in the afternoon near Huron Woman's river and opposite Huron Woman's Islands. In the distance was seen Keweehaw Peninsula, closer than they had expected from previous information. Douglass wrote in his diary that they found an old Indian campground with many wigwams and a lot of drying fish. Close by was a recent Indian grave covered with bark. The Indians had deposited the handle of a war hacket, a rattle, a headbroad, and seven marks showing that he had distinguished himself in battle seven times.

On the twenty-fourth, they crossed Huron Bay, went around the point and crossed Keweenaw Bay. The wind was high and Dr. Wolcott, Forsyth, and Douglas had to join in the paddling in order to make progress. The canoe shipped water and Douglass wrote he was drenched by the time they reached the mouth of Portage River. They waited for another canoe. When the rest reached them the next morning, they began the portage of the peninsula.

A wide river of little current, the portage soon opened into a lake, going upstream across the peninsula and was marshy. Near its head, the voyagers carried their canoes and supplies across a short passage. They reach another small lake and a swamp land. Douglass found carnelian, chalcedony, prehnite, and what he believed to be zeolite among the pebbles of the subsequent shore. Because of the portage and the wind, they were delayed there and Douglass was able to collect flowers including the pitcher plant.

Westward across the southern shore of Lake Superior, they arrived at the mouth of the Ontonagon River and the site of a Chippawas village. The Indians saluted the American flag with shots and crossed the river to welcome them. A major objective of the Cass Expedition was to see Copper Rock and they persuaded four Chippewas to guide them there, up the river from the camp. Cass and a few scientist went, taking enough supplies with them to spend the night. Once the way up, they examined an Indian weir for sturgeon fishing, catching them with hooks, making a barrier on the river to keep them coming in on the red clay water where they could not otherwise be seen. From evidences seen on the bank, Douglass concluded that the river occasionally overflowed. The river then began to wind and when the time came, a camp was made.

On the next day, they struck their tents about four in the morning and found the river further upstream more rapid. Shortly, the governor's canoe "ran against a snag which tore a considerable hole in the bottom, and were obliged to lose about an hour in mending it." At the rapids, the walking party of ours started out with two soldiers and expedition Indians, leaving Cass and Mackay to await their return. The walk was hard with the pointman running through the rough country. They passed through a ravine which was dark. [4]

Undergrowth was almost suffocating and they were greatly fatigued. They reached their goal. Douglass was disappointed. The rock was much smaller than had been represented, but as noted by Douglass many travelers and scientists had cut off samples from the rock and it was made much smaller by this process. Still it was not an island nor was it on an island as some wrote. Indeed it was but "a large pebble on the main shore near the water." After viewing it for awhile, the members of the expedition proceed back to the base camp on the lake. [5]

At this point, a band of Indians came to visit and to dance with belts of wampum work, dressed mainly in leggings and breech cloths. Some wore American shirts. They were painted. They made music with their rattle and tambourines. Chanting and dancing, they made quite a show for the explorers. Douglass described the dance in his journals.

The Cass Expedition made about 50 miles on the first of July passing Iron River and reaching Porcupine Mountains, which were estimated at 1,000 feet high. They first saw them at a distance of 65 or 70 miles while back at the Keweenaw Peninsula. Douglass saw a formation of older red sandstone with a dip of 25 or 30 degrees at first and as they proceeded the degrees had been more pronounced. The shore was high, made up of rocky sandstone starts. Because of the slowness of the soldiers' canoe, they camped earlier and allowed them to catch up. The campsite was poor, but such was life.

They passed the first of the Porcupine mountains on the next days trip and saw plenty of interesting scenery along the river. Douglass noted the presence a waterfall of 70 to 89 feet, carrier pigeon of great number and easily killed with clubs. Montreal River flow marked a bend, and they were soon going northwest once again until they reached pass Bad River where it was more northward. They stopped on Madeline Island, then called St. Michael's Island, where Michael Cadote had his fur trading post. Cadote was back in Michilimackinac, but the natives were eager in their stores of silver and copper, very vague and unsatisfactory. They were saying what they thought the whites wanted to her and gain presents. Off again, they were at the South West Company's establishment on St. Louis River on the fifth of July.

Douglass found a marshy terrain on the lower St. Louis River, "but afterwards the flats on the shore became more elevated and dry and present the appearance or rich river bottoms." He saw wild roses and blue pea. Elm formed most of the forests with birch and hemlock on the highlands. At the establishment they were welcomed by either Pierre Cotte or Joseph Cotte. The trader had a fine field of potatoes, but he could not get other vegetable seeds, he complained. There was an Indian coffin on a frame, exposed to the air. Zebulon Montgomery Pike had seen them among the Osages over a decade earlier and Douglass had read his account of the trip.

Beginning on the sixth of July 1820, the expedition began its portage upriver. They first had to pack the baggage onto the crew and sixteen extra Indians hired for this work. These extra Indians showed a degree of strength which for the relatively soft Americans were marvelous. One in particular was strong. He would, Douglass wrote, "shoulder at a load tow kegs of bacon weighing not less than 125 pounds each and a bag of flour or corn nearly a hundred pounds more, and with this he would walk or rather trot off in style which would have fatigued me had I been perfectly unloaded." His mother also carried heavy loads, for instance, her large birch canoe of a size fit for an Indian family and their goods. Children too would carry as much as they could on these pottage, on back and in hand. [6]

The morning of the seventh of July was rainy, but they went ahead although they had to go through deep mud frequently. Douglass, himself, felt more able on this second day to carry his load with less fatigue than the previous day, despite the continued rain. He wrote that the Indian women outdid themselves in carrying things on this second day. And so the portage continued until they could launch their canoes downstream once again on fair water. They had seen falls, burnt forests, more rain, and rocky streams. Passing the Rapid au Glukey, short and brisk, Douglas noted the rich soil, the best seen thus far. Trees in the vicinity were the aspen, lind, bass, soft and sugar maple, elm, white and swamp ash, birch, and oak chiefly. There were also an occasional spruce, hemlock, and white pine. The undergrowth was made up of willow, alder, haze, chokecherry , white thorn, gooseberry, and many wild roses, which brightened up the countryside.

Taking leave of the St. Louis, which came from the north, they turned south to ascend the Savannah. There were many snags, but the water was sufficiently deep. There were swamps, along the way. Rain and mosquitoes plagued them but they were tired enough to considered unleavened bread to be a real luxury and a wet earth bed a solid comfort. Insects continued to plague them and were almost intolerable. They arrived at Sandy Lake once again, at the post of the fur company and were told they had made a uncommon progress from the Sault St. Marie. Their arrival surprised the factors and natives.

After councils with the Indians of Sandy Lake, they left on July 17, 1820, to ascend the Mississippi River for its headquarters. They made good progress despite the current. Mosquitoes plagued them along the way, one "actually pierced a glove of tolerably thick beaver leather." Passing Swan Creek, they noted its rapids and were soon encamped for the night. More rain slowed their start on the next morning. They passed a number of small brooks, Trout River, Prairie River, and sandy shores covered with pines. The route was generally westward. They reached the headquarters they sought and were happy to be then homeward bound. The way was quicker now. Stopping off at Sandy Lake once again, they were soon headed down river for Prairie du Chien, and there we shall leave them for their more familiar journey to civilization. [7]

---

[1]Jackman, *American*, pp. 22-36. See pp. 37-38.
[2]*Ibid.*, pp. 36-37. Quotes on p. 36.
[3]*Ibid.*, pp. 38-41, 44-51. Quote on p. 51.
[4]*Ibid.*, pp. 51, 53-59, 61. Quote on p. 57.
[5]*Ibid.*, p. 58. Quote on p. 58.
[6]*Ibid.*, pp. 62-71. Quote on p. 69, 71.
[7]*Ibid.*, pp. 71-78, 81-86. Quote on p. 81.

Chapter XXVII

JACKSON

When Jackson decided to accept the presidential offer for him to become governor of Florida, he had several reasons that lead him to accept. One of these was the chance to appoint friends and people, he respected, to offices under his governorship. However, when Monroe decided to make all of the appointments himself, Jackson felt he had received a body blow. High up in this regard was Captain Richard Keith Call, whom he wished to appoint. He had met him when Call was a third lieutenant in his army and had fought at Horse Shoe Bend. Call had recommended himself to Jackson since he had soldierly bearing and action. All of the men, of the company Call was in, had deserted in mass. Call was the only man who did not, who remained and continued to fight. From that point on, Jackson esteemed Call. As a captain, Call served again with Jackson, this time in the First Seminole War, and afterwards.

Call had come to Pensacola to be a lawyer after the province became an American territory and corresponded with Jackson regularly. Andrew and Rachael Jackson enjoyed his letters and the Jackson-Call friendship continued. He wanted to give Florida the benefit of Call's ability, but since Monroe made the appointments there was nothing he could do. Call was successful as an attorney and his Pensacola friends wanted him to run for the position of delegate to Congress for Florida. Call felt it was too early to undertake a political career. Jackson said Call made a good decision. When he was financial secure, it would be time to launch a political career. Had he served in the government and not have the funds afterwards, his retirement would find him deserted by his friends.

However, he was a brilliant lawyer and honors were to come his way. Monroe made him a militia brigadier general, which was Jackson's idea, and a councilman of Pensacola and of the annual legislative council in St. Augustine. During the summer of 1823, friends called upon him to run for Congress. He agreed. Although he had opposition and was not known in East Florida, he won a majority. A successful political career was launched. Because Florida was not yet a state, he did not have the vote. He worked hard and gained for Florida a number of appropriations for internal improvements of roads, bridges, canals, and light houses. He arranged for the building of an $100,000 navy yard and depot on the west coast.

He was re-elected a number of times. Although popular in Florida, Call had many enemies and was lacking in the necessary political abilities needed to be successful at home. Once he developed a dislike for someone, the rupture was permanent. He had the sponsorship of Jackson and did well. However, his hostility to Van Buren was later to end his political career. Meanwhile, he received help from John H. Eaton as well as Jackson. His initial success was due to this help. Without it, he might have failed Florida and been returned to a law office. His enemies included John Randolph of Virginia.

He was replaced by Colonel Joseph M. White in 1825. After this, he made money in real estate, was involved in politics, and served in Cuba as Jackson's special agent to obtain the Florida archives. He failed in this last and returned to Florida. His family died and he served in the Second Seminole War. He was unjustly accused of not coming to General Clinch's aid, which caused a controversy and severe censure and criticism. Later as commander and governor of Florida, he ran into great difficulties. [1]

The gospel on the frontier was often carried by circuit riding preachers. The Methodist ministry is an example of that promotion of the words of Jesus and the traditions of the church. One historian opens his account that the picture of the midwestern frontier was neither accurate nor complete "unless the itinerant Methodist preacher is placed in the immediate foreground. So ardent was the early preacher in the pursuit of his labor that he waited neither upon the manner nor the means of his going. His activity was as mobile as the fluctuating edge of the frontier." He preceded the wagon treks; he was a pioneer. Preachers "pushed into the new territory along with the hundreds of other restless spirits; he was on hand at every house raising, corn husking, and tree felling; he was present at the weddings, births, and deaths. Being one of the same class as those to whom he was to minister, he had, by his own nature and social status, a perfect understanding of pioneer habits, feelings, and prejudices."

Itinerant preachers had a large territory upon which he was turned loose. It was a long term work. It was a hard life, one of privation and difficulties. But there was generally a welcoming in every home and hovel. "His arrival was of high moment, and with genuine hospitality the host offered his coarse fare of wild meat, and cornbread or hominy. Yet occasionally from the more prosperous class the preacher met with a cold refusal." One preached asked for a stay at the house of a widow of means, only to be told that she entertained no cattle like he. The minister sang a song and she relented. He spent a rare comfortable night. They were always out in the weather in their long ranged travel.

Wherever there was a stationary lay preacher, the circuit rider would find cooperation. There were local meeting houses. There were occasional interruptions when a bear or wild turkey was chased. Rowdies sometimes tried to break up the sermons and classes. Preacher at times had to use force to bring order back to the meeting. Sometimes, the ministers served as law officers and doctors. Most often it was with herbal remedies. They could use the formula medicine created by Lorenzo Dow with claims for its grand cures. Dow was an itinerant minister.

They were not generally educated and had to rely upon a few sermons. Since they were on circuit, they could use sermons over and over again, each time to a new audience. The people were so eager for the religion of their past, that the preachers were successful and did much good. In 1821, Peter Cartwright could not point to a single literary man among the 280 preachers of the west. He had his temporary congregation sing, and he appealed to the emotions. Converts were many and Methodism thrived. There was no room in the circuit route for wives and the preachers remained bachelors for years. They could only marry when they retired. There was much hardship and sacrifice, but the circuit preachers were doing the Lord's work and that was their reward. They survived in the wilderness and did good. They had to be happy with that. [2]

Due to the primary needs of the frontiersman, the Western towns needed merchants to become established in their communities. Real estate promoters recognized this and often offered free town lots to any settler who would erect a store building. They expected to draw two or three merchants to assure the founding of their town. The stores would form a center, where farmers could get supplies. Hopefully these communities would attract doctors, lawyers, and teachers. In many cases the doctor in the frontier town would often open a drugstore selling glass and paint as well as drugs. Lawyers preferred to live in county seats and state capitals where there was more business and courts.

Many of the frontiersmen had varied interests. For instance, Ninian Edwards was not only a lawyer and farmer, but he was a real estate speculator, operated sawmills and gristmills, and owned and supervised five stores in Illinois and three in Missouri. He turned politician also. Edwards was a governor when Illinois was a territory and then when it was a state. Next, he served as United States senator.

As a general rule, merchants served more than one function. Their stock of retail goods and groceries freed the farmers from the need to be an artisans and to raise a large variety of food products and provide groceries and items such as salt that they could not provide on their own. Merchants brought to the West goods produced by specialists in the East and in Europe. Because of the lack of bankers on the frontier, merchants kept money on deposit from their customers. Most of the settlers did not have capital or money to be protected and for the majority, the merchants served as a barter center, where farmers could sell their produce and orators in exchange for products they could not produce. They also provided credit for farmers. The rates were high but although money short the farmers produced a surplus and could afford the interest and prices this engendered. Merchants shipped the farm crops to commission merchants and used the funds to pay their bills for goods sold or to be sold to the settlers.

Merchants generally had only a basic education, but they were well read. They usually dropped out of school early to clerk in a store. What education they had took, indeed was superior to modern day education in the basics, and they were good at the mercantile necessities of arithmetic, reading, writing, and penmanship. Among the goods, they stocked were books of classical subjects such as Herodotus and Josephus and more modern works such as those of Shakespeare, Byron, Cervantes, Scott, Fielding, Hume, Smollett, Milton, Defoe, and Bunyan. During the winters when people stayed home because of inclement weather, they had time to read. Also, they were postmasters and read newspaper and periodicals that came through their hands. There was time the year around to talk to their customers about what they learned, gathering prestige. Because of trips to Philadelphia for dry goods, they were well traveled. [3]

In his early years, Abe loved to read and took time out for it, whenever he could. He worked as a youth, but was considered lazy because he spent time reading. His father could bray to his neighbors that Abe was smart, but generally he despised learning and was concerned about his son's time spending in learning. However, he did not like to interfere. Thomas could belt Abraham at times, but Abe did not complain. Father and son were not close nor was their much understanding between them. Both men were good natured and liked people, but there was a gulf between them. Young Lincoln loved to talk and would spend much time telling jokes, stories, and deliver up what he had read. He was never boring and people loved to listen to the boy and adult. He did not join any church, but was well versed on the Bible and religion and attended church. His memory was almost perfect and loved to repeat the sermons almost verbatim after they got home. He liked to gather in groups, but was not overly friendly to girls. When fifteen, he began to make speeches. [4]

John Woods described the Americans in his book of life on the Illinois prairieland. He wrote that most Americans "are well acquainted with law, and fond of it on the most trifling occasions. I have known a law-suit brought for a piggin or pail, of the value of 25 cents. ... Another failing in their character is drunkenness; and they are extremely quarrelsome when intoxicated. Many of them are sometimes truly industrious, and at other times excessively idle. Numbers of them can turn their hands to many things, having been accustomed to do for themselves in small societies. They are a most determined set of republicans, well versed in politics, and thoroughly independent. A man who has only half a shirt, and without shoes and stockings, is as independent as the first man in the States; and interests himself in the choice of men to serve his country, as much as the highest man in it, and often from as pure motives,--the general good, without any private views of his own." [5]

In Kentucky, as in Tennessee, a central problem faced the people, especially the landowners. The panic was harming the state's economy. The planters needed relief from creditors. However, creditors wanted their money and opposed any relief. Creditors were in a minority so when election time came they were received less than one third of the votes for their candidates. There was a good turnout for this election of almost three-fourths of eligible voters. [6]

At Fond du Lac, Governor Lewis Cass had an African American interpreter between himself and the natives. That language specialist was George Bonga, who worked as a voyageur for the American Fur Company and had a Chippewa wife. After his stint for Cass in 1820, George became a prominent and wealthy independent trader noted for his tremendous size and strength as well as a gentleman and a man of ability doing what he did best.

George was half-Indian himself, the son of Pierre Bonga, who started as a servant of fur trader Alexander Henry. In his turn, Pierre was the son of Joas Bonga and of Marie

Jeanne, slaves belonging to Daniel Robertson, a British commandant on the frontier. George's mother was a Chippawa Indian maid when she married Pierre. The pair had George, Jack, and a daughter. Pierre was in charge of a fort in 1803 for a time, jointly with another man. There was a Bonga, most likely Pierre who was a principal trader living with the Chippawas. Later, George Bonga was an interpreter in a 1837 treaty negotiation at Fort Snelling. [7]

One New Yorker, the humanitarian John Pintard, a patriot of modest means, mentally alert and eager for the betterment of mankind, wrote his opinions in this paragraph to his daughter near New Orleans. She was married to a doctor. "I told you," he wrote, "I think that Master Samuel Bayard has gone to pass the winter with his Uncle Nicholas at Savanna. I received a very affectionate and descriptive letter from him depicting, in vivid colors, the first impression of southern manners and customs on the mind of a northern youth, which as you know by experience are not the most favorable. The contrast between freedom and slavery is shocking to one totally unaccustomed to consider and treat a Negro as inferior in the scale of creation; repugnant as these scenes are to his sensibility; still he applauds and justly, the planters for their liberal genuine hospitality. The Georgians are outrageous about the Missouri Compromise and impute everything, but justice and humanity, with conscious scruples of an outrageous violation of the national constitution, to us northerners, as tho' we were actuated by unworthy motives. In the justification of slavery they would extend the curse to every region of the United States, which God forbid." [8]

Josiah Quincy described Harvard University of 1820 in his 1883 book that "few realize that college life sixty years ago was just a year longer than it is now. Cambridge was not deserted during the vacation; while at present from July to October everybody is off and all the rooms are vacant. The students' apartment of my day were not so attractive that one would wish to linger in them. I cannot remember a single room which had carpet, curtain, or any pretense of ornament. In a few of them were hung some very poor prints, representing the four seasons, emblematic representations of the countries of Europe, and imaginative devices of a similar nature. Our light came from dipped candles, with very broad bases and gradually narrowing to the top. These required the constant use of snuffers."

The college furnished the fuel of wood, which had been cut from Maine land owned by Harvard. The wood was brought by the college sloop, the "Harvard." Authorities praised themselves for the wisdom of these transactions. "It was not until Dr. Bowditch, the great mathematician, was given a place in the government that this arrangement was quietly abandoned. This eminent gentlemen succeeded in demonstrating to his associates that it would be much cheaper for the college to buy wood from the dearest dealer than to cut it on its own lands and transport it in its own sloop. It is strange how long-established methods of obtaining the necessities of life will continue, when a little thought will show that better ones may be substituted."

After discussing the coming of anthracite coal to Harvard at another time, Quincy continued, writing that there were two college clubs which were limited to those with the highest scholarship. These were the Phi Beta Kappa and the Hasty Pudding Club. He gives the place of honor to the Medical Faculty Club, "a roaring burlesque upon learned bodies in general and the college government in particular. In this association was to be found some of the most excellent fooling that I have ever met. We had regular meetings, conducted with mock decorum, at each of which a pseudo professor delivered a lecture on some topic of medical interest." There were clubs in which the sole function was an occasional bacchanals of drinking. [9]

Around 1820, Baltimore and Philadelphia had the bulk of trade with the western territories and states because of migration patterns, connection, and geographic closeness. Industrially developed Philadelphia had the leadership in goods produced. Within twenty years, however, New York City had made great inroads on their markets and city merchants in the middle states feared that New York would gain a monopoly. Merchants in the city were receivers of a shift in population growth advantage. Upper Mississippi Valley territories and states developed in New York merchants had ties with that area and received goods from New York.

Investor attention swung to developing anthracite coal deposits in the Quaker city to the detriment of investments in wholesaling and production. Again New York City benefited. Because of the Erie Canal goods could be shipped more cheaply from the city to the northwest with it competitive edge. Freight rates dropped when the canal came into operation. Philadelphia responded with its own canals which protected trade with the West, but it lost some market shares close to New York City over the years. Because of the growth of Chicago and its waterway connection with Buffalo and New York City, the metropolis on the Hudson had another advantage. [10]

Billy Caldwell, born at Detroit around 1780 to an Irish colonel in the British Army and a Potawatomi chief's daughter, was educated as a Catholic. He was one of the Indians in the Old Northwest who were hostile to the Americans in the War of 1812, but came over to the America side after the death of Tecumseh at the Battle of the Thames where Billy claimed to have fought.

Caldwell became a trader and joined a large number of Potawatomi in adopting white man's way of life. Thomas G. Conway wrote about the next phrase of Billy's life: "About 1820, he made his home at Fort Dearborn, where he became known as a friend of the white people. Because he aided in preventing trouble between the whites the appellation Sauganash, which means Englishman. When the first local election was held in Chicago on August 7, 1826, Caldwell was elected justice of the peace. Although three-fourths of the voters were pure and mixed-blood Indians, this was a significant achievement of status vis-a-vis the white community because his victory indicated the indulgence of the latter."

He became an entrepreneur bidding for contracts and working with the whites for the removal of his Potawatomi Indians relatives. In 1829, he was a negotiator for the Treaty of Prairie du Chien and profited from the transaction. Afterwards, he remained at his village near Chicago. He helped keep the Indians in hand during the Black Hawk War of 1832. The Potawatomi from Indiana would not accept his leadership through in 1834.

Caldwell received additional annuity for his services in the Chicago treaty. In 1835, Caldwell went west and gained a mission for the Potawatomi near Council Bluffs. He gathered power in his hands and died on September 27, 1841. [11]

Edwin Forrest proved the ablest of Shakespearean actors and was especially prominent in roles the English playwright's tragedies. This Presbyterian actor was born on March 9, 1806. His father was from Scotland and his mother was American. The former worked for the United States Bank as a runner until his death. The boy early caught tuberculosis and was overprotected. He learned rhymes. Edwin amused the workmen of a brother's shop by youthful recitation. By this means he was introduced to the entertainment world. When ten years old, Edwin had to go to work, ending his schooling for the counting house. He wanted to become an actor and spent some of his worktime at the theater, and an indulgent employer told him that acting would be his ruin. He stayed at work only one year or so, turning to acting.

Since Edwin outshone his brothers and sisters at reciting, William introduced him to Alexander Wilson, a noted ornithologist, who was impressed and recommended Lemuel G. White, Philly elocutionist, to teach the boy speech in the hopes that he would become a preacher. Father William saw security for his son in that, and scrimped and saved that the boy would have lessons. Edwin's voice grew strong.

On November 17, 1820, he played his first important role as Young Norval. This was in his hometown and birthplace of Philadelphia at the Walnut Street Theatre. This early performance did not prove a success for him, but he tried all the harder, which effort was to bring great success. After all, he was only a boy and had not gained the seasoning of experience in acting. He continued acting and gradually got better and better. This required some traveling. Still he was not much of a success. At the time, he was most suited for low comedy. When an editor predicted great things for the youth, the editor was called a madman. His best role so far was as a blacked-up Othello in Louisville. Soon he entered the circus business as a tumbler and rider. This lasted for one year. Often he was laughed at. He endured. Forrest was definitely a fighter against the odds at which he was to win. [12]

[1]Martin, Sidney Walter, "Richard Keith Call, Florida Territorial Leader," *Florida Historical Quarterly*, 21 (1943), 332-351.

[2]Posey, Walter Brownlow, *The Development of Methodism in the Old Southwest, 1783-1824*, Tuscaloosa, Ala: Weatherford, 1933, pp. 35-47. Quote on pp. 35, 36.

[3]Atherton, Lewis E., *The Frontier Merchant in Mid-America*, Columbia, Mo: University of Missouri, 1971, pp. 15-19, 28-32.

[4]Beveridge, *Lincoln*, I, 65-83.

[5]Angle, p. 81. Quote on p. 81.

[6]Mathias, Frank F. and Shannon, Jasper B., "Gubernational Politics in Kentucky," *Register of the Kentucky Historical Society*, LXXXVIII No. 3 (Summer 1990), 245ff.

[7]Porter, Kenneth Wiggins, *The Negro on the American Frontier*, New York: Arno Press and The New York Times, 1971, pp. 142-144.

[8]Pintard, *Letters*, 352-353. Quote on pp. 352-353.

[9]Quincy, Josiah, *Figures of the Past*, 1883.

[10]Atherton, *Frontier*, 1971, pp. 80-85.

[11]Conway, Thomas C., "An Indiana Politician and Entrepreneur in the Old Northwest," *Old Northwest*, 1 (March 1975), pp. 51-61.
[12]Brown, Thomas Allston, *History of the American Stage,* New York: Dick & Fitzgerald, 1870, pp. 129-130.

Chapter XXVIII

SCOTT IN AMERICA

About this time, Scott came out with his very best and most famous novel *Ivanhoe*. This is greater unity of time and character. Its construction is tighter and its characters are fever drawn. It is historical fiction at its best, in which Scott is the most noteworthy of the genre. The work takes place in the time of Richard the Lion-hearted and he is one of the chief characters of the novel. This and others were to be widely read in America.

Shortly Scott published *Kenilworth*, a historical novel centered around the life of Robert Dudley, earl of Leicester, in court of England's Elizabeth I. The story has its basis in the numbers and traditions of time covered. The characters are well delineated, and it takes a while to learn who were the villains, so involved is the story in life-like character. Scott created a realistic setting and understanding of English events. The portrayal of Elizabeth is most real to life. Leicester is the chief character in the story and his rival is only sketched in. This is one of the better novels from the genius of Scotland's novelist.

Even better still, with greater action and a more sympathetic plot, *Old Mortality* is an adventure novel and love story. It takes place in the time of Charles II and William and Mary in the lowlands of Scotland which Scott so dearly loved. There was a happy ending and twisted plot like all of Scott's historical novels with the hero in deep trouble and on the wrong side of history. It is the tale of military action which provide the framework of the tale, although the characters are somewhat one-dimensionial. One of the lesser of his novels, *The Talisman* had an unknown Scotsman as hero and the Holy Land as a background and the Crusades as subject. Saladin and Richard I played a major role in the book when both were contending for Palestine. As in most of his novels, the hero makes a mistake that lands him in trouble. This work came out in 1825 with another novel of the Crusades, *The Betrothed*. [1]

In 1820, Adams and Calhoun discussed privately the issue of slavery. Calhoun recognized as just and noble the Northerner's idea that slavery was contrary to the Declaration of Independence and abusive. However, Calhoun attempted to enlighten Adams why slavery was socially necessary to the South. Since only blacks did domestic labor, a man who hired whites to work in his house would lose his character and reputation among fellow Southerners. The same would be case also if he hired white labor to help him with the farming. This guaranteed equality among whites. Calhoun said it was unlikely to end the Union. However if it did, Southern would have to ally themselves with the English. It was clear to Adams that the North would re-used force to resist this and to Calhoun that Northern force would turn Southern communities into military communes.[2]

English traveler W. Faux described in 1820, Clay as "a tall, thin, and not very muscular man; his gait is stately but swinging; and his countenance, while it indicates genius, denotes dissipation." Clay was known as an orator, but he lacked the finer points of oratory. The eloquence of the man flowed as a torrent, irregular and sometimes obstructed. Fire and vigor made up or lack of fluency and grace. His actions are not keyed to his speech but when "he speaks he is full of animation and earnestness; his face brightens, his eye beams with additional luster, and his whole figure indicates that he is entirely occupied with the subject on which his eloquence is employed." Clay's oratory is still most pleasing and is very convincing.

Clay was able to organize well with a quick mind which cut through obscure and complicated subject with ease. His mind was penetrating and acute. He had a fertile invention, good memory, and a fine and discerning judgment. Seldom at a loss "to amplify and embellished, he but rarely fails to do justice to the subject which has called forth his eloquence." The man was intellectually superior to his associates. [3]

It was time for change in Old Boston. Because of its growth, the old town meeting government was failing. In 1820, there was an amendment which passed with John Adams' vote for one to enable freemen in large towns and in cities to for representative governments to vote taxes and expenditures and pass other laws. Josh Quincy was accurate when he stated the old method and its results in large communities.

He wrote some time later about Boston when he stated the case for change. "When a town meeting was held on any exciting subject in Faneuil Hall those only who obtained places near the moderator could even hear the discussion. A few busy or interested individuals easily obtained the management of the most important affairs in an assembly in which the greatest number could have neither voice or hearing. When the subject was not generally exciting, town meetings were usually composed of the selectmen, the town officers and thirty or forty inhabitants. Those who thus came were for the most part, drawn to it from some official duty or private interest, which when performed or attained, they generally troubled themselves but little or none at all about the other business of the meeting."

In this way, it was said that the business of the town was run by a few with little say about the running of the city or a chance to judge upon the participants. The election of representatives besides the general selected remedied that. The freeman of Boston had more to say in their government after the change. This new structure was approved in a vote ratio of 2.7 to 2. in 1822. John Phillips was voted mayor and the mayoral-council form of government was instituted. He was a compromise choice and got the new government off to a good start.

But second mayor Josiah Quincy was the molder of Boston under the new government. A reformer, he gave the city clean streets for the first time. Mortality rates improved as a partial results of his move. He reorganized the fire and police services. Everything was kept quiet by no more than eighteen police and watchmen in service at any given hour. He had trees planted and a public garden created. There began at this time, a girls school which proved successful, but Quincy ended that. He preferred to have these girls in private schools since the parents of most of these girls could afford private schooling for their female children. It was his pleasure to pay host to Lafayette when he came to América for his triumphant visit, honored by all Americans in his old age. Rarely had so many Americans agreed upon any one thing as the cheers for the Frenchman who along with Washington rested well in the hearts of the American people during the Monroe administration. [4]

The premier intellectual in the United States during his age, Ralph Waldo Emerson, saw the light of day on May 25, 1803, in the parsonage of his father the Reverend William Emerson in Boston. The elder Emerson was away at the time. That morning he had listened to one of his colleagues give the Election Day sermon and had dinner with the governor of Massachusetts. When he got back home in the mid-afternoon, his wife Ruth presented him with his son. The parents named his after his maternal uncle Ralph, who was a supercargo of merchandise on a ship bound for China. One of William's ancestors was a Waldo family head. They had sought religious asylum in England and had come to America. Massachusetts' governor ate with them the next day.

Preacher Emerson was chaplain of the state senate and artillery company in Boston. His children were forbidden to play outside the fence of the parsonage and were brought up to recite passages from such great writers as Shakespeare, Milton, Pope, and Addison. Then on May 12, 1811, Waldo's father died. Besides the education he got at home, Emerson attended Boston Public Latin School. Although he did only passably satisfactory in school, Emerson showed talent as a poet. At age fourteen, he passed the entrance examinations and entered Harvard in the class of 1821. [5]

Emerson emphasized that all men had much in common. At the same time or throughout the centuries there were common thoughts and experiences. They had manifold ties with the dead and the living. The teacher noted that the present man can think what Plato thought or felt. Historians recorded the works of this common mind. There are seeds contained in mankind that have put forth in previous and present empires. Because of these sprouting ideas, changes can occur from time to time and he developed. What people have experienced, others have at will experienced before and after them. [6]

As can be observed in Emerson's work, his writing is a long series of pretty sentences with little fact and idea in them. This pleased the ears of his followers, but even in his day there was a critical view of his efforts. One commentator, devoted to Emersonian poetry, wrote that the line between his poetry and prose, which he so often traversed was faint, elusive, and indefinite. His friend Alcott noted that his works were analogical rather in logical. Critics accused Emerson of being inconsistent in his prose and poetry alike. Emerson's writing was " a disarrayed jumble of shining thoughts." [7]

Daniel Drake, American physician and educator-author, was born on October 20, 1785, in Plainfield, New Jersey. His family early moved west and in December of 1800, Daniel was apprenticed to Dr. William Goforth of Cincinnati from whom he gained a knowledge of medicine. At times, he slept under the counter of the apothecary shop. On August 1, 1805, Goforth gave Drake a certification which told the world that Drake was qualified to practice medicine. In October, Drake went on horseback to Philadelphia for formal lectures in the medical department of the University of Pennsylvania. The spring of 1806, found him back in Mayslick, Kentucky, and the spring of 1807 in Cincinnati to take over Goforth's practice.

A successful physician, Daniel played a role in community affairs, becoming a member of the first debating society, of a dramatic group, and chairman of the first committee which proposed a circulating library there. On December 20, 1807, he married Harriet Sisson, a beautiful and talented lady. He wrote an article on a Mayslick epidemic published in *The Philadelphia Medical and Physical Journal*, then a pamphlet on Cincinnati, printed in 1810. The pamphlet described the town and its environs and was so well received that he worked on a larger work on the Miami river valley of Ohio. It was published in 1816. After taking an doctor's program at the University of Pennsylvania, he got his MD on May 11, 1816, and was offered a professorship at Transylvanian University of Lexington, which he accepted.

In a controversy at Transylvania charges were made against Drake and he published a pamphlet answering them with great logic and success. Having resigned, Drake marched back to Cincinnati and in 1819 succeeded in having the Medical College of Ohio incorporated. Next, he had Cincinnati College incorporated In 1820, he opened his medical college and directed its affairs. He founded a hospital in 1821. Expelled from his college for an unknown reason, Drake returned to Transylvania University.

Drake defended Clay in 1825 and became a professor at Jefferson Medical College at Philadelphia. He was known as an able lecturer. In 1839, he went to Louisville Medical Institute where he taught for ten years. He traveled widely. In 1850, his *A Systematic Treatise, Historical, Ethnological, and Practical on the Principal Diseases of the Interior Valley of North America, as they appear in the Caucasian, African, Indian and Ewquimaux Varieties of its Population* was published. It was widely praised. He died in Cincinnati on November, 1852. In 1870, long after his descriptive letters of Kentucky were published as *Pioneer Life in Kentucky, 1785-1800*. It was an interesting book and was republished in 1941.

In 1820, the widow Ann Mercer Davis remarried and the new step-father sent David Davis to live with an uncle in Annapolis. David Jr.'s father David Davis had been a physician and planter when his son was born. Ann had been born to a rich planter and was the senior Davis' distant relative. She married at age fifteen after schooling at Linden Hall at Lititz, Pennsylvania. Married three years, she had happy hopes for the future since her husband had shown great promise. Born into slave holding stock, young

David was nursed by slave nanny. This was the custom for the time and place. He was to grow up to become Lincoln's political manager.

The first playmates of David's were the slave children of The Rounds, Mercer plantation. He to grow up in comfort and with negative feelings on both slavery and abolitionists. This was unusual for descendants of slaveowners, but was the case for a number of people in the nineteenth century. Like all people born into such families, David developed a fiery temper. Slave owning family members had bad tempers with their slaves as a rule. It was part of the price slaveowners had to pay for slavery. Hard on slaves, slavery could also be hard on the owners and their families. It was ill-suited for life as well as liberty.

His stepfather was Franklin Betts, a bookseller and stationer in Baltimore. Born in western Massachusetts, he had studied for the Episcopal ministry. It has been suggested that Ann met Franklin at church. She was deeply religious and interested in Heaven and did not concern herself with material things, except as provided by being rich. Like women in the nineteenth century of her class, she was not interested in matters of family finance. This was not the woman's job in upper class families. Only in lower class families were women busy in shopping and buying and needed to be careful with money. Someone always paid the bills for upper class women.

She had no concern with her son's estate of five thousand dollars, but Franklin had its management and the welfare of David was left to relatives like Reverend Henry Lyon Davis, the uncle who preached in St. Anne's in Annapolis. He married Jane Winter of a prominent Maryland family. David's cousin was Henry Winter Davis who also made his mark in America. The care of David was divided between the uncle and the guardian. This resulted in David being boarded at a school run by Isaac Sams near Ellicott City, Maryland. Ann had had five children by Franklin and he was not wanted there. [8]

In 1820, there was another agricultural society founded. This was in southern Virginia, at Clarksville. The group was named the Roanoke Agricultural Society. Their object was to promote the interests and improvements in husbandry and rural economy. There meetings were quarterly and the topics of discussion were of course the tariff which they opposed as a undue tax upon themselves, never mind the advantages to the nation or to others. They also talked about the best method to cultivate the soil and feed livestock. They decided upon the best manures for the enrichment of the soil. Other items up for their own self-education were crop rotation and the proper use of lime. Another issue at hand was agricultural education, which were just beginning to come into its own. Other groups were to be formed at Williamsburg, Fincastle, Rockbridge, Winchester, Jetersville, and Ayletts. This was just the beginning of such organizations and county fairs. [9]

[1]Scott, Sir Walter. *Ivanhoe, Kenitworth, Old Mortality, The Talisman, Quentin Durward*.
[2]Capers, Gerald Mortimer, *John C. Calhoun--Opportunist: A Reappraisal*, Gainesville, Fla.: University of Florida Press, 1960, Rep. Chicago: Quadrangle, 1969, pp. 71-72.
[3]Faux, *Memorable*, 28-30.

[4]Crawford, Mary Caroline, *Romantic Days in Old Boston: The Story of the City and of Its People During the Ninetieth Century*, Boston: Little Brown, 1923, pp. 1-13.
[5]Allen, Gay Wilson, *Waldo Emerson: A Biography*, New York: Viking Press, 1981, pp. 5-10, 15, 24-28, 38-39.
[6]Emerson, Ralph Waldo, *Collected Works of Ralph Waldo Emerson*, New York: Greystone Press, n.d., pp. 1-2.
[7]Benton, Joel, *Emerson as a Poet*, New York: M.F. Mansfield & A. Wessels, 1883, p. 31. Quote on p. 31.
[8]King, Willard L., *Lincoln's Manager: David Davis*, Cambridge, Mass: Harvard University Press, 1960, pp. 1-7.
[9]Turner, "Virginia," 81-82.

Chapter XXIX

SETTLING TEXAS

On January 17, 1821, the provincial government in New Leon approved the petition of Moses Austin. They issued instructions that Moses Austin was to settle his three hundred families in Texas near the Colorado River. His settlers must either be Catholics or agree to become Catholics beforehand. They were required to present credentials attesting to their good character and habits and take an oath to obey and defend the government and person of the Spanish king. It was hoped that these settlers would augment agricultural, arts, and industry. Moses Austin was to be their governor. [1]

When news of this reached the Austins, Moses was on his death bed. It was up to Stephen F. Austin to go to San Antonio to make arrangements. In June, he went on steamboat to meet the escort sent by Martinez. With him went several men to explore the territory granted to his father. He sold Moses' servant Richmond and proceeded to Texas with the escort. His party soon numbered sixteen men. Martinez welcomed him cordially, recognizing Stephen as Moses' heir. Details were ironed out. Austin made tentative plans with Bastrop and Erasmos Seguin for arrangements for his settlers to trade with the Indians. He visited the area and went to La Bahia on the coast, the other important community in Texas. Gaining useful knowledge of the territory, Austin returned home to gather up his settlers. [2]

Back in New Orleans, Austin advertised for emigrants with full information on the conditions of the grant and that they were to meet. The land cost them nothing but the payment to Austin of twelve and a half cents per acre by installments. This compared to a much higher charge by American land offices. Land was cheap in Texas even for that day. No wonder so many men wanted to farm in Texas. This was a grand opportunity. Austin also undertook to aid poor emigrants out of the money that he received. He was not in it to become rich. His services were reward along with the money that he was able to pocket. This was a grand undertaking and followed by that of other impresarios to follow Austin's example.

The only major problem was to find transportation for the families that soon began to settle near the coast of the Colorado and Brazos river valleys. A schooner, *The Lively*, was gained to transport provisions, arms, ammunition, seed corn, and agricultural implements for settlement, along with eighteen emigrants. Austin traveled by land to the area, but was unable to connect with the schooner's arrival. Instead, he reached San Antonio to find that because of the change in government from Spain to one in Mexico City, he needed to go to Mexico City to save his grant. Wilkinson and Hayden Edwards were already there to achieve concessions like those of the Austins. A Mexican committee was appointed to frame a general law of colonization. Austin told them that he wanted a special law for his colony but the committee rejected this idea. Finally, such a law was passed and approved by Mexican Emperor Iturbide and promulgated on January 4, 1823. Under it, Austin had no problem in getting matters arranged for his colony. [3]

The reviewer in the *North American Review* was definitely in favor of internal improvements when he reviewed three books on such measure in the state of North Carolina and its history. For the people of the times, there were few subjects of deeper interest than the subject. "While as a nation we are growing in wealth, in physical strength, and moral worth, we are laying a foundation for respectability and happiness, which will not easily be shaken. The strongest safeguard of the liberties of the people is intelligence; the best security of their morals is industry; the surest pledge of their future greatness is a wakeful spirit of enterprise, and a generous emulation. Under a government like ours, and in a country like the United States, everything depends on manly, spirited, and well regulated exertion. It is the genius of our government to encourage enterprise of every sort, without interposing any more checks, than are essential to preserve its own stability, and secure to all an equality of rights and privileges." [4]

Every community and state had this opportunity with public spirit, enlightened zeal, and honorable ambition. There must be mutual action. "The most direct and powerful means," he wrote, "of improvement rests in the states individually." A knowledge of internal conditions and wants could be easily arrived at. Each had full authority for improvements. Although prudence and economy are estimable virtues, a narrow policy in which there were no internal improvements was false economy. It would always keep the citizens in poverty. "He is the truly economical man, who disposes of his means judiciously, but liberally, for beneficial purposes. Property must not, he preached, be kept inactive. Internal improvements must be made for future prosperity, in his view. He would have more taxes for the building of roads and canals and for education. He deplored the lack of debate on his subject. [5]

There was an anxious concern on the part of many Americans to see the slave trade suppressed. One of these Americans was Congressman Joseph Hemphill, chairman of the House Committee on the Slave Trade. A sticker for legislation, however, the representative wished to peruse the Constitution and laws on the subject. By this referral, he noted, "the earnestness and zeal with which this nation has been actuated, and the laudable ambition that has animated her councils to take the lead in the reformation of a disgraceful practice, and one which is productive of so much human misery."

Hemphill felt slavery could not be suddenly ended, and the Constitution had allowed slaves to be imported down to 1808. After that, it was up to Congress to prohibit the slave trade. In 1794, Congress had forbidden American ships from carrying slaves to a foreign country. In 1798, the federal legislative tried to prohibit importing slaves into the Mississippi Territory under penalty of freeing the slaves so carried to be strong and hurtful.

There was a couple of other prohibitions on the question of the slave trade, and then in 1807, Congress prohibited the slave trade, beginning on the first of January of 1808. In order to prevent the further importation of slaves, there were penalties of heavy fines, long imprisonments, and forfeitures of vessels. Congress authorized presidents to suppress the slave trade with armed vessels on the high seas. In later years, Congress made similar laws and provided, in 1819, to authorize them to return seized imported slaves to Africa. There was to be an agent on the coast of Africa to receive the slaves. Next, American citizens were subject to the death penalty as pirates if they transported, or played a role in transporting blacks to make them slaves.

Foreign nations had acted to suppress the trade, but neither they nor the Americans had been able to end the slave trade. However, American naval forces, under Captain Trenchard for instance, captured slave ships off Africa and sent them to America to be condemned, which they were. From Washington's time to 1821, it was estimated that one million and half blacks were taken from West Africa and slavery in the two Americas. Americans read of the many deaths of blacks on crowded and inhumane slave ships. Close observers felt than until the slave trade ended there would not no civilization in Africa. Hemphill believed that civilized nations must co-operate if the slave trade was to be ended. Hemphill suggested action off the very coast of Africa, before the slave ships were dispersed to their ports of call in their most inhumane trade. [6]

Led by the Virginians, many Southerners talked coolly and deliberately about secession. However, they might be satisfied with limiting the powers of the federal government. They were unhappy not only with the attack on slavery during the Missouri issue, but with the increase of federal actions with new claims and pretensions. The central government had established a national bank and the Supreme Court acted to increase its jurisdiction. In particular, the state of Virginia had been called before the bar of justice in a case. Virginians declared that according to the Constitution, states could not be sued in federal cases. The Supreme Court thus had no jurisdiction. [7]

In the early years of the century, Britain, France, and Russia took an interest in the Greeks, who were under Turkish rule. Russia was to sponsor the Greek Alexander Ypselantes revolt, Napoleon had taken an interest in Greece, and Britain had extended their influence to the Greek homeland when Richard Church took Zante, an Ionian island. Poets and travelers developed an increase interest in ancient and modern Greece. The Greeks themselves began talking about independence. An imperialistic feeling about Greece had long existed in Russia and under Napoleon was developed in France and affected England. Basically however, the interest in Greek independence had more and more influence in Europe after the Napoleonic wars were ended. The British were concerned that Russia would dominate an independent Greece. Church, after varying adventures in Europe, dreamed of a free Greece and plotted as an official of Naples. He trained Greeks in military skills and encouraged them.

The Greek independence movement had a prelude in Russia. While Abe was still a small boy, in 1814, the Friendly Society was founded at Odessa to promote a Greek uprising against their Turkish masters. At this time, Ali Pasha of Joannina asked the Greeks to join him against the Sultan. The Greeks did not respond to the Pasha, but many eminent Greeks joined the Friendly Society, soon headed by Prince Alexander Hypselantes of Moldavia and Wallahia, a Russian army officer. This prince marched into Turkey, but was unable to raise a revolt. They fought bravely, but the attempt ended in failure.

When the Russian plot to free Greece failed in March of 1821, it resulted in a series of events which was to free the Greeks after a long and troubled war. Turks seized influential Greeks and the Greeks massacred Turks in Greece. Revolution spread. The Ottomans had their hands full in the empire at the time and the Greeks revolutionaries enjoyed initial success. However, Greek democracy as it fast developed, was weakened by the Greek desire to lead and not be led and local feeling further divided them. This was to weaken in a bloody war in which there were atrocities on both sides. On the other hand, they were good at guerrilla warfare. [8]

In that far distant land of Greece, Archbishop Germanos raised the standard of the cross on April 2, 1821, as a signal for a general uprising of the subject Greeks against their Turkish masters. From the first, the Christian Greeks had the advantage of a quality sea power over the larger ships of the Turks. Greek sailors were superior. Most of the crews of Turkish ships were Greeks and when they left, the Sultan had to rely upon impressed crews of dock-laborers or peasants. Early Greek successes on land also spread the revolt. After their victories, the Greeks slaughtered Turkish men, women, and children. Shortly, Turks under Omar Vrioni, an Islamic Greek, were successful. When the Greeks destroyed Turkish reinforcements in the defile of Mount Oeta, Vrioni retreated northward from Athens to Thessaly. In their turn, the Turks massacred Greeks. Twenty days after the revolt, they had killed Patriarch Gregorios of Constantinople. Christendom rallied behind the Greeks in spirit and supplies and then with volunteers.

The war continued in the spring of 1822, with a systematic suppression. The Greeks were more organized and stopped the Turkish advance. Then the Greeks fell to civil war among themselves. They fell to fighting over the financial aid Lord Byron brought to Greece. At this point, Sultan Mahmud asked Mehemet Ali, pasha of Egypt to bring his army and navy to crush the rebels. Ali did so and managed by his superior organization and mastery of war to defeat the Greeks, who had used money from Europe and America unwisely. Soon the Greeks were seemingly doomed. Only Lord Cochrane and General Richard Church could save them, and the latter Englishman received Greek authority and proceeded to aggressively pursue victory. Their general assault on the Ottoman camp failed. It looked as if Greek independence was doomed. [9]

News of an outbreak of insurrection in the Greek provinces in Turkey had reached the United States at the beginning of the summer of 1821 and rapidly spread. Americans hailed the movement for independence and were immediately sympathetic. The early British fear that this would lead to an undesirable annexation to Russia was noted in America. [10]

The people of frontier Detroit were unmoved when they heard of the Neapolitan and Piedmont insurrections. Their newspaper's editor doubted that free principles would catch on in Europe. When they learned of the Greek revolt the first of June, the frontiersmen were cautious. Celebrating the fourth in 1821, there were no toast for Greek freedom. Before the end of July, they had hope awakened in their hearts. Editor J.P. Sheldon felt there was a chance when he noted the ferocious enthusiasm of the Greeks. His readers were interesting in his view that if this was to be guided with wisdom and prudence by experienced leaders, the result would be happy. When they learned that a Greek woman had paid for a fleet and took charge in an effort to free her country, they became excited. They were increasingly interested in and supported by their sentiments. Within several months, these westerners advocated American mediation between Turks and Greeks and recognition of Greek independence. Later, the newly formed Thespian Society took up the Greek cause in Michigan. [11]

There were four Kentuckies. There were the rural and community states of the eastern mountains and the rural and urban lives of the middle and western meadows and hills. The mountaineers were little changing and isolated. The richer westerners were developing and in contact with the world. In the mountains, there were few slaves and neighborhoods very much alike with people being the independent frontier types who had settled for so long in the rugged terrain. In the other Kentucky there were more urban areas and more prosperity and culture.

Writing about both, F. Garvin Davenport noted that "although isolated, the mountaineers could not escape completely from the institutions of the world beyond the ridges. The long arm of the law reached far up the valleys and country court was held at regular intervals in the foothills even before court houses were constructed. Jails were built to confine mountaineers who broke the law although many criminals escaped unpunished into the wilderness." The law forces punished but also acted as guardians for orphans and ill-treated children. The woman had a difficult life, doing as much work as her husband. Courtship was grand and the weddings were festive occasions, much of the bright spot in the drudgery of living. When strangers came they were at first considered with suspicion and when proven enjoyed all the hospitality that the people could give. Self-sufficiency was very important.

"Superstitions old and new supplanted actual knowledge. They continued to build their homes of logs, with chimney and fireplace made of rock slabs and mud. Roofs were constructed of split boards and windows were not considered a necessity. The timbered slopes provided fuel and water came from springs or shallow wells." Gourds were used to make up household items and when at their most prosperous farmers could own a few cows. Corn was the main product.

Urban society generally followed the lines of rural society in the rest of Kentucky in this time. Frontier influences were strong in the towns and cities of Kentucky, but there were better opportunities and more culture. There were societies and fraternal activities. There was some manufacturing, wholesale and retail stores, newspaper and magazines, and inns and coffee shops. There were also the negative citizens who were so visible in civilizations. There were also other troubles such as the presence of hordes of hogs in the streets, where they ran wild for public use. They were often collected and sold at public auction. There were also difficulties with stray dogs and goats. Sanitation was poor and there were odors.

People made an effort at self-improvement however and there were relief programs. Industry in all of its meanings was encouraged. There was entertainment in dances and in horse racing. People were well dressed and there was the Christmas season to enjoy. Drinks of all kinds were enjoyed by the mass. Taverns did a good business. There were political and social lectures and meetings, and military musterings, exhibits and seances. There were plays and churches. And central and western Kentucky were full of slaves. [12]

Iturbide had been a general of great ability in the Spanish army in Mexico and had played a large role in suppressing the revolutionaries. The viceroys lauded his successes and felt more secure because they had such a general. Suddenly, on February 24, 1821, he switched sides. He issued a plan for independence. He was now on the side of the patriots. The news reached Spain and the beleaguered monarch (by Spanish liberals) decided to send a Irishman to be the viceroy of Mexico, the sixty-second in the line since Cortez's victory over Montezuma brought Mexico to the Spanish empire and a viceroy was established soon afterwards.

In August, Juan O'Donoju arrived at Vera Cruz to assume the viceroyal position. He found that it was a lost cause and he agreed to meet Iturbide, with the aim of founding a kingdom with a member of the Spanish royal family as king. Iturbide had other plans however. He wished to be the ruler himself, much on the order of Napoleon. Iturbide entered Mexico City on his charger, where he was greeted royally. A tired viceroy took ill and died and Iturbide went on to declare himself emperor of Mexico. Stephen F. Austin learned of Itubide's February declaration on the way to San Antonio near the Guadalupe. [13]

John Pintard wrote on March 17, 1821, that in New York state Governor Clinton was a prime mover in the establishment of agricultural societies. His political foes there were so incensed against him that they would destroy everything to replace Clinton. In this idea, they were working in the legislature to recall the law promoting agriculture. They were endeavoring to end other beneficial programs of his making. Their hatred knew no bounds and reason. Everything good he was for, they opposed. Hatred had made them insane as it often does. It seemed that the peaceful citizens were unable to prevent mobs in the streets and things were getting out of hand. Pintard felt that no matter were Clinton destroyed, he would have given luster to New York and his work would shine forever.

Large numbers of people were being put in jail for their unpaid debts. In 1820 in Boston some 1,442 debtors went to jail. Because she owed six to eight dollars and could not pay, a Springfield girl of nineteen with infant were put in jail. One debtor in jail was blind and owed six dollars. He had a family dependent upon him and they were in sad straits while he resided in jail. Owing a few dollars, an aged veteran of Bunker Hill was put in Salem's jail. A few were rescued. The Marblehead Infantry raised $22.18 to gain the release of a sixty-eight-year-old veteran of the Revolution. A large number were simply released on bail or freed out right. Others obtained the liberty of the jail yard.

At the time there was no bankruptcy law. Merchants were working to get such laws since it would allow them to get fresh starts and opportunity. Many could not pay their debts because their capital was all tied up. Farmers were land poor and unable to pay at the moment. Land poor meant that you owned valuable land, but little or no cash. Great wealth in land often precludes being rich in available money. There were modificatiochanges in creditor rights in the post-Revolutionary period and debts were less pressed or larger numbers would have been in prison for unpaid debts. [14]

[1]Kennedy, *Texas*, pp. 307-308.
[2]Barker, *Austin*, pp. 30-37.
[3]Kennedy, *Texas*, pp. 309-313.
[4]"Internal Improvements of North Carolina," *North American Review*, January 1821, p. 16. Quote on p. 16.
[5]*Ibid.*, pp. 17-20. Quotes on p. 17, 17-18.
[6]*America State Papers for Foreign Affairs.* Quote on p. 90.
[7]Brown, Everett Somerville ed., *The Missouri Compromises and Presidential Politics, 1820-1825, From the Letters of William Plumer, Junior, Representative from New Hampshire*, St. Louis: Missouri Historical Society, 1926, p. 41.
[8]Dakin, Douglas, *British and American Philhellenes During the War of Greek Independence, 1821-1833*, Thessalonki: 1955, pp. 5-19, 22-25, 28-32; Miller, William, *A History of the Greek People*, London: Methuen, 1922, pp. 11-12.
[9]*Encyclopedia Britannica*, 1911, XII, 493-495.
[10]Dupre, Huntley, "Kentucky and the Greek War of Independence, 1821-1828," *Filson Club History Quarterly*, XIII (1930-9) pp. 98-99.
[11]Lagoudakis, Charilaos, "Greece and Michigan," *Michigan Historical Magazine*, XIV (1930), 16-20.
[12]Davenport, F. Garvin, *Ante-Bellum Kentucky: A Social History, 1800-1860*, Oxford, Ohio: Mississippi Valley Press, 1943, pp. 1-5, 21-36. Quote on p. 3.
[13]Wharton, Clarence R., *The Republic of Texas: A Brief History of Texas from the First American Colonies in 1821 to Annexation in 1846*, Houston: C.C. Young, 1922, pp. 30-31.
[14]Coleman, P.J., *Debtors*, 1974, pp. 42-44.

Chapter XXX

KEAN

One of the greatest actors of all time came to America at this time. He was short and unpossessing, but he carried playgoers to such heights, especially in Shakespeare. Edmund Kean was subject to drinking sprees and would disappear for days with a concentration on that sport of the dissolute. The actor could become deranged. He was impulsive and unconventional in a romantic age when that was acclaimed. He was most Byronic and such an actor that he moved the world in emotion. Kean made the living Shakespeare even more alive.

His American tour began in New York on November 29, 1820, as Richard III. His fame was so great that the theater was sold out long in advance. Many in the audience were skeptical. How could anyone swept all cultural England off its feet like Kean had. They soon found out. Kean received ovation after ovation during the progress of the play. He was so popular that he was held over for four weeks, a first for the time and place. He played the roles of Othello, Shylock, Hamlet, Lear, and Richard II. He was Sir Giles Overreach and Brutus and Sir Edward Mortimer. His performance as Brutus was in a play written for him by John Howard Payne.

Kean was an extraordinary power as an actor and could express great passion. He did have a strange manner, but he had his gestures and looks down to the most subtle detail. He spellbound them and electrified them. His role was consistent in every performance. Long hours were engulfed with practice for his parts. A great personality, he projected an illusion that he was indeed the man in the role he enacted. It was not Richard III he was portraying but Kean. He was Richard III in person, that is he was living flesh, living the part as himself. The audience felt it was Kean that these events were happening to; the great illusion that can be presented in theater but never in movies.

He made friends wherever he went and was soon in Philadelphia. A success there was so great that the audience demanded something new, a curtain call. Manager William B. Wood thought this destroyed the illusion, but the people did not think so. Wood soon observed in Kean a major weakness of character. Kean fell to going with new friends dinning and celebration when he should have been resting for the next day. This was a serious mistake. The actor knew this but did not resist. He should have been aloof. His drinking on these nights did him great harm and his health was overextended. His friends enjoyed the prestige, but Kean himself did not benefit. Next, he acted in Boston. Everyone talked of him, but suddenly he wore out his welcome. Attendance dropped off and he refused to act without a crowd. This angered Americans and they were tired of Kean and acting anyway, so he soon left for England. The news had reached England and they turned against him. Popularity is sand. Kean had begun a long decline. Soon it accelerated and he was broken by a willful public. [1]

Meanwhile, in April of 1821, there was a riot at the Walnut Street Theater in Philadelphia where Edmund Kean was playing a return engagement. He was probably drunk and did not do his part as well as the public was accustomed to seeing actors perform. The audience hissed and groaned him, crying for Kean to leave the stage. Kean did not stand for this; no one was calm. He turned and called them cowards and other harsh words. However, when the uproar continued, Kean had to leave the stage. The acknowledged leader of the youth, William Bingham, Jr., got up from his seat in the box amid his fellows, and took the side of Kean, but he and his friends were thrown off the box and fell to the floor of the stage. Suddenly the lights were extinguished and the riot ended in the darkness. Years later, after Kean had refused to perform in Boston because the audience was too small, the people of Philadelphia revived their umbrage; he was pelted when he took the stage in the city. Those were troublesome years for the dramatists. [2]

On March 31st, Penieres, a Frenchman, received a commission to be a subagent to the Florida Indians, without Jackson's approval. Some government officials and citizens in Washington thought that Penieres had more experience with Indians than the others who wanted the job. However, those who were closer to the situation thought that this was not the case. Jackson had not arrived at his governor's post yet, and Captain John R. Bell was in charge, as selected by Jackson. Bell was thus in charge of Indian affairs also, but no one told him about Penieres. Bell was surprised when he learned of the activities of Penieres and reacted. He noted in a letter that he had news of a French gentleman being on St. John River saying that he was an authorized agent assigned to explore and hold talks with the Indians.

This was the first time, Bell had heard of that and he ordered the man brought before him. When Calhoun got around to informing Bell, the acting governor found nothing favorable to him in the man brought before him. There was a definite barrier since the Frenchman could not speak English or the Indian tongues. Penieres had no understanding of the Indians and thought the Seminole to be lazier and dirtier than any Indians he had ever seen. Further, Penieres did not understand the American liberal Indian policy of this time in the nation's history. Indeed, he seemed completely incompetently prepared for his job. [3]

Despite the efforts of Governor Miller in the previous year, the Osage Indians opened up warfare against the Cherokee and others in April of 1821. This was preceded by attacks on Cherokee hunting parties the past winter. The Osage murdered and plundered them and forced other Cherokees to abandon the hunts. Cherokees still hoped that they might obtain pacific terms, but in early April, the Osage attacked in force, nearly four hundred strong. The American commanding general prevented them from crossing over the Arkansas River at Fort Smith. Four Quapaws were decoyed over the river with signs of friendship and the Osage murdered three. Osage Indians murdered also four Delaware. Cherokees deterred a further Osage advance. Next, the Osage plundered some white families of guns, horses, cattle, hogs and other articles.

Meanwhile, Secretary of War John C. Calhoun gave orders to Major William Bradford at Fort Smith to use his efforts to maintain peace between the two tribes. Bradford made such efforts and kept the two tribes apart, reporting back to the War Department in the capital. He appealed to their fears and also told them that it was contrary to the wishes of the United States government. [4]

When John Tyler Jr. decided to retire from Congress, Andrew Stevenson ran. Tyler warmly supported Stevenson and the legislator handily won election without opposition. Andrew had not wished to be a congressman in 1821, since it was against his will and interests. However, the public demanded it, and he decided to stand for election without opposition. The lack of a contest overruled his wife's wish that he not enter Congress. Among the other new members of the time was James Buchanan from Pennsylvania. He served for thirteen years, until he was defeated in the election of 1833, a stormy political year. He took his son along with him, wishing to direct him toward a legal career. Stevenson found tutors for his son and the son later went to college, graduating from the University of Virginia in 1832, when his father was Speaker of the House of Representatives. [5]

A man named William Bechnell about whose early life nothing is known, formed an expedition to trade for horses and mules and catch animals of every description in the southern Rockies. His party left Franklin on August 18, 1821, with a trip to the Arkansas River. On October 21, they reached the mouth of the Purgatorie River in the mountains. They turned south toward Raton Pass into Spanish territory. They were welcomed in Santa Fe and made their profit. Shortly later, he led a large expedition in which he founded the Santa Fe Trail as it existed for the years ahead. He later traveled on the Missouri River and moved to Texas in time to participate in the revolution there. [6]

Word of the Texas venture of Austin spread rapidly throughout the western states and territories. It was most interesting and there were many who decided they would like to take up settlement in Texas. Pioneers seeking cheap land and new vistas were telling each other about the opportunity in the Mexican province. Moses had earlier mentioned that those interested outnumbered the required three hundred allowed by the Spanish government. Mrs. Moses Austin had written Stephen that "everyone has the highest opinion of his plans, and many are only waiting until they know he has made the establishment, when they mean to follow him."

Stephen wrote on October 13, 1821, after a visit to Texas that, that he had received almost a hundred letters from men in Kentucky and Missouri about settlement. He was convinced that he could bring fifteen hundred Americans to farms and plantations in Texas if that many would be settled. Three weeks later an Arkansas legislator wrote

Stephen F. Austin that the idea was all the rage and that he could raise fifty people for Texas. Many would come to Texas if there was no governmental disruption there. And this was only the beginnings of a large flood of information about the many who wished to move to Texas to farm. Among the multitudes who wanted to go immediately, there were many with questions about the land, its government, and many other requests about the land, especially about whether their faith would receive toleration. [7]

The *Lively* headed to Texas, sailing by way of Galveston Bay where it encountered a pirate ship. This vessel, however, fled and the captain of the settler's ship was left to view a schooner, which had been scuttled upon the beach. There was no more organized piracy action at Galveston as it had been in the days of Lafitte, but there were still a rare pirate operating at the end of the days of multi-piracy. Interestingly enough, it went out about the time the Spanish were being driven out of the New World. Lafitte had been expelled from Galveston a few years before by the United States government.

Because of storms at sea, it did not land as expected at the Colorado but unloaded at the mouth of the Brazos. Some days later there was another ship landing at the river, the New Years Day contingent of settlers. The *Lively* then sailed away and the settlers gathered everything up and began to go. Another ship, this one from Mobile had been wrecked and its passengers William Morton and his family had escaped and found the opportunity to join the *Lively* party. They all went up the bank and founded Richmond, the first Austin impresario town in Texas. [8]

On August 1, 1821, in Philadelphia, S.R. Overton sat down to write Andrew Jackson what he had learned from Pennsylvania politicians who were dabbling in presidential politics to end the fragmentation of their party and create political influence for themselves. Their upright governor, Joseph Hiester, had cut them off from state patronage and they sought national plums for the future. Overton wrote Jackson that Pennsylvania's dominant party had decided to run him for the presidency in 1824. The politicians had been collecting materials to decide the feasibility of and to promote a Jackson race. Overton was authorized to state that Jackson had their support. He was more popular and had greater claims on the highest office in the land than anyone else. [9]

The people in Norfolk were excited in November of 1821. There would be a real treat in town with the arrival of Junius Brutus Booth, in the role of Richard III. Booth already had a great name for himself in America and now when he reached Norfolk there was a letdown until he started acting in their theater. His rendition of the ill-fated king was highly acclaimed and applauded. The reason for the previous disillusionment was Booth's age. He was then twenty-five and looked younger. They saw a mere lad in an old straw hat and linen roundabout gawking at the scenery. When he acted all this was forgotten and the people who went to the theater whether well dressed ladies from the waterfront or the elite of the old city appreciated this. This proved the highlight of theater in Norfolk, Virginia, for in the years ahead the people lost their delight in theater and the old building fell into disrepair until it became in 1833 a Methodist church and in 1845 a victim to a fire. [10]

The slave Denmark Vesey, born in either Africa or the Caribbean, had a good deal of education when he was brought to South Carolina, and he gained more while there. Education for slaves went against the grain of slavery, but some slaveowners had their slaves taught to make them of greater use to them. There were strong laws against teaching the slaves, but because of custom, these were often ignored. After the Vesey incident, there was more strong feeling against any teaching of slaves, but the Vesey revolt did not change things that much. The oppressed were eager for learning and some of them picked it up from children or by self-help. Education could open the road for the slaves and also teach doctrines contrary to the best interests of slave society, like freedom and equal rights. Education was to open the way to Vesey's rebellion and proved the correctness of those who did not want slaves who could read and write correctly in the dangers.

Looking back in time, Dr. Alexander Garden, a church rector had given formal schooling for education and conversion from 1743 to 1764 or so to African Americans. At one time, this school had up to sixty pupils. However, half a century later, only a few masters wished their slaves educated since it would lead to their freedom. Most religious instruction was forbidden territory also, although four faiths worked hard for the teaching of religion to slaves. The faiths were the Methodist, Baptists, Episcopalian, and Presbyterian. The Baptists spread the word through their local associations and the Methodists used a society for this purpose. Episcopals and Presbyterians lagged behind. The simple and emotional nature of the first two contributed to black conversions. Many masters thought it to be their command duty, so more learned Christianity than learned to read and write, by a far greater margin.

Vesey was a slave for a long time, when suddenly he won a lottery prize of $1,500. With $600 of this, he purchased his freedom and joined the half-world of being a freedman, still with a lot of restrictions and free. He cherished this freedom, and became a carpenter at the nice pay of $1.50 a day in Charleston. He was rich compared to most African Americans and responsible. He met many African Americans slaves and freedmen in the course of his employment, which often took him to outlying areas to work or prepare ship timbers. Soon after he became free, the state legislators tightened up the fetters on the slaves by making it much tougher for them to gain their freedom. This was an effort to dry up the source of freedmen to protect slavery and to lessen the influence of freedmen on slaves. After 1810, slaves were becoming more valuable and the whites wanted to keep them in slavery to toil for them.

Having more freedom than most African Americans in the South, the white people who respected him thought him beyond ambition and well satisfied. However, there was a personal resentment and discontent underneath. He had freedom of movement but a limitation in that his freedom was not such as to command dignity. Besides his children were all slaves since the various wives--some at the same time--were slaves. Under the code all African Americans belong to the same slavery if they were slaves, even though their father--like Vesey--was free or even white. This did not lead to self-respect. For him, the degradation of blacks was an affront to the race. His first action was to encourage African Americans that he met to better themselves, to improve their lives. He used the Bible to show the slaves that slavery was unjust. By December of 1821, he began to talk of direct action. Trouble was ahead. [11]

While Lincoln was celebrating Christmas at age twelve in Indiana, Clara Barton was being born in North Oxford, Massachusetts. Their paths were to cross during the Civil War. At the time the lady was an angel on the battlefield caring for Union soldiers, in particular helping the wounded. Clarissa Harlowe Barton was born on the twenty-fifth of December of 1821 to farmer Captain Stephen Barton, a local leader and veteran of the Battle of the Thames, and his wife Sarah Stone. Both parents were very intelligent and worked at giving their sons and daughters and education at home as well as in school. Although Clara was shy, she was adventurous, especially on horseback. This ability to ride fast and expertly was to save her life during the war. When a child, she had listened eagerly to the war tales of her father, little knowing she would see much of battle. [12]

She had four older brothers and sisters who taught her joyously. The little child learned to read at age three. In the winter of 1824, Stephen carried her to Colonel Richard C. Stone's school one mile and a half down the way. At age eight, her father moved the family down the hill to the 300 acre farm at the bottom, a much better farm on the banks of the brook-like French River. Her two brothers bought the old farm on the hillside. In the years that unfolded, the brothers prospered and then bought better farms on the river bank. Her self education continued. Her riding skills learned at this time was to help her escape pursuing rebels in the Civil War. She nursed her injured brother David for two years until steam baths cured the aliment of his fall. This close care was hard on Clara's health and it was soon her turn to recover her normal strength.

In 1829, her father sent her to a boarding school, but Clara became sick in the place and returned home. The strange place and its 150 strange girls proved too much for the girl because of her super-sensitivity. Her family taught her mathematics. Two able teachers, Lucien Burleigh and Jonathan Dana, taught Clara history, language, composition, and English literature by Lucien and philosophy, chemistry, and Latin by Jonathan. During vacation time, Clara Barton learned to weave cloth. Idleness was not for her. In time, she worked in the nearby mills until two weeks later they burnt down. For the next eighteen years she taught school. The schools roughnecks respected her because of her athletic endeavors on the school ground and she had no trouble from them. In the fifties she worked as a government clerk in Interior in the capital. [13]

About this time, Abraham was old enough to take a bag of corn to the mill to be ground. He went on horseback and enjoyed the trips. Young Lincoln went to the school of Azel W. Dorsey and learned penmanship and excellence in spelling so well that he did the writing for everyone in the settlement of Pigeon Creek. Later, he went to the school of William Sweeney for a short time. This comprised the finish of his formal education, amounting to a year of education. [14]

Also in the year 1821, David Crockett in Tennessee ran for state legislator and won with his down to earth campaign. He gave speeches full of rough country vernacular. He made outlandish boasts with humorous anecdotes. He attacked his enemies with harsh words. Using common language, he put forth an image of being a self-made man, and played up an illiteracy which he had long since escaped. The electorate voted him in office, but once there he proved a poor legislator. After this, he turned to hunting bear as an avocation, leaving his effective wife managing the farm. He was used to hunting instead of work and promptly re-entered politics, winning a term in the legislature at this time in the western district as a champion of squatters' rights. He ran for Congress and lost to win two years later.

Crockett was born in 1786 to a poor farm pair, fifth of nine children. They moved several times and then ran an inn for two decades with reasonable success. His only education came from parental instruction; but his father wanted him to go to school. Crockett was not interested. Instead, he worked at age twelve as a cattle driver. When his father threatened him with a beating if he did not go to school, David ran away from home. He worked as a teamster and farmer assistant, and then odd jobs. David earned enough money to pay off some of his father John Crockett's debts.

He subsisted in near poverty for three years, fell in love, and lost the girl. This decided him to go to school. He knew then that he needed to get an education to get anywhere in the world. While attending school, he successfully proposed and was jilted while engaged. A deep depression plagued him in the next nine months. At age nineteen, he fell in love again, courted, and then married Mary "Polly" Findlay. They farmed over the years. In 1813, he enlisted for Jackson's Creek Indian Expedition. In 1814, he joined the Florida campaign during which he missed the chief fighting, but he was later to brag about his military experience. He returned home to find his wife dying. She left behind three of their children.

Elizabeth Patton and Davy married. Her dowry financed a career in politics and his hunts. She managed the farm well and David successfully speculated in land, owned a gunpowder factory and a distillery. He was elected a county magistrate and a lieutenant colonel of the militia. It was then that he ran for the legislature. [15]

Edenezer Snell was a Federalist in politics and a squire and businessman in economics. He was socially erect and a Congregational deacon with extreme Calvinist views in religion. His chief claim to fame, however, was that he was the grandfather of William Cullen Bryant, whose father the doctor Peter Bryant was liberal in his Calvinist views. The doctor had more influences in the teaching of his son than his father-in-law. Indeed, he was a member of the state legislature and an august Unitarian.

William grew up to profess that everybody must face death in accords of their religion for death was much on the ground that man's mind is a world of man's failures and of nature. His first great poem was published in 1817 anonymously as "Thanatopis" in the *North American Review*. Impressed by God's handicraft, nature, Bryant took a religious turn into his father's liberalism. He met Richard Henry Dana, Sr., and formed a friendship. In 1821, Bryant published a book of poems which critics in the *North American Review* praised. Bryant's chief subject was nature. The poet went on to become an editor and a wealthy man from investments in a newspaper and New York real estate. [16]

It was John Quincy Adams who said in 1821 that one-half of congressmen were seeking executive offices for themselves and the other half were trying to gain positions in the federal government for relatives. All of this made things difficult for Monroe and other presidents to whom the same appeals were made. Niles was to write in his newspaper that there were sixty members of Congress applying for office and he threatened that he would publish the names of those who had success in their applications. When one auditorship was vacated and the president had an opening to fill, five senators and forty-five representatives asked for that single job. The job was evidently easier work than their then demanding work in Congress. There were good paying jobs out there and they wanted them. Congressional pay was low and many relied upon their pay to benefit from the financial needs of life. [17]

Martin Van Buren was recently elected to the United States Senate when in 1821, he got the idea of establishing a political machine in New York state. At the time, the Federalist party in New York was past history and the De Witt Clinton Republican had lost the confidence of the people of the state. Van Buren was the logical successor of the Jeffersonian Republican. Seizing his opportunity, he built up the Republican party with patronage, which the new constitution of that year had granted to the governor and legislature. However, he realized that he and his friends must win elections to regularly rule the state.

Lacking in jealousy and eager to make use of men a ability and those whose talents on the way up, the new senator selected a small coterie of friends in the state capital and rewarded and promoted new talent to build up his organization. He would delegate the management of the party to these friends and organize from the lowest level to the highest. Since there was a vacuum, Van Buren Republicans soon had control of the governorship, the legislature, and judiciary. [18]

Private banks were not wanted in many new agrarian states. For instance, when they were admitted to the Union, the states of Indiana, Illinois, and Missouri prohibited banks except for the one in each state that was owned and operated by the state government. Western agrarians were hostile to banks and corporations. This authorization in the state constitution was not taken advantage of until the mid-thirties. Indeed, there were state government banks in such places as Delaware, where there was also private banks for the people to deposit at will and borrow when they were considered good credit risks. Farmers were important customers when they bought land. Indeed the state controlled bank in Delaware was named the Farmers Bank of the State of Delaware. It was established in 1807. [19]

---

[1]Morris, Lloyd, *Curtain Time: The Story of the American Theater*, New York: Random House, 1953, pp. 18-28.

[2]Oberholtzer, *Philadelphia*, II, 43-44.

[3]Mahon, *History*, pp. 32-33.

[4]Carter, *Territorial*, XIX, 285-286, 308-310, 344-345.

[5]Wayland, *Stevenson*, pp. 56-57.

[6]Parrish, William E., "Bechnell, William," Lamar, *Reader's Encyclopedia*, pp. 84-85.

[7]Barker, *Austin*, pp. 83-87.

[8]Wharton, *Republic*, pp. 42-43.

[9]Klein, Philip Shriver, *Pennsylvanian Politics, 1817-1832: A Game Without Rules*, Philadelphia: 1940, p. 119.

[10]Wertenbaker, Thomas J., *Norfolk: Historic Southern Port*, Durham NC: Duke University Press, 1931, p. 130.

[11]Lofton, John, *Insurrection in South Carolina: The Turbulent World of Denmark Vesey*, Yellow Springs, Ohio: Antioch Press, 1964, pp. 3-25, 50-52, 75-82, 131-134.

[12]Ross, Ishbel, *Angel of the Battlefield: The Life of Clara Barton*, New York: Harper, 1956, passim.

[13]Epler, Percy H., *The Life of Clara Barton*, New York: Macmillan, 1915, Rep. New York: Macmillan, 1946, pp. 6, 9-25.

[14]Beveridge, *Lincoln*, I, 62-63.

[15]Utley, *Encyclopedia*, pp. 112-113.

[16]Spiller, Robert E. etal, *Literary History*, 1963, 294-305.

[17]Fish, Carl Russell, *The Civil Service and the Patronage*, Cambridge, Mass: Harvard University Press, 1920, pp. 59-60.

[18]Remini, Robert V., "The Albany Regency," *The New York History*, XXXIX (October 1958), 341-344ff.

[19]Hammond, Bray, "Banking in the Early West: Monopoly, Prohibition, and Laissez Faire," *Journal of Economic History*, VIII No. 1 (May 1948), pp. 4-5.

Chapter XXXI

FRIENDS FOR JACKSON

The first serious consideration of Jackson as president began in the winter of 1821-1822 when his friends began to talk about making him president. In January of 1822, one of the Nashville newspapers began to press for a Jackson presidency. One of Jackson's friends however secretly worked to have Clay elected. Judge John Overton wrote Clay on the sixteenth of January that "as far as I know the public mind, you will get all the votes in Tennessee in preference to my man whose name has been mentioned." Then when Pleasant M. Miller suggested running Jackson so as to gather electoral votes in Tennessee, Alabama, Mississippi, and Louisiana away from Crawford and Clay so as to help John Quincy Adams win the election, the shifting Overton decided to back Jackson. His objective was probably to defeat the opposing faction in Tennessee. [1]

John Anthony Quitman, American lawyer, legislator, governor, congressman, general, and sectionalist, was born on September 1, 1799, in Rhinebeck, New York, to the Reverend Frederick Henry Quitman and his wife Anna. Frederick was born in 1760 in the west German duchy of Cleves, educated at the University of Halle, and settled in Curacao in the Dutch West Indies. There he met and married Anna, daughter of the island governor. After over a decade, they sailed to the United States and took up an American Lutheran ministry west of Albany. Soon they moved to Rhinebeck. Frederick kept busy caring for his flock, living a modest life. His formal training led him into a leadership role in the state church organization. As a rationalist, he spoke against predestination and a cruel Calvinist God.

The young John had a childhood of play and education, often intermingled. He made violins and collected birds, insects, and reptiles. His schooling was intense and successful and Frederick wanted his son to enter the ministry. While studying in Hartwick Seminary, John taught both elementary and secondary students, even those older than himself. Demanding though his life was, John made time for a social life of parties, picnics, sleighing, and ice-skating. In 1818, he went to Philadelphia and taught English at the Catholic academy at Mount Airy College. Teaching was dull and he did not want to preach. Quitman decided to take up a legal career in the West. After the school year was over in 1819, John went to Chillcothe, Ohio, and studied law. He and his mentor moved to Delaware, Ohio, where the land office was. It was there that he became a militia captain.

Shortly after his admission to the bar, Quitman headed southward. On December 3, 1821, he reached Natchez and began his successful law career in style. Long intent on a gentleman's life, he soon found the Mississippi town and its surrounding plantation a place for him to excel professionally, economically, and socially. Quitman accepted slavery and was soon defending the institution. Quitman married into the Natchez aristocracy when he took the marriage bonds with Eliza Turner on December 24, 1824. The couple toured the North and visited the Quitmans the next summer. They had a daughter and moved into a brick mansion on about 31 acres of land called Monmouth, near the Natchez-Washington Road.

Seeking an important political career, Quitman started by becoming a militia major. The militia of Mississippi had declined, so he and forty odd men established a volunteer city militia, headed by Quitman, to defend Natchez, which lacked a police force. Also, he worked to end dueling in the country by establishing a court of honor. His political career had its foundations and the people accepted John as a leader in the community. In order to further consolidate his standing, he joined the Masons and quickly advanced to Grand Master. He joined the Trinity Episcopal Church, where the town's elite worshipped. In 1827, Quitman successfully ran for the state legislature. In Jackson, Quitman was active and gaining influence. Quitman worked hard for the interest of Natchez. Because of an appointment to state chancellor, in charge of equity courts, Quitman withdrew from his re-election bid.

In 1832, Quitman attended the second Mississippi constitutional convention as a conservative delegate. The members consistently outvoted Quitman and his fellow conservatives. They were intent upon reform. Quitman wanted the chief state officials selected by the legislature rather than popularly elected. The convention thought otherwise. In a final vote of the delegates, they voted the new constitution into law. His fear of democracy was without effect, since the voters showed restraint at elections in the years ahead. [2]

The power of a secret organization, Free Masonry, finally brought against itself strong opposition. It has been estimated that a majority of outstanding men of the United States belonged to Masonic lodges when the Presbyterian Church Synod of Pittsburgh at its January meeting in 1821 condemned Free Masonry as unfit for professing Christians. Sporadic denouncements continued during Monroe and then Adams administration, until the sudden disappearance of a Free-Mason from Batavia named William Morgan. It was reported that Morgan was preparing an expose of the order and had been killed by unknown Free Masons. Members of the order made accusations that their opponent had gotten rid of Morgan, but the people felt the Masons had been guilty of foul play, which was later proved some members had.

Newspapers in the northern states wrote about the incident and large numbers of citizens began to act against the secret and supposedly threatening society. At local meetings, committees were formed to investigate the lodges and protect the communities.

The fact that the Free Masons dominated politics and therefore was considered subversive and unrepublican was a leading charge. Alert to the dangers of special interests, Stevens was in the vanguard of the anti-Masonic movement in Adams county. He recognized that a single issue platform was politically weak, but his life's experience brought him into the nascent party and kept him there even though the Whig Party beckoned forth on the horizon. Unfortunately the leaders of the Whigs included Free Masons in their number. [3]

Jefferson Davis' father had a problem. He wanted his son to be well-educated but there were no good schools at hand. Most of the teachers were untrained. Most of the students did not want to learn. He would have to send his son outside the county at age ten. There was a school in Adams County, called Jefferson College. Its principal was James McAllister, a man of learning. Then Bostonian John A. Shaw established Wilkinson Academy nearby. This would be good for Jefferson Davis, and he was brought home from Jefferson College to be entered there. However, Davis was to learn that his son was so averse to learning and so resentful of strict discipline of Shaw that he came to his father for sympathy. The father was to prove very wise.

Mr. Davis listened to what his son had to say. Then he told the youngster that it was for Jefferson to elect whether he wanted to work with his head or his hands. No son of his could be an idler. The boy chose to take a job. Mr. Davis sent him to pick cotton on the plantation. After one day of working in hot weather in a busy cotton field, Jefferson decided that this was not for him. His father sent him back to school. He applied himself seriously thereafter and proved a good scholar. When Shaw told Jefferson's father that the young lad was ready for college, Davis sent his son to Transylvania for a liberal education under Holley. It was an excellent place for education. Jefferson Davis became a friend of Clay's son and met the great man. He then went to West Point. [4]

Fanny Wright D'Arusmont, American author and reformer, was born on September 1795, in Dundee, Scotland, to James Wright and his wife. They died before Fanny was two and one half years old and Fanny fell heir to the fortune. The father had been son of a rich merchant in Dundee, an articulate liberal, and correspondent of noted men of science and letters. He had attended the University of Dublin.

The young child was sent to England to live with a maternal aunt. Fanny was unhappy there and spent her time in the aunt's library reading widely. When she was sixteen or seventeen she read Carlo Botta's history of the United States during the Revolution. From that time forth she was intensely interested in the young nation. She could find so little information on the country, she feared Botta's work was a romance, but a check with an atlas reassured her that the nation existed. She became imbued with the idea of freedom ands later of social reform, ideas which were to last her a lifetime.

At age eighteen, back in Scotland for a visit, she was given the privilege of reading books in the Glasgow University library. There she read everything she could on the United States. Meanwhile, she was developing a sensitive social consciencelessness, especially for the poor and aged.

When she came of age, she stayed in Scotland where she boarded with Mrs. Rabina Craig Millar who had been in America for two years. This whited her interest in things American. She decided to go to the United States and her younger sister Camilla followed her in this as in other things. They went out and Fanny led her sister to New York, Philadelphia, and the interior for the better part of two years. During this time she saw produced a play of Swiss independence that she had written. It was a success, but played only three evenings. Thomas Jefferson read it and wrote Fanny expressing his enjoyment of it and his respect for her.

The sisters were well received, liking as they did the Americans and being liked in return. This helped give Fanny a rosier view of America than many British travelers had. Fanny wrote Mrs. Millar in Scotland a series of long letters which she soon published as *Views of Society and Manners in America* in 1821 in New York and London. Other editions followed. It was translated into Dutch and French. Her stress on a society which was new had been a great effect on European views for some time. She also became famous.

Fanny developed a good friendship with Jeremy Bentham and a close one with Lafayette. She and her sister attended Lafayette on his 1824 tour of the United States, a home coming of sorts. When he returned to France, they stayed in the United States where she became interested in social engineering by means of settlement. She tried to uplift and bring opportunities for black slaves. Her programs generally ran into trouble. She continued with efforts for communal settlements. Going on lecture tours and writing she stressed education as the major hope for social betterment. In 1831, Fanny was married to a Frenchman named Guillaume Sylvan Casimir Phiquepal D'Arusmont. The marriage failed and the couple divorced. She supported Jackson and worked for reform. She died in Cincinnati on December 13, 1852, after a lonely retirement. [5]

The West prospered and new states were admitted to the Union. Ohio had been admitted in 1803. The state was populated by Virginians and Scot-Irish and German emigrants from Pennsylvania and became Republican. They established their state constitution with a figurehead governor in adherence with Republican fears of executive government. Suffrage belonged to white males who paid taxes or who worked on country roads. There was a Federalist minority who held the balance of power at times when Republican factions disagreed. Prosperity and a rapid increase in population--its representation in Congress was more than doubled by the census of 1820--were encouraged by wildcat banking and speculation until a depression began in 1818.

The year before, Indiana became a state in the Union, a party of settlers under George Rapp, calling themselves Rappites, came from Pennsylvania to establish a community where all land was held in common. This community was sold to Robert Owen in 1825, who called the town New Harmony. All did not go well and dissension was early a hallmark of the settlement until Owen gave up on his project in 1827. New Harmony did give birth to such progressive movements as equal rights for women, free schools, and free kindergarten. Southerners populated most of Indiana and Illinois, which followed Indiana as a state.

Several southern states were admitted to Union. Louisiana with its large French population became a state in 1812, almost a decade after the Louisiana Purchase. Mississippi became a state in 1817 with two-thirds of its lands still in Indian hands. Western rambunctious energy in the state found an outlet in brigandy along the Natchez Trace and later in filibustering expeditions elsewhere, Alabama became a state in 1819, increasingly settled by cotton farmers who founded plantations worked by African American labor.

Transportation across the country was aided by the building of roads and the use of steamboats. The National Road across to Wheeling had been interrupted by the War of 1812, but as soon as peace was obtained, construction continued until the stone-paved road reached Wheeling in 1818. From there, the Ohio River provided the main course through to the West. For settlers from Ohio to the broad highway of the river had to be traded at some point for the roads of the interior with their tree stumps providing trouble for the traveler. Flatboats provided the main means of river transportation until they were replaced by river steamboats. The *Enterprise* made it first trip from New Orleans to Louisville in 1815 in twenty-five days, a fantastic rate of travel for those accustomed to poling kneel boats up the Mississippi. Improved vessels in the next ten years cut that time to a week. In 1819, there were thirty-one steamships plying their trade on the rivers from Wheeling to New Orleans. Boone's old Wilderness Trail was no longer used by pioneers who preferred the National Road and the ship ride.

Speculation and freewheeling were prominent occupation for the Westerners. Land warrants traded hands fast, each purchaser hoping to get a better price than he paid. Much of the eight million acres in Illinois and Missouri granted to war veterans remained uncultivated while the warrants traded hands. Specie had migrated eastward and there was little cash available for trading purposes. Amateurs established banks everywhere, printing paper money needed for trade on the filmiest security. Others traveled from town to town intent upon fraud. They established offices, issued paper money in return for promissory notes, sold them to businessmen at a discount to cash, and skipped town. The businessmen, confident that they had made a bargain by getting the notes so cheap, were left holding the bag when they found out that the bank notes were worthless.

Trapping still provided adventure and profits for some, but most preferred the safety of home. Indians in the north and Spaniards in the south kept fur trading activity to a minimum among the Americans. Astor controlled the competition of Oregon and the Canadians soon controlled the fur trading of the West, whiles Astor gained control of the trade around the Great Lakes. Depression encouraged fur trading late since while manufacturing goods fell in price, fur prices remained steady, creating greater profits for fur trading.

Major Stephen H. Long led an expedition into the awakening West in 1819-1820. He traveled up the Missouri to the Platte River, west and then south to Pikes Peak and then down to the Canadian River. In his report on the area covered, he characterized it as a useless land. The region became known as the Great American Deserts; this discouraged its settlement for several decades. The treeless plains were not the American idea of cultivable land since they were used to clearing forests before planting and consisted that this type of land was the only fertile land. New methods, new implements, and new crops were later to change all this.

White Floridians had a problem. They lived with their slaves in the vicinity of free African Americans, former slaves, only paying annual tribute to their Indian "masters." Slave runaways in Florida could travel a short distances to virtual freedom, only having to pay "rent" in the form of tribute and perform military service to the Seminole in whose lands they lived. In 1821, an Indian agent said of the blacks in Seminole lands were a group of lawless freebooters. He knew that they had attacked whites on numerous occasions and were a danger to the settlers of Florida and the planters of Georgia. It would be necessary to remove them to the west. However, he realized that the Seminole, who were attached to their protégés, would never consent to such measures. Because of this the entire community of reds and blacks would have to be removed.

This idea did not suit the planters who wanted to repossess their slaves and not to move them further from their reach. Floridian officials claimed that the African Americans taught indolence to the Indians. This was not the case, neither worked as hard as the whites because they lived to suit themselves and not to gain great possessions like the European descendants of the then United States. For while, Indian removal was a weak force; it took the thirties for it to gather up important steam as a movement under the sponsorship of Andrew Jackson. [6]

About this time, Governor William Carroll of Tennessee and Felix Grundy were listening to a long sermon of Presbyterian preacher Gideon Blackburn in Nashville. Blackburn was so spell-binding and interesting that the people did not mind the three and a half hour length of the perforation. At the end, Carroll turned to Grundy and asked how he stood such a long sermon. Grundy replied that he could have listened to Blackburn until midnight. Blackburn was noted for his lengthy sermons. On another occasion he held forth for two hours in a steady but not heavy rain in a graveyard. They listened intently and did not worry about the soaking. Blackburn himself got wet but he did not finch what he considered his Christian duty.

This was not especially unusual, for in that day and before that time long sermons were the rule among ministers, but rarely in the rain, not for over three hours. People of that day who attended the services took their religion seriously and listened to the preachers, not as a matter for social prestige, but for instruction and guidance. It was also entertainment for all of it serious content. Political speeches too were long and attended by large numbers. People enjoyed listening to those who could speak well, give perforation, religious or political, or humorous. They heard them all out. [7]

About this time, a young African American boy and his brother, Ira Aldridge and Joshua Aldridge, took advantage of the opening of Brown's Theatre on Mercer Street in New York City. They took to the stage, but their religious, straw vending father, Daniel Aldridge found it out and came to the theater and took them away. His father had intended Ira to be a minister. He would have no lapses. But, Ira was already sure that he wanted to be an actor, and he later acted and was internationally known as a great actor in such parts as Othello. Ira was going to the African Free School, where he was as a true actor, awarded prizes for declamation. Soon he was to go to such shows as those at Park Theatre, where a small and backside area was restricted for African Americans. They could not watch the plays in the lower and most of the upper levels.

There had appeared in 1818 at the Park, an English actor who was to play the role in the life of Ira Aldridge. His name was James William Wallack. Wallack's brother Henry Wallack, a year older than James was also to help the young man. Both were actors. James had taken the role of Macbeth. He also acted in the parts of Hamlet and Richard III among many others. His first appearance in New York City was on September 7, 1818. Henry came across in the next year and in the following season appeared as Rob Roy in the adaptation from Scott's novel *Rob Roy*. This brother played the parts of Shylock and of Othello. The great tragedian Edmund Kean came from England about that time to play major roles in Shakespearean drama, which was acted so much at this time.

In the autumn of 1822, English comedian Charles Mathews arrived to act as Goldfinch in *The Road to Ruin*. The roles lasted for several months and he used his American experiences to write a book of sketches entitled *A Trip to America*. Meanwhile, the new Park Theatre had opened up with room for 2,500 people and improved lighting. The new patent oil lamps in three chandeliers lit up the hall. Each of the chandeliers contained fifteen lights. It was the wonder of the age for auditoriums. [8]

On November 25, 1821, the Park Theatre Company performed the Mordacai Manuel Noah play *Marion, or the Hero of Lake George*, a drama of the Revolution, drawn around the Battle of Saratoga. It was a popular drama. For ten years, it was acted on the stages of Philadelphia, New York, and Boston. His hero was Marion, who was a fictional patriotic leader. He was in constant peril of his life through, a true to life plot of warfare. This was followed in the next year by Noah's *The Grecian Captive, or the Fall of Athens*, which play took advantage of the playgoers interest in the Greek Revolution. When Noah wrote it, Athens had yet to fall, but Noah added this ending to make a better drama. He Americanized the characters. He had other popular plays in this period, including *The Siege of Tripoli*. [9]

[1]Sellers, Charles Grier Jr., "Jackson Men with Feet of Clay," *American Historical Review*, LXII (1957), 539ff.

[2]May, Robert E., *John A. Quitman: Old South Crusader*, Baton Rouge, La: Louisiana State University Press, 1985, pp. 2-41, 50-57.

[3]Woodley, Thomas Frederick, *Great Leveler: The Life of Thaddeus Stevens*, New York: Stackpole Sons, 1937, pp. 35-37.

[4]McElroy, Robert, *Jefferson Davis: The Unreal and the Real*, 1937, Rep. Smithmark, 1995, pp. 8-19.

[5]Baker, Paul R., "Introduction," Wright, Frances, *Views of Society and Manners in America*, Rep ed. Cambridge, Mass: Harvard University, 1963.

[6]Porter, *Negro*, pp. 141-142.

[7]Posey, Walter Brownlow, *The Presbyterian Church in the Old Southwest, 1778-1838*, Richmond: John Knox Press, 1952, p. 47.

[8]Marshall, Herbert and Stock, Mildred, *Ira Aldridge: The Negro Tragedian*, London: Rockliff, 1958, pp. 23-31.
[9]Quinn, *History*, pp. 151-153.

Chapter XXXII

SECOND TERM

In his early youth, Abe doubtless heard of General Andrew Jackson, hero at New Orleans and a mighty frontiersman. The boy was almost six when the general defeated the British at New Orleans on January 8, 1815. When Lincoln was born, Jackson was forty-one. Both were born into poor families in southern states and Abraham was to study law as Andrew had done. A number of years later, Lincoln next heard of Jackson in the Florida controversy. Jacksonian administration of affairs in Florida was criticized. All this was ready news on the frontier where Jackson was a hero. In a number of years, Monroe was to retire after finishing his second term and the contest was seriously discussed in 1821, three years before the election. Frontiersmen were talking about a campaign by Henry Clay of Kentucky, but soon westerners were also discussing a Jacksonian bid. The Overton faction of Tennessee wanted to return to power and chose the popular Jackson to carry them to victory. This was the beginning of a Jacksonian candidacy.

The trouble with the economy was no sooner over than political dissatisfaction increased. Monroe won his second term overwhelmingly in 1820, but not everyone was satisfied. No sooner had the country watched the inaugural for the president's second term, than there was a discussion of who would be next. In Tennessee the talk about the presidency and the contest of 1824 got serious in 1821. At that time, the talk had shifted to the candidacy of Henry Clay. While this was happening, Jackson, worn out, returned to his Tennessee plantation from Florida, listened to the discussion, and formulated his own views of what was best for the nation.

Chief among Jackson's complaints was the bad treatment and abuse he had received over his administration of affairs in Florida. He was not one to easily forgive his enemies. Jackson believed that his governing of Florida was enlightened and that his critics were blinded by personal corruption. Monroe might entrust Florida to Jackson, but he could not now complain, since he never sent instructions and never disapproved of the governor's acts, which were always reported to him. Still, the enmity between Jackson and Monroe had continued on the part of both men.

When the newspapers began to note various corruptions in the government and when Jackson read them he tied the corruption to the treatment he had received. Both were mixed in the future president's mind. The people who had opposed him were guilty of malfeasance. National corruption accounted for the abuse of patriots. Jackson believed this and it was a central issue in subsequent years. He read also about corruption in the Bank of the United States, information which influenced his views when he reached high office.[1]

Felix Grundy, breaking away from Tennessee's Erwin faction, also abandoned Clay to support Jackson. Grundy introduced the Jackson resolution in the Tennessee house and Carroll's faction dared to oppose the popular hero, so the resolution passed unanimously. Tennessee's Jackson was nominated for the presidency. Jackson's good friend Hugh Lawson White did not believe the sponsors were serious. Others suspended a political maneuver to increase Adams' chances. After all, Henry Clay or John Quincy Adams were the choice of most of Jackson leaders. Considering results for state elections, the maneuvering was unsuccessful. Miller was unable to defeat Williams and his followers and friends put up Jackson's name. Jackson won the senate seat by a vote of 35 to 25. People generally trusted Jackson. Sam Houston was enthusiastic about the prospect and predicted the people and not a caucus would make him president. [2]

On January 28, 1822, Ezekiel Webster wrote his younger brother Daniel Webster that he "never did like John Q. Adams. He must have a very objectionable rival I should not prefer." Adams was at the bottom of the rung of the ladder almost for Ezekiel. However, the Adams were never popular in terms of friendships. Ezekiel noted that he thought "it would be very difficult for any candidate to divide the vote in New England with him. Although he may not be very popular, yet it seems to be in some degree a matter of necessity to support him, if any man is to be taken from the land of the *Pilgrims*. I should really prefer Calhoun, Lowndes, Crawford, Clinton & fifty others I could mention--but this is a high matter & it is very uncertain what political feeling may prevail three years hence." Calhoun at that time was much of a national candidate and not yet sectionalized, although he was known as a Southerner.

Almost two weeks later, Ezekiel wrote about New Hampshire politics. He informed Daniel that "the nomination of Judge Woodbury puts Hill into hot water. He has not hesitated in choosing his course--and that is to write against the Judge. I think you will be very much edified in reading the Patriot. It will be very refreshing after a severe day's labor. I took on like a spectator at a bull baiting, pretty indifferent who is the conqueror or the victim--I have no tears to shed for either." Hill was the editor-publisher of the Concord *Patriot* and an ally of Woodbury generally, but the two men were also friendly rivals. Their political partnership did not suit them well, but they usually had no other choice. Each benefited from the other most of the time. [3]

On March 8, 1822, having decided that now was the time to recognize the independence of the Hispanic colonies, now that Florida was American and now that they had demonstrated by and large that they could remain free, Monroe asked Congress for the necessary measures. Since most congressmen had long been willing and interested in the welfare of the new republics, they acted fast for the legislature. They past the recommended law and it was signed by Monroe on May 4th.

President Monroe's special message to Congress proposed the recognition of Hispanic American countries. It was clear by this time that the nations to the south in the Americas had established their independence and were free of Spain, subject to further protection. He also asked for money to maintain diplomatic missions in those nations. Congress would not act before this because of the negotiation about Florida. With that territory American, they need no longer avoid offending Spain. And of course the prevailing sentiment in Congress had long been in favor of the independence of the colonies. Clay had won his case for recognition at last and on March 18th, the House of Representatives adopted a resolution for recognition. They also passed an appropriation bill for providing $100,000 for the expenses of the diplomatic missions, Monroe wanted sent. The Senate voted for the resolution and money bill shortly after the House.

Then there were delays by both president and Congress. It was almost a year later before action was completed on the many things that needed to be done. Monroe had wanted Jackson to go and then Ninian Edwards, but both men declined one after the other. The president then sent Joel R. Poinsett. More delays followed and Poinsett did not go to Mexico City for some time. He was received on June 1, 1825. This was lost time which hurt the United States and gave Britain an equal start in gaining Mexican support. [4]

About the end of March, in Charleston, Rolla Bennett, a slave to Thomas Bennett, the governor, talked to an intimate friend. He asked him to join an uprising to kill the whites. The unnamed African American delayed giving an answer. Later, he to told Rolla that he should take care because God says we must not kill. Rolla called him a coward and laughed. Rolla then said they could have help from Haiti and Africa if they would make their first step. Of course, this was not true since the insurrectionists could expect no help from abroad. The slave asked to be left alone for he would defend his master if they came to kill him. Called a coward, the slave said he would go to their meeting. The plotters were saying not only that Haiti and Africa would aid them, but the Congress had freed the slaves and the planters would not free them. When the slave asked what would be done with the women and children, Rolla answered that they would know what to do with the wenches. The rebel then told that the uprising was well organized at that time. Mingo would come up from James' Island and another force would seize Powder Magazine. A third force would take the United States' Arsenal on the Neck. In all there would be a terrible massacre. [5]

On April 21, 1822, a New Yorker who signed himself "Patrick Henry" wrote Henry Clay in an attempt to promote De Witt Clinton with the Kentuckian. They writer stated that they must put aside passion to avoid doing the wrong thing and operate on reason. He claimed to be Clay's friends and interested in Clay's elevation above all others. Clay must not allow Crawford to be elected to the presidency since that would stand in the way of Clay. Should Crawford be defeated how he would never rise to the high office because of his lack of literature and weight of character. Since Adams was too cold, he could not be elected. The New England would not carry New York, Pennsylvania, Ohio, or Kentucky. If Clay supported Clinton, he would return the favor and make Clay vice-president or secretary of state. There he could be out of the turmoil and follow Clinton to the presidency. Also, he averred that Clinton and Clay shared the same views. [6]

An Ohio trader named Hugh Glenn, and Jacob Fowl Fowler, from Kentucky followed the Arkansas River to near its head quarters and then south to Santa Fe. Glenn got a trapping license and with three other men plus Fowler worked the Colorado headwaters of the Rio Grande in early 1822. At this same time, Captain William Becknell, an long time Indian fighter and veteran of the War of 1812, arrived at Santa Fe about the same time. They returned to Missouri, arriving on January 30, 1822.

Becknell was able to tell the merchants of the American frontier that they had gone west to trade with the Comanche Indians when they met Mexican rangers. The Mexicans encouraged them to go to Santa Fe where they made a big profit from the small amounts of merchandise they brought. Since the goods which had to come around about from Vera Cruz, they were the most expensive so the Mexican could get a bargain with these overland purposes. And now, Becknell was able to say, American traders were welcome in New Mexico since the Mexicans had obtained their independence. Others were eager to go and soon there was a regular trade. Becknell made another journey in which they crossed a waterless land and almost died of thirst.

Chief Richard Fields and his Cherokees wanted title to their land in East Texas and a treaty with the Mexicans. On February 1, 1822, Fields wrote Alcalde James Dill of Nacogdoches that he wished "to fall at your feet and humbly ask you what must be done with us poor Indians. We have some grants that were given us when we lived under the Spanish Government and we wish you to send us news by the next mail whether they will be reversed or not. And if we were permitted we will come as soon as possible to present ourselves before you in a manner agreeable to our talents. If we present ourselves before you in a rough manner we pray to you to right us. Our intentions are good toward the government." [7]

The Cherokees knew that for the more cultured Mexicans and Americans their manners might seem out of place. They were farmers who were not educated or trained in the best of society. But they wanted to live in peace and cultivate their own laws and election of chiefs. Fields had just replaced Bowles by election where two auditors presented their respective candidates and the warriors lined up for a vote count in two lines. Fields was elected in this manner over an opponent. His dedication to his people meant dealing with the Mexican government, but he and his people wanted their own laws and government which they were used to at home in the east and west alike.

However, they faced strong obstacles which was presented at the first when the alcalde or judge-mayor did not reply to his letter. Like was necessary, Fields went over Dill's head. He took Bowles and twenty Cherokees to San Antonio to see Jose Felix Trespalacious, who was governor of the province. He asked the governor about a title to the lands the Cherokees were now living upon.

The governor and chief reached an agreement that the Indians might go to Mexico City to press his case. Those Cherokees who were not going with Fields were to return to East Texas and report to their people about the agreement. The Indians were to prevent cattle rustling on their part and punished those Cherokee who stole cattle. Kunetand would become chief in Fields' absence. Meanwhile, they would have possession of the land they had settled upon. They would have the rights of a citizen and work under that government and laws of Mexico and take up the defense of that Empire (as it was under Iturbide) if and when necessary. they could trade in everything but arms and ammunition with Indians who were considered friendly to Mexico. They signed it on November 8th.

The governor wrote a letter to his superior in Saltillo to the south. Commandant Caspar Lopez was informed of the enthusiasm of Trespalacious about the Cherokee. The governor "said that they numbered about one hundred warriors and two hundred women and children and that they worked for a living, made their own clothes from cotton which they wove into cloth, raised horses and cattle, and used firearms. He said that many of them understood English, He believed that they would be useful to the province." [8]

Going on to Mexico City, they arrived there in early 1823. They found there a revolution in which Agustin de Iturbide was overthrown and a triumvirate was established with Guadalupe Victoria, Nicholas Bravo, and Pedro Celestino Negrete as its members. Fields appealed to them but due to the lack of a colonization law, the three leaders could do nothing. Meanwhile, the Mexican government continued to support the Cherokees since the latter had had no money for their trip. He asked for approval of the treaty signed in San Antonio. Impresario Austin was there for a Mexican approval of his grant, made by the Spanish before Iturbide. Hayden E. Edwards, Robert Leftwich, and Green DeWitt were in the city. They probably all met. At any rate, when the Indians ran out of money, Edwards paid their expenses, for which he was later reimbursed by the Mexican government.

The Cherokee were met with a disguised hostility. With "a natural jealousy toward strange Indians they were postponed and dismissed with some indefinite and perhaps illusory promise." Mexican minister Lucas Alaman was a maker of these promises but he had already decided that they should not receive a grant. Still he promised. When the Cherokees headed for home, Alaman wrote the new commandant general at Saltillo, Felipe de la Garza, to "be very careful and vigilant in regard to the settlement of the Cherokees...until the publication of the General Colonization Law...although the benefits to arise from it, cannot be extended to them." [9]

In March and April of 1822, Governor James Miller was on tour up the river to settle the differences of the Osages and Cherokees in the southern United States. The Osages stated they wished peace on any reasonable terms. First along his line of march was the Cherokee tribe. There he found two war parties had left to battle the Osages. He stayed awhile and talked to a number of the old and principal chiefs, but they were not open to peace. They would rather wait for the Cherokee war parties to return. Should they be successful and had no deaths, they would talk about a peace. Miller headed forth to Fort Smith on the western line of Arkansas, where he learned nothing of any war parties.

Nathaniel Philbrook, who was the subagent for the Osage, went to the Osage town. He found them in real distress. They were open to attack since they had no ammunition. With no bullets, they also could not kill any animals for meat. Poor and watched, they begged Philbrook for peace. Sub-agent Philbrook returned to where the Cherokees were encamped and wrote the governor that they would talk about an armistice, until they had a chance to meet the Osage chiefs for peace talks. Miller thought Fort Smith would be the place for peace talks. In his letter to Calhoun, the governor of Arkansas wrote about annuities and of the territory to be granted to the various tribes.

The secretary of war replied that "the continuance of hostilities between the Cherokees and Osages, notwithstanding all your efforts to prevent it, is much to be regretted. It is believed that nothing short of the interposition of the government, by military force, will put an end to it: for this however, there is no authority." There was a bill, he noted, "at the last session of Congress, which would give such authority, but it did not pass--it is probable that it will be done at the next session. In the meantime you will continue your efforts to make peace, and if that he still impracticable, you will endeavor to render the effects of the war as little injurious as possible to our citizens in its vicinity." [10]

The Moravian Brethren held slaves, but they were very kind to them and saw to their material and spiritual welfare. Beginning in the 1730s, they had sent missionaries among the slaves of the Caribbean to Christianize them with great results. Soon they sent missionaries to the indigenous people throughout the globe. They reaped a rich harvest with their Christian and liberal attitude toward people. Soon Black congregations led by white ministers existed in many diverse places. They were to establish settlements in British North America. Their center there was at Wachovia in North Carolina. It flourished and they bought slaves for their plantations.

Not only did individuals own slaves but the Church itself owned them and rented them out to tradesmen and other proprietors. Many slaves actively sought out membership in the Church to the satisfaction of the Moravians. They were socially assimilated with the white Moravians but stood apart and were not used.

All did not go well in Eden. By the 1790s some of the white people began to sit apart from the African Americans. These disliked the slaves. At first, ministers tried to change their racism, but within a decade they abandoned the effort. Church boards then erected a barrier by banning the slaves from certain rituals and designating a separate cemetery for the slaves. They followed the trend of the time and did not resist it. The African Americans were restless and there was a white blacklash. This was natural since the idea of liberty for all peoples began to change to that for whites only in the minds of the Americans. The revolutionary period was passed and a new era was upon America.

In January of 1822, the idea of separate churches was founded. They cited difficulties and tensions. The slaves had different feelings. Some welcomed the idea, while others felt bitter over the segregation. The ones who were happy about the change, had tried as early as 1819 to have black-only religious gatherings. Segregation among the Moravians were now an accomplished fact in the congregations. Others fell into line.

Moravians were no longer to be as different than the whites elsewhere in the South. The slaves had begun to feel ashamed at meeting with the whites. The African Americans said that "we black people love each other and are happy to see each other and therefore will gladly come to the meetings which will be held for us." They still did not have African American ministers though. This would be for the future. [11]

[1]Remini, Robert V., *Andrew Jackson and the Course of American Freedom, 1822-1832*, New York: Harper & Row, 1981, II, 1, 12-16; Sellers, Charles G. Jr., *James K. Polk: Jacksonian, 1795-1843*, 1957, p. 88.

[2]Sellers, *Polk*, pp. 88-91; Schlesinger, Arthur M. Jr., *History of American Presidential Election, 1789-1968*, New York: Chelsea House, 1971, pp. 361-362; Day, Donald and Harry Herbert Ullam, *The Autobiography of Sam Houston*, Norman: University of Oklahoma Press, 1954, pp. 24-25.

[3]Webster, Daniel, *The Letters of Daniel Webster*, ed. Van Tyne, C.H., 1902, Rep New York: Haskell House, 1969, pp. 89-91. Quotes on pp. 89-90, 91.

[4]Rives, George Lockhart, *The United States and Mexico, 1821-1848*, New York: Charles Scribner's Sons, 1913, Rep. New York: Kraus, 1969, pp. 45-48; Wayland, *Stevenson*, pp. 60-61.

[5]Starobin, Robert S. ed., *Denmark Vesey: The Slave Conspiracy of 1822*, Englewood Cliffs, NJ: Prentice Hall, 1970, p. 18-19.

[6]Hopkins, James F., ed., *The Papers of Henry Clay*, Vol. 3: Presidential Candidate 1821-1824, Lexington KY: University of Kentucky, 1963, pp. 196-198.

[7]Clarke, *Chief Bowles*, pp. 19-20. Quote on pp. 19-20.

[8]*Ibid.*, 18-22. Quote on pp. 21-22.

[9]*Ibid.*, pp. 22, 24. Quotes on pp. 22, 24.

[10]Carter, *Territorial*, XIX, 437-440. Quote on p. 440.

[11]Sensbach, Jon F., "Culture and Conflict in the Early Black Church: A Moravian Mission Congregation in Antebellum North Carolina," *North Carolina Historical Review*, LXXI (October 1994), 403-407. Quote on p. 407.

Chapter XXXIII

ASHLEY'S EXPEDITION

William H. Ashley and his partner Andrew Henry set out to developed the fur trade up the Missouri in the spring of 1822. They had been long time friends and both were ambitious for success and position on the frontier and elsewhere. Born in Virginia, Ashley came to Missouri as early as 1805 and settled below St. Louis, where he met Henry and was a witness to the latter's wedding and was a consular when the Union broke up after only eighteen days. Although, Ashley was slight of frame, medium in height, and had a thin face with its prominent nose and jutting chin, he commanded respect from the first. One could tell that he was intelligent and forceful. Soon, he was made a captain in the St. Genevieve militia and justice of the peace for his district. Time passed and Ashley became a lieutenant colonel of the Sixth Regiment of Washington county and Henry became major of his First Battalion, when war broke out between America and Great Britain.

Before the war's end and the good friends moved to Washington County to profit from lead mining. Andrew engaged in the lead mining business and William began a powder manufactory. Prospering, Ashley became a full colonel in 1819. In 1822, he was made a brigadier general after serving as Missouri's first elected lieutenant governor. A success, Ashley wanted more and he and Henry picked the fur trade, which Henry knew well as early as 1808, being a partner in the old Missouri Fur Company and had built a post on the Snake River, a tributary of the Columbia. Dissension divided the trade but Henry had his experience to show for his efforts.

There was a four way competition for the furs of the Missouri valley so Ashley was not the only one organizing, but he hoped to be first in the field. Reorganized in 1820, the Missouri Fur Company had been preparing an expedition under Robert Jones and Michael Immell to reoccupy its territory. Known as the "French Fur Company" to its rivals, the firm of Berthold, Pratte, and Chouteau was preparing a sixty man party to build a Fort in Sioux country and to trade as far upriver as the Mandans. French traders had come to the United States and found American partners for the fourth fur company prepared to take a round back journey around the interior by land from the source of the Mississippi westward.

The company's men were divided into two parts. Henry led an advance party up the river on April 3, 1822, and Ashley followed with the rest on May 8th. They had not gotten sufficient men for the expedition and there were other problems. The keelboats used proved clumsy, but it was difficult any way to go upstream, with oars, poles, and sails. Because the river had a twisting course, sails were useful only rarely and only for a short period so the strength of the boatmen, phenomenal and well noted, was essential for traveling. Low banks covered with tall timber and a mat of wild grapevines and tangled brush made the way difficult and sometimes impossible for the Americans. The worst came to worst and the *Enterprise* keelboat was swept under in an accident, losing its $10,000 cargo, a hard blow for the expedition. So they had to wait for Ashley to raise enough money for new supplies. This done they continued upstream.

Jedediah Strong Smith, traveling with Ashley's expedition, was surprised at the vast hordes of buffalo in the interior. They reached the Sioux, Rees, and Mandans in that order and Smith, on his first trip west, began learning about Indians. On October 1, 1822, they arrived at the confluence of the Yellowstone and found there Henry's fort, recently constructed and they prepared for a winter stay, while Ashley went downstream to prepare a second years' outfit.

The Rees had been hostile since last seen and now Ashley was leading his band into their territory. He arrived at the two Ree villages on May 30, 1823. He was careful and indeed remained careful but this did not protect him as much as he would have liked. In front of the towns was a large sound bar on a horseshoe bend with the current in front. The Rees were on the right bank or south of the river. Ashley anchored his boats in mid-channel, and went forth to parlay with chiefs Little Soldier and Grey Eyes. When invited, Grey Eyes boarded the skiff. Grey Eyes said there would have to be a council. That night, he returned and said the Rees would remain friendly and would trade.

Ashley told Grey Eyes that he would like to trade for some horses for a crew of say forty or fifty to go overland up the valley. The Indian agreed to trade horses for goods and said that Ashley might pitch his tent on the beach on the next morning to receive the horses. On the next day, he purchased about nineteen horses and more than two hundred until in the early evening one of the chiefs wanted to trade for guns and ammunition. This early turn made Ashley very weary and he had his men maintain an alert that night with the breaking off of trade.

It was near morning when a severe windstorm hit with a hard rain and flashes of lightning and because of this it was impossible to take the horses away. Principal chief, the Bear, sent Ashley an invitation to come visit him. Brave Ashley went and he was treated well. Little Soldier told him that the Rees would attack him before his trading expedition left. He told Ashley he had best take the horses across the river. General Ashley, believing it was a stratagem to have the horses moved from under the guns, did nothing. Meanwhile, some of the men went into the village seeking bed partners and one Aaron Stephens was killed. When they learned this, the men, a motley crew, felt various concerns about their safety and there was no unity of opinion and resolution. Then in the early morning the Indians attacked the shore party, killing and wounding all of the horses and killing a number of the men.

Smith and his party were in a bad situation and soon yelled for boats to take them on board, but the boatmen were paralyzed.. Then Ashley managed to get two skiffs started for the shore. When they reached the shore, the Smith group was so mad that they fought on and the two boats left. Finally, they broke for the river and swam to safety. Jim Clyman swam hard, but he was swept downstream with the strong current. Reed Gibson rescued him and saved his life only to fall victim to a Ree bullet. Clyman made it to the bank and escaped by running for safety. The boats picked him up and Gibson died. Fifteen died and nine were wounded and survived. It was the worst disaster known in the history of the fur trade. [1]

The Ashley party used keel boats, barely suitable for the river travel. They were very large for the day, often as large as seventy-five feet in length and fifteen feet in width. When loaded, they drew two or three feet of water. Men propelled them using poles against the river bottom and walking along the gunwales to push them along. Some twenty to twenty-four pole pushers acted in unison and the boats could be fitted with a sail. There was a super-structure which provided cabin and storage space. Covers along the sides could be raised in protection during an attack. One or two small canvases were kept abroad for use.

The Missouri River was not an easy stream to travel. There were sand bars and snags which were hard to avoid since it was uncharted. Because of the spring rise of melted snow, the time that Ashley and Henry traveled, the flooded river offered particular troublesome movement. As we have been one large boat with its $10,000 worth of merchandise was ripped by a snag and sank. The crew barely escaped and the cargo could not be rescued. [2]

Jedehiah Strong Smith, American trapper and explorer of the far west, was born on January 6, 1799, at Jericho (now Bainbridge) New York to merchant Jedehiah Smith and his wife Sally Strong, both of easy New England stock. As a boy, Jedediah Strong Smith hunted deer and squirrels. When he was eleven or twelve, the family moved on to Eire county, Pennsylvania. He found a mentor and friend in Dr. Titus Gordon Vespasian Simons. One daughter and one son of the elder Jedediah married into the doctor's family shortly. Both families moved to the Western Reserve of Ohio by 1817. At about his majority, the young Jedediah made his way to northern Illinois where he spent the summer and fall of 1821, and then down the Mississippi until he reached St. Louis in the spring of 1822. [3]

The father of Ulysses S. Grant was a successful tanner named Jesse Grant, born poor, and his mother was the daughter of an independent farmer. She was named Hannah Simpson and was a maidservant of God with a strict sense of duty, believing in the total depravity of mankind and predestination. Her religion was Presbyterian in her youth, but she became a Methodist when the Simpsons moved to Ohio from a farm near Philadelphia. The future general was born on April 27, 1822, ten months after Hannah's marriage to Jesse. They moved to Georgetown, Ohio, not far from the Point Pleasant birthplace of Ulysses, seeking better opportunity in the summer of 1823.

Young Grant grew up to be most honest in a society which admired lying in the interest of one's pocketbook. Neighbors considered the boy to be stupid because he was honest. However, his ability for horsemanship and breaking colts earned him praise. A lack of popularity among the boys of the town and its environs did not result in many fights because he did not get excited. He was quiet especially after his taunting of his best friend led to that boy spurring his horse so hard that the animal reared. Grant was poor in his studies, but was fortunate enough to have the formal education that Abraham Lincoln lacked. Grant capped his education with four years at West Point, which he did not enjoy. Largely ignored, the cadet did attract attention as a horseman, but was only an average student in the Military Academy. [4]

Like Lincoln, Andrew Johnson was born in a log cabin and into great poverty. His native Raleigh was a raw settlement in North Carolina when Johnson entered the world on December 29, 1808, weeks before Abraham. For this, there was to be a special tie between the two men when they met much later in life. The well designed town in the woods was established as the state capital, but the governors would not live there. Andrew's father died when he was three. His mother remarried a poor man again.

Because there were no public schools, Andrew had no formal education, but he loved to listen to men read to apprentice tailors and workers of the tailor shop in which he was soon employed. The hours were long and the owner was not indulgent and after a scrape, the Johnson brothers ran away from the tailor shop. Andrew found employment in tailor shops in Carthage, North Carolina, and then in Laurens, South Carolina. By this time, he had learned to read and spent hours reading. Then Johnson headed west. He reached Knoxville and headed south down the Tennessee. In time, Andrew settled in Greeneville in the hills of East Tennessee where he met and married Eliza McCardle. The marriage took place on May 17, 1822. [5]

About this time, in April of 1822, certain congressmen took a major interest in internal improvements. Late in the month, the House passed a bill to resolve the problem of keeping the Cumberland Road maintained. Weather and vandals had played havoc with some sections of the road. The House would provide its upkeep by providing the collection of tolls on the roads. The Senate took up the bill. Some senators argued that it was unconstitutional and vetoed it after the Senate passed the bill. When Monroe said money could be given to the states for roads and canals if the states built and maintained them, the nationalists prepared a bill for surveys for roads and canals. James brother Philip Pendleton Barbour led the attack on the proposal with states rights arguments. He failed and the House passed the survey bill in February of 1823. John Taylor said in the Senate that the proposal was a Trojan horse, but most senators voted in favor of the survey bill if Monroe signed it into law. [6]

General Edmund Pendleton Gaines, at the headquarters of the Western Department at Louisville, Kentucky, took part in the Osage-Cherokee peace process. He had had experience with Indian negotiations before this. Born on March 20, 1777, in Culpeper

County, Virginia, he early saw frontier service when his family moved into Tennessee. When he was eighteen, he saw service as a lieutenant in a rifle company organized to fight the Indians. In 1797, Edmund entered the army as an officer. His first notable operation was to survey a road from Nashville to Natchez for 1801 to 1804.

Next Gaines received the command of Fort Stoddert. A captain in 1807, he was the arresting officer of Aaron Burr and was a witness at the trial. Tiring of army life, he studied law and practiced in the Mississippi Territory, while on a long leave which was common enough at the time. However, when the War of 1812 broke out, he went back into the army and during the next year became a colonel. He commanded the regiment which covered the American retreat at the battle of Chysler's Field in 1813.

Serving as an adjutant general, he was put in command of Fort Erie which sustained a long and vigorous British attack in a war with many American defeats. A seriously wounded Gaines was promoted to brigadier-general with a major-general brevet. The war was over before he recovered, but in 1817, he treated with the Creek Indians and served with Andrew Jackson in the campaign against the Creek and Seminole tribes. [7]

While in command in Louisville, General Gaines wrote a message to the two tribes stated in firm tones that their war should continue no longer. The president required and requested that each nation should stop and bury the hatchet. They should not delay in making peace on just principles. He told them that the was coming to visit Fort Smith on the fourth of August and desired to meet with the principal chiefs of both Indian nations. He told them of the laws of the United States against war with neighbors, which included the Indians. Monroe saw no just cause for the spilling of further blood. Gaines reported to the president. Suddenly the efforts of the peacemakers were successful. Governor Miller had achieved a settlement. [8]

On May 25, 1822, in Charleston, Peter (also known as Devany) went to market. Since his master, Colonel J.C. Prioleau, was absent, he strolled down to the wharf below the fish market to spend some time looking at the ships. The slave William Paul and he got to talking about a vessel and he earnestly said that did he know something serious was about to take place. The answer was no. William said that there was to be action in which many slaves were determined to right themselves by shaking off their bondage. Peter was horror struck but still feeling good ties with his master and wishing no change, he hurriedly left William Paul. Peter appreciated his master's kindness, so when a black friend of his told him to tell the colonel what had transpired, he did so. [9]

Prioleau returned on Thursday, May 30th, heard Peter's story and questioned him. The colonel then informed James Hamilton, intendent of Charleston, that he had information of a slave insurrection. Hamilton immediately called a meeting of the City Council for two hours later. He asked Governor Thomas Bennett to attend. Meanwhile, Prioleau informed the Pauls so that they could put all of their males slaves in the guardhouse, pending an investigation. The council and governor listened to the tale of Peter and ordered William Paul in for questioning.

William admitted talking to Peter and denied saying anything about a slave uprising. He was put in the guardhouse and quizzed with possible other persuasions until he was confessing. On the basis of this, they arrested Peter Poyas and Mingo Harth. They searched their belongings and found a letter which referred to deliverance by God as Daniel had been delivered. This did not alert the captors and since the two laughed about the charge, they released them, but kept a watch on the two. William then said that there was a wide plot for a massacre of whites and Ned Bennett volunteered to be examined if he was suspected. He had been named by William.

There was a blind alley at that point, but Major John Wilson of Charleston sent out his mother's blacksmith slave George to find out what he could about the plot. George belonged to a Methodist class for African Americans. A dark mulatto man, he could read and write and was of excellent character. On June 14th a friend of his brought him information that led George to inform the major that there was definitely a revolt in prospect. Time was important since it was to take place Sunday, two days away, a date almost one month earlier than planned due to the arrest of Peter Poyas. Major Wilson hurried to Hamilton's house, told him the intelligence and Hamilton informed the governor. This set off meetings and an increase of the town guard and militia preparations. This action was to prevent the uprising. Vesey, faced with such strength, decided not to act. However, the plot was not dead. It could be delayed to a more opportune time. Meanwhile, the investigation continued. [10]

On the next day, Vesey entertained Peter Poyas, Ned Bennett, and other insurrection leaders. A plantation slave was there by the name of Frank Ferguson. He was from the James Ferguson residence in town. Frank had just arrived from a visit to the owner's plantation in St. Johns parish where he had just arranged that John O. and Pompey should lead a column of revolting slaves down to Charleston when the word was given. Vesey sent out Jesse Blackwood to go and give the word to these two men. Jesse went forth but was stopped by the third patrol he met. Meanwhile, twenty to thirty slaves reached Vesey in Charleston, escaped from another plantation in a canoe.

It was then that it was decided to await events. They prepared even as the horizon looked dark for an uprising the next day. By this time the whites were alarmed and the revolt looked dead in the water for the conspirators. Then Vesey and the others were arrested and confessed. A number were executed. This ended the Vesey "insurrection." At this time, it received almost no publicity, the news being suppressed in order not to encourage the slaves into a repeat later. The African Americans were left to their dissatisfaction with their life and their good cheer about their condition. [11]

The claims issue between the United States and France had its beginning in the decrees of Napoleon whereby English and American ships would be seized and their cargoes confiscated. The United States protested without effect, although sometimes empty promises were made of redress. When the United States declared war against Britain, there was another declaration of war against France but it failed by two votes in the United States Senate. In November of 1812, an American minister in Paris, Joel Barlow, went to meet Napoleon on the way back from Russia, and Vilna, Poland, to lay before him the demand for indemnity, but a stunned Napoleon, after great losses in Russian snows, was too much in a hurry to stop off and went directly to Paris. Barlow trudged behind and reached Cracow only to die of constant exposure and fatigue on December 24, 1812. The French emperor would not acknowledge the legality of the American claims, but made some promises, which after Napoleon's downfall, was left to succeeding governments.

Albert Gallatin, a man of refinement, was sent to the court of Louis XVIII to press the claims to the new foreign minister Armand E. Du Plesris de Richelieu, who wished to cultivate understanding between France and the United States. The American arrived in Paris on July 9, 1816, where he learned that the French government finances were in bad order and that a loan for the payment would have to be heavily discounted. Richlelieu told Gallatin that his government was in no condition to pay the claims at this time. He feared that other nations would forward their claims also should any part of the American claims be paid. At this point, Gallatin made a formal presentation of American claims, based upon the law of the nations. It would not have to be paid immediately given the state of French finances. When France liquidated the final debts of its European creditors, the American prevented any remark being made to preclude a later discussion of the claims. These were the claims he kept before the French view.

In December of 1821, there was a change in government, but the claims were unpopular with all parties. Gallatin once more presented the question of the claims before the French government. He suggested either a full payment or the reference of the whole case to a joint commission. It was decided that the claims settlement would have to await a decision upon a commercial treaty. This was negotiated in final form and was then signed on June 24, 1822. Still there was no settlement of claims although the Monroe and the Adams administrations were interested in resolving the issue. [12]

While the common man was speaking out for economic equality, he was also concerned with education for his children. Many a man and wife were to talk about this with hopes for opportunities denied them, which would accrue to their offspring. There were some public schools, but they were poorly staffed. There were some even in small communities, but they did not attract good teachers nor were they consistently maintained, as witness the youth of Lincoln. Pennsylvania's journalist William Duane spoke out for their opportunity and noted that his state's schools lacked method. He suggested using the Pestalozzi system.

Five years later, an African American woman named Matilda, wrote that these days were gone. Ignorance blinded men and the "diffusion of knowledge has destroyed those degrading opinions, and men of the present age allow that we have minds that are capable and deserving of culture." Women had an influence on their men and youths and needed education if they were to properly use this. One answer was domestic tasks and the reading of books when finished with the daily grind. [13]

[1]Morgan, Dale Lowell, *Jedediah Smith And the Opening of the West*, Lincoln: University of Nebraska Press, 1953, 1967 ed., pp. 19-20, 26-33, 38-41, 50-56.

[2]Alter, J. Cecil, *James Bridger: Trapper, Frontiersman, Scout and Guide*, Columbus, Ohio: Long's College Book, 1951, pp. 6-7.

[3]Morgan, *Smith*, pp. 23-26.

[4]Anderson, Nancy Scott and Anderson, Dwight, *The Generals: Ulysses S. Grant and Robert E. Lee*, New York: Alfred A. Knopf, 1988, pp. 21-30, 53-56.

[5]Trefousse, Hans L., *Andrew Johnson: A Biography*, New York: W.W. Norton, 1989, pp. 17-28.

[6]Lowery, Charles D., *James Barbour*, 1984, pp. 136-139.

[7]Carter, *Territorial*, XIX, 441; *Dictionary of American Biography*, IV (1), 92-93.

[8]Carter, *Territorial*, XIX, 441-442. 460.

[9]Starobin, *Denmark Vesey*, pp. 17-18.

[10]*Ibid.*, p. 42; Lofton, *Insurrection*, pp. 147-151.

[11]Lofton, *Insurrection*, p. 151ff.

[12]McLemore, Richard Aubrey, *Franco-American Diplomatic Relations, 1816-1836*, Baton Rouge: Louisiana State University Press, 1941, Rep. Kennikat Press, 1972, pp. 1-9, 12-14, 25-28ff.

[13]*Annals of America*, V (1821-1832), 32-35, 225-226.

Chapter XXXIV

GREEKS

Americans learned of events in Greece generally through London and in the eyes of the English. On August 17, 1822, they read in *The Albion,* a weekly on events in the British Empire and the world, that the Russians were indignant at the barbarous massacre of the Greek hostages, but would not go to war with the Turks as a result of that atrocity. The editor quoted in the weekly stated that he knew he was taking the unpopular side of the issue in believing that mediation between the powers Russian and Turk should not be withdrawn. The Briton noted the arduous and delicate duties of Viscount Strangford in the negotiations, who had acted with singular prudence and success. Sio Island was enjoying peace and prosperity and should have remained so in the eyes of the editor. The ambassador mentioned was the British ambassador.

On August 24th, Americans learned that the constitution of Greece had been formulated. The Greek orthodox religion was established as the state religion but religious freedom was established. Everyone was equal under the eyes of the law and all might aspire to high station. All were to contribute to the national process. Nothing was said about freedom of the press, but journalists were allowed to sit in on the proceedings of the legislative. Power was divided by the legislative and executive powers. Like Britain, the legislative body shall chose the ministers of state. Prince Mausosordato was to be head of state and the executive. [1]

In Russia and Turkey, there was conflict, peaceful so far and unmarred by violence despite their differences in Turkish Greece. The editor felt that it was a certainty that there would no longer be a war in Europe. He wrote for American consumption that Turko-Russian differences were compromised and the Russian guard was back in St. Petersburg. He then erupted with a statement for the Greeks and extermination of the Turks.

The news from Greece and Turkey was filled with violence in both areas of the Ottoman Empire. Not to be fully recognized as truth was the Greek victory over the Turks in the passes of Thermopylae on July 8, 1822. The Sultan's forces were said to number 70,000 men, 50,000 of which were casualties or prisoners. Of the resulting fugitives, 4,000 were rallied by Choorschid Pasha and escaped. Shortly news came from

Greece that tended to prove that there was no battle at Thermopylae. Indeed news came from Vienna, about hard fighting in favor of the Turks elsewhere. Word reached western Europe that Athens fell to the Greeks, who allowed the Turks of that city to keep half of their valuables and all of their clothing and bedding for a return to Asia paid by Greeks. Since some preferred to remain, these were offered protection.

More certain were events in Constantinople which could be viewed and reported upon by westerners. The elite troops of the Ottoman Empire, the western Janizaries marched through the streets of that capital committing terrible excesses along the way to the Grand Vizier's palace and the Seraglio. Asiatic troopers were called in and they attacked the Janizaries, killing 200 of their number. The rest fled to be executed or banished. There was more news. Things looked bad for the Greeks with only three strongholds with a lack of provisions and ammunition. Word came elsewhere of Turkish advances.

Before this, the Greek troops in Argos had forced the Turks to retire one day in great disorder and at great loss and the second in an orderly withdrawal. Turkish losses were great. More reinforcements reached these Turks and they advanced once again. On the ninth of August, Tcher Hadji Ali headed his cavalry and led his troops to force a passage, at whatever cost. He fell at their head and soon the Turks broke away. The Greeks collected their booty and pursued the Turks toward Corinth. The news of these battles did not reach New York until late October or early November. [2]

Meanwhile in the United States, Governor William Carroll of Tennessee found time to build a political machine, whose aim was to elect Jackson president. The young lawyer Sam Houston worked with Carroll for this end. From Murfreesboro, on August 3. 1922, Houston wrote to Jackson that a resolution had just passed the state senate recommending Jackson to be president of the United States. He alluded to Jackson's reserve on the matter and stated that the crisis must be dealt with. Something must be done about the corruption of the nation. Houston had no faith in the heads of department in Washington and wrote that Jackson could expect no friendship from the gentlemen in Washington. Actually there was no corruption. Houston told the general that he was before the eyes of the nation, and had nothing to fear and everything to gain. Jackson was a faithful guardian and would be the popular choice from a groundswell and not from a caucus in Congress, Houston predicted. Jackson wisely kept his council and allowed his friends to work for him. He was publicly quiet. [3]

On August 2, 1822, Kentucky born Mississippi politician Thomas B. Reed wrote his friend Henry Clay that he had lost popularity in Mississippi because of his stand on the question developed from the Seminole War. Reed would have preferred Clay, but he now had no popular support. Finally Reed was forced for his political survival to support that other westerner, Andrew Jackson. Clay had such a small following in the state that no ticket was offered to men of Mississippi to vote on. [4]

In Illinois, there was a gubernatorial election. The state was without parties and there was no great national principles upon which the voters could decide the election. Particular to the year in the state was one issue, slavery, but this was not defined. Joseph

Phillips, state chief justice, was the most prominent candidate running. He was pro-slavery with supporters from early settlers from the slave states. Those men who were dissatisfied with Phillips ran Edward Coles, who was anti-slavery. When Coles gained a large measure of strength along the Wabash, the Philiips party selected Thomas C. Browne, an associate justice, to run to take votes away from Coles and enable Phillips to win. Browne was also pro-slavery. A fourth candidate also ran. The voters elected Coles by a plurality of fifty votes over Phillips. Had not Browne entered the contest, Phillips might have won. Getting Browne to run was a serious mistake for pro-slavery politicians.

The Coles policies included the need for a sound metallic currency, a canal construction program, and the abrogation of slavery in Illinois. He required a law against the kidnapping of free African Americans in the state to sell them into southern slavery. The southern interests made every attempt to get a convention to meet, a convention to change the Illinois Constitution, with failure at first. Finally, they succeeded in the legislature. An appeal to the electorate was made by both groups.

There issued a most heated debate-campaign of pro-slavery against anti-slavery forces which split families and friendships. Both sides used newspapers and other printed materials to fight it out tooth and nail. Governor Coles led the anti-slavery people with aid from outside the state. People were divided as each side did what it could to win the call of the convention to remake the constitution. It was a long contest of 18 months, but it finally came to a vote on the first Monday of August of 1824. The pro-slavery faction received a vote of 4,950, while the anti-slavery won 6,822 votes against the convention. Unfortunately the pro-slavery faction swarmed to support Jackson for president, taking with them large numbers of anti-slavery voters, and soon controlled the state of Illinois. [5]

James Monroe received an interesting offer in September of 1822. Underground leaders in Cuba said they would revolt should the United States make their island a state in the American Union. Monroe was cautious should such an acquisition result in British countermeasures and result in reopening the slavery question since Cuba would become a slave state. The word on Cuba spread through the United States and rumors reach the capital of Great Britain. When George Canning heard of the offer, he was very disturbed, realizing that it would be a blow to his Government. Americans concerned themselves when Canning sent a squadron to Cuban waters for the limited purpose of checking not Cuban acquisition by the United States but corsairs operating out of the island. Six weeks later, Spain said the raiders would be defeated and the squadron sailed away. By then the Americans had reacted, warning the Spanish Government not to cede Cuba to Britain. [6]

News of pirates operating off the coast of Cuba reached officials in the United States. These renegades were taking American ships, seizing cargoes and making their passengers into hostages to be ransomed. This was intolerable and orders were given out for the dispatch of warships to crush the pirates of the Cuban shore. Lieutenant William Howard Allen sailed the sloop *Alligator* to clear the seas there of the marauders. He sailed from New York on August 13, 1822, but for three months found nothing.

Then on November 9, 1822, he sailed into the port of Matanzas on the north coast of Cuba east of Havana. As he was about to order his sailors to lower the anchor, he learned that a gang of pirates had just captured an American brig and schooner. They would return the officers if paid a ransom of $7,000 in a bay fifteen leagues away. Allen ordered his men to sail to that bay. He found the pirates in three small vessels, one with a red flag. The American saw the prizes. Because the water was too shallow, the Americans rowed the boats from the *Aligator* and captured a pirate vessel. The pirates fatally wounded Allen in the encounter. [7]

On October 5, 1822, Henry Clay and his supporters thought Jackson would have to withdraw from the contest for the presidency. Clay wrote Landon Cheves, who had just resigned the presidency of the Bank of the United States, that the nomination of Jackson would be withdrawn. Governor William Carroll of Tennessee had written Clay one month earlier that Clay would receive unanimous support in his state. The Kentuckyian expected a sweep of the western states. He expected Pennsylvania's adherence to his fortunes would be the key. The people of that arch stone state preferred him to any other, and especially to William Crawford, he believed. His supporter John Sloane of Ohio wrote that Clay stood in high esteem in Sloane's part of the state. Only Clay's pro-southern sympathies during the Missouri controversy kept him from an even greater standing in Ohio. Should Pennsylvania drop John C. Calhoun, Sloane expected Clay to carry that state too. [8]

Seeking support for Jackson, Major William B. Lewis wrote George Poindexter on October 10, 1822, to solicit his advocacy of General Andrew Jackson. The Mississippian was not interested then, but on May 4, 1823, Poindexter had changed his mind. In a letter to Jackson, he asked for his aid to secure the vacant federal judgeship in Mississippi. He hoped that American voters would reward the general with the presidency. When the judgeship went to Peter Randolph, Poindexter endorsed Adams. He claimed, however, that he supported John Quincy Adams because Jackson would not win the presidency. [9]

On November 18, 1822, Kentucky legislators met in caucus to nominate Henry Clay for the presidency. They considered it the most suitable recommendation that they could make. They expressed the warm affection and the strong confidence in this their fellow citizen. In proposal of Clay, they felt that the time had arrived for a westerner in the high office. The legislators appealed to the magnanimity of the whole union to favorably consider "their equal and just claim to a fair participation in the executive government of these states." However, it was not only an appeal for westerners in the presidency, but one for character in government. The legislators believed that they had the interests of the nation in view and would see the talents of services of Clay justly rewarded. [10]

John C. Calhoun, who also wanted to be president, wrote Nicholas Biddle on December 2, 1822, that, being solicitous of the success of the Bank of the United States, he was glad to learn of Biddle's nomination to the presidency of the Bank, hoped he would be elected, and wished to cooperate with Biddle to aid the banks. Biddle replied that he cordially thanked Calhoun for his sentiments and wrote that the unfortunate bank "has from its birth been condemned to struggle with the most perplexing difficulties, yet even with all its embarrassments it has sustained the national currency and rescued the country from the domination of irresponsible banks, and their depreciated circulation. The time has perhaps arrived when it may combine its own and the country's security with a more enlarged development of its resources and a wider extension of its sphere of usefulness. To this object...my own exertions shall be anxiously directed." [11]

With the fear of the Vesey incident still in mind, and fearing that free African Americans from ships would infect the slaves with ideas of freedom, the South Carolina legislature got into motion. On December 21, 1822, the legislators passed an act which was stringent and abusive of the rights of African Americans. this law "required that free Negro employees on any vessel which might come into a South Carolinian port be imprisoned until the vessel should be ready to depart; that the captain of the vessel pay the expenses of their 'detention' and take them away from the state; and that upon the captain's failure to do this, they be deemed 'absolute slaves' and sold."

Shortly, the police arrested and jailed free seamen of the African race. An American captain of one of the ships sued stating that such detention was a violation of the United States Constitution. A lower court judged this illegal imprisonment constitutional and the state supreme court would not overrule the judgment. Masters of other ships petitioned Congress but did not get relief. British minister in Washington Stratford Canning protested vigorously when the black mate and four black seamen, free men, were imprisoned under the law. The British ship was from Nassau. The captain paid for their imprisonment and left, informing Canning. Four months passed and Adams wrote Canning that the difficulty had been removed.

Adams had spoken to South Carolina congressmen Joel R. Poinsett and James Hamilton and they got their state government to end the reinforcement of the law. In August of 1823, arrests were again made at the insistence of the South Carolina Association, whose mission was to press the enforcement of the black code. The law was defended as the right to regulate foreigners and to maintain police regulations.

Then, on August 7, 1823, Supreme Court Justice William Johnson, in Charleston as circuit judge ruled that the South Carolina Act was in violation of federal rights to regulate commerce. He opposed any nullification of the national laws, this one in the Commercial Convention of 1815. This caused much excitement in Charleston. Because it was dangerous to slavery and in contravention of their way of life, the newspapers suppressed the news of the opinion. However, it shortly appeared in pamphlet form.

Johnson, a native of Charleston, was attacked and answered back. Senator Robert Y. Hayne of the state was angry and people who spoke to him had to change the subject to another. The legislature back home compromised and suggested that the seamen not be allowed to go ashore. However, in fact, the government enforced the imprisonment of the seamen. This led to British protest in London. London would protect the rights of its citizens. Adams conferred with Monroe and Attorney General William Wirt. The latter supported the decision of Johnson and Adams tried again to end the situation, but his reasonableness did not avail him of anything with a determined state government in South Carolina. There Adams and Wirt was criticized in the great heat that

Charlestonians were most capable. It rested and the state had won. They continued their actions against the federal law with impunity. There was no Jackson or Lincoln to step in and enforce American law and justice. [12]

A certain A.E. Miller of Charleston, South Carolina, wrote an anti-abolitionist book which he published in 1822 and dedicated to the legislature of that state and members of that City Council. He took a sectional stand of the South and the West against the North and the East. The abolitionists' country had participated, he reminded his readers, in the slave trade and were not reproaching the rest of the country of an exaggerated evil and did not correctly represent that peculiar institution. They defamed and slandered the slaveholders and in the progress almost ended in shaking the republic. Only Clay's calm and temperate intervention prevented the danger. Miller blamed the intemperate zeal of a few for a possible calumny.

The Southerner wrote further that "the people of the North and East, are, or they affect to be, totally ignorant of our situation, and yet they insist upon legislating for us upon subjects, with a knowledge of which they appear to be wholly unacquainted. This is neither fair, nor honorable, nor wise, nor prudent. It must be recollected, that every state is sovereign and independent within the circle of her own territory, and that her citizens have an indisputable right to frame whatever laws their intelligence may deem necessary to its prosperity and happiness, provided they do not conflict with any of the great fundamental principles of the Federal Constitution."

Not only were slave states dictated to, but they were "slandered in their public prints, denounced in their pulpits, and calumniated in pamphlets and orations." On top of this, white and black missionaries preached peace in slave states and delivered fire-brands of discord and destruction and in secret stirred up trouble among the African American population. This led to insurrection. Instead of supporting a Southern repression of bloody rebellion, the abolitionists misrepresented Southern motives, defamed Southern character, and ridiculed and reviled Southern laws. [13]

[1]*The Albion*, August 17, 1822, pp. 70, 78.

[2]*Ibid.*, September 7, 1822, p. 95, October 5, 1822, p. 127, October 19, 1822, p. 143, November 2, 1822, p. 158.

[3]Day & Ullom, *Autobiography*, pp. 24-25.

[4]Miles, Edwin A., *Jacksonian Democracy in Mississippi*, Chapel Hill: University of North Carolina Press, 1960, Rep. New York: Da Capo Press, 1970, pp. 6, 8.

[5]Washburne, E.B., *Sketch of Edward Coles*, (1882), 57-198.

[6]Perkins, B., *Castlereagh and Adams*, 1964, pp. 308-309.

[7]Butler, William Allen, *A Retrospect of Forty Years, 1825-1865*, ed. Butler, Harriet Allen, New York: Charles Scribner's Sons, 1911, pp. 12-13.

[8]Hopkins, *Clay*, pp. 291-295.

[9]Miles, *Jacksonian*, p. 8.

[10]"Recommendation of Henry Clay for the Presidency, Frankfort, November 18, 1822," Schlesinger, I, 392-393. Quote on p. 392.

[11]Biddle, Nicholas, *The Correspondence of Nicholas Biddle dealing with National Affairs, 1807-1844*, Boston: Houghton Mifflin, 1919, 28-29. Quote on pp. 28-29.

[12]Hamer, Philip M., "Great Britain, the United States, and the Negro Seamen Acts, 1822-1848," *Journal of Southern History*, I, No. 1 (February 1935), 3-12.

[13]Miller, A.E., *A Refutation of the Calumnies Circulated Against the Southern or Western States, Respecting the Institution an Existence of Slavery Among Them*, 1822, Rep. New York: Negro Universities Press, 1969, pp. 7-14. Quotes on pp. 10-11, 11.

Chapter XXXV

THE SMITHS

The father of Gerrit Smith, the famous abolitionist, was Peter Smith, a fur trader and real estate speculator. His mother was Elizabeth Livingston who was second cousin to Chancellor Livingston. She was kin by marriage to the Van Renssalaers, the Schuylers, and the Tenbroecks. Peter was a successful businessman and had a great start as one time partner of John Jacob Astor, both of whom got their beginnings as poor clerks. At first, they kept a small store and traded first hand with the Indian traders. During the summer months, the partners would go to Albany by sloop up the Hudson River, and walk on foot across rivers and swamps, over mountains, and through forest to reach the tribes.

They would pay for the furs, which the Indians had trapped during the winters when fur would be full and rich, with wampum made of beads, shells, and bits of glass. Happy with their pay which passed for money in Indian eyes, the natives would help the traders transport the skins on their backs and by canoes to Albany. From there the partners would ship them to New York City to sell. When the partners dissolved their business, Astor bought property in the city and Smith purchased acres in upper state New York. Each man prospered greatly with Astor taking the lead.

Born in Utica on March 6,1797, Geritt had a good education at the academy at Clinton and entered Hamilton College, from which he graduated with honors in 1818 as valedictorian. He kept up to date in his reading, especially the *Letters of Junius*. His early biographer wrote about Garrit that the young man's "manners were open, his bearing was cordial, his action graceful and winning. His popularity was universal, and the social turn of his disposition carried him into the games, entertainments, collegiate and extra-collegiate amusements of his companions." Shortly after his graduation, he married wealthy Ann Backus, the daughter of the president of the college. She died of dropsy of the brain after seven months of marriage. He remarried in January of 1822 to Ann Carroll Fitzhugh.

In the latter years, young Garrit Smith was managing his inheritance and his father's amity. Also in 1822, his father came to a close call with death which shook up the old man so much that Peter turned to religion. To his contemporaries, Judge Smith was a hard, sharp, and shrewd man. Henceforth, he became a dispenser of religious tracts with an interest in the welfare of others in their religious lives. He thanked God for his mercies and had Reverend Comstock pray for him. Peter Smith became a preacher of sorts with the aim in life to spend widely in tracts to give the Christian message. He soon ran out of tracts. [1]

There was still popular interest concerning the presidential candidacy of Jackson, but Jackson himself did not consider it likely. Important leaders in the nation were not seriously considering Jackson for the presidency, since there were many more important candidates in the field already. These candidates had followings and position for above those of Jackson and if popularity with the people was ever considered, they had enough popularity with the people to suit serious politicians. [2]

In Maine, the ruling clique of the Republican party wanted Crawford to succeed Madison, but John Quincy Adams was popular in Maine and when the party held its caucus in January of 1823, the majority prevailed and the Republicans worked for Adams. The influential Portland *Argus* opposed Adams, but the people did not listen and Adams won three to one. The *Argus* was to oppose Adams in the next election also. [3]

Edward Coles, American governor of Illinois, was born on December 15, 1786, in Albemarle County, Virginia, to John Coles, a Revolutionary War colonel, and his wife. Edward's pre-collegiate education was given by private tutors. His father then sent him to Hampdon Sidney until 1805 when he sent him to finish at William and Mary College where he fractured his leg and fell behind in his studies. Edward left the summer of 1807 before the first and graduating examination. Back on the plantation, he read and studied history and politics. In 1808, John turned the plantation over to his son Edward.

While in his earlier college days young Coles considered the question whether or not man has property rights in his fellow man, reading everything he could on the subject. Listening to lectures, he formed his answer. Soon he could not longer reconcile the declaration that all men are born free and equal with the American social proposition which had enslaved persons. By this time, Coles decided that he could not longer own slaves himself or live in a slave state. So, he accepted an appointment as private secretary to James Madison. This job lasted six years.

After the end of the War of 1812, Coles explored the Old Northwest to decide where to settle his African American slaves in their freedom. Upon returning to Virginia, Madison sent him to Russia to settle a particularly difficult misunderstanding. Coles explained the situation to Alexander I and the emperor recalled the offending minister from the United States. His mission accomplished, Coles traveled westward through Berlin to Paris, where he met Lafayette. Next he toured Great Britain and returned home. In 1819, he took his slaves to Illinois and freed them. Three years later, he was elected governor of that state as we have seen. [4]

John Greene was acting in the role of Snake in the Restoration comedy of "School for Scandal" in December of 1822, when he made his first appearance in his home town of Philadelphia This was at the notable Chestnut Street Theatre John had been born in the city and started his dramatic career as Octavian in "The Mountaineers." This was in Frederick to the west of Baltimore, in Maryland. He celebrated his career in marrying

Anne Nuskay, born in Boston on March 23, 1800, who had come to Philadelphia to play in "School for Scandal" as Maid. The career of the Greenes was not very distinguished. They were to retire in Nashville, where John leased the Nashville Theatre to act and manage. He died when he was engaged in Memphis and Mrs. Greene died in time after him. [5]

With the death of his father, young Stephen F. Austin inherited the impresario grant with but one flaw. The Spanish had lost Mexico in a revolution and the Mexicans were now in control. He went to Mexico City to make arrangements with the republic only to find out that Agustin de Iturbide had declared himself emperor. It took almost one year to get the grant from Agustin I, but when the emperor was overthrown, Austin had to start all over again. He talked to congressmen and it took until 1824 for him to get his grant. [6]

Meanwhile in 1822, near Vermont's New York line, Greeley in a family of need, learned that a Whitehall printer was looking for an apprentice in his newspaper business. He set out on foot for eight hilly miles to apply at the community just across in New York. The printer looked him over and said that he was too young. It was four years later when he got a second chance. In 1826, Horace Greeley heard that an apprenticeship needed filling on the weekly *Northern Spectator* in East Poultney with its two thousand people and six sawmills. Young Horace headed for the town, which was a dozen miles away. The newspaper manager Amos Bliss was in his backyard planting potatoes when he heard Greeley ask him if he was the man in charge of the printing office. Bliss said yes he was and asked Horace questions to test on his general knowledge and was satisfied. He sent him to his foreman for his judgment. The foreman was favorable and after further questions, Bliss hired the boy.

With Zac Greeley's approval Horace left his parents who were soon on the way to Pennsylvania. It was a sad parting. The boy boarded at Harlow Hosford's Eagle Tavern, just off the green. His host was concerned about Horace because he ate heartedly and talked a lot. Amidst the drinking in the tavern, he lectured against drink and tobacco use. The friends he lost on the issue, he regained by supporting the policies of John Quincy Adams, who had found the favor of the people in East Poultney. The men listened to Horace who was full of news, especially on Washington politics. As the years passed, Greeley took part in many a debate in the schoolhouse and visited his folks in Pennsylvania twice on foot. Near the close of his apprenticeship, the troubled *Spectator* closed and Horace joined the Greeley family in the Alleghanies of Pennsylvania. After a few printing jobs could not be found near the Greeley homestead and Greeley went to New York City for his fortune at a time when primitive trains were getting their limited start. [7]

With his famous newspaper advertisement for enterprising young men interested in the fur trading occupation, William Henry was launched into the pages of history. Born in about 1778 in Powhatan County, Virginia, he moved to Missouri in his mid-twenties in 1802. He was successful in business, land speculation, the military and in politics. Basically, he handled supply and marketing from St. Louis and left Henry to go into the field. Soon he himself was to take to the field as we shall see. His use of whites to trap as free agents or employees, he angered the Indian trappers who were used to trapping and bringing the pelts to white posts. Their livelihood was being threatened, the militant Blackfeet were the chief enemy of Ashley's method, but it gave new vitality to the trade and fixed trapping patterns for the next two decades. It was innovation at its best. [8]

There was a new invention in the printing trade. Daniel Neall of Pennsylvania built a vertical printing press. It required one person to operate it. He could supply the paper, provide the pressure, and removed the printed sheets. The machine would take care of the rest. It used its acting and re-acting powers to supply the types with ink. It would maintain its motion and prepared for a new impression. This was done in a less time than it would be for two hands in the common made, to perform half that service. [9]

James Polk entered some land speculations with his father, making part of his payment in the form of legal services. However, politics was his chief interest and everything he worked out pointed to a political career. There was circuit riding, where he met judges, lawyers, and leading men throughout middle Tennessee. He was brought before voters in crowded courtrooms by his legal speaking. Financial success gave him an independence. Also he met politicians at the Tennessee legislature. Money and politics furthered his future as a politician.

In his private life, James made strides with friends, both men and ladies. It was important for his political career to be considered a regular fellow and he had more than one woman friends. Finally Polk married Sarah Childress, a woman of finished and finest qualities, who had been well educated. Sarah went to fashionable schools and learned the piano, which her wealthy father could afford. Her father was a planter. He had been a land speculator, a tavern keeper, and a wealthy merchant and had recently died.

After the end of the special session in 1822, Polk declared for the election contest for the position of legislator and ran a hard race in 1823. He used his energy and determination wisely for he defeated an entrenched politician. In the legislature, Polk joined Governor William Carroll's forces and was soon the leader of his anti-bank and pro-reform program. Polk was also involved in a land grant battle to preserve educational funding lands for Tennessee in opposition to Overton and Blount interests. Grundy and Polk were at odds on most issues, Polk being against toll roads involving his Tennessee constituents between Columbia and Nashville and for a national road from Buffalo to Washington and then New Orleans. He was on a committee to petitioning the routing of this road through Tennessee. At the same time, Polk supported Jackson for president for election in 1824. Running for Congress in 1825, Polk won in a field of five by a substantial margin. In doing so, he defeated Jackson's old enemy Andrew Erwin, the leader of the Erwin faction. [10]

After being taught by Dame Prentiss, Oliver Wendall Holmes was happy to be under the tutelage of a man. Mr. Bigelow did not always appear in the morning because of migraine headaches but young Oliver was being educated at home listening to the elders talk and reading out of the two thousand book library of his grandfather and father' accumulation. Oliver never opened the books of sermons, but loved the English classics and historians. He read poetry for its contents. He had lost interest in religion, although of course he went to church. Above all else Oliver loved to talk and could hardly be shut up. [11]

Meanwhile, in Mexico City on February 21, 1823, Emperor Iturbide dissolved the Congress, giving them ten minutes to evacuate. He ruled with an appointive Junta for a while and then ruled alone. It seemed that Austin would do well for the emperor validated Austin's colony. The young American felt all would be well and he prepared to leave Mexico City. Suddenly Iturbide fell. Santa Anna and Bravo had led a rebellion which quickly swamped the emperor's boat. This put Austin into a spot again. Now he had to get things cleared with the new government. [12]

In Boston, on January 23, 1823, Massachusetts Republicans met to nominate John Quincy Adams for the presidency. Their numbers consisted of legislators and delegates from towns in the state without representatives. A committee, drawn up earlier, reported to the assembled men that the time for electing a successor for James Monroe was too far to know what the conditions of the country would be or who was most useful to the nation in the presidency. It was time enough for them to see that Adams had great qualifications for the high office to be elected in the next year. They declared their feelings for the information of the nation. Their confidence in the republican principles of Adams, his public and personal integrity, his experience, his great services, and his exalted talents was unlimited. [13]

With a groundswell of support for Andrew Jackson in Pennsylvania, the general adhered to his policy of making no expression of availability for the office of president. To him like earlier presidents in Washington and Jefferson, the office sought the man and not the man the office. Washington did not want the presidency but accepted it only out of duty. Jefferson was a reluctant candidate. Jackson wanted the office, but neither said nor did anything to gain it. However, he expressed gratitude for a public expression of respect and confidence at a public notice of his military services. He asked for no reward of public office for his contribution to the national good. Content to be a spectator, Jackson continued his rule of neither accepting nor declining public office. [14]

The outpouring of interest and support for Jackson throughout the nation surprised the Tennessee politician. Further surprise overwhelmed them. Jackson expressed his economic view early. There was dismay; most of the Tennessee politicians believed differently and were upset to support a man who was against their personal interests. Even more concerned, Monroe and the presidential candidates in his administration felt they had to do something to curb this movement.

John Quincy Adams acted promptly. He suggested naming Jackson to be the United States minister to recently independent Mexico. Monroe backed this idea and asked Eaton if Jackson would accept. Eaton did not know. Without checking with Jackson, Monroe made the appointment. Jackson turned him down. Accepting would have been a mistake and Jackson would have caused Monroe trouble in such a mission. He was not a diplomat and would have been antagonistic to the Mexicans. There was no reason to go to Mexico when things were going so well at the beginning of his campaign for the presidency.

At the very time Jackson was cheered by the declaration of Pennsylvania Republicans backing him. This was the key to Calhoun's northern support and now it went to Jackson. Calhoun stared defeat in the eyes. Jackson thought it hurt Clay and Crawford also. Further, Jackson stated that if the people in the southern states of Alabama, Mississippi, and Louisiana followed Pennsylvania's Clay and Crawford would be further hurt.

Then came the hitch. Should the Overton faction be unable to gain the senatorship, and they were having trouble finding a suitable candidate, this would reflect negatively upon Jackson's popularity in his home state and hurt the race. Major Lewis and John H. Eaton managed Jackson's acceptance of the national senatorship from Tennessee. [15]

Over the months the Jackson name worked its magic and the strong support grew. His support spread to Maryland. Calhoun's supporters were concerned about Jackson's popularity in Baltimore. Internal improvements was a major issue faced by Jackson and later one of the issues closest to Lincoln in Illinois. Henry Clay, Adams, and Calhoun were all supporters of roads and canals and spending federal money on these projects. William H. Crawford and Jackson were moderates. Monroe was opposed. That Jackson was a moderate on the issue did not hurt him. His popularity cut across the issues. [16]

[1]Frothingham, Octavius Brooks, *Gerrit Smith: A Biography*, New York: G.P. Putnam's Sons, 1878, Rep: New York: Negro University Press, 1969, pp. 6-19, 22-23, 27.

[2]Seller, "Jackson," pp. 537-538.

[3]McCormick, Richard P., 1966, pp. 51-52.

[4]Washburne, E.B., *Sketch of Edward Coles, Second Governor of Illinois and of the Slavery Struggle of 1823-4*, 1882. Rep. Negro University Press, 1969, pp. 13-53, 57.

[5]Brown, Thomas Allston, *History of the American Stage*, New York: Dick & Fritzgerald, 1870, pp. 149-150.

[6]Meyers, John Meyers, *The Alamo*, New York: E.P. Dutton, 1948, p. 49.

[7]Hale, W.H., 1950, pp. 8-14.

[8]Utley, Robert M. (ed.), *Encyclopedia of the West*, New York: Wings Books, 1997.

[9]*Albion*, January 25, 1823, p. 255.

[10]Sellers, *Polk*, pp. 63-66, 72-92, 98.

[11]Bowen, *Yankee*, pp. 36-40.

[12]Wharton, *Republic*, pp. 51-53.

[13]"Presidential Nomination of John Quincy Adams, Boston, January 23, 1823," in Schlesinger, *History*, I, 394-395.

[14]"Andrew Jackson to the Dauphin County Committee. Feb. 23, 1823," in Schlesinger, *History*, I, 396.

[15]Remini, *Jackson*, II, 50-51 and 408 n. 33.

[16]*Ibid.*, II, 1, 12ff; Haller, Mark H., "The Rise of the Jackson Party and Maryland, 1820-1824," *Journal of Southern History*, 307-309; Benton, *Thirty Years*, I, 21-23.

Chapter XXXVI

PRESIDENTIAL BUG

With the approach of election year 1824, conflict among cabinet ministers was endemic and made it hard for Monroe to effect consensus among them. The British Government was campaigning to gain a united effort among the great nations for action to destroy the slave trade. Americans were, however, sensitive on that matter since it dealt with England whom they could remember as an aggressor on the sea the previous decade and before. Americans did not want the British to search their ships, even for slaves from Africa.

However, with a soften of this idea by the spring of 1823, Monroe instructed Adams to write Minister Richard Rush to negotiate on the matter. Congress wished harmony on the issue. Monroe thought that this would be an agreement against the slave trade would lead to other resolutions of Anglo-American problems. Crawford was happy about such an idea, but Adams thought that it would run counter to the right of American vessels to be free from searches at sea. However, Canning accepted the proposal with few changes and the cabinet gave Monroe whole hearted support on the measure. The House of Representatives adopted, without a dissenting vote, a resolution against the slave trade.

Then John Holmes of Maine and Martin Van Buren of New York, two Crawford supporters, came out with denunciations of the treaty. They then wanted a modified treaty, limiting the right of search to African coastal waters. Monroe sent a message to Congress but it did not do enough good and the Senate added the amendment to the treaty and passed it. Canning led Parliament to reject the amended treaty. Then he closed talks on other issues. Crawford's supporters and maybe Crawford himself ended a promising beginning. At least Crawford would not intervene when asked by Monroe. For Crawford it must be said that he was in the throes of medical problems. [1]

Early favorite William H. Crawford suffered a series of defeats starting with a lack of response outside the South. His sole support in the North and Northwest came from New York where Van Buren's faction favored his candidacy. Then he fell ill and was debilitated. He might have had a paralytic stroke or maybe a drug overdose of medicine for his erysipelas. When he stated his determination to fight on, his followers rallied. Everyone knew he was sick, but his aliment was kept from the public. He gradually improved but he still was affected by a partial paralysis. More trouble followed. Van Buren tried to gain a caucus nomination from the legislature in Albany, but failed. However, New York legislators approved the idea of congressional caucuses to nominate candidates. Crawford was relying upon such a group, expecting its approval. New Yorkers stated that Congress was the best way the contest could reflect national interests. Also it would lessen sectionism. In the months ahead the caucus method was subject to attack, notably from legislatures in Tennessee, Maryland, and Alabama. [2]

Monroe's secretary of the treasury had great credentials for the presidency. He seemed the natural heir of the Jeffersonians. William Harris Crawford was Virginian born even, but moved to Georgia in 1783 at age eleven. There he became a lawyer. In 1802, he was elected to the state legislature and in 1807 to the United States Senate. Crawford was a diplomat to France before becoming secretary of war and then to treasury post. He had strength in only two counties. In Monroe county, the voters had immigrated from Georgia and were avid supporters of Crawford county. In Wilkinson county, they supported Crawford because Crawford's foe George Poindexter was unpopular there. Crawford was known for his innate conservatism which did not appeal to Mississippi voters. [3]

While American readers knew they liked Cooper's *The Spy*, the American critics awaited English reviewers to decide whether it was a good book or not. Only a few wrote of the books as an admirable work. Impressed by the English culture, they visited English leaders in culture to be impressed by them. Word got around that Cooper wrote interesting books, that they were good stories of action and danger, works of American character and the American scene. They could relate, admire, or hate the hero and villains. Natty Bumppo made his first of five appearances in Cooper's third novel, *The Pioneer*, which came out in February of 1823. People rushed to the bookshops and bought copies. By noon on the first day, they had bought 3500 copies. A leading reason for first sales of such numbers in a limited market was the appearance of the shooting of a panther about to strike the heroine from the book in the newspapers. [4]

This work includes the usual love story, involving Elizabeth Templeton, daughter of a judge and landlord, and the usual dangers and well drawn characters. The judge character was based on Cooper's father, but the tale is of course fiction. The locale was the sources of the Susquehanna in mid-state New York. *The Pioneers* had the favor of *The Spy*, but the philosophy expressed are purely Leatherstocking. As usual Cooper write well, but this is not his best book. That place is reserved for *The Last of the Mohicans* deservedly his most popular novel. As usual also his chief heroine is brave and virtuous. [5]

On June 7, 1823, Thomas Lincoln joined the Pigeon Baptist Church by transfer from the Kentucky church. He was well thought of in his church and in April of 1824, the church board appointed Thomas to attend a church conference. Later in the year, he was named to a discipline committee to visit and reconcile a couple who had separated. The church would not accept a divorce. In June of 1825, he was a trustee and was placed upon a trustee committee of three to make arrangements to repair the church. The next committee he was on interviewed those people who were not in good standing in the church. By then Sarah Lincoln had been received in the church and married Aaron Grigsby on August 2, 1826. She died in childbirth on January 20, 1828. In September, Thomas Lincoln resigned as trustee of Pigeon Baptist Church. The Lincoln later had their differences with their church, but they came to an agreement with the church and Thomas was on another reconciliation committee. In 1829, Abe worked in James Gentry's store. [6]

British interest in the Americas was to keep Spain or any other European nations away from the ex-Spanish colonies. The patriots of Hispanic America had been struggling for a decade or so for their independence from Spain and the British government feared that the movements from Mexico to Argentina would be crushed by the Holy Alliance in Europe. Canning tried to get French assurances that France, which had been crushing a Spanish rebellion, would not ask for and get any colonies in the New World as indemnity or as spoils of war.

At this same time, the American government feared that Great Britain wanted Cuba for herself. Calhoun would go to war with Britain for the third time if that island nation was seized by King George's government. Adams countered that the United States could not prevent Cuba's seizure by England. Monroe was in favor of a mutual Anglo-American agreement not to take Cuba. The advisers of the president would not support this idea. Calhoun thought that nothing would come of it, while Adams felt it would involved American participation in European politics.

The Americans decided upon a unilateral action and on April 28, 1823, Adams instructed the American minister to Spain to say that the transfer of that island to any other power would be repugnant to the United States. He advised Hugh Nelson to consult with the Spanish minister of foreign affairs on the matter. In addition that if Spain would give Cuba away, it would be considered against the interests of the United States. America would resist such a move by arranging the people of that island declaring its independence. It was known at that time that the people of Cuba wanted to retain their ties with Spain. [7]

During this summer, William H. Ashley led his newly recruited party of seventy beaver trappers from St. Louis to the Upper Missouri. The group included such future greats as mountainmen as Jedediah Smith, Jim Bridger, Hugh Glass, Tom Fritzpatrick, Jim Clyman, and William Sublette. On June 2, 1823, about 600 Arikaras, hostile from the first to the whites and a barrier on this section of the river, attacked the fur traders. They forced Ashley and his men downriver, having killed fifteen and wounding twelve others. Ashley sent a brave man along to report what had happened, to Fort Atkinson.

Colonel Henry Leavenworth was commander there and immediately acted to raise a force to come to Ashley's aid and punish the Arikaras. He had been an officer veteran of the War of 1812. Now he led his Missouri Legion with its over one thousand men including volunteers from the Missouri Fur Company. The main part of this force was the 600 Sioux allies. They arrived at the Arikara village and on August 14, ended the skirmishing and started an assault begun by cannon bombardment which played havoc with the crudely barricaded lodges. The Arikara fled in mass, but Leavenworth failed to pursue.

Because of this hated timidity, the victory turned into psychological defeat. He was viewed harshly and the Indians thought the whites lacked power and will to subdue them. The Upper Missouri remained closed for awhile. Later the Arikaras were leveled by smallpox, leaving them with only one thousand or so people. Other tribes lost great numbers of lives due to this epidemic of 1837. What were left became friendly with the whites and soon served them as scouts in Indian campaigns.

When the Indians of the Missouri blocked Ashley, he sent fur traders due west to the Rocky Mountains where they harvested a rich beaver fur crop. The way was largely by land transport in the place of the great rivers of Missouri and others in the northern area of the Great Plains. Ever innovating, Asley established a new system. He would have camps or rendezvous meetings where trappers could gather and form an annual supply caravan. They wintered in the country and trapped in spring and fall, to bring their pelts to civilization each summer. There they could rest and relax, enjoying life, before resupplying for the next years trips into the wilderness. Supplies also went to them by mule train overland up the Platte and across South Pass. Ashley sold out in 1826 and settled into a mercantile business and a political career once again, being a representative in Washington from 1831 to 1837. [8]

Originally, Major Henry, had hoped to camp at Three Forks for the winter, but he had to change his plans and settle in at the Great Falls of the Missouri in the land of the Blackfeet Indians. They halted at the mouth of the Yellowstone. General Ashley returned to St. Louis to finance and supply his expedition and to recruit some more men to better blanket the fur country. Major Henry supervised the building of a fort on the tongue of land between the Missouri and Yellowstone on high banks. The several log cabins were surrounded by a stockade.

When the heavy winter snows fell, the men were often confined and learned to prepare food and cook and make their own clothing. There were hunts, usually for a few buffalo still left in the area. Skills with a rife were developed. Skills with Indian sign language and spoken language were acquired. Further, there were hunting and exploring excursions and the Indians proved friendly in their villages. Profitable time was engaged in by trading. In the spring of 1823, they met other trappers and traders from the states who had wintered in the region. The Blackfeet expressed dissatisfaction with the encroachment, but there were no fights.

Henry moved out his trappers with the first breaking up of the river ice to get the earliest start possible to trap and trade. Some trappers went ahead of the main body when the Blackfoot Indians outnumbered them, killed four whites and drove the rest out of the country without their pelties. The very same thing happened to others operating for the Missouri Fur Company.

Holding his men at the fort, Henry was alarmed at the report of young Jedediah S. Smith who came to the fort with a seasonal friend. Ashley sent him with news of a bad defeat at the Arikara villages and a request for all the men the major could spare. Henry led about eighty of his men down river below the villages where the Cheyenne River met the Missouri. All of the rescuers reached Ashley to learn that he had sent 250 troops and the Sioux joined Ashley to punish their old enemies, the Arikaras, who had in fifteen minutes devastated Ashley's party who had to swim for the keel boats. Fourteen men were killed and nine were wounded. [9]

After the Ree disaster, Ashley sent a letter and group to Fort Atkinson to authorities there, shocking Colonel Henry Leavenworth and peppery Indian agent Major Benjamin O'Fallon. Leavenworth had a proven record for brave and energetic service in the War of 1812, but his officers thought he was too much of a politician who could not be counted on to take necessary actions. O'Fallen consulted with Joshua Pilcher, acting partner of the Missouri Fur Company on the Missouri. Wanting action on the problem, Pilcher was glad for the opportunity to quell the Ree or Arikaras for they had tried to waylay his boat and rob his clerk. Pilcher offered the aid of his company for an expedition.

Because Leavenworth wanted O'Fallon to keep the local Indians quiet, Pilcher was sent to represent the Indian Office. Having no cavalry, the colonel gained the services of the Sioux to lead the attack upon the Ree until he could bring the artillery to bear on the village. This is what indeed happened. On June 22, 1823, the expedition got started. One of the boats was wrecked on a snag and another one had difficulties which threatened the end of the military expedition. They reached Fort Recovery. Pilcher learned of the deaths of four more of Ashley's company to warring Blackfeet and the lost of some of his own employees, seven men including Immell and Jones to other Blackfeet. Meanwhile, Henry brought down the furs of the first year and passed the Ree villages ignoring their signals for a parley.

On August 8, 1823, at a point twenty-five miles below the Ree villages, Leavenworth disembarked his men and marched them ten miles with the Sioux as cavalry. Orders were given to Major A.R. Woolley to proceed up river with the Missouri Fur Company men. After their arms were checked, ammunition passed out and strips of white muslin given to the Sioux to wrap around their heads to distinguish them from the Ree, the march was continued on the ninth. The Indians were put in front to attack the Ree if they marched forth from their towns and to keep them from fleeing. Sioux forces were eager for battle and rode fast ahead of the Americans to kill Ree. The two old enemies fought for an hour before the army could reach the plain half a mile from Ree towns.

Fortune was slightly in favor of the Ree when the Americans arrived, but the latter were unable to fire because of the mixture of fighters. There nothing they could do before their artillery arrived. Reaching here at sunset, the boats provided the artillery but nothing could be done until morning. Ten to fifteen Ree were killed that day and two Sioux were killed. On the morning, the Sioux scattered in the garden and in the hills, while the artillery raked the villages killing many Rees and doing great damage.

Preparations were made for firing rifles at the stockade to see if it could be assaulted and he retired to report on the favorability of an assault. His withdrawal might be thought to be a retreat, a signal to the Sioux that the Americans could be attacked. He countermanded the assault orders making Captain Bennet Riley furious. Here was his chance for promotion after eight or ten years of doing nothing and maybe no chance for the next ten years. That night however the Ree sued for peace saying the troublemaker chief Grey Eyes had been killed. Peace was then made. One night soon afterwards the Ree fled quickly and left the battleground to the Americans and the Americans returned to their fort. [10]

Meanwhile to the South, the Spanish authorities gave Austin broad powers of government. He was to govern and administer justice and command a militia force. They quite wisely instructed him with these functions. Austin exulted confidence. The leader of the Americans in Texas drew up a code of laws and administered them with justice. He threw out a number of miscreants in his colony during the ensuing years.

Returning to his colony in the summer of 1823, he found it disintegrating, so he had to take strong steps to keep those remaining and settle new people on the granted lands. It was a heavy responsibility but he carried it well. "Many of the original immigrants had returned to the States because of the hardships, and the new recruits had not arrived. He went at his work bravely, and conditions soon began to change. His zeal for his colonists knew no bounds."

He founded a town called San Felipe de Austin on the Little Brazos River and it became his capital. Because of the scarcity of priests, the colonists were left to carry on their own religious ways, although obstensively Catholic by requirements that the colonists all be Catholic. Priests were so rare that they had to marry by bond before the notary public and then when the priest arrived were married officially and wholesale. Some burnt their bonds and dissolved their marriages before the ceremony time arrived with the priest. [11]

Mr. F.W. Johnson visited the town in its early days He described it as "though the principal town in the colony, was but a small place. However, it could boast a tavern, store, and blacksmith shop and a few American and Mexican families." He went into the store with its stock "of two or three barrels of whiskey, some sugar, coffee, salt and a few remnants of dry goods, in value not exceeding five hundred dollars." He found there a number of men who were playing cards, drinking, or eating pralines, and talking. They used some Mexican words for ranching and generally enjoyed themselves. This store proved a social center as well as a retail outlet for the pioneers.

He described the agriculture of the place as follows: "We arrived at the busy season of preparing for and planting. Those of the settlers who had sufficient teams were breaking prairie, others were clearing what was called weed prairies, and bottom lands sparsely timbered, but with a thick growth of weeds. When the ground is cleared, holes are made a proper distance with a stick, and a corn-seed put in the holes and covered. This done, it is left to grow and ripen and received no other work, except to knock the weeds; the ground thus prepared and planted will yield twenty-five or thirty, sometimes forty, bushels per acre." [12]

Mississippians favored John Quincy Adams as a major candidate for the presidency before Jackson entered the race. Some of Jackson's popularity rubbed off on Adams when the latter's adherents used the argument that Adams had championed Jackson in the Seminole campaign in Florida. Although the New Englander did not elicit warm sympathy from voters in general, his abilities were well recognized and won him support. The Mississippi legislature was equally divided between Adams and Jackson, but the delegation to Washington DC was pro-Jackson. [13]

[1]Ammon, "Executive Leadership," pp. 124-126.
[2]Hopkins, J.F., "Election of 1824," pp. 367-369.
[3]Miles, *Jacksonian*, p. 6.
[4]Grossman, *Cooper*, pp. 28-29.
[5]Cooper, James Fenimore, *The Pioneers*, New York: Dodd, Mead, 1958, *passim.*
[6]Pratt, *Lincoln*, pp. 5-7.
[7]Ford, Worthington Clauncey, "John Quincy Adams and the Monroe Doctrine," *American Historical Review*, VII No. 4 (July 1902), 676-680.
[8]Utley, *Encyclopedia*, pp. 16-17, 20.
[9]Alter, *Bridger*, pp. 8-14.
[10]Morgan, *Smith*, pp. 59-77.
[11]Winter, *Texas*, p. 31. Quote on p. 31.
[12]*Ibid.*, pp. 32-33. Quotes on pp. 32-33.
[13]Miles, *Jacksonian*, pp. 6-8.

Chapter XXXVII

THE MONROE DOCTRINE

Days after the Arikara Battle, Henry was leading his bands of trappers in the fur country. Hugh Glass and his companion Bill were setting traps on a stream running from the Black Hills. The two men passed through cherry thicket when Hugh saw a grizzly bear using his nose to ferret out pig-nuts and motioned to his companion to come up. They proceeded carefully, stopped, aimed and fired their rifles to badly wound the bear. Their hope to kill the animal was unanswered and the bear charged them. They ran, but the thick brush hindered them. This was no problem for the bear, whose weight and strength carried him through the brush.

Hugh and Bill burst across the bluff, but Glass fell, tripping over a stove. Getting up, he was confronted by the bear. He fired his pistol into the animal and plunged his knife into the bear as the bear began to maul him. Ferocious in his pain, the bear tore the trapper's head and body with tooth and claw. Glass fell. A frozen Bill then fled, sure that Glass was dead. He returned to camp with the sad news.

The captain of the band sent Bill and another man back to the site. They found a dead bear on the body of a still breathing Glass. Hugh had skin badly lacerated into strips and the two men thought he would soon die. They collected his arms, his hunting shirt, and moccasins after pulling the dead bear from his body and turned back to camp to report that Glass was dead. Meanwhile, Glass was still alive and eating the meat of the grizzly for several days until he had strength to crawl. He carried raw meat with him down the river, suffering from his wounds and barely able to move. Many days later, he made the fort some eighty miles away, having lived on roots and berries, and received the medical attention and rest he needed and had needed for so many days. He was greatly scarred and almost unrecognizable. [1]

Adams wrote on July 22, 1823, that if the Russians wished to lay at Fort Ross on the western coast "the foundation for an exclusive territorial claim of Russia to the Northwest Coast, down to the very borders of California..., it is time for the nations whose rights are affected by this project effectually to interpose." The idea of Russian dominance in the trade and fishing of the Pacific Ocean was unacceptable. There could, perhaps, "be no better time for saying, frankly and explicitly, to the Russian

Government, that the future peace of the world, and the interest of Russia herself, cannot be promoted by Russian settlements upon any part of the American Continent."

This however was a secondary part of the prevalent discussion that lead to the Monroe Doctrine. This was the first time that Adams mentioned Fort Ross in his correspondence or diary. Since it was no little noted by Adams it was clear that it had no real influence upon the idea of the Doctrine. Still, there were protests from the British and American Governments to that of Russia on the incursion at Fort Ross. Even then for both Monroe and Adams it was of minor importance. [2]

Foreign secretary George Canning summoned American minister to Britain, Richard Rush, to a meeting at the end of Downing street in his office there. It was August 16, 1823. Canning and Rush exchanged greetings and Rush sat down for the discussion, opening the event by mentioning Russian claims to the North Pacific. There was no rise there from the Englishman, so Rush led the conversation to Latin America by asking if there was any chance of the revolutionaries holding out in Spain against the French. Canning was vague. Rush noted "that should France ultimately effect her purposes in Spain, there was at least the consolidation left, that Great Britain would not allow her to go farther and lay her hands upon the Spanish colonies." Canning replied by asking what Rush thought his government would say to the American government going band in hand with the British government in acting to prevent this.

Rush hesitated. Although he had instructions from home that emphasized "the common interest in blocking European action in the Americas," he did not want the responsibility of taking action without further instructions from Secretary of State Adams. The diplomat avoided a reply. Canning ignored a like question of what was the British position regarding the former colonies and did Britain intend to exchange ministers with the new countries. The Englishman would not lend its offices to mediate as Britain had before, but would do nothing to prevent the solution of the dispute between Spain and Spanish America. After he left office, Rush sent a report back to Adams via the fastest ships, that of the Black Ball company out of Liverpool.

Six days later, on the twenty-second, Canning's letter on the subject, reached Rush. The English leader wrote that the recovery of the colonies by Spain was deemed by his government to be hopeless. Britain would recognize them when time and circumstance seemed apt. Still they would not interfere with amicable negotiation. Britain wanted no Spanish territory in America and would not be indifferent to the seizure of these lands by other powers. Should America's policy be substantially the same then could be, Canning asked, and would Rush issue concurrent declarations or sign a joint statement to this effect? Rush did not commit himself. Although Rush kept pleading lack of instructions Canning pressed on noting that events might get ahead of them.

Finally in replying to Canning eloquence, Rush stated that both governments wanted to keep France or any other European power from taking the Latin Americans over. The difference between the countries, Rush said, was that the Americans had recognized the Hispanic nations in the new world while Great Britain had not done so. Should Britain recognize the states, than Rush would sign the joint statement. Canning declined because, he said of "the uncertain condition, internally, of these new states, or, at any rate, of some of them." There matters stood. [3]

The Russian Tsar Alexander I wanted to keep the Americans neutral in the Spanish-Latin American conflict. He gave orders to his envoy in Washington to replay his plans not to accept any envoys from free Latin American nations. The envoy also had a message from the Tsar that he wished the Americans would not act in any manner other than neutrality in dealing with the rest of the Americas. These thoughts were expressed by Baron de Tuyll to John Quincy Adams. In return, Adams said the reply would have to await the president's return, but that the American neutrality could depend upon the neutrality of European countries. Tuyll also wanted to publish his note in the semi-official Washington newspaper. Adams preferred for him to send it and the Americans reply to Congress. The baron decided to wait for the reply. [4]

Monroe read two dispatches about October 17, 1823. The first was from Canning which told the president about the designs of the Holy Alliance against South America. The British Foreign Minister proposed that the United States and Great Britain cooperate in protecting the Western Hemisphere against Continental Europe. Monroe drew from it two questions. Should the United States entangle itself in European politics and war? Was it a case of London supporting liberty against despotism. He had not reached the answer to the first and the second was assured. Canning's proposal was, he felt, an opportunity for the United States to express its view that European interference of Hispanic America would be an attack on the United States. He wrote Jefferson for his and Madison's advise on the matter. [5]

On November 13, 1823, Adams worked on his list of suggestions to Monroe for his annual address to Congress. Once finished, Adams took the memorandum to the president at the White House. There he found a president deeply worried about the Holy Alliance's desires to return Hispanic America to Spain and fearful that that group of European nations might carry its desires to fruition. Calhoun, learning about the fall of Cadiz to French troops, was alarmed and pessimistic about possibilities of a Holy Alliance conquest of Spanish America.

Adams was optimistic, believing that the governments of the Spanish ex-colonies were strong enough to withstand assaults. At the end of a cabinet meeting, the secretary of state Adams told them, in his words, that he "thought we should bring the whole answer to Mr. Canning's proposals to a test of right and wrong." Only the South Americans "had the right to dispose of their condition." Adams would issue a proclamation to that effect in answer to Channing's proposals.

With the passage of weeks, Canning became cool to the proposed joint communiqué and Rush saw Canning the next time. The Britisher said nothing about South America. Rush concluded that there would be no more diplomatic dialogue on the matter. News had just reached England of a conference between Argentina and Spain and the destruction of what remained of Morales' royalist army in Columbia. Rush would not for his part raise the discussion back to Hispanic American affairs. England's Canning had communicated with the Frenchman Prince de Poligno and obtained a disclaimer for his part. The French government stated that it was believed that the ex-colonies of American could not be subjugated and that it would not take any military action to subdue the Spanish ex-colonies. Rush did not know about this until later. Adams did not know this until the doctrine had been pronounced. [6]

Cowkeeper was a distinguished chief in East Florida. He had two sons who were chiefs. Payne was the civil chief of the Seminole and Bowlegs was the military chief of this Indian tribe. When Payne died, he was succeeded by his eldest, a Seminole named Solachoppo or Long Tom. This last died young of the white man's disease dissipation. His younger brother, Micanopy, then followed Long Tom as civil chief.

This Cowkeeper had owned many cattle and slaves, one of whom was his interpreter Abraham. This Abraham knew English well and accompanied Cowkeeper to Washington to talk with the president. When the old chief and Abraham returned to Florida, Cowkeeper set Abraham free. He was to become an important person among the Seminole. Sensible and shrewd, Abraham became a leading adviser of the chiefs. There was another Indian of note, a Creek, who came from Alabama where he had participated in the Fort Mimms massacre in 1811. After Jackson completed his campaign, Jumper was one of the Creeks seeking refuge in Florida among the Seminole. Jumper married well, taking as his spouse the sister of Micanopy. [7]

On one Saturday in the month of September in 1823, thirty enslaved and free African Americans gathered near Salem, North Carolina, to build a churchhouse for their one year old congregation. First, they stacked their logs, boards, and shingles on a plot of land near their cemetery. They then began to build with the logs and then boards, pounding nails to hold them into place. The work was finished by day's end. They were Moravians and had endured their increasing discrimination with fortitude and a happy nation. The idea for the separate house of worship came from the white churchpeople and the funds to build it also came from them. This was the beginning of some independence for them. [8]

Americans were sadden to learn reports of a massing of Turkish armed forces coming out of Turkey to crush the Greeks which finally appeared in early October issues of *The Albion*. There was little new and nothing which the Americans could count upon for truth. However, there were encouraging reports. [9]

By September of 1823, Weed was head of the Rochester branch of the new People's party, but since he was deeply in debt despite good pay, he became a legislative solicitor or lobbyist. Rochester businessmen sent him to Albany to get a bank charter. He got it and became acquainted with the legislators. This benefited his political position. Weed took part in the move to nominate Samuel Young as governor, but the Regency themselves nominated Young and the People's Party needed to look elsewhere. When the Regency removed Clinton from his job as canal commissioner. Clinton became a martyr and was nominated for governor once again. Weed was responsible for uniting the wings of the party by getting Tallmadge to run for lieutenant governor. Weed ran for the state assembly. Both Clinton, Tallmadge, and Weed won.

Meanwhile, Weed had managed a maneuver that put New York in Adams corner and leads to the presidential contest of 1824 being thrown into the House of Representatives for decision. In 1825, he attended that year's session of the legislature. His party was in power and he was engaging. Most of internal improvement bills passed the house but were lost in the Democratic senate. Weed joined the Democrats and other People's party in blocking Ambrose Spencer as senator. Weed supported Albert H. Tracy as senator but Tracy was not elected. After a fruitless trip to Washington to gain political favors, Weed returned to Rochester and bought the *Telegraph* from Peck on borrowed money. Weed was soon to become an anti-Mason party supporter.

On the 5th of October of 1823, supporters of Jackson met in Philadelphia's county courthouse and adopted a series of resolves. It was the duty and right of the people to select their own candidate for president. They would not be interfered with or dictated to in this matter. The people thought and acted for themselves separate from the self-constituted aristocracy. In accordance with this resolve, they wanted General Andrew Jackson to be their president and would organize for the promotion of the candidate. [10]

Support for Jackson in Pennsylvania spread rapidly from the western counties to Philadelphia. It had reached Philadelphia, when in October of 1823, a democratic group of politicians and citizens passed at the court house strong resolutions promoting Jackson for the presidency, because he was a uniform and consistent democrat and qualified as a statesman as well as a soldier. He would govern wisely in peace and triumphantly in war. They confided in his moderation, virtue, and firmness. To these citizens, he supported the rights of man and the suffrage of all men. After these declarations, the men began to organize. Their opposition was Calhoun, but Jackson's popularity swept aside Calhoun's lieutenant for all of their hard work. Within a few months, George M. Dallas dropped his support of the South Carolinian leader and presented a resolution calling upon local delegates to the March Harrisburg Convention to vote for Jackson at that state-wide meeting. [11]

The legislators of South Carolina met on November 19, 1823, and resolved to support John C. Calhoun for president. It was time for the expression of sentiments of every section in the land. According to their opinion, Calhoun was a man of distinguished talents and public services. He was devoted to general administration, had the views of the South in mind, had been zealous in the late war with Great Britain, and was a man of integrity. For these values he stood, entitled to the favor of the people. [12]

The Jacksonian party in Maryland developed out of a coalition of dissident politicians. This group was an inclusive alliance of former Federalist leaders, friends of John C. Calhoun, Republican leaders for Crawford, young men on the move, and Jackson leaders. The latter were painfully aware of their lack of a distinctive economic and legislative program. It was a personality cult thing. They stressed Jackson's qualifications for the high office, but the truth was that he was a war hero and it was this that made him. The Federalist party had made its last stand in 1821 and was no more. There was only one party in Maryland and the coalition held no power, but this party followed the Federalists into division and crumbling. Now that there was no competition, people lost interest in organized parties.

In 1823, the friends of William H. Crawford were working for his candidacy and late in that year they planned to use a congressional caucus to make him the official choice of the national Republicans. People in Maryland opposed the caucus system and there were protest meetings by the male citizens of the state. The organizations in whose meetings protests were voted for were fire companies, others were formal county meetings. More organizations established their opinions on this matter. As for as most Marylanders were concerned, caucus selections were out, but three congressmen defied the Maryland General Assembly to attend the Crawford caucus and supported him. Major General Samuel Smith led the Crawford forces in the state. Crawford was the hero of the wars against Britain and a long time representative and senator, but Smith was unable to build much Crawford support in the state.

Calhoun had some support in Maryland and the prominent lawyer and public official, Robert Goodloe Harper, was a Calhoun leader in the state. They had hopes of gaining Maryland for Calhoun in 1824. Still they were surprised and discomfited by Jackson's growing popularity in the city of Baltimore. They were later to back Jackson themselves, but this is a story for the next year. Maryland Federalists were to be fascinated by Jackson also. Should Jackson win they had hopes of ending their isolation. [13]

[1]Alter, *Bridger*, pp. 22-35.

[2]Perkins, *Monroe Doctrine*, pp. 5-9. Quote on p. 7.

[3]May, Ernest R., *The Making of the Monroe Doctrine*, Cambridge Mass: Harvard University Press, 1975, pp. 1-7.

[4]Bergquist, Harold E., Jr., "John Quincy Adams and the Promulgation of the Monroe Doctrine, October-December 1823," *Essex Institute Historical Collections*, 111 (January 1975), 38.

[5]James Monroe to Thomas Jefferson, October 17, 1823, in Ford, Washington Chauncey, *John Quincy Adams: His Connection with The Monroe Doctrine (1823)*, Cambridge, Mass: John Wilson, 1902, p. 7.

[6]Ford, Worthington C., in *American Historical Review*, VIII No. 1 (October 1902), pp. 28-29, 689, 691. Quotes on p. 29.

[7]Williams, John Lee, *The Territory of Florida: or Sketches of the Topography, Civil and Natural History, of the Country, the Culture, and the Indian tribes from the First Discovery to the Present Time with a Map, Views, & c..*, 1837, Rep: Gainesville, Fla: University of Florida Press, 1962, p. 214.

[8]Sensbach, "Culture and Conflict," p. 401.

[9]*The Albion*, October 4, 1823, p. 127.

[10]"Declaration of Support for General Andrew Jackson, Philadelphia, October, 1823," Schelesinger, *History*, I, 399.

[11]Hopkins, "Election," pp. 366-367.

[12]"Presidential Nomination of Secretary of War John C. Calhoun, Columbia, November 19, 1823," Schlesinger, *History*, I, 400.

[13]Haller, Mark H., "The Rise of the Jackson Party in Maryland, 1820-1829," *Journal of Southern History*, pp. 307-311.

Chapter XXXVIII

OSAGES

There was more trouble with the Osage Indians on the frontier. Indian trader Antonio Barraque and eleven or twelve hunters were attacked on November 17, 1823, by over eighty Osage Indians on the Blue River. With them were a Mr. Wilbourn and seven other Americans. The Indians shot down four of the Americans and badly wounded two more and a black, Barroque's property. Colonel Matthew Arbuckle wrote General Gaines that the Osage had a long time policy of maltreating the whites and robbing horses and other white property. Yet it is probable that they would not have committed the late act of hostility, had it been possible to restrain Americans from hunting in their country. The Choctaws made war upon the Osage from white settlements on the Red River, Americans trespassed on their lands, and United States effort to bring the two tribes to peace had led to the outrage.

The Osage wished to settle their dispute with the Cherokee by their own means. The young men especially did not know the strength of the American nation like the old and had seen only scattered whites. The Osage thought that their nation was the strongest one on earth and they could raid as they wished. The chiefs were advisers only and could not restrain the warriors, but in this case the leaders of the nation turned over the murderers to the Americans. Two of them were sentenced at their trial to be hung. [1]

While the United States was a weak republic of about ten and one half million people and Europe was a powerful group of nations at peace and many times more populated with only an ocean between the two continents. Monroe had prepared to challenge Goliath, counting only the help of Great Britain, although the British had only indicated their interests in the cause of Pan-American independence. Eight years after the last major European war, European nations had developed their armies and navies. They were once again financially strong. The nations interested in expanding or recovering their colonies in America numbered five. Governments in Great Britain, France, Spain, Denmark, and Holland stated their aims publicly and privately. Other nations such as Austria were in agreement to help Spain to reconquer its Spanish colonies recently freed. [2]

Henry Clay became a friend of Hispanic American governments and their people. A strong defender of the rights of man in the world led him to demand fair treatment for the Americas. Finding things and men to praise, he talked of their command of the sciences, their possession of universities, and of their writers. Americans had very little interest in the countries to the south. Clay deplored their ignorance and that of the Europeans alike. The Kentuckian would not impose upon the Hispanics United States principles and liberty, but noted that they had established this and asserted their rights.

The people had undertaken a glorious struggle and he recognized it in ringing tones. It was to the best interests of the United States that they succeed. They must be free but he wanted them to adopt neutrality in foreign affairs. Clay deplored those people in the United States who claimed that these countries would be rivals with Americans in agricultural productions and thought only in terms of the economic benefits of policy toward them. It was a matter of principle and not money. He knew more about Argentine history, for instance, then his fellow legislators knew. [3]

After a long period of insurrections and warfare in Hispanic America, the United States became the first outside power to recognize the independence of the new Hispanic countries to the south of the United States. Europe disapproved of this step, but could do nothing in the face of a hostile Great Britain, who although they criticized this step, at heart favored independence and even more used this state of affairs to trade and loan to governments. Great Britain would not support the European powers and, instead, sought an ally of the United States. The two English speaking nations had a great deal in common in their desire for trade and commerce, which gave them an acute interest in Latin America.

Jefferson and Madison answered Monroe's inquiry about the Canning proposals with their advise for him to accept the proposals. John Quincy Adams was against such a step, to avoid ensnaring the United States into a position where they could not take any territory from Mexico or Cuba. Adams did successfully make a stand against European interposition of the Americas to the Czar. On December 2, 1823, Adams won an everlasting victory. He formed the Monroe Doctrine in that the United States would stay out of European affairs and would have European countries stay out of affairs of the American continent. In time, the Europeans recognized the American nations. [4]

At this time, President James Monroe issued his Monroe Doctrine in a speech read before Congress. There were nine points, He declared that the Americas, both continents, were free and independent. As sovereign nations, they were not open to further colonization by the European powers. For their own part, the Americans forswore taking part in European Wars. This was followed by the nation until World War I. This was not as emphasized in American history as was the statement of an independent Americas. The government and people of the United States shall consider European attempts to extend their political systems to be a threat against our peace and safety. For her part, America would not interfere with existing colonies. This lasted seventy-five years.

To go even further, America would regard European attempts to control or oppose any nation on the continents of the western hemisphere to be unfriendly acts against the

United States. American people and happiness would suffer from foreign efforts to force their systems on the people of the nations. Of course, the United States would not object if a nation accepted or made a monarch of their own free will, without interference from abroad. They would leave the nations to the south to their own devices and opposed Spanish efforts to subdue them. He hoped that the other powers would not interfere and follow the American example in this statement. For their part, the government of the United States would not interfere with internal affairs. Besides the Americans would recognize existing or de facto government in the world.

In addition Monroe noted that "if we look to the comparative strength and resources of Spain and those new Governments, and their distance from each other, it must be obvious that she can never subdue them. It is still the true policy of the United States to leave the parties to themselves, in the hopes that other powers will pursue the same course." He did not say that a combined Europe might be able to do this conquest. However, Monroe knew that with England opposed, this could never take place or be attempted. The European continent needed control of the seas which Britain had. And the British were clearly opposed to such an endeavor. It was this muscle of London that made the Monroe Doctrine possible.

Foreign reaction was strong. Canning in London supported Monroe. The Spanish were very angry when they read the declaration. They wanted the glory of Spain and could not care less for the Hispanic Americans. This was to be proved in Cuba for the next seventy-five years. Chateubriand of Paris said that Monroe should be resisted. The leading Paris newspaper scoffed. Prince Metternich of Austria bitterly condemned the Doctrine. Hispanic American countries were joyful. Simon Bolivar expressed his cheer and Brazil offered an alliance with the United States.

The Czar obliged the Americans by withdrawing his claims to the land south of Alaska. Alexander I had a soft spot in his rigid heart for the Americans. He sustained the Monroe Doctrine. Many American newspapers supported Monroe and support grew over the months and years ahead. Soon, it was considered one of the greatest principles of American policy. The president himself was to consider it his greatest accomplishment. Adams might well have considered it to be his best, along with the treaty ending the recent war with Great Britain. [5]

Canning's reaction to the American Monroe Doctrine was strong. He did not need the United States to keep out the other European powers of the Americas. Who were the Americans to dictate policy for London? Who were the Americans to be able to act to accomplish what London could do by itself? It must have been clear to Canning that in his view the Americans were hanging on to the British coattails in the matter. The people of the United States outside the Monroe Cabinet did not suspect that this was the English reaction. They appreciated London's stand on keeping Europe out of Latin America.

Canning saw that the Americans would deny Britain's its own interest in increasing British power in the western hemisphere. On February 8, 1826, Canning was to privately write that "the avowed pretension of the United States to put themselves at the head of the confederacy of all the America, and to sway that confederacy against Europe, (Great

Britain included), is not a pretension identified with our interest. By this time, Canning had instituted a diplomatic campaign against the United States to subvert any Hispanic sympathy towards the United States. He wanted to prevent any alliances or looking to the United States for help. As a nationalist, a true Briton, he forwarded the interest of the two main islands of Britain. And, of course, the upper class of his nation. Indeed, he was successful in promoting British interests and influence. He based this on the power of England before the Spanish colonials revolted and since. [6]

When Adams placed the non-colonization doctrine in his briefing papers for Monroe, the president included them in his message to Congress. This was in only one paragraph in the document and was not considered to be of great importance at the time. Most newspapers in their reports on the message, often at length, ignored the non-colonization doctrine which was later to become so important in American history. Three fairly important papers made brief comments on the idea.

The *National Gazette and Literary Register* of Philadelphia praised the minor doctrine. The editor said that this asserted principle "has a very comprehensive meaning; forms quite an epoch in our relations with Europe, and cannot fail to have produced a new sensation in all the leading courts." The editor thought it might have surprised and startled the Russian minister to the United States. "We do not know whether it be expected that Russia will renounce any of her pretensions in regard to the Northwest coast; but if she do, it will be the first instance of her retracting a claim of right, real or fictitious, in the whole course of her history since the era of the great Peter's reign."

The editor of the New York *Spectator* thought it seemed a broad one. However, on second thought, he expressed approval for its justice and intrepidity. He could not comment on this further, because he had not an idea of just what the president was saying and how it would effect Britain and Russia's claims in Oregon. "Where the president avows the neutral course the administration will pursue in the event of any renewed attempt that may be made by Spain and Portugal (unaided by other Powers) upon the revolted American colonies. In this view of the case, what cause can any European nation have of complaint?" The only change the United States could make would be by conquest or purchase. The third paper, the *Albion* of New York was edited by an Englishman and he was hostile. This Briton thought it would be preposterous for America to limit England in the continent. [7]

The issue of the Greek Revolution found its way to Congress when Daniel Webster spoke on December 8, 1823, before the Senate in favor of moral support for the Greeks. Although he admitted that a country should tend to its own concerns, Webster thought the maxim should not apply to the situation at hand. Because America was a free republic with a half century of experience, the nation was compelled to take a part in the world's events. He noted that "the age we live in, and our own active character, have connected us with all the nations of the world; l and we, as nation, have precisely the same interest in international law as a private individual has in the laws of his country." Having struggled ourselves, we must give others involved with our very principles the cheering aid of the American example and opinions. We are safe from the conflict across the wide Atlantic and he would not have us send armies to Europe, the force of public opinion must be expressed. [8]

Sympathy for the Greeks in their fight for independence was wide-spread in the western world. In the United States, memorialists wrote the Congress from New York City on December 19, 1823, that they had seen the heroic efforts of Greeks to efforts of Greeks to affect their rescue from human bondage and felt that Americans must give assistance as well as good wishes. They believed that the Greek cause was the highest concern to the interest of the human race. Their object in writing Congress was to petition Congress to recognize Greek independence. This did not have to happen immediately however. The New Yorkers left it to the discretion of the government. They believed that Americans thought that the Greeks had proven themselves and vindicated their rights to equal nationhood. [9]

Settled in his mind that the senatorship was his duty, Jackson undertook the long trip to Washington. Along the way, he was greeted by people. His popularity was obvious, which would have pleased those who wanted to see him made president and would have alarmed those who feared his economic views. Andrew took the stagecoach to avoid people. He was only partially successful. At other places, he had to travel by horseback since no stagecoach was available. After a long journey of nine hundred miles, he arrived at Washington. It was the morning of December 3, 1823.

Jackson found the electoral contest wide open, but could be well satisfied with his popularity. He was the center of attention and had a good chance to come out on top. To improve matters, he began to patch up old quarrels with important public men, with General Winfield Scott, Thomas Hart Benton, and Henry Clay. [10]

Five families got abroad the raft. All were kin except for a solitary man with the party. They shoved the raft off and crossed the Sabine River to the other side. They were now in Texas and the date was the day before Christmas in 1823. The thirty-three people continued on into the interior of the Mexican province. A. M. Highsmith was an experienced frontiersman, having served in the War of 1812 as a ranger and scout and he led his son and his relatives deep into central Texas. His son was Benjamin F. Highsmith, quickly to become an Indian fighter. Ben was born in Lincoln County, Mississippi, on September 11, 1817. [11]

The Highsmiths settled on the Colorado River two miles above the site of La Grange, on the western bank at a place called Castleman's Spring for John Castleman. Soon afterwards the Indian began to press on the small settlement and the families there moved down to the settlement of Zaddock Woods and Stephen Cottle. The Indians were still too close and the cumulative people went to Rabb's Mill. After a few years the hitherto before friendly Comanche Indians came to the settlement of Rabb's Mill and informed the settlers there that they must leave Comanche territory or be killed. The families could not stand up to the Comanches and migrated.

In 1929, the settlers scattered. Most went to Old Caney and Columbus, but the Cottles went to Jesse Burnham's and the Highsmiths went to Elliot C. Burkner's. In 1830, Highsmith went on a trading trip to San Antonio with James Bowie, William B.

Travis, Ben McCulloch, Winslow Turner, Sam Highsmith, and George Kimble. They toured the frontier town with its grass-covered houses upon their arrival on April 1, 1830.

From the area of the lower Colorado River, settler W.B. Deewees wrote on December first to Austin. He detailed their sufferings on the Texas frontier. Chief among them was a want of provisions. "There have been a great many new settlers come on this fall, and those who have not been accustomed to hunting in the woods for support, are obliged to suffer." Single men had to reside with families in the settlements. "We remain here,, notwithstanding the scarcity of provisions, to assist in protecting the settlement.

We are obliged to go out in the morning, a party of us, to hunt food, leaving a part of the men home to guard the settlement from Indians, who are very hostile to us." They did not go alone, but in companies. This made hunting more difficult and the game was scarce so that they often returned empty-handed. The children were going without food. The women did not complain, but they showed their feelings with their looks. They kept cheerful and often helped mount guard with the muskets against the Indians. The friendly Tonkawa Indians supplied them with needed deerskins for clothes. Deerskin were the common material for clothing, even for the women. [12]

The western regions of Virginia were made up in part of settlers from Pennsylvania and Ohio and held few slavers. They were unhappy about the voting arrangement in which the slaves counted for representation, the east and central area holding the predominant strength in the legislature. They demanded special legislation which would even the vote. This led to a hostility against the peculiar institution of slavery. Many influential men in the state of Virginia were opposed to slavery and in 1823, they came close to gaining gradual emancipation. The major obstacle was solving the question of what should be done with the slaves when free. [13]

William H. Keating, professor of mineralogy and chemistry at the University of Pennsylvania, traveled with Stephen H. Long's 1823 expedition and looked at Chicago with dour predictions for its future. He disagreed with Henry H. Schoolcraft's favorable conception of Chicago and its possibilities written in 1821. Fort Dearborn, Illinois, was abandoned a few months after Keating visited it. He wrote that its founding was necessary to intimidate the hostile, and powerful tribes in the area. It worked. The fort was left since it was no longer needed. There was still an amiable Indian agent. Supplies was needed for the Indians because of the growing scarcity of game. [14]

James Fenimore Cooper put his personal experience into good use when the wrote *The Pilot*, published in 1823 when Lincoln was fourteen. In his first chapter, Cooper introduced Captain Barnstable and his sweetheart Katherine Plowden on the rocky coast of England. Then the author added to the sense of mystery and an action scene with its suspense and dangers from the elements. On the passing of this dangerous passage, it become even more secure that this is an American ship. The characters are well done with youth and maturity contrasted. It well might be that the actors on this literary stage are somewhat wooden, but the times called for heroic men and women who have set personalities. This is an adventure story and action is king. In this type of literature, people are not complex.

Shortly, the officers of the frigate were called upon to an consultation about a land expedition which is the main action of Cooper's book. A sub-plot is revealed, which was the rescue of the two young ladies whom Barnstable and Griffith loved. Cooper uses romance to entwine the plot. As could be expected in the novelist's work, the women are outspoken and patriotic to the American cause. The lead English character is Colonel Howard, loyal to the English monarchy and the divine rule idea of the king being present and his subjects children who must obey their national father, granted by birth by their Heavenly Father.

We get to know the pilot better in his meeting with his once upon a time lady-friend Alice Dunscombe, a companion to the ladies loved by Barnstable and Griffith. There is action once again and plenty of capture and escape in the Cooper manner. The action and romance continues in subsequent pages and the mysterious Pilot is poorly covered. Even at the conclusion, little more is known about the pro-American pilot than when we first meet him in Cooper's pages. It has been suggested that the pilot as a fictionalized John Paul Jones, but the character of the pilot like the other people of the novel is pure fiction.[15]

[1]Carter, *Territorial*, XIX, 570, 572, 576, 719.
[2]Wheeler, Joseph and Grosvenor, Charles H., "Our Duty in the Venezuelan Crisis," *North American Review*, CLXI No. 5 (November 1895), p. 628.
[3]Sterling, Carlos Marquez, "Henry Clay: Forerunner of Pan Americanism," *Americas*, XVI (May 1964), 4, 6.
[4]Bemis, S.F., *A Diplomatic History*, 4th ed., 1955, pp. 196-211.
[5]Wilson, Charles Morrow, *The Monroe Doctrine: An American Frame of Mind*, Princeton: Auerbach, 1971, pp. 23-24, 35-40. Quote on p. 35.
[6]Williams, Mary Wilhemine, *Anglo-American Isthmian Diplomacy, 1815-1915*, Washington: American Historical Association, 1916, pp. 27-28. Quote on pp. 27-28 n. 5. See Wait, Eugene M., "Warriors and Revolutionaries: The Argentine Revolution, 1806-1816," MS: the best English language book on the subject, in its examples.
[7]Perkins, *Monroe Doctrine*, pp. 13-16ff. Quotes on pp. 15,`15-16.
[8]*The Annals of America*, V, 109-109.
[9]*American State Papers-Foreign Affairs* V, 251-252.
[10]Remini, *Jackson*, II, 53, 59-62.
[11]Sowell, A.J., *Early Settlers and Indian Fighters of Southwest Texas*, New York: Arogsy-Antiquarian, 1964, 2d ed., pp. 1-2.
[12]Winter, *Texas*, pp. 37-38.
[13]*Confederate Military History*, 1899, III, 19.
[14]Angle, pp. 8ff.
[15]Cooper, James Fenimore, *The Pilot*.

Chapter XXXIX

VARIOUS

One of the issues that was facing Jackson as the election loomed on the horizon and would be a primary problem with people on both sides of the issue during his later presidency was the subject of internal improvements. A popular idea, it made a hero of New York's governor De Witt Clinton when he was the main sponsor for the building of the Eire canal. Other men could look at Clinton and wish for some popularity with the voter. Still there were opponents, men who based their opposition upon constitutional grounds believing that the constitution did not allow internal roads and canals to be made, that there was no provisions for this construction in the primary law of the nation, and that only the states could legally build such roads and canals.

President Monroe presented a study of the question in a state paper for Congress explaining his negative opinions on the issue. Congressional attempts to persevere and repair, even would be unconstitutional, in Monroe's thought since it would require the same powers necessary for a general system. Looking at the negative side the president noted the difficulties of preparation, the need to secure rightaway and to have laws to prosecute disgruntled landowners who would destroy segments because they were forced to sell land or because the project did not run through their territory. Funds would be required for constant repairs. He foresaw conflicts between state and federal government. Indeed Monroe examined the constitution, seeing in it six powers which seemingly would be the basis for approval, but which he argued would not sustain those who argued that the constitution would allow it.

Proponents for internal improvements argued that the legal right of the federal government to build them was the grant to establish post offices and post roads. Monroe and others argued that only existing roads and post offices came under this head. This was surely not what the founding fathers had in mind. The second power was that to make war which included building roads for the betterment of military protection, to tie the nation closer together, and to generally promote protection. To this Monroe disagreed. Thirdly was the power to regulate trade which was clearly to support the nation behind internal improvements.

The fourth power was one for the general welfare which Monroe said would be no power at all, but which clearly provided power to build the improvements legally speaking. Monroe rightfully disdained the fifth power, to make necessary laws to support the powers, because clearly it was not a grant of power. Six gave the power to dispose of land granted to the federal government by the state and make laws for them, which as Monroe rightly said had nothing to do with building roads and canals. It seems that only the first two granted the required power, but that should have been sufficient. [1]

An upsetter of tradition and established religion as it was seen then, anticlerical Alexander Campbell was educated in the Presbyterian Church, but when his first child was born, he began to deviate from his Presbyterian faith. He rejected infant baptism and in June of 1812, he had his family baptized by immersion. He organized the Brush Run Church and became a spokesman for the Baptists. He prospered as a preacher of note and in 1823 engaged in a debate with Presbyterian pastor William McCalla near Washington, Kentucky. He did well as the Baptist champion, but to show his changing views to the religious foundings, the church of the first century, he made a short address to the Baptists he was championing.

He said that "Brethren, I fear that if you knew me better you would esteem and love me less. For let me tell you that I have almost as much against you...as...against the Presbyterians. They err in one thing and you in another; and probably you are each nearly equidistant from original apostolic Christianity.

Campbell attacked tradition, creeds, confessions, associations, and reverend titles. He told his followers to espouse Biblical teachings only. However, his disciples stayed within the associations in order to convert others to his views. He believed that a person could not initiate the process of conversion by narrations to the congregation of the person's Christian experiences. There was no need of a crisis in life to lead to conversion. One must become a Christian first to receive the light in the Scriptures. Attempting to relive, as he thought, early Christian worship, we would take up a collection for the poor on Sundays. During this time, Campbell published *The Christian Baptist*. [2]

Benjamin Franklin Wade, American senator and advocate of black rights, was born on October 27, 1800, in Shoemakers' Lane in Feeding Hills, Massachusetts, to James Wade and his wife Mary Upham Wade in addition to a large and active family. There were eleven children in the family which was headed by a poor farmer, so much so that there was a great demand for early farm work and a hiring out as chore doing on neighboring farms. Benjamin was the second youngest and like his older brothers and sisters lost good education from the poverty of the family. Still his eldest brother was educated enough to become a physician, such as there was at the time. The younger children had less chance for an education.

Benjamin retained much of his puritan ancestry; the determination and hard work of his forebears was evident in his life. With a modicum of formal education, is mother and her few books were available for learning. He did not take well to formal religion.

Lacking interest in the teaching and hard life of true religion, he was further tainted in the times by having Deist beliefs, which are common in our era.

The older brothers of the family with sister Nancy and her husband, went west to Andover, Ohio, located near the state line with Pennsylvania. They soon sent for the rest of the family and supplied them with a wagon to make the trip. The family followed including Benjamin. Hope beckoned, but the young Benjamin found the life to be rough. Still he undertook it in good spirits and worked hard in several fields. Besides farming in the summer and teaching school in the winter, he cleared forests, hunted game, and drove cattle to market in Philadelphia. The latter netted him $12 (then a sizable pay) and expenses along the way.

In 1823, at the age of twenty three, he ended one of his cattle driving trips and went to Watervliet, New York, the home of his eldest brother James Wade, a successful physician. He liked the place but after beginning a physician education, learned that this was not his field. Rather than depending upon relatives, Benjamin taught school to earn his way and once finishing his stint at a medical education, returned to the west, where he worked as a laborer on the Eire Canal. When he had earned and saved enough, Wade returned to Ohio, where encouraged by the youngest Wade, Edward or Ned, undertook the study of law. Studying under the best Ohio had to offer in Canfield, he made his way to legal work at Jefferson, Ohio, and was under way.

Doing well in legal search and limited only by difficulties in public speech which he was to overcome, he became known for his abilities. The prominent Joshua Giddings took Wade into partnership and Wade was underway toward success. Wade often had to travel east on business. Soon he overcame shyness and speech difficulties and the future was ensured. He surmounted all obstacles and was launched upon a career which was to lead to politics. Wade was always a radical for the rights of the oppressed and always a reformer. He hated the exploitation of any and all. To him government existed to protect the weak from the strong. Although a Whig and then a Republican, Wade never hesitated to depart from party positions, long range or short range. Issues counted most with him and on these he was frank.

As a politician with the Whig and showing his talents, Wade was soon nominated and elected to the county office of prosecuting attorney. He gained 1,664 votes to his Democratic opponent's 487 votes. In that office he continued to prove himself and was nominated and elected to the state senate, gaining 1,302 votes to his Democratic opponent's 575 and headed for Columbus, Ohio. There he took his own course. Wade began to promote anti-slavery causes in the midst of harsh treatment for blacks in his state of Ohio and worse in the South. [3]

Roger Brooke Taney was born on the family estate of Battle Creek Plantation on March 17, 1777. He and his father got along well together. Michael Taney, although impatient when teaching his children in their lessons, took great pleasure in teaching his sons how to ride, swim, fish, row, sail, skate, and to shoot ducks and geese in season. Monica, his mother, had sound judgment and by her example showed herself pious, gentle, affectionate, retiring and gentle. Her reproofs were gentle and affectionate.

Schools were scarce in Maryland at the time and at eight Roger went to a school three miles away, taught by an elderly man, who was well disposed, but relatively ignorant. He taught basic reading, writing, and arithmetic from Dilworth's spelling book and the Bible. Financially poor, the old man had to cultivate a few acres of poor land to get by. During bad weather, the children stayed at home. The school had about thirty students.

When the teacher had taught Taney boys all that they could learn from him, Michael Taney sent his son to board with a Hunter, a Scotsman who kept a grammar school ten miles away. The Scotsman had a reputation of being a fine classical scholar. Roger began his studies of Latin under the man, but within a few months the teacher became insane and the school was broken up. With this avenue of education done, Michael Taney employed private tutors for his children. The first tutor died of tuberculosis and the second knew little Latin and no Greek.

The best tutor was the third. David English was a graduate of Princeton and later, he edited a newspaper and served as a bank official. This tutor suggested one year later that the boy be sent away to college. He went to Dickinson College at Carlisle. His stay there was successful and he entered one of the two secret literary society in which he gained the honor by vote of members to give the valedictory address. He wanted to become a lawyer and his father wished so too, so in the spring of 1796, Taney went to Annapolis to read law in the office of the able jurist Jeremiah Townley Chase. Three years later he was admitted to the bar.

His father wished him to practice in Calvert county at home and so after a maiden effort in Annapolis which saw him win his first case, he came home. His father wanted him to be elected to the House of Delegates at Annapolis and so he was. He served upon many committees, special committees, and he chaired some of them. Taney took a special pride in supporting the law which arranged for the building of a canal between the Chesapeake and Delaware bays, opposed by the Baltimore interest. Taney was defeated in the next election. The Jeffersonian Republicans won the state, due partially to the unpopularity of John Adams in Maryland. Michael and Roger Taney decided it would no longer do for Roger to remain in his home county and Michael suggested Frederick to which the younger Taney went.

At the time, Frederick was the second largest town in Maryland, second only to Baltimore. Taney was to live there and practice law for nearly a quarter of a century. Five years after his arrival Roger married the sister of his friend, Frances Scott Key. In 1816, the electoral college of Maryland chose Taney a state senator, in which position he served for a number of years and expressed himself as a hard money man.

In 1823, Taney, destined for greater things, removed to Baltimore, where he practiced law and was elected counsel for the Union Bank of Maryland and one of its directors. This close association had a negative influence upon Taney. A former Federalist, Taney became a Jacksonian in the election of 1824 and 1828 and became one of the leaders of the Democratic Party in the state of Maryland. [4]

The half horse half alligator vainglory Mike Fink decided to go on a trapping trading expedition formed by Ashley in the spring of 1822. He and his close friends Carpenter and Talbot, seeking adventure, served as boatmen, trappers and hunters on the journey and helped built Henry's fort. Next, the three men with in others including Smith spent the winter at Musclehall River. Things went well until Fink and Carpenter fell to arguing about a woman back in the states. This heated quarrel was patched up, but Carpenter felt Fink was holding a powerful bitterness against him and indeed such was the case. Winter meant a four foot freeze on the Missouri, and spring did not come until April when Indians were present for a visit.

When they reached the Yellowstone in 1823, the quarrel broke out once again and patched upon. By the way of showing the absence of hard feelings, Mike proposed once again that they fire at cups of whiskey on their heads. A coin toss decided that Mike would be first to shoot. Carpenter told Talbot he would be killed, but he could not back out. One had to die sooner or later. He stood still with the cup on his head. Pacing off the usual seventy, leveled his rifle, lowered it briefly to say "Hold your noodle steady, Carpenter, and do not spill the whisky, as I shall want some presently."

Fink shot Carpenter through the forehead, an obviously sure shot, blew the smoke from his muzzle and said, "Carpenter, you have spilled the whisky!" Months later Fink bragged about his murder in the presence of Talbot, who drew Carpenter's pistol and shot Mike dead, through the heart. Thus lived the criminal life of an unhealthy sport. His legend was to grow and end up in a Walt Disney movie in competition with Davy Crockett, who got the best of Fink. The movie did not cover Mike's misbegotten life and the two never actually met. [5]

Anson Jones, president of the Republic of Texas, was born on January of 1798 near Great Barrington, Massachusetts, the thirteen of fourteen children of Solomon Jones and his wife Sarah Strong, descended from Colonel Sir John Jones and Catherine Cromwell through their son William Jones. Catherine, Sir John's wife, was the sister of the Protector. Sir John Jones was deputy governor of New Haven and Connecticut from 1683 to 1698. Solomon was left an orphan at age seven and lived a life of poverty switching from rocky farm to rocky farm.

Anson learned the alphabet and first principle of learning at a small country school taught by his older sister Sarah. Then he walked five miles a day to school at Egremont Plains for a short while before being taught by the Episcopal rector of Great Barrington, the brother of Bishop Griswold. At fourteen years old he wanted to fight Britain in the new war, but his father, who had fought at Bunker Hill and seen Burgoyne surrender at Saratoga, sent him to Lenox Academy for courses in languages and mathematics. He had worked hard all day and studied at night, being the son of a poor man.

His mother died and the family broke up. Anson was old enough to work and his father and three older sisters decided he should become a physician although the boy wanted to be a printer. He embarked upon his studies at Litchfield, Connecticut, with the then method of direct studies under a practitioner. After a difficult time of it and some side teaching, Anson passed his examination on September 5, 1820, before the Oneida Medical Society. He settled at Bainbridge but failed as a physician, lacking business to exist; moved to New York City as a merchant, was sued for back debts.

On the way to Harper's Ferry in 1823, Anson stopped off at Philadelphia. He failed to build up a business there and went to Venezuela, where he made a success for two years. Plagued by a shyness and an uncertainty, Anson had had troubles in adjusting to the world, but Caracas brought out success in Anson which led to improvement in the man. The Jones that left Caracas was a stronger and more capable man than the one who arrived.

Since he was ill-trained in the progressive thought beginning to develop, he decided to finish his education in the new medical school being founded by Jefferson College in Philadelphia. He finished his courses and graduated. He joined the Masons and expanded both his acquaintance, but his clientele failed to improve. A success in the Masons, he rose to high offices and organized Philadelphia Lodge number thirteen. He was elected Grand Master of all the Old Fellows in Pennsylvania. Still, he felt himself a failure as a doctor and got into personal trouble with his fellow Masons.

Anson went to New Orleans as a partner in a mercantile house which its owner Thomas J. Spear was extending to New Orleans. Unfortunately Spear was a rascal and the business fell apart with Jones the victim. He was told by Texans that Brazorias needed a doctor. He went to Texas. [6]

And there is the story of a plain pioneer farmer. Joseph Crow Goss was born in Rowan County, North Carolina, on October 21, 1804, to David Goss and his wife Abigail Crow Goss. At age of eight, he moved with his parents to the frontier in Illinois. He went with them to Gosport, Indiana, in 1823. Marrying four times, he had twelve children by two wives. He farmed and raised stock, making most of his money raising sheep, cattle, and hogs. Priding himself on the fine horses he raised, he sold chickens, turkeys, ducks, tobacco, honey, buttermilk, kraut, meat, and vegetables from his farm.

Joseph made trading trips to New Orleans by flat boat and to Baltimore and St. Joseph by horse teams. He took pork products to New Orleans and imported various goods from Baltimore to Gosport, Indiana, where he loaded saddles and bridles for sale to the Indians at St. Joseph, Missouri, about 1840. In 1844, he made a trading trip to Balltown, Missouri, where he sold goods to the natives.

Selling his farm in Indiana, Goss went to Kansas in 1858 with Durham cattle and Southdown sheep, the first purebred livestock to be brought to Kansas. He was one time owner of the La Cygne House, the second hotel in La Cygne, Kansas. He laid low during the trouble with the Missourians before the war and in 1864 had to hide out in the woods from Price raiders. His inclination was to work hard all of his life. [7]

In Maine, the ruling clique of the Republican party wanted Crawford to succeed Madison, but John Quincy Adams was popular in Maine and when the party held its caucus in January of 1823, the majority prevailed and the Republicans worked for Adams. The influential; Portland *Argus* opposed Adams, but the people did not listen and Adams won three to one. The *Argus* was to oppose Adams in the next election also.
[8]

---

[1]Benton, *Thirty Years*, I, 21-27.

[2]Birdwhistell, Ira V. (Jack), *Gathered at the River: A Narrative History of Long Run Baptist Association*, Louisville: Long Run Baptist Associations, 1978, pp. 23-27.

[3]Trefousse, Hans Louis, *Benjamin Franklin Wade: Radical Republican From Ohio*, New York: Twayne Publishers, 1963, pp. 17-32.

[4]Steiner. Bernard Christian, *Life of Roger Brooke Taney: Chief Justice of the United States Supreme Court*, New York: William & Wilkins, 1922. Rep. Westport, Conn: Greenwood Press, 1970, pp. 8-21, 25, 29-33, 36-38, 41-43, 59-62. 81-87.

[5]Morgan, *Smith*, pp. 46-49.

[6]Grambrell, *Anson Jones, passim.*

[7]Heuss, Lois, *Frederick Goss of Rowan County, North Carolina and His Descendants*, 1968, pp. 157-159.

[8]McCormick, pp. 51-52.

INDEX